R - Jenkins

LECTURES ON
FOREIGN HISTORY
1494-1789

By J. M. THOMPSON
F.B.A., F.R.Hist.S.

BASIL BLACKWELL, OXFORD
1965

First edition 1925
Second edition, revised 1930
Seventh impression 1954
Revised and reset 1956
Third impression 1964
Reprinted 1965

PREFACE TO FIRST EDITION

These lectures were given at Magdalen during the winter terms of 1921–1924. The audience consisted of undergraduates in their first year, many of whom had read little English history, and less foreign. Most of them were taking the Previous Examination in Modern History, the intention of which was to supply a background of European history against which they might afterwards set up a more detailed study of English history in the Final School.

In such circumstances it was the first duty of a lecturer not to be dull, so that his audience might wish to go on studying the subject. His second duty was neither to teach too little history, lest his audience might learn nothing from him; nor too much, lest they might learn nothing for themselves. His third duty was to refer his hearers, so far as possible, from his historical statements to the sources from which they were derived, so that they might realize that the essence of history is not the learning of facts, but the judging of evidence.

The lectures were written before delivery, and have been revised, but not essentially altered, since.

In order to avoid footnotes, short references to authors quoted have been inserted into the text, and italicized: a list of these and other books used will be found at the end.

Thanks are due to Mr. W. C. Costin, of St. John's, for his kind help in reading the proofs.

PREFACE TO REVISED EDITION

The opportunity of revision has been taken to modify (it was not always easy), some references to contemporary events which were appropriate when these lectures were first delivered thirty years ago.

CONTENTS

LECTURE		PAGE
I	A Survey of Europe in 1494	1
II	The Renaissance	13
III	The Italian Wars	25
IV	The Rivalry of Francis I and Charles V	36
V	The Reformation	48
VI	The Counter-Reformation	63
VII	The Netherlands Revolt	78
VIII	The French Wars of Religion	95
IX	Henry of Navarre	113
X	The Thirty Years' War	126
XI	Richelieu	140
XII	The Minority of Louis XIV	157
XIII	Louis XIV—Home Affairs	169
XIV	Louis XIV—Church and Foreign Policy	187
XV	The Regency	205
XVI	Louis XV	223
XVII	Northern Europe, 1640–1740	238
XVIII	The Wars of Polish and Austrian Succession	254
XIX	Frederick the Great, and the Seven Years' War	266
XX	Enlightened Despotism	281
XXI	Louis XVI	300
XXII	Conclusion	314
	List of Books	335
	Index	343

LECTURE

A SURVEY OF EUROPE IN 1494

I

The period of history covered by these Lectures is a long one—nearly three hundred years (1494–1789). It is long, and it is important; for it coincides with the education of Europe, from the time when it went to school at the Italian Renaissance to the time when it came of age at the French Revolution.

To cover so much ground, we shall have to limit our survey to the essential events, the indispensable people. To keep a due sense of proportion, we must look at European history from some particular point of view. What shall this be? I think we shall find that it had best be, in the main, French. The period begins and ends with French dates: 1494 is the invasion of Italy by the French King, Charles VIII; 1789 is the meeting of the Estates General, which started the French Revolution. For the greater part of three centuries French culture, French diplomacy, and the French army set the fashion to Europe. Of the books dealing with the period, those most worth reading are written by Frenchmen, and assume that France is the centre of interest.

One word about books. The Humanist philosopher Paracelsus had a short and pleasant way of dealing with this subject. He used to begin his lectures by lighting some sulphur in a brazier, and throwing into it the works of his predecessors, with the words 'Sic vos ardebitis in Gehenna'—'Thus will you burn, as your books are burning, in the flames of Hell' [*Paget*]. I should be sorry to foretell such a fate even for the compilers of historical handbooks who do so much to spoil history. Nor is it the Lecturer's business, but that of the College Tutor, to recommend a course of historical reading. If I mention particular books, it will be for particular reasons; and with no intention to prescribe these, or to proscribe others. In general, what I would say is this. You don't study history to learn historical facts, but to acquire historical judgment. It is not learning which makes a historian, but discernment. Historical truth, if that means a complete account of an event as it really occurred, is hardly ever attainable. But historical truthfulness is much more important, and is within the reach of all. Only, to attain it, you must go to school under the best historians. This was the advice that *Erasmus* gave to a student friend. 'Read first the best books on the subject which you have in hand. Why learn what you will have to unlearn? Why overload your mind with too much food, or with poisonous food? The important thing for you is not how much you know, but the quality of what you know.' And then he goes on to give some practical advice, which I would rather have you take from him than from me. 'Divide your day, and give to each part of it a special occupation. Listen to your lecturer; commit what he tells you to memory; write it down if you will, but recollect it, and make it your own. Never work at night; it dulls the brain and hurts the health.' (But notice how early Erasmus got up, and how hard he worked in the morning.) 'Remember above all things that nothing passes away so rapidly as youth.'

II

I have said that our centre of interest must be France. But first, by way of introduction, we must try to take a wider view. We must realize the extent of our subject. We must attempt a survey of the whole field.

Let us start from Oxford, and travel rapidly round Europe, to see what is going on. 'Rapidly,' you may think, is hardly the word for the fifteenth century. Travel was certainly slow in those days. But it was not specially difficult. There were regular routes for trade and travel, both by land and sea. Already English scholars frequently rounded off their Oxford or Cambridge education with a visit to Paris or to Padua. Continental scholars returned the compliment. In the seventeenth century English travelling companies were acting Shakespeare in several parts of Europe. There was no need to take Baedeker's *Manual of Conversation* with you when you went abroad; for all educated people could speak Latin, and they were 'more like citizens of a common country than they have ever been since' [*Froude*].

It is the year 1494. First, what is happening here, in Oxford? Oxford is, of course, a walled town, with gates barred at night across the High (by the Eastgate Hotel) and the Corn (by St.

Michael's Church): at Smith Gate there is a chapel, now (1925) embodied in the new buildings at Hertford. But life is sufficiently safe, and the town sufficiently crowded, for important buildings to be rising outside the walls. Magdalen is nearly finished; and two years ago (the year in which Columbus discovered America) they started building the Great Tower.

This College (and others no doubt were like it) was not in a very good state at this time. At a Visitation held in 1507, 'it appeared that many of the Fellows kept dogs, one of them also having a ferret, and that they made frequent poaching expeditions: some of them recommended the Junior Bachelors and Scholars to hunt "by day and night." The use of Latin in conversation, enjoined by the Statutes, had been laid aside' (I am afraid it is still), 'There were factions in the College, and several members were in the habit of wearing arms.' Nor was that all. The Vice-President of the College was accused (among other crimes) of dabbling in black magic: he had, it was said, 'baptized a cat,' as a means of discovering hidden treasure. He afterwards became a bishop [*Wilson*].

What kind of education would you have got, if you had come up to Oxford in 1494? You would probably have begun by reading the *Doctrinale* of Alexander, a Latin Grammar written in rhyming hexameters: the ingenious author also wrote an Arithmetic in the same style. Then you would have gone on to Logic, studied in the *Parva Logicalia* or 'Little Logicals'—so called, Sir Thomas More suggested, because it contained so little logic. If you had survived this fare, you would have ended, I expect, with the staple food of medieval teaching—Aristotle, with the accumulated mass of commentaries upon him. In your last year, if you were of a theological turn of mind, you might have attended the lectures of the newly-appointed Lady Margaret Professor of Divinity, on the 'Quodlibetical Questions of Duns Scotus,' and would have considered (this is only the first of twenty-one problems) 'whether in the Divine Persons essentials belong more immediately to the divine essence than notionals do?' [*Lupton*].

It was against this kind of education that the new teachers, the scholars of the Renaissance, were beginning to protest in 1494. Colet's Oxford lectures on St. Paul (1496–1504) introduced a new method and point of view into the teaching of theology. The Oxford which Erasmus visited, and described in his letters (1499), was a meeting-point of two civilizations and two schemes of life—medievalism and modernism.

Next, what is happening in England? Politically speaking, England in 1494 is already 400 years ahead of the rest of Europe. Since the eleventh century it has been virtually one country under one king—a condition which France and Spain are only just reaching, and which Italy and Germany will not reach for another 400 years. It has the only effective parliament in Europe, and the only limited monarchy which remains limited during the seventeenth and eighteenth centuries. Its kings have suppressed the arbitrary power of the nobles without transferring it to the crown. By losing their continental possessions they have learnt the uselessness of foreign conquest. England in 1494 is peaceful and orderly, and the richest country in northern Europe.

III

Now let us cross the Channel to France. We must hire horses at Oxford, unless we prefer to walk, and go by the Wycombe road (no more than a cart-track) to London; cross the river at London Bridge; and then on by Gravesend, Rochester, and Canterbury to Dover. Once across the Channel (in a small sailing boat, as quickly as the wind allows) we can travel for about £50 a year, provided that we do not fall in with highwaymen or horse-thieves, or waste our money on tennis, fencing, or dancing. The inns are excellent in France, in Germany shocking. So long as we keep to the main routes, and avoid war areas, we can travel safely, and in tolerable comfort [*Erasmus*].

What is the state of France in 1494? First—because so much history depends on this—notice its geographical unity. France was meant by nature to be a single country under central control. It is a large, fertile plain, with easy-going rivers, and no internal barriers, sloping down from a semi-circle of mountains—Ardennes, Vosges, Jura, Alps, Cevennes, and Pyrenees—to its Atlantic coast. The only part of the country seriously divided from the rest is the Rhone valley; and there you will find traditions of political independence surviving down to the present day.

Secondly, in 1494 France has just achieved the political unity strong government, if it is to do its best. They will not be ruled by their equals, but they almost worship their kings. Who those kings were, and what they did for their country, we shall see.

IV

Let us now turn to Spain. It is easier said than done. If we go by land, we shall have to find a way over or round the Pyrenees —the most serious mountain barrier in Europe, cutting Spain off, century after century, from the political and religious ideas of its northern neighbours. If we go by sea, either from Genoa to Barcelona, or from Antwerp to Corunna, we shall still have a long and difficult climb from the coast on to the bare and windy uplands which form the central mass of the country, before we find our way to its ancient capitals, Toledo and Valladolid.

To understand what kind of country Spain was (and is) we must go back to the time of its re-conquest from the Moors. Everyone who goes to Spain should visit one of the most beautiful buildings in the world, the Mosque at Cordova. It is a cool and shadowy forest of marble, built (as the Moors knew how to build) both for the practice of religion and as a refuge from the heat. In the middle of it a clearing has been made—the marble trunks felled, the stone branches lopped off—and an ugly church in the Renaissance style inserted, to fit a Mohammedan building for Christian worship. Such has been the history of Spain. In the tenth century, when France was a patchwork of feudal states, Spain was under the heel of Moorish conquerors. Cordova was their capital. It was a University city, five times as populous as Oxford, where Moors and Christians studied side by side. Its leather-work and jewellery were known all over the world. But the military power of the Moors was already declining. The Spaniards were re-conquering their country from the north towards the south, bit by bit. First, from the mountainous Kingdom of the Asturias (the one unconquered part of old Spain), the Douro valley, the Kingdom of Leon; then the Ebro valley, Catalonia and Aragon; then the uplands of Castile, so-called from the castles ('castillos') which were built to harry the retreating Moors; and last, Andalusia, the valley of the Guadalquivir, opening on to the western seas. Aragon looked eastwards, and reversed the Roman conquest of Spain by extending its power which its geography suggests. It has not been an easy business. Five hundred years ago, in the tenth century, France was a patchwork of feudal states, as Germany still is in the fifteenth—twelve secular states and seven ecclesiastical, each with the right to make war, coin money, and administer justice; and with no link between them except an elected king. It took 500 years to turn these nineteen Frances into one—350 years under the Capet kings (987–1328), and 150 years under the Valois dynasty (1328–1483). The Capets made the crown hereditary, and Paris the capital of the country. In their wars against England (1154–1258) they created French patriotism and the French army. Sometimes by marriage or by purchase, sometimes by less regular means, they so extended their rule that by 1328 France already included fifty-nine of its modern eighty-seven departments, and only four large provinces were still independent—Flanders, Brittany, Burgundy, and Guyenne. Under the Valois kings this unity was endangered by fresh wars with England. But when in 1491 Charles VIII made a political marriage with Anne of Brittany, and added her estates to the French crown, the map of France became very much the same as in 1914.

The chief difference that you would notice was on the eastern frontier, where the Franche Comté (as it was called), or East Burgundy, was still in the hands of Austria. This was because the Dukes of Burgundy, the last holders of a group of states scattered up and down the Rhine valley, had just died out. Their Netherlands domains and East Burgundy had passed, through his marriage with Mary of Burgundy, to Maximilian I of Austria. France had retained West Burgundy. Each power coveted what the other held. The 'Burgundian policy' of the Hapsburgs plays a large part in the sixteenth century. In the seventeenth and eighteenth Bourbon diplomacy turns on the same question, and attempts to secure, at the expense of the old Burgundian territories, a 'natural frontier' for France on the left bank of the Rhine. It was the same question again in 1870, and again in 1914.

The French people in 1494, so far as we can judge them on our way through the country, have already the national character that their history will so often illustrate. They are vain, witty, quarrelsome, and changeable: great lovers of liberty, but greater lovers of success. Their character as well as their country calls for to the Balearic Isles, Sicily, Sardinia, and Naples (1229-1435). Castile looked westwards. Starting from Seville and Cadiz, Spanish sailors joined in the development of Africa, and in the discovery of America. The New World was to be a colony of Castile.

This history of conquest and re-conquest left its mark upon the people. The Spaniards at the beginning of the sixteenth century were the best soldiers in Europe, and the most devout Christians. They had sacrificed political liberty, culture, and freedom of mind in order to arm themselves against the infidel. The end of the struggle left them proud, ignorant, cruel, and fanatically orthodox. There remained little restraint upon the arbitrary power of the king, except the arbitrary power of the clergy.

In 1494 Spain, as a single country, is not yet twenty years old. Its union came about by the marriage of Ferdinand, the heir of Aragon, and Isabella, the heiress of Castile. On their accession in 1475, these 'Catholic kings' held between them three-quarters of the whole peninsula. Two years ago (1492) they conquered Granada, the last home of the Moors. Only last year (1493) a Genoese adventurer sailing under the Spanish colours came back from a mad voyage to the west with tales of a new Spain to be conquered overseas, and of gold enough to make old Spain the richest country in the world. With its wealth, its fighting power, and its centralized monarchy, no country in Europe, in 1494, was better prepared for supremacy.

V

Italy in the sixteenth century imported foreigners, as it does today. 'I think verily,' writes an English traveller in 1549, 'that in one region of the world again are not half so many strangers as in Italy: specially of gentlemen whose resort thither is principally under pretence of study. All kinds of virtue may there be learned: and therefore are those places accordingly furnished' (notice this) 'not of such students alone as are most commonly brought up in our Universities—mean men's children, sent to school in hope to live upon hired learning—but for the most part of noblemen's sons, and of the best gentlemen, that study more for knowledge and pleasure than for curiosity and lucre' [*Howard*].

Evidently, then, we shall be in good company on this part of our journey.

It is a curious contrast, when we sail from Barcelona, and land at Genoa or Naples. After passing through three countries which are nations, and have kings, we find ourselves in the one which first taught Europe the lesson of law and order, of empire and government, but which has now no unity, no patriotism, no central control. 'From the fall of the Roman Empire to the second half of the nineteenth century Italy was nothing more than a geographical expression: during the Middle Ages and in modern times there was no more an Italian state than there was a Greek state in the ancient world' [*Malet*].

In place of one Italy, there were three. The south formed a separate state, and fell under foreign control. It was conquered, as England was, by the Normans, and at the same time (1040-80). Afterwards the Kingdom of the Two Sicilies, as Naples and Sicily came to be called, was held both by France and by Spain. In central Italy the Papal States formed a belt across the peninsula, cutting off north from south, and hindering any attempt at national unity. 'The Church,' wrote *Machiavelli*, 'being on the one hand too weak to grasp the whole of Italy, and on the other too jealous to allow another power to do so, has prevented our union beneath one head, and has kept us under scattered lords and princes.' North Italy fell into foreign hands, as the South did: but the invaders did not hold it successively; they held different parts of it at the same time. The old rivalry of the Italian Republics was complicated and embittered by the quarrels of their foreign conquerors, France, Austria, and Spain.

Italy then, in 1494, is the home of all the arts—the art of painting, the art of diplomacy, the art of war: but it has made government too a mere art, with no honesty, or principle, or patriotism in it. We shall see how its political weakness made it the prey of stronger powers. But we shall also see how captive Italy took Europe captive, and how the love of beauty and of learning was carried from it into every country north of the Alps.

VI

From Italy let us too cross the Alps into Germany. It will not be so difficult as to cross the Pyrenees. Three great river-systems lie behind the Alps—that of the Rhone to the west, that of the Rhine to the north, and that of the Danube to the north-east. Several great passes leading to these valleys, such as the Mt. Genèvre in the west, the Great St. Bernard in the north-west, the Septimer in the north, the Brenner in the north-east, were well known to the Romans, and used all through the Middle Ages. In 1494 Venice holds the lower Adige valley, the natural approach to the Brenner; and unless we have the right to use the Venetian trade-routes we had better go another way—from Milan past Lake Como, and then either by the Valtelline and some lesser passes (just outside Venetian territory) to the Brenner and Innsbruck; or by one of several passes to Zürich and Basle.

Whichever way we go, we shall find no political Utopia north of the Alps. We shall pass from anarchical Italy into polyarchical Germany. There is, indeed, an Emperor in Germany. The Holy Roman Empire is, in 1494, more than 500 years old. Otto was crowned Emperor twenty-five years before Hugh Capet was elected King of France. But in point of political development, if France is 400 years behind England, Germany is 400 years behind France. For whilst the French kings have been making one France of seventeen provincial Frances, the German emperors have been struggling in vain to prevent the break-up of Germany into 'the Germanies' (as the French call it); and that not a mere nineteen large provinces, but three or four hundred small states. There is an old Elizabethan house at Conway, which is said to have 365 windows, one for every day of the year: they fit into the architectural scheme of the building, and give light and air to its many dark rooms and dusty passages. But the 365 states of Germany, with their 365 ruling Dukes, Counts, Margraves, Archbishops, and Electors (not to mention the Free Cities), let in nothing but weakness and confusion. There was not too little government: there was too much. 'Each state, each prince, prelate, and imperial town possessed the right of managing all its internal affairs, its courts of justice, its commercial regulations, its internal taxation and legislation, and its foreign alliances' [*Stubbs*].

Was there no central control? Some, but not much. Each state was nominally a fief of the Holy Roman Empire; and the Empire had an elaborately ineffective government of its own.

'For the election of the Emperor, and some other high business, there was the organization of the Seven Electors' (a committee consisting of the heads of three ecclesiastical states—Cologne, Trèves, and Mayence, and of four secular states—Bohemia, the Palatine, Saxony, and Brandenburg); 'for national deliberation and legislation, and for the voting of general taxation throughout the German portion of the Empire' (for there were non-German fiefs in Italy and elsewhere) 'there was the Imperial Diet' (a parliament without a House of Commons); 'for the preservation of peace between the several states there was the organization of the Circles' (that is, groups of states so arranged as to separate the most powerful); 'and for arbitration between the princes or states in the way of appeal there were the Imperial Chamber and the Aulic Council' [*Stubbs*]. The nearest parallel that I can think of to the Holy Roman Empire is the University of Oxford. The Chancellor is our elected Emperor. We have not one but many bodies of Electors. Convocation is our Diet, the Hebdomadal Council our Imperial Chamber, the Vice-Chancellor's Court our Aulic Council. All the formal rights under the constitution belong to the University; most of the real liberties remain with the Colleges, the names of whose Heads and the customs of whose members are almost as varied as those of the German principalities. The Emperor occasionally attempted to assert himself: it produced about as much effect as a University Commission.

But you must not suppose that the Holy Roman Empire was dead. In 1436, about fifty years before the date of our visit to Germany, the Archdukes of Austria began to be elected Emperors as a matter of course. Austria was ambitious. Its motto followed the five vowels, A E I O U—in Latin, 'Austriae est imperare orbi universo'; or, in English, 'Austria's Empire Is Over the Universe.' It was a Catholic country, too, the Pope's chief protégé north of the Alps. And its geographical position made it the natural guardian of the gate of the Danube against the increasingly dangerous advance of the Turks.

In 1494 the ruler of Austria was an able and ambitious man, Maximilian I. It was his policy of state marriages (himself to Mary the heiress of Burgundy, his son to Joanna the heiress of Spain) which founded the world-wide empire of his grandson,

Charles V. He consoled himself for his phantom rule in Germany by the dream of making himself Pope. His tomb is in the great church at Innsbruck, surrounded by bronze statues of the heroes of Germany. The effigy, like the Empire, is a wonderful work of art; but there is no body beneath it. Maximilian was buried elsewhere. The Empire was a cenotaph.

VII

We might extend our imaginary tour beyond Germany into Russia, Scandinavia, and the Netherlands. But I doubt whether we should find much to add to our picture of Europe in 1494. It will be better to stop here, and to summarize what we have learnt. What we see everywhere is the break-up of the political and social system of the Middle Ages, and the beginning of 'modern times.' The form of government which presides over this change is monarchy. Wherever a strong rule has been set up, it is that of a king who has suppressed or absorbed rival powers—the feudal nobility and the Church. Sometimes, as in England, the crown allies itself with the people against the nobles; sometimes, as in France or Spain, it gets the better of both. In England the monarchy remains constitutional: in France and Spain it becomes absolute. What we are to trace, from the beginning of the sixteenth century to the end of the eighteenth, is the rise and fall of absolute monarchy, the fall and rise of popular freedom.

Notice, secondly, a very important result of the suppression of the feudal nobles. It leaves a gap in society by which the new middle class, the commercial and trading part of the community, can enter in. Their arrival is all-important. They come to trade and to make money: they stay to bring political liberty, enlightenment, and social revolution.

Thirdly, we are looking at the beginnings of the modern nations. You might call a man an Italian in 1494, meaning that he came from Italy; or a German, to distinguish him from a Turk: but the name Englishman, Frenchman, or Spaniard was not a mere label. It meant that its bearer was one of a people who stood together, fought side by side, shared a common tradition, and were ready, at a pinch, to sacrifice their private interests for a common end. The city loyalty of ancient Greece or medieval Italy, the tribal loyalty of the German nations, the industrial loyalty of the Trade Guilds, were taking shape in a new emotion and policy called patriotism. And patriotism was already beginning to take the place of religion.

Lastly, the cult of patriotism put into the hands of the Government not only a weapon against its enemies much more deadly than gunpowder, but also a hold over its own people which for the first time made the State the rival, and not merely the partner, of the Church. This was specially significant at a time when the Renaissance was also robbing the Church of its long monopoly of learning and art, and undermining its appeal to a supernatural authority.

Four features, then, of Europe in 1494—centralized government, a middle class, national feeling, and the separation of Church and State; or (if you will) absolutism, commercialism, patriotism, and secularism—show that the medieval is already turning into the modern world.

1556 that Europe and Charles were beyond fear of a great disaster.

And this was not all. We might have supposed that, in face of such a danger, Francis would patch up his quarrel, and join in a crusade. On the contrary, Europe was scandalized to see his Most Christian Majesty allying himself with the infidel, and using the danger of Europe to extract better terms from his Austrian rival. At the moment of the battle of Mohacz a French envoy arrived in the Turkish camp, asking the Sultan's help against the Emperor. In 1535 Francis and Solyman signed commercial capitulations, and an offensive and defensive alliance. In 1543 French and Turkish fleets, with their base at Toulon, co-operated in the blockade and bombardment of Nice.

No wonder, then, that Charles failed in his task. After thirty-seven years of constant work, constant travelling and fighting, he abdicated. His huge Empire was split up. Germany he gave to his brother Ferdinand; Spain, Italy, and the Netherlands to his son Philip; as though to say, 'It is too much for one man.' He himself retired for the little that was left of his life to a Spanish monastery. There he read and wrote political dispatches, and interested himself in the affairs of the Inquisition—he could not conquer the habit of work. There was another habit that he could not conquer. It is said that he shortened his days 'with surfeits of sardine omelettes, eel pies, pickled partridges, iced beer, and flagons of Rhenish wine, relieved by copious draughts of senna and rhubarb, to which his horror-stricken doctor doomed him as he ate' [*Motley*]. There was always something epic about Charles, even in his appetites. He might have had for his epitaph, 'He sometimes spared others; himself he never spared.'

VII

We have dealt with the causes and character of the rivalry between Charles and Francis. What, now, were its results?

First, Europe was saved from a Hapsburg hegemony, and the principle of the balance of power was set up. The force of circumstances, adroitly used by Francis, had been too much for Charles's unwieldy empire. It was never revived again. But the fear of it lived on. You will find it in the background of the French Wars of Religion, and of the Thirty Years' War. The policy of Francis was resumed, and his work completed, by Henry IV, Richelieu, and Mazarin. France was built upon the ruins of Spain. Its own ruin began when, at the opening of the eighteenth century, there were Bourbons upon both the French and Spanish thrones, and Louis XIV was suspected, with better reason than Charles V, of designs upon the liberty of Europe.

The second result of the contest was the Franco-Turkish entente, which, in one shape or another, has lasted almost to the present day. What were its effects? It lowered the tone of international diplomacy. It prevented the expulsion of the Turks from Europe. It gave France, for more than a hundred years, a monopoly of trade in the Levant, and a permanent sphere of influence in the Nearer East. This alliance was perhaps one of the most significant fruits of the Renaissance. It marked the end of the medieval order, when the Catholic unity of Church and State stood solidly against the infidel and the heretic. It showed that religion was no more the motive of politics than of trade; and that its place was being taken by *raison d'état,* or national self-interest. It was that which coupled the Most Christian King with infidel allies in the sixteenth and with Protestant allies in the seventeenth century. This may seem reasonable enough to us: to the men of that time it was revolutionary.

Thirdly, the contest between Charles and Francis contributed very much to the progress of the Reformation. During the critical years, when Lutheranism was growing in Germany, and Calvinism in France, the two heads of Catholicism in north Europe were too busy fighting one another to pay much attention to the new heresy. When at last they stopped fighting, it was too late to do so. You can see this clearly from *Calvin's* correspondence. He is more afraid of what Charles may do to the Protestants in Germany than of what Francis may do to the Protestants in France. But he dreads them both. His chief hope is that they may keep each other employed. His chief fear is lest either of them may prove victorious, and so be free to persecute the Protestants; or may both agree to patch up their quarrel, and make common cause against the heretics.

One last result, which applies not merely to the struggle between Charles and Francis, but to the whole period of the Italian Wars. Whilst France was giving its attention to Italy

RESULTS

and the Nearer East, and spending its resources to maintain the balance of power in Europe, Spain and Portugal, and to a lesser extent England and Holland, were opening up the Far East, and initiating a new balance of power in America. A short comparison of dates will illustrate what I mean:

EUROPE	AMERICA	FAR EAST
1494. Charles VIII in Italy.	1492. Columbus's Voyage.	1498. Vasco da Gama in India.
1499. Louis XII in Italy.	1497. Cabot in N. America	
	1500. Cabral in Brazil.	
1520. First War of Francis and Charles.	1520. Magellan's Voyage.	1520. Portuguese Embassy at Peking.
1529. Turks at Vienna.	1529. Cortés in Mexico.	
	1532. Pizarro in Peru.	

True, between 1531 and 1534, Cartier, under Francis' patronage, made three voyages to North America, and founded French colonies on the St. Lawrence. But it is pretty clear what is happening upon the whole. Just as in the eighteenth century the British Empire was built up while Europe, and particularly France, was occupied with the wars of Frederick the Great, so now the Spanish and Portuguese empires were founded while France was occupied with Italy and Austria. And behind both events lies the great discovery which was handed on to England from Portugal and Spain—which France never quite realized, and Germany learnt too late: the discovery of the influence of sea power upon history.

LECTURE V

THE REFORMATION

I

We have seen that when the Renaissance crossed the Alps it became scientific instead of artistic, constructive as well as critical, and took on a new moral and philosophical character. It thus carried the revolt against medievalism into fresh fields. Every nation had something to contribute to the new order; and the contributions of the strong, successful states were not necessarily or in fact the most important. Feudalism, the political and social system of the Middle Ages, was developed into absolute monarchy in France and Spain. Scholasticism, the medieval system of thought, was transformed by international scholars and thinkers into modern science and learning. It remained for Catholicism, the religious system of the Middle Ages, to be broken up and put together again in the shape of modern Christianity. This was the work of the Reformation; and most of it was done in Germany.

II

First, as to the causes of the Reformation. How are we to select or classify, where so many things contributed to such a vast movement? I will content myself with three causes which were specially important in Germany, and leave you to infer the rest. They are papal finance, the condition of the religious Orders and the publication of the New Testament.

By papal finance I mean this. The Roman Church at the beginning of the sixteenth century was organized and managed as a business concern. It is always a difficult question, how far it is proper to receive wages for religious work, or to exact payment in return for spiritual privileges. But all conscientious men feel (and they felt the same in the sixteenth century) that it is wrong to make a profit out of religion. And it is undeniable that under Julius II and Leo X the Papacy was doing so. Two of its most scandalous transactions were the sale of benefices, and the trade in Indul-

PAPAL FINANCE

gences. Read Luther's *Address to the Christian Nobility of the German Nation* [*Wace and Buchheim*]. No second-hand account gives half so good an impression of the causes of the Reformation. Part I of the Address is a refutation of the Roman position under three heads. Part II suggests Agenda for a General Council—the temporal power of the Papacy; the expenses of the Papal Court, and of the Cardinals' establishments; the financial exactions by which these are met—for instance, the tax called 'Annates,' originally raised to fight the Turks, but now spent at Rome; more and more benefices falling into papal hands, and sold to the highest bidder; the payment made by newly-appointed archbishops for the 'pallium'—and so forth. In Part III Luther specifies no less than twenty-seven points in which reform is necessary. As he is writing to the German princes he includes a few for their special benefit—as, for instance, a demand for University reform, and a protest against the luxury and immorality of German society. But most of his twenty-seven articles are directed against the Papacy, and call for the abolition of its worldly privileges and its financial exactions, amongst which the sale of benefices again occurs. This was simony, and in itself a great scandal. It was also, as Luther knew, a point upon which the German princes felt particularly sore. They disliked all the best Church appointments being in the Pope's hands. They did not see why the fees paid upon taking up a benefice, or its income during a vacancy, should not go into their own pockets.

The trade in Indulgences, the immediate cause of Luther's protest at Wittenberg in 1517, needs a little further explanation. It was not a new question. The business went back to the year 1300, when Pope Boniface VIII expounded the doctrine that the superabundance of Christ's sacrifice formed an inexhaustible treasury [infinitus thesaurus] of grace, the spending of which had been entrusted to the Church in the form of grants giving total or partial remission of the punishment due, or the penance to be done, for sin. He accordingly decreed that in 1300, and every hundredth year after, anyone who went on pilgrimage to the Church of St. Peter and St. Paul outside Rome, and made a penitent confession, should receive full pardon for his sins, and full remission of any punishment they deserved. In 1343 Clement VI, finding this a popular institution, altered it from once a century to every fifty years. In 1476 (and this was the crux) a Bull of Sixtus IV not only extended these Indulgences from living penitents to souls in Purgatory, but also turned a religious concession into a means of raising money. I will translate the important words. 'We therefore allow and make this Indulgence: if any relations, or friends, or other faithful Christians, with pious intention, and on behalf of such souls as are exposed to the fire of Purgatory, shall within the said ten years give a certain sum of money to the restoration fund of the Church of X, we hereby decree that such plenary remission shall be effective and favourable for a relaxation of penalties for those souls on whose behalf they have made the said payment.' If there were any doubt as to the meaning of these words, it would be set at rest by the prospectus of this and other Indulgences put out by the authorities of the Church of X; it is a very commercial document, especially recommending one form of policy which gives plenary remission 'whenever a man thinks he may be going to die, even though he does not actually do so'—as, for instance, in shipwreck, or siege, or time of plague. 'This,' the document ends, 'is an unprecedented provision, especially for those who go to sea' [*Kidd*].

When Julius II in 1510 and Leo X in 1514 wanted money for the building of New St. Peter's at Rome, these Indulgences were adapted for the foreign market, especially in Germany: and little remained except to demand cash payment from the purchaser. For an extra fee you could now choose your own confessor; and he could impose as penance a further contribution to the building fund. This was the traffic against which Luther protested. You will allow that he had a good case. And here too he could count on the support of the German princes. The sale of Indulgences meant a constant drain of money from their estates for the benefit of Rome. So much for papal finance.

The second cause of the Reformation was the bad condition of the clergy, and especially of the religious Orders. This too was an old complaint; and it was the more serious because the religious Orders had many of them been founded for the very purpose of reforming the society which they now disgraced. The feeling against them had been growing since the fourteenth century (when you find it, for instance, in Chaucer), and was

CLERICAL IGNORANCE

coming to a head in the sixteenth. It was always, I think, the chief popular grievance against the Church. As to contemporary evidence, the most famous of all attacks on the monks was a sham correspondence, making fun of their ignorance, immorality, and bad Latin. The book came to be published in this way. A few years before Luther's Wittenberg protest, Reuchlin, one of the first Hebrew scholars of the Renaissance, had been put on his trial for unorthodoxy by the monastic theologians of Cologne. After his acquittal he published the letters of sympathy he had received during the trial, under the title of *Clarorum Virorum Epistolae*. Ulrich von Hütten, Luther's most militant supporter, hit on the idea of completing the discomfiture of the monks by publishing imaginary letters of sympathy written to Ortwin Gratius, one of the obscurantists of Cologne: and he called the book *Epistolae Obscurorum Virorum*, which I suppose might not unfairly be rendered, 'Letters of some shady persons.' It is impossible to extract the full flavour of the book—it is rather strong at times—from a quotation, or to reproduce the dog Latin in which it is written: but here is one of the letters, making fun of monkish superstition. 'Henricus Schaffsmulius to Ortwinus Gratius . . . I want to ask your reverence what you think about the following point. Supposing that on a Friday, or some other fast day, one eats an egg, and there is a chicken in it? The other day we were sitting in an inn at Campus Florae having a meal, and ate some eggs; and when I opened one egg I saw that there was a chicken in it. I showed it to my companion. "Eat it up quick," he said, "before the landlord sees it. If he does, you will have to pay half-a-crown or five shillings for it: for in these parts it is the custom to pay on the nail for everything set on the table; they won't take anything back. And if he sees there is a young chicken in the egg he will say you must pay for the fowl as well as the egg; and he will reckon it full-grown, however small it may be." So I swallowed the egg as quick as I could, chicken and all. Afterwards I remembered that it was a Friday: and I said to my companion, "You have made me commit a mortal sin, in eating meat on a Friday." "Oh, no," he replied, "it is not a mortal sin, or even a venial one. A young chicken like that is reckoned part of the egg, until it is hatched out." And he told me that it was the same with cheese that had maggots in it, or with insects in cherries, beans, and so on. They could all be eaten on Fridays, and even on Vigils of the Apostles.' And so the book goes on. It is of course a parody, and no fair account of the whole class attacked. But the evils were sufficiently serious —ignorance, superstition, loose living—and the attempt of the Church to reform these abuses is sufficient evidence that they existed.

For the third cause of the Reformation I should take the publication of the New Testament. This we have already mentioned when dealing with the Renaissance. The invention of printing enabled the Greek text of the New Testament (for scholars), and (for less educated people) translations of it in French, German, Italian, and other languages, to obtain quick and wide circulation. The prejudices to be overcome were at first immense. The Vulgate, the authorized Latin version of the Bible, had been used so long that every word of it had come to be thought sacred: and when in 1522 the Spanish University of Alcalá published an Old Testament with the Vulgate in the middle, and the original Hebrew and the old Greek Septuagint translation on either side of it, the editors compared this arrangement to Christ crucified between two thieves. But the greater the prejudice against first-hand knowledge of the Bible the greater its effects, if widely spread. This was the object of Erasmus's famous edition of the New Testament—in Greek, with a new Latin translation opposite—which appeared in 1516. 'I wish,' he says in his Preface, 'that even the weakest woman should read the Gospels, and the epistles of Paul; I wish that they were translated into all languages, so that they might be read and understood, not only by Scotchmen and Irishmen, but also by Saracens and Turks. I long for the farmer to sing portions of them to himself as he follows the plough, for the weaver to hum them to the tune of his shuttle, and for the traveller to beguile with their stories the tedium of his journey' [*Seebohm*]. Erasmus, however, was not content to let the Bible speak for itself. He introduced each Gospel and Epistle with a preface of his own; and added notes and paraphrases in which he pointed to the contrast between the teaching of Christ and the practices of the Church. This, for instances, is his comment on the passage in Matthew xxiii, dealing with the Scribes and Pharisees: 'You may find a bishop here and there who teaches the Gospel, though life and teaching have small agreement. But what shall we say of those who destroy the Gospel itself, make laws at their will, tyrannize over the laity, and measure right and wrong with rules constructed by themselves? Or those who entangle their flocks in the meshes of crafty canons, who sit not in the seat of the Gospel, but in the seat of Caiaphas and Simon Magus, prelates of evil, who bring disgrace and discredit on their worthier brethren?' Or, on Matt. xxiv, 23 ("Lo, Here is Christ"): 'I saw with mine own eyes Pope Julius II at Bologna, and afterwards at Rome, marching at the head of a triumphal procession, as if he were Pompey or Caesar. St. Peter subdued the world with faith, not with arms or soldiers or military engines. St. Peter's successors would win as many victories as St. Peter won if they had St. Peter's spirit.' This kind of commentary might not suit the 'Cambridge Bible for Schools.' But the case was urgent, and Erasmus was determined that new readers of the Gospel should not miss its modern application. Nor did they.

III

It is time now to leave the causes of the Reformation, and come to the man who actually began it. I will not stop to give an account of Luther's life, which is in all the books [e.g. *Smith*]. But I will pick out one or two points which may help to explain him, and then go on to the movement to which he gave origin and expression.

Before he became a Reformer, Luther was a peasant, a monk, and a scholar; he experienced conversion; and he went on a pilgrimage to Rome. His peasant origin explains his manliness, his lack of refinement, his simple way of dealing with complex problems. His monastic training left him devout, and rather superstitious, with a strong leaning towards orthodoxy outside those matters in which his conscience made him a rebel. Nor was he a mere agitator: all his life he was a great reader of books, and for many years a prolific writer. As a monk he had studied the Bible and the Fathers; as a lecturer at Wittenberg he read Lefèvre, Erasmus, and many other mystical or humanist writers. He was a self-educated man: his opinions might be crude; but he had formed them himself, and was prepared to stand by them.

Then he had suddenly discovered, like St. Paul, that though he could form his own mind, he could not save his own soul. He went through a vivid experience of conversion, and found salvation in the text, 'The just shall live by faith.' This conviction gave his life the centre it needed. Round it he built his theology: upon it he based his moral courage. He feared nothing but not to preach his faith. Finally, soon after his conversion, Luther visited Rome; and it was the shock of what he saw there—the crying contrast between the New Testament in his heart and the old Church before his eyes—that turned him into a Reformer.

The Reformation might have come about if Luther had done no more than challenge the sale of Indulgences. But it would not have taken the course it did unless he had also become a great and popular writer. We know something about the circulation of his books. The number of German works printed in 1518, including Luther's, was a hundred and fifty; three years later they were more than six times as numerous. It was in 1520 that Luther began publishing his chief theological works; and the rapid increase from that date is largely attributable to his own writings, and those to which they gave rise [*Smith*]. We have also a letter from Froben, Luther's publisher at Basle, dated 1519, in which he says that six hundred copies of his latest 'Lucubrationes' have been sent to France and Spain, as well as to all parts of Italy, to England, and to the Netherlands; that they are being sold in Paris, and read even by students of the orthodox Sorbonne. Practically the whole edition is sold out. 'I never knew a book,' says Froben, 'sell so well' [*Kidd*]. It was a favourable moment for publication. To be educated then was to know Latin; and any book published in Latin had an international circulation, like a cinema film nowadays. Luther and Erasmus must have had reading publics unrivalled until the eighteenth century, when French became what Latin had been, and made Voltaire and Rousseau international. It was an age, too, of translations, of national as well as European demand: and everywhere printing-presses were springing up to supply food for the new appetite. But it was not merely the demand for books, or the interest in theology, which secured Luther his circulation; but also his style. Michelet compared it to a mixture of Moses and Rabelais. As those two authors never collaborated, I cannot tell whether it is a good comparison. But that Luther's style is vigorous, eloquent, wordy, and rather vulgar, you can judge for yourselves, even from an English translation. It was a new way of treating theology, in the sixteenth century; and it made an immense appeal.

Let me mention three other points, closely connected with one another. Politically, Luther was a conservative, and stood for the rights of the German princes against their own subjects, as well as against the Pope. The discontented knights of 1523, the rebellious peasantry of 1524, got no sympathy from him. Unlike Calvinism, which became a disintegrating force in politics, Lutheranism played into the hands of the government, and became a State religion.

Again, as in politics Luther supported the Government, so in ecclesiastical matters he was what we should call a 'strong Churchman.' In 1519 he was willing to drop his attack on Indulgences, and to submit to the Pope. 'I testify,' he writes, 'before God and his whole Creation, that I have never wished, and do not wish today, in any way to impair or destroy the power of the Roman Church . . . I fully believe that the power of this Church is supreme' [Kidd]. And though later he threw over the Pope, Luther never surrendered the Catholic system. He bitterly opposed the innovations in Church order and customs introduced by more advanced 'Lutherans' than himself—Carlstadt, Munzer, or the Anabaptists. Like John Wesley, he was never really a member of the sect called by his name.

One more point. The upshot of Luther's teaching was to dethrone the Pope and to enthrone the Bible. Authority was not destroyed; it was only transferred. Orthodoxy was not impaired: it was refounded on the Scriptures. But on what Scriptures, and how interpreted? Those which Luther thought important, interpreted in Luther's way. For instance, Philip of Hesse quarrelled with his wife, and wanted to marry again. As a Catholic, he would have gone to the Pope, and paid for a divorce. As a Protestant, he went to Luther, who, without any payment, referred him to the example of Abraham, and allowed him to keep both wives at the same time. True, this caused something of a scandal. But no Protestant doubted that such matters must be settled by authority, or that the principle of authority which Luther set up was sound.

IV

Luther's great protest came about in this way. In 1514 Leo X needed money for the building fund of St. Peter's, and proposed to raise it, in his cynical way, by the sale of Indulgences. He accordingly entered into an agreement (and nothing shows better the character of papal finance) with Albert, Archbishop of Mayence, and with a big banking firm, the Fuggers of Augsburg. Albert owed the bank a large sum of money, which he had borrowed from them to pay the Pope when he received his archbishopric. The bank was now to undertake the sale of Indulgences. Half the receipts were to go to the bank in payment of the archbishop's debt, and half to the Pope, to build his new cathedral. The actual business of selling the Indulgences was put into the hands of one Tetzel, who carried out a kind of 'national mission' to advertise his wares. We have a contemporary account of Tetzel's methods: it comes from a mining village called St. Annaberg. 'It is incredible what the ignorant and impudent friar gave out. He said that if a Christian had committed incest, he had only to drop a coin into the Pope's Indulgence box, and the Pope had power in heaven and on earth to forgive the sin; and if he forgave it, God must do so too. Item, if they contributed readily, and bought grace and indulgence, all the hills of St. Annaberg would become pure solid silver. Item, as soon as the coin tinkled in the box, the soul for whom the money was paid would go straight to heaven. The Indulgence was so highly prized that, when Tetzel entered a city, the Papal Bull was borne on a satin or gold-embroidered cushion, and all the priests and monks, the Town Council, the schoolmaster and his scholars, men, women, maidens, and children, all went out to meet him with banners and tapers, with songs and processions. All the bells were rung, and all the organs struck up. He was conducted into the church, and a red cross was erected in the middle of the building, and the Pope's banner displayed. In fact, 'God himself could not have been welcomed and entertained with greater honour' [*Kidd*]. This was the kind of thing that roused Luther, and no wonder. His famous 'Theses,' nailed to the church door at Wittenberg in 1517, were in form no more than questions for discussion: they were in fact a comprehensive denunciation of Tetzel, the Papacy, and all their works.

Charles V was at this time in Spain, and had not yet been elected Emperor. How did he hear of Luther, and what did he think of him? In October, 1520—and the date shows how slowly news travelled in those days—*Peter Martyr*, writing from Spain, transcribes a long letter that he has received from his friend Valdes at Brussels about a fearful portent [prodigium horrendum] which has appeared in Germany. He goes on to quote a full account of Luther's 'Theses,' and the burning of the Pope's Bull. 'I am terribly afraid,' wrote Valdes, 'that this evil will spread too widely for us to be able to apply any remedy to it.' The next news, which is also from Spain, shows that Valdes was right. In April, 1521, Charles received a letter from his old tutor, now his Regent in Spain, Adrian of Utrecht. It ended as follows (but I have had to prune the Cardinal's style): 'A person named Martin Luther has been properly and justly condemned by the Holy See for a number of errors and heresies. Nevertheless he obstinately persists in diffusing and spreading the said errors and heresies by writing in districts subject to the Empire, to the great dishonour and disservice of God, and of our holy mother the Church: besides which it is a blemish and insult to your Majesty, since everyone knows your Majesty's fervent intention to oppose all who act contrary to our Lord Jesus Christ and our holy faith. And so I beg you, Sire, most humbly, to make the whole world understand that you are the enemy of the enemies of Christ, and of the holy faith ... or at least to defend your own honour, by prohibiting and preventing this wicked and pestilent fellow from openly and publicly corrupting the said holy Catholic faith; and to send and transfer the same Martin Luther to his judge, our holy father the Pope, for just chastisement, and the punishment he deserves. Your very humble servant, A., Cardinal of Tortosa' [*Gachard*].

This letter did not reach Charles until he was already at the Diet of Worms (April, 1521). There he saw and heard the heretic for himself. Luther had come to the Diet more than half expecting to be made a martyr: but his safe conduct was respected, and he was allowed to go away into ignominious retirement. Honesty was the Emperor's best policy; and Luther's political position was stronger than that of John Huss. But Charles must also satisfy the Pope; so he made a declaration pledging himself to use all his power for the suppression of Lutheranism. 'My predecessors,' he said, 'the most Christian Emperors of the German race, the Austrian Archdukes, and Dukes of Burgundy, were until death the truest sons of the Catholic Church. They have left behind them the holy Catholic rites, that I should live and die therein; and so until now, with God's aid, I have lived, as becomes a Christian Emperor ... A single monk, led astray by private judgment, has set himself against the faith held by all Christians for a thousand years or more, and impudently concludes that all Christians up to now have erred. I am therefore resolved to stake upon this cause all my dominions, my friends, my body and my blood, my life and my soul' [Kidd].

Charles, I am sure, honestly hated the Lutheran heresy. He was known to be a devout Catholic. 'Every day in his life,' says the Venetian envoy, 'he has heard one, and often two, masses. At present (1557) he hears three ... He attends sermons at the great Church festivals. ... He reads the Bible every day, makes his confession and communion four times a year, and gives alms to the poor ... I have heard it related as a fact, and as a notable evidence of his religious zeal, that when he was at Ingolstadt, and near the Protestant army, he was seen at midnight in his tent, kneeling before a crucifix, with his hands clasped in prayer' [Badoaro]. To such a man it was a matter of conviction, as well as of policy, to declare war on Lutheranism.

V

But what could Charles do? His difficulties were immense. The only policy which his conscience allowed him—the extirpation of Protestantism—was rendered practically impossible by the political character of Germany, the popularity of Luther's appeal, and the uncertain relations between the Emperor and the Pope.

First, the political state of Germany. The minute and varied subdivision of the Empire made it as easy to propagate heresy there as it was difficult to eradicate it. There were always princes who would turn Protestant because their neighbours were Catholic, or remain Catholic because their neighbours were

Protestant. A preacher of heresy who was prosecuted in one state could always flee into another. A long apprenticeship in caballing had taught the princes how to form leagues in order to attack one another, or to defy the Emperor. Any strong policy that issued from Vienna was certain to be opposed at Nuremberg, at Dresden, or at Berlin. If it was to be imposed by force, that could only be by the use of foreign or mercenary troops. Indeed Charles himself visited Germany as a foreigner, and did not spend there more than eight or ten out of the thirty-seven years of his reign. Such conditions left him little chance of a successful religious policy.

Again, public support made Luther irrepressible. At the very moment when the Emperor and Diet (at Worms, 1521) were publishing their ban against him, and burning his books, the Venetian ambassador wrote home, 'I cannot tell you how much favour Luther enjoys here ... In truth, had this man been prudent, had he restricted himself to his first propositions and not entangled himself in manifest errors about the faith, he would have been ... adored by the whole of Germany' [*Contarini*]. And Valdes writes to Peter Martyr at the same time to say that Germany is as little likely to listen to the Emperor as to the Pope; and that, in spite of his prohibition, Luther's books are being sold with impunity in every village street [*Peter Martyr*]. In face of this passive resistance Charles was powerless. His decrees were as useless against paper and ink as the Pope's Bulls were against Protestants. He might and did attempt a theological compromise. The Colloquy of Ratisbon in 1541 was one step in this direction: the Interim of Augsburg in 1548 was another. But both attempts failed, owing to the bitterness of party feeling, not only between Catholics and Protestants, but also between one body of Protestants and another. The only settlement which could be reached, and that not till thirty-eight years after Luther's protest at Wittenberg, was a mere truce (the Peace of Augsburg, 1555), which left Germany divided into hostile camps, and arming for a thirty years' war.

Napoleon is reported to have said that Charles might have solved all his difficulties by becoming a Protestant. An easy solution for a realist of the eighteenth century, who was ready, if it would serve his turn, to profess Mohammedanism; but for

Charles an impossible one. He was a convinced Catholic, king of the most Catholic country in Europe, and secular partner of the Pope. How could he, or why should he sacrifice so much for the unification of Germany? And the country itself was half Catholic. Is there any likelihood that Charles would have united the whole of Germany, where Gustavus Adolphus failed to unite even the Protestant north?

A third and unexpected difficulty that Charles had to face was the attitude of the Popes. In 1521 he was on friendly terms with Leo X, and this is reflected in his declaration at Worms against the Protestants. The same year Leo died. His successor, Adrian VI, Charles's old tutor and viceroy, disappointed his patron by taking Francis' side in their quarrel, and listening to Francis' offer of help against the Turks. The Emperor grew less anxious to oblige such an ungrateful Pope, and the proceedings against the Lutherans languished. Clement VII, who succeeded to the Papacy in 1523, was at first friendly. But the victory of Pavia in 1525, which set Charles free to deal with the Protestants, also earned him the jealousy of the Pope. They took opposite sides in the League of Cognac (1526); and in 1527 came the fatal sack of Rome by a renegade Imperial army. The next year, indeed, they were reconciled, and in 1530 Charles went straight from his Coronation at Bologna to deal with the Lutherans at the Diet of Augsburg. But by this time the Protestant states of Germany were too strong for coercion, and too stubborn for compromise. I don't think that Charles ever gave up his intention to crush Lutheranism. But had he succeeded, it would have been regarded as a victory for the Church: and he did not feel inclined to do so much for an unfriendly or intriguing Pope. The Popes, for their part, disliked Charles's power in Italy, and distrusted his independent type of Churchmanship. But, if he failed to crush the Protestants, their jealousy was very largely to blame.

Taking all Charles's difficulties into account, I think we shall feel more surprise at his attempting so much than at his achieving so little. He fought a losing battle for Catholicism single-handed, not only against the Protestant Princes of Germany, but also against the official head of Catholic Christendom.

see the foolishness of the whole scheme. For the sake of problematical conquests in Italy Charles sacrifices possessions at home which he can never regain—bags full of gold to Henry VII of England, to Ferdinand of Spain the district of Roussillon in the Pyrenees, and to Maximilian of Austria two of the most important frontier provinces of France, the dowry of his wife Mary of Burgundy—Artois and the Franche Comté. Nor were these sacrifices of much use. Whatever promises of neutrality might be made, French interference at Milan would be resented by Maximilian, who regarded it as a fief of the Empire; at Naples by Ferdinand of Spain, who hoped to regain that old outpost of Aragon; and everywhere by the Pope, who did not intend the balance of forces in Italy to be upset by any power except his own.

The Italian wars which began in 1494 lasted, with hardly an interval, until 1559—a period of sixty years. Their history falls into five periods, which I will summarize very shortly.

First (1494–1498), *Expedition of Charles VIII*. He easily reaches Milan, Florence, Rome, and Naples (1495). Then a league is formed against him between the Emperor, the Pope, the King of Spain, Venice, and Ludovico of Milan, the very man who had invited him into the country. The battle of Fornovo (1495) secures his retreat. By 1497 his last troops are withdrawn. In 1498 Charles is dead.

Second (1499–1504), *First expedition of Louis XII*. He defeats and captures Ludovico at the battle of Novara; reaches Rome and Naples; and partitions South Italy with Ferdinand of Spain by the Treaty of Granada (1500). But there is soon a dispute about the terms of partition, and he is driven out of the country (1504).

Third (1508–1515), *Second expedition of Louis XII*. This time he is invited into Italy by Pope Julius II, to join with Austria and Spain in his League of Cambrai against Venice. The French army does the bulk of the fighting, and defeats the Venetians at Agnadello (1509). Julius thereupon forms a Holy League with the Swiss and Henry VIII of England to drive Louis out (1511). The French win the battle of Ravenna, but are defeated at the second battle of Novara, and have to evacuate the country (1512). In 1515 Louis is dead.

C

Fourth (1515–1546), *The Italian Wars of Francis I and Charles V.* In 1515 Francis I of France invades Italy and wins the battle of Marignano, which enables him to make a Concordat with Pope Leo X, and (by the Treaty of Noyon, 1516) to keep Milan. But a second campaign in 1520 leads to his defeat and capture at Pavia (1525); and the concessions of territory which he is forced to make by the Treaty of Madrid (1526) are hardly undone by subsequent wars and the Treaties of Cambrai in 1529 and Crépy in 1544.

Fifth (1552–1559), *The last wars,* and final settlement between Henry II of France and Philip II of Spain by the Treaty of Cateau Cambrésis in 1559.

But with these two last periods we must deal more in detail at a later stage.

IV

I said that these Italian wars illustrated the transition from medieval to modern methods of fighting. Let me explain a little more fully. One knows how, when a child tries to draw a battle-picture, he is apt to put in, without any feeling of incongruity, ancient Greeks and modern Frenchmen, Norman bowmen and the Royal Horse Artillery, Red Indians and South Sea Islanders, fighting side by side. Something of the same kind happened in the Italian wars. Mounted knights in full armour charged men armed with cannon and arquebus. Phalanxes of Swiss pikemen found themselves attacked by 'artifices du diable,' as they called them—primitive bombs, 'stink-pots,' 'tanks,' and the like. Cavaliers who, once unhorsed, were too heavily armoured to rise again, and who, according to the gentlemanly customs of medieval war, were allowed (for a consideration) to go home, and fight again another day, were now brutally stabbed as they lay. The old professional mercenaries measured swords with the new national amateur infantry. Bayard, the pattern of medieval chivalry, fought his last campaigns on fields where the fore-runners of modern scientific generals—Gaston de Foix or Gonzalvo da Cordova—won their first successes. There could be no doubt in what direction military art was moving. Guns which in the Hundred Years' War measured three or four feet in length, and had a range of a hundred to a hundred and fifty yards, were now from ten to twenty feet long, and carried proportionately far: some of the siege guns were so heavy that they could only be drawn by teams of fifteen to twenty horses. The arquebus still took three minutes to load and two to fire, and its range was only from a hundred and fifty to two hundred yards, so that the longbow and cross-bow could still be used against it: but it had come to stay. There were now in the field not only national French cavalry—the heavy-armed 'Gens d'armes,' with their lance and sword and axe—but also national French infantry, fighting side by side with Swiss and German 'lansquenets'—professional mercenaries. In 1515, after defeating some of these Swiss gentry at Marignano, Francis I cleverly contrived that in future they should sell themselves to nobody but the King of France. They became the royal body-guard of the Louvre and of the Tuileries, as they are still the papal body-guard at the Vatican. In the later eighteenth century they were the only troops upon which the French monarchy could depend. It was they who defended the Tuileries against the revolutionary mob in 1792, and were massacred almost to a man. They were not finally abolished till 1830; and to this day, when you visit a French cathedral, the military-looking verger who shows you round is called a 'Suisse.' As to tactics, sixteenth-century armies still fought in long lines, face to face, and this practice continued down to the eighteenth century. The chief novelty in these wars was the 'frightfulness' practised by the foreign troops, who, disregarding the rules of the game drawn up by the Italian "condottieri", refused quarter to their prisoners, put garrisons to the sword, and tortured civilians in the search for loot.

The brutal business of war had then few of the modern alleviations. We know this from the memoirs of the most famous French physician of the sixteenth century, Ambroise Paré, who learnt his business on the Italian battlefields. 'There was in his time no organized medical service. The King took with him his own physicians—priests, or clerks in Holy Orders—who also served as chaplains to the army. A host of barber-surgeons, irregular practitioners, and quacks followed the troops with drugs and ointments. Women skilled to suck or dress wounds went in and out of the camp. The soldiers had their own rough and ready remedies for gunshot wounds—Paré notes one, which was a drink of gunpowder stirred in water... With the use of powder and shot came the belief that gunshot wounds had a special virulence: and the treatment with boiling oil was practised by general consent long after Paré, within forty-eight hours after his first sight of fighting, had discovered the folly of it.' Paré mentions, among other popular medicines, powdered mummy, which was imported from Egypt, and much prized as a remedy for 'inward bruise,' and 'unicorn's horn' (several substitutes for which were on the market) as an infallible antidote to poison. [*Paget*].

V

What were the results of these Italian wars? First, as regards France, which started them, and was mainly responsible for keeping them going. By 1559, at the end of sixty-five years of almost continuous fighting, a few fortified places in Savoy and Piedmont were all of Italy that remained in French hands. One invader after another had the same experience—it was a country easy to overrun, but impossible to hold. All Charles's romantic dreams, all Louis' material ambitions, all the picturesque enterprises of Francis, ended, as the old French chronicler put it, 'in glory and smoke'. We have seen how much France paid, at the beginning of the wars, for freedom to invade Italy. At the end of them, instead of Milan or Naples, France had gained, in the north Calais, and in the east the three bishoprics (better known in later days as the three fortresses) of Lorraine—Metz, Toul, and Verdun. Modern French historians have written many homilies on this text. They have blamed a policy which wasted the national resources so far from home, and in a country which could never be held. The true line of expansion, they point out, was eastwards and northwards, towards the 'natural frontier' of the Rhine and the Scheldt. There is much truth in this from the point of view of later French history. But I think that these critics are a little obsessed by the experiences of 1870 and 1914. In the sixteenth century France ran no serious danger of attack from the east. The one front upon which she could most easily meet her rivals was North Italy. Nor was it territory that her kings needed so much as fame. And to get that, they must play their part on the public stage, in the intellectual and artistic centre of Europe, where there were writers and painters to advertise their deeds. In that part of their aim, at any rate, they were successful.

Secondly, how was Italy itself affected by the wars? A contemporary historian describes 1494 as 'the most unfortunate year for Italy, the very first, in truth, of our disastrous years, since it opened the door to numberless and horrible calamities, in which it may be said that a great portion of the world has subsequently shared' [*Guicciardini*]. When Charles VIII was marching over the Alps, Savonarola, the prophet and social reformer of Florence, announced that he was coming 'as a scourge upon the cities of Italy, to punish them for their sins.'

As to the scourge, he was not far wrong. But there is little evidence that it produced any repentance or improvement. Italy still went on in its old selfish, immoral way. The presence of foreign enemies in the country may have saved it from Turkish attacks; may even have saved it from the ambitious designs of Machiavelli's hero, Caesar Borgia. But France came to plunder, not to save, as she did again just three centuries later, under Napoleon. Only now she did nothing, as he did, for the unity and good government of the country. On the contrary, all hope of the unification of Italy was postponed for over three hundred years.

Thirdly, how did the Italian wars affect the position of the Papacy? The Popes of the sixteenth century were neither spectators nor umpires of the struggle, but active participants in it. Alexander VI intrigued for and against the French invader of his country, cursing him when he was free to curse, blessing him when he could not afford to do otherwise. Julius II formed one league of foreign powers against Venice to extend the Papal States, and another with Venice to expel the foreigner. Erasmus saw him, on horseback, in full armour, leading his troops against Bologna—a man most fit for war. At a time when many people were learning to judge the Church by the New Testament, such conduct could not go unchallenged. The worldly, political, and military part played by these men as rulers of the Papal States was one of the causes of the Reformation. Yet most people, I think, still regarded the Temporal Power of the Papacy as necessary to its spiritual supremacy. They were less scandalized at the idea of a Pope fighting than at the idea of anyone being found to fight against a Pope. The Papacy, I must say, made full use of this prejudice. It shot down its enemies and excommunicated them at the same time. And the very success of these methods made it hated, at a time when it might have been the one champion of peace and justice in a violent and treacherous world.

Lastly, it is often said that the Italian wars did one great service to civilization—they carried the Renaissance into the countries north of the Alps. How far is this true? Of course, these wars took many people to Italy who would not otherwise have gone there. Many of them brought back among their loot pictures, books, jewellery, and other products of the Renaissance. The reign of Francis I saw a considerable vogue of Italian architecture, Italian art and culture, in French society. Lyons, the half-way house from Paris to Milan, became a trading centre and a home of Humanism. In Montaigne's household Latin was always used in conversation, even by the maidservants [*Tilley*]. But the rank and file of the French armies in Italy were not of the class to profit much by contact with Humanism. Even Charles VIII, though he brought back Italian gardeners and plasterers from Naples, seems to have been more struck by a cageful of lions at Florence than by all the artistic treasures of that city. Burchardt, who showed him round Rome, does not suggest that he found much to admire there. The *Vergier d'honneur,* a long poem written to celebrate the expedition, mentions little but fighting and jollification. One odd sidelight on this point may be added from the diary of a citizen of Paris during the reign of Francis I. This is the entry: 'In the year 1517 Monsieur de la Vernade, Knight, forwarded to this city of Paris a dead serpent boiled in oil, called a crocodile, which had been given to him at Venice by the city magistrates. This serpent, on his return, he presented to the church of St. Anthony at Paris, and had it fixed upon the wall, where it still remains. This serpent was captured near Cairo, when the Nile was in flood. It was found dead' [*Journal d'un Bourgeois de Paris*]. I suspect that preserved crocodiles appealed more to the ordinary man of that time than the art and literature of Italy.

Nor can one suppose that these wars made it any easier for peaceful travellers to go to and fro across the Alps. There were always in peace time a great many of these, as you can tell from the letters of Erasmus—scholars visiting Padua or Bologna, ecclesiastics travelling to Rome on church business, merchants and ambassadors going to or coming from Venice. It was by such means, rather than by military invasion, that the real riches of Italy were carried across the Alps.

LECTURE IV

THE RIVALRY OF FRANCIS I AND CHARLES V

I

During the first three periods of the Italian wars, with which we have now dealt, Italy was the prey of French and (to a lesser extent) of Austrian and Spanish invaders. During the fourth and fifth periods, with which we have still to deal, it becomes the fighting-ground of Francis I and Charles V. The drama of which they are the protagonists has more than temporary importance. We are in fact watching, in the rivalry of Francis and Charles, the earliest form of that Franco-Austrian enmity which was the mainspring of European diplomacy till the middle of the eighteenth century, when it was transformed, with even more momentous consequences, into a feud between France and Prussia. It is therefore essential to inquire, at the outset, what Francis and Charles stood for, and why their interests came into conflict.

II

The French people did not realize that they had lost their liberties until they regained them under the Revolution. Looking back from the experiences of 1789, they interpreted French history as a struggle of the people against the Crown to recover rights which in England we had never lost. The last French king to acknowledge these rights was Henry IV: one of the first to ignore them was Francis I.

In appearance and manners Francis was, like his contemporary Henry VIII, and his descendant Louis XIV, every inch a king—athlete, sportsman, poet, man of the world; a great talker and a great eater; a thoroughly charming, self-satisfied, and self-indulgent person. His sister Margaret wrote a poem about him, which I have tried to translate:

FRANCE UNDER FRANCIS I

'Is he handsome? Yes, he is rose and white,
Brown-haired, fine in figure and height;
He shines on earth like the sun in the sky,
Brave, valiant in battle, both prudent and spry;
He is modest and kind; though a King, always caring;
Though none is so strong, yet full of forbearing' [*Batiffol*].

Sisters are not always so complimentary. Anyhow, a king like this was a new experience for France, after the deformed Charles VIII, and the invalid Louis XII—a change like the coming of the Renaissance, of which Francis was a typical product. And if one reads contemporary accounts of the magnificence of Francis' Court, and of the pageants and festivities that enlivened Paris in his time, one understands why later generations looked back to these years as an Elizabethan age of France.

Below this sparkling surface momentous changes were going on in the government and social condition of the country. The monarchy, which had been paternal, and almost constitutional, became more and more absolute. The local jurisdiction of the nobles was gradually replaced by that of King's officers, later called *Intendants*, responsible to the Crown alone. The provincial *Parlements* (courts of law, with the duty of registering royal decrees) were deprived of their rights of remonstrance. Civil offices were sold to the highest bidder; and after his concordat with the Pope in 1516 the King was able to nominate to most of the high ecclesiastical posts in the country. He thus secured an obedient clergy and Civil Service, and prepared the way both for the Gallicanism and for the Absolutism of Louis XIV. The actual government of France was in the hands of the King and the King's set, whoever they might be at the moment; and was carried out through ministers made and dismissed at the King's pleasure.

One must not think that these changes arose out of, or became part of, the constitution of the country. *Mme de Staël* heads one of the chapters in her account of the French Revolution with the question, 'Was there any French Constitution before the Revolution?' and practically answers 'No.' At any rate, nobody knew what it was, or consciously acted upon it. It was like English law. It had no existence as a whole; it simply consisted of parts. It had no principles; it was built up by practical decisions upon separate points. It was a case-made constitution. And in France, in the absence of any effective Charter, or Parliament, or public opinion, it was the kings themselves who decided each case as it arose, and in the interests of absolutism. Francis I begins this process; it continues under Louis XIII; its climax is the reign of Louis XIV; its catastrophe the execution of Louis XVI.

French society during Francis' reign is changing even more rapidly than the French constitution. The great 'seigneurs' are becoming idle aristocracy. Their local functions and fees go to the Intendants. They are impoverished by rising prices, and by attendance upon an expensive Court. Their duties disappear, and their life becomes a daily round of privilege. The army and the church are the only occupations still open to a gentleman. Meanwhile the rising middle class, unhampered by social traditions or family pride, was used by the Crown as a weapon against the nobles, and as a stepping-stone to absolute power. Below the nobles, below the clergy, below the middle class, came the peasantry, the great bulk of the population, whose duty it was to do the work left undone by the privileged classes, and to pay the taxes from which they were exempt. These poor people were already in a state of degradation which made the brilliancy of the Court a farce, and national prosperity an idle dream.

In this growth of arbitrary government, this suppression of local and social responsibility, this unfair distribution of public burdens, and unhealthy relationship of class to class, we can already see the germs of the French Revolution. But what Francis saw, I think, was something very different—the advantages of a despotic government, a powerless aristocracy, and a subservient people. And when, in 1515, he invaded Italy, and was victorious at Marignano, when in 1516 he treated upon equal terms with the Pope, he may well have thought himself without a rival in Europe.

III

But three years later, in 1519, the whole situation was changed by the death of Maximilian, which made Charles I of Spain also Charles V of Austria, and a young man of nineteen found himself the greatest prince in Europe. His father was Philip, son of Maximilian of Austria and Mary of Burgundy; his mother was

THE EMPIRE OF CHARLES V

Joanna, daughter of Ferdinand of Aragon and Isabella of Castile. From Ferdinand he inherited Aragon, Sardinia, Sicily, and Naples; from Isabella, America and Castile; from Maximilian, Austria and all other possessions and claims of the house of Hapsburg; from Mary of Burgundy, the Franche Comté, and what through him became the Spanish Netherlands. Look at the map, and you will see at once how the union of all these territories threatened to upset the balance of power in Europe.

Nor was this all. Among the Hapsburg claims which Charles inherited was one of quite recent origin. Since 1438 the rulers of Austria had always been elected to the dignity of Holy Roman Emperor. In 1519, in spite of the rival candidature of Francis I and Henry VIII, Charles was duly elected in the place of his grandfather Maximilian. No doubt this added much to his responsibilities, and little to his power. But it gave him unequalled prestige, it was a certificate of orthodoxy, and it ensured him the support of Germany, if ever he led Austria, as the champion of Europe, against the Turks.

What kind of man was Charles, who, at an age when we are just leaving school, succeeded to this tremendous position? We have portraits of him at various ages. At thirteen 'he gives natural evidences of an excellent disposition. People say that there are plenty of clear signs in him of justice and rectitude. Although he is still a boy, he can't stand flattery or falsehood, and will have nothing to do with men of this character. Everyone says that he has a seriousness beyond his years. He is equally unassuming in his laughter, his movements, his gestures, and his conversation' [*Peter Martyr*]. This promise was fulfilled. Charles was always serious, strenuous, unassuming; a sportsman, a man of the world, a good soldier, and a shrewd diplomatist. Right at the end of his life we have a more personal portrait. 'He is of moderate height' (reports a Venetian ambassador) 'and has a grave look. His forehead is broad, his eyes blue, with a look of energy, his nose aquiline and a little bent, his lower jaw' (the Hapsburg jaw) 'long and projecting, so that his teeth don't meet, and one can't hear the ends of his words distinctly. His front teeth are few and bad: he has a good colour, and a short beard bristling and white, well proportioned to his figure' [*Badoaro*]. To complete this picture I will add a letter written from Augsburg in 1551 by an

English author and traveller, Roger Ascham, to his friend Mr. Raven, Fellow of St. John's College, Cambridge. 'I have seen the Emperor twice,' he says; 'first sick in his privy chamber, at our first coming. He looked somewhat like the parson of Epurstone. He had on a gown of black taffety, and a furred night-cap on his head, Dutch-like, having a seam over the crown . . . I saw him [also] sitting at dinner, at the feast of the Golden Fleece: he and Ferdinando [his brother, the King of Hungary] both under one cloth of Estate; then the Prince of Spain [his son, Philip]; all of one side, as the Knights of the Garter do in England . . . I stood hard by the Emperor's table. He had four courses; he had sod beef very good, roast mutton, baked hare . . . The Emperor hath a good face, a constant look: he fed well of a capon. I have had a better from mine hostess Barnes many times in my chamber. He and Ferdinando ate together handsomely, carving themselves where they list, without any curiosity. The Emperor drank the best that ever I saw; he had his head in the glass five times as long as any of us, and never drank less than a quart at once of Rhenish wine.'

Both Charles and Francis had their portraits painted by the great Titian. Francis he only pictured side-face, from a medal, but made him treacherous as well as charming. Charles sat for him several times, and every portrait makes the little man look rather formidable. Charles had few of the showy qualities of Francis; but he had a better head and a bigger heart.

IV

What were the causes of rivalry between these two men? Personal antipathy—their unlikeness in character and ideas— is not sufficient explanation. Nor was it merely that Francis owed Charles a grudge for defeating him in the election to the Empire in 1519, or for imprisoning him at Madrid in 1525. It needs more to explain a feud which lasted nearly forty years, and survived as an international quarrel for two-and-a-half centuries.

On the French side the real cause of trouble was this: Francis felt himself in danger of 'encirclement' by the Hapsburg Empire. The union of the Franche Comté with the Empire had removed the last barrier between the two Powers. From Artois in the north to Burgundy in the east, and again throughout the length of the Pyrenees, the French frontier was menaced by the soldiers of Austria and of Spain. More: French unity was incomplete. France was only half a nation, so long as great parts of Burgundy and of the Netherlands, racially or geographically continuous with her own territory, were in the hands of a foreigner.

Charles, for his part, was by birth a Fleming, and by family tradition a Burgundian. He could not give up his ancestral possessions: he would prefer to consolidate them by the recovery of Western Burgundy. He wanted to be buried at Dijon, by the side of his grandmother's ancestors. He was not grasping, but he was ambitious. His motto was, 'Plus Oultre,' 'Further still'; or sometimes 'Non dum,' 'Not yet'; and his device the Pillars of Hercules.

If Charles was the victim of a policy which he did not invent, and of which he would have disapproved—the world-empire designed by Ferdinand and Maximilian—Francis was the instrument of a theory which he only half understood—the Balance of Power in Europe. This theory was a natural consequence of the formation of national units of government at the end of the fifteenth century. The question was bound to arise, How would the new nations group themselves, for commerce and for war? You get the first groupings in the League of Cambrai and the Holy League, organized by Pope Julius II to turn the balance of power in Italy in his favour. It was a new thing when this theory was invoked against the union of Spain and Austria, and when not only Protestant England but also infidel Turkey was thrown into the scales. Francis, whether he knew it or not, was the forerunner of William of Orange in the seventeenth and of William Pitt in the nineteenth century—in organizing coalitions against any power that should threaten a hegemony of Europe.

V

I will only summarize the wars of Charles and Francis, as I did the earlier wars in Italy. They fall most easily into six groups of summer campaigns—for we have not reached the time when armies (except during a siege) kept the field in winter.

The first 'war' ran from 1520 to 1526. Francis, defeated and captured at Pavia, became a prisoner in Spain; and only secured his liberty by signing away West Burgundy and Flanders at the

Treaty of Madrid (1526). The correspondence that went on during Francis' imprisonment makes three things quite clear: first, that the only real obstacle to peace was Charles's demand for the cession of West Burgundy, and Francis' refusal to surrender it: secondly, that, when at last Francis promised to give it up, he stated publicly that he had been coerced into doing so, and did not consider himself bound by his word: and thirdly, that the Pope was prepared to absolve him from his oath; from which we may conclude that there were 'scraps of paper' in the sixteenth as well as in the twentieth century [*Champollion-Figeac*]. At the end of the second war (1526–1529), by the Peace of Cambrai, Francis remained in possession of West Burgundy. Between this war and the next he reorganized his army on a territorial basis, recruiting seven 'legions' in seven provinces of France. At the end of the third war (1536–1538) he gained Savoy. The fourth war (1542–1544) brought no advantage to either side: the Treaty of Crépy (1544) confirmed the Treaties of Madrid and Cambrai. In 1547 Francis was dead, and his personal quarrel with Charles at an end. There remain, however, two wars, some mention of which is needed to complete the series. In the fifth war (1552–1556) Charles was opposed by Henry II of France, who, at the Peace of Vaucelles, deprived him of the key positions in Lorraine—the 'three bishoprics' of Metz, Toul, and Verdun. In 1556 Charles abdicated his throne, and the last war (1557–1559) was fought between Henry II and Charles's successor, Philip II of Spain. By the Treaty of Cateau Cambrésis in 1559 France kept the three bishoprics, and gained Calais and Boulogne; but surrendered all her Italian claims beyond a few frontier-forts in Savoy. Spain kept Milan and Naples.

Though I have included these last two wars in the series that opened at Pavia, and in the general period of hostilities going back to 1494, it must be noticed that in one respect they are very different. Henry II had his own grudge against Charles: he could never forgive the harsh way in which he had been treated in the Spanish prison where Charles held him hostage for his father's good behaviour. He was no less determined than his father had been to shake off the Austro-Spanish grip upon the French frontiers. But he seems to have realized—and to have been the first French king who did so—that the danger-point was not in

Italy, but on the east and north-east frontiers of France itself. He knew what he wanted: he kept what he got: he only fought to make a profitable peace. Calais and Boulogne secured the Channel coast againt England. Metz, Toul, and Verdun blocked the gap by which France could most easily be invaded from the east. The eastern frontier was pushed further back, and Paris began to have more breathing space. Thus Henry restored the foreign policy of France to its natural lines, and turned the long-drawn disaster of the Italian wars into a definite and enduring advantage.

VI

In 1519 Charles had the world at his feet. In 1556 he abdicated, worn out by ill success. Why did he fail?

The chief reason was the size of the weapon he tried to wield. France was a single country under single control. Its king could count on the service of its nobles, the wealth of its merchants, and the patriotism of its common people. But Charles could count on no common language, or interests, or religion, to keep together the Germans, Spaniards, Flemings, and Italians who peopled his 'ramshackle Empire.' Spain was the nucleus of his power, and the recruiting-ground of his best troops. Spending about half his reign there, he became increasingly Spanish in outlook, and retired to a Spanish monastery for the last months of his life. But it took ten years to pacify and reorganize Spain after the 'revolt of the Communes,' with which his reign began; and a still longer time to exploit the full wealth of the American gold-mines. Charles envied Francis the ease with which he could fleece his rich sheep: he was constantly in need of money; and the pension which he granted to Erasmus was very irregularly paid.

In Germany Charles was a foreigner, and never mastered more than a few words of the language. He disliked its Protestantism: he disliked the independence of its princes: he disliked the embarrassments of the Emperor's position, which gave him no power to impose taxes, or to raise troops. In Italy he was not only a foreigner, but also an invader. Though crowned by the Pope, he could never forget, nor the world forgive, the fatal sack of Rome by the Imperial troops (1527).

Only in the Netherlands was Charles really at home, understanding and understood by the people. The province was well governed by the princesses who acted as his Regents. Occasional troubles, such as the rebellion of Guelders, or the revolt of Ghent, were firmly but sensibly dealt with. And if Charles's reputation for orthodoxy led him to introduce the Spanish Inquisition, his common sense made him take care that no serious use should be made of it in a country which provided him with two-fifths of his entire revenue. In a word, he treated Flemings as Flemings, and they remained loyal to Spain: his successor Philip treated them as Spaniards, and they rebelled.

Such was the Empire over which Charles attempted to reign. Even a modern ruler, with railway and aeroplane, post office and printing press at his command, could hardly do it. For Charles it was impossible. Nor was he even free to attend to the business of government. Three difficulties constantly distracted his attention, and dissipated his forces—the Reformation in Germany, the contest with Francis, and the danger of invasion by the Turks. With the second of these we have already dealt: with the first we must deal subsequently; only the third concerns us here.

Seventy years before the date of which we are speaking, at the time of the fall of Constantinople (1453), appeals had been made to the Pope to lead a fresh crusade against the Turks. Then the Turks had paused. Now they were advancing again. From the beginning of his reign we find Charles instructing his French ambassadors to represent to Francis the danger of a Turkish invasion, and to ask help in the defence of Christendom. In 1521, the year after the accession of the great Sultan Solyman, Charles received urgent letters from the King of Poland and the Queen of Hungary, saying that the Turks had captured Belgrade, and were advancing across the Hungarian plain. Hungary, as the Queen urged, and as Charles well knew, was the 'bulwark of Christendom,' and he could not neglect her appeal for help. In 1522 the Turks captured Rhodes. In 1525 they renewed their invasion of the Danube valley. In 1526 they routed and killed the King of Hungary at the battle of Mohacz, and overran the whole country. In 1529 Solyman appeared before the walls of Vienna. Hungary became an infidel province, and the churches of Buda were turned into mosques. It was not until Solyman's death in

1556 that Europe and Charles were beyond fear of a great disaster.

And this was not all. We might have supposed that, in face of such a danger, Francis would patch up his quarrel, and join in a crusade. On the contrary, Europe was scandalized to see his Most Christian Majesty allying himself with the infidel, and using the danger of Europe to extract better terms from his Austrian rival. At the moment of the battle of Mohacz a French envoy arrived in the Turkish camp, asking the Sultan's help against the Emperor. In 1535 Francis and Solyman signed commercial capitulations, and an offensive and defensive alliance. In 1543 French and Turkish fleets, with their base at Toulon, co-operated in the blockade and bombardment of Nice.

No wonder, then, that Charles failed in his task. After thirty-seven years of constant work, constant travelling and fighting, he abdicated. His huge Empire was split up. Germany he gave to his brother Ferdinand; Spain, Italy, and the Netherlands to his son Philip; as though to say, 'It is too much for one man.' He himself retired for the little that was left of his life to a Spanish monastery. There he read and wrote political dispatches, and interested himself in the affairs of the Inquisition—he could not conquer the habit of work. There was another habit that he could not conquer. It is said that he shortened his days 'with surfeits of sardine omelettes, eel pies, pickled partridges, iced beer, and flagons of Rhenish wine, relieved by copious draughts of senna and rhubarb, to which his horror-stricken doctor doomed him as he ate' [*Motley*]. There was always something epic about Charles, even in his appetites. He might have had for his epitaph, 'He sometimes spared others; himself he never spared.'

VII

We have dealt with the causes and character of the rivalry between Charles and Francis. What, now, were its results?

First, Europe was saved from a Hapsburg hegemony, and the principle of the balance of power was set up. The force of circumstances, adroitly used by Francis, had been too much for Charles's unwieldy empire. It was never revived again. But the fear of it lived on. You will find it in the background of the French Wars of Religion, and of the Thirty Years' War. The policy of Francis was resumed, and his work completed, by Henry IV, Richelieu, and Mazarin. France was built upon the ruins of Spain. Its own ruin began when, at the opening of the eighteenth century, there were Bourbons upon both the French and Spanish thrones, and Louis XIV was suspected, with better reason than Charles V, of designs upon the liberty of Europe.

The second result of the contest was the Franco-Turkish entente, which, in one shape or another, has lasted almost to the present day. What were its effects? It lowered the tone of international diplomacy. It prevented the expulsion of the Turks from Europe. It gave France, for more than a hundred years, a monopoly of trade in the Levant, and a permanent sphere of influence in the Nearer East. This alliance was perhaps one of the most significant fruits of the Renaissance. It marked the end of the medieval order, when the Catholic unity of Church and State stood solidly against the infidel and the heretic. It showed that religion was no more the motive of politics than of trade; and that its place was being taken by *raison d'état,* or national self-interest. It was that which coupled the Most Christian King with infidel allies in the sixteenth and with Protestant allies in the seventeenth century. This may seem reasonable enough to us: to the men of that time it was revolutionary.

Thirdly, the contest between Charles and Francis contributed very much to the progress of the Reformation. During the critical years, when Lutheranism was growing in Germany, and Calvinism in France, the two heads of Catholicism in north Europe were too busy fighting one another to pay much attention to the new heresy. When at last they stopped fighting, it was too late to do so. You can see this clearly from *Calvin's* correspondence. He is more afraid of what Charles may do to the Protestants in Germany than of what Francis may do to the Protestants in France. But he dreads them both. His chief hope is that they may keep each other employed. His chief fear is lest either of them may prove victorious, and so be free to persecute the Protestants; or may both agree to patch up their quarrel, and make common cause against the heretics.

One last result, which applies not merely to the struggle between Charles and Francis, but to the whole period of the Italian Wars. Whilst France was giving its attention to Italy and the Nearer East, and spending its resources to maintain the balance of power in Europe, Spain and Portugal, and to a lesser extent England and Holland, were opening up the Far East, and initiating a new balance of power in America. A short comparison of dates will illustrate what I mean:

Europe	America	Far East
1494. Charles VIII in Italy.	1492. Columbus's Voyage.	1498. Vasco da Gama in India.
1499. Louis XII in Italy.	1497. Cabot in N. America	
	1500. Cabral in Brazil.	
1520. First War of Francis and Charles.	1520. Magellan's Voyage.	1520. Portuguese Embassy at Peking.
1529. Turks at Vienna.	1529. Cortés in Mexico.	
	1532. Pizarro in Peru.	

True, between 1531 and 1534, Cartier, under Francis' patronage, made three voyages to North America, and founded French colonies on the St. Lawrence. But it is pretty clear what is happening upon the whole. Just as in the eighteenth century the British Empire was built up while Europe, and particularly France, was occupied with the wars of Frederick the Great, so now the Spanish and Portuguese empires were founded while France was occupied with Italy and Austria. And behind both events lies the great discovery which was handed on to England from Portugal and Spain—which France never quite realized, and Germany learnt too late: the discovery of the influence of sea power upon history.

LECTURE V

THE REFORMATION

I

We have seen that when the Renaissance crossed the Alps it became scientific instead of artistic, constructive as well as critical, and took on a new moral and philosophical character. It thus carried the revolt against medievalism into fresh fields. Every nation had something to contribute to the new order; and the contributions of the strong, successful states were not necessarily or in fact the most important. Feudalism, the political and social system of the Middle Ages, was developed into absolute monarchy in France and Spain. Scholasticism, the medieval system of thought, was transformed by international scholars and thinkers into modern science and learning. It remained for Catholicism, the religious system of the Middle Ages, to be broken up and put together again in the shape of modern Christianity. This was the work of the Reformation; and most of it was done in Germany.

II

First, as to the causes of the Reformation. How are we to select or classify, where so many things contributed to such a vast movement? I will content myself with three causes which were specially important in Germany, and leave you to infer the rest. They are papal finance, the condition of the religious Orders and the publication of the New Testament.

By papal finance I mean this. The Roman Church at the beginning of the sixteenth century was organized and managed as a business concern. It is always a difficult question, how far it is proper to receive wages for religious work, or to exact payment in return for spiritual privileges. But all conscientious men feel (and they felt the same in the sixteenth century) that it is wrong to make a profit out of religion. And it is undeniable that under Julius II and Leo X the Papacy was doing so. Two of its most scandalous transactions were the sale of benefices, and the trade in Indulgences. Read Luther's *Address to the Christian Nobility of the German Nation* [Wace and Buchheim]. No second-hand account gives half so good an impression of the causes of the Reformation. Part I of the Address is a refutation of the Roman position under three heads. Part II suggests Agenda for a General Council—the temporal power of the Papacy; the expenses of the Papal Court, and of the Cardinals' establishments; the financial exactions by which these are met—for instance, the tax called 'Annates,' originally raised to fight the Turks, but now spent at Rome; more and more benefices falling into papal hands, and sold to the highest bidder; the payment made by newly-appointed archbishops for the 'pallium'—and so forth. In Part III Luther specifies no less than twenty-seven points in which reform is necessary. As he is writing to the German princes he includes a few for their special benefit—as, for instance, a demand for University reform, and a protest against the luxury and immorality of German society. But most of his twenty-seven articles are directed against the Papacy, and call for the abolition of its worldly privileges and its financial exactions, amongst which the sale of benefices again occurs. This was simony, and in itself a great scandal. It was also, as Luther knew, a point upon which the German princes felt particularly sore. They disliked all the best Church appointments being in the Pope's hands. They did not see why the fees paid upon taking up a benefice, or its income during a vacancy, should not go into their own pockets.

The trade in Indulgences, the immediate cause of Luther's protest at Wittenberg in 1517, needs a little further explanation. It was not a new question. The business went back to the year 1300, when Pope Boniface VIII expounded the doctrine that the superabundance of Christ's sacrifice formed an inexhaustible treasury [infinitus thesaurus] of grace, the spending of which had been entrusted to the Church in the form of grants giving total or partial remission of the punishment due, or the penance to be done, for sin. He accordingly decreed that in 1300, and every hundredth year after, anyone who went on pilgrimage to the Church of St. Peter and St. Paul outside Rome, and made a penitent confession, should receive full pardon for his sins, and full remission of any punishment they deserved. In 1343 Clement VI, finding this a popular institution, altered it from once a century to every fifty years. In 1476 (and this was the crux) a Bull of Sixtus IV not only extended these Indulgences from living penitents to souls in Purgatory, but also turned a religious concession into a means of raising money. I will translate the important words. 'We therefore allow and make this Indulgence: if any relations, or friends, or other faithful Christians, with pious intention, and on behalf of such souls as are exposed to the fire of Purgatory, shall within the said ten years give a certain sum of money to the restoration fund of the Church of X, we hereby decree that such plenary remission shall be effective and favourable for a relaxation of penalties for those souls on whose behalf they have made the said payment.' If there were any doubt as to the meaning of these words, it would be set at rest by the prospectus of this and other Indulgences put out by the authorities of the Church of X; it is a very commercial document, especially recommending one form of policy which gives plenary remission 'whenever a man thinks he may be going to die, even though he does not actually do so'—as, for instance, in shipwreck, or siege, or time of plague. 'This,' the document ends, 'is an unprecedented provision, especially for those who go to sea' [*Kidd*].

When Julius II in 1510 and Leo X in 1514 wanted money for the building of New St. Peter's at Rome, these Indulgences were adapted for the foreign market, especially in Germany: and little remained except to demand cash payment from the purchaser. For an extra fee you could now choose your own confessor; and he could impose as penance a further contribution to the building fund. This was the traffic against which Luther protested. You will allow that he had a good case. And here too he could count on the support of the German princes. The sale of Indulgences meant a constant drain of money from their estates for the benefit of Rome. So much for papal finance.

The second cause of the Reformation was the bad condition of the clergy, and especially of the religious Orders. This too was an old complaint; and it was the more serious because the religious Orders had many of them been founded for the very purpose of reforming the society which they now disgraced. The feeling against them had been growing since the fourteenth century (when you find it, for instance, in Chaucer), and was

CLERICAL IGNORANCE

coming to a head in the sixteenth. It was always, I think, the chief popular grievance against the Church. As to contemporary evidence, the most famous of all attacks on the monks was a sham correspondence, making fun of their ignorance, immorality, and bad Latin. The book came to be published in this way. A few years before Luther's Wittenberg protest, Reuchlin, one of the first Hebrew scholars of the Renaissance, had been put on his trial for unorthodoxy by the monastic theologians of Cologne. After his acquittal he published the letters of sympathy he had received during the trial, under the title of *Clarorum Virorum Epistolae*. Ulrich von Hütten, Luther's most militant supporter, hit on the idea of completing the discomfiture of the monks by publishing imaginary letters of sympathy written to Ortwin Gratius, one of the obscurantists of Cologne: and he called the book *Epistolae Obscurorum Virorum,* which I suppose might not unfairly be rendered, 'Letters of some shady persons.' It is impossible to extract the full flavour of the book—it is rather strong at times—from a quotation, or to reproduce the dog Latin in which it is written: but here is one of the letters, making fun of monkish superstition. 'Henricus Schaffsmulius to Ortwinus Gratius . . . I want to ask your reverence what you think about the following point. Supposing that on a Friday, or some other fast day, one eats an egg, and there is a chicken in it? The other day we were sitting in an inn at Campus Florae having a meal, and ate some eggs; and when I opened one egg I saw that there was a chicken in it. I showed it to my companion. "Eat it up quick," he said, "before the landlord sees it. If he does, you will have to pay half-a-crown or five shillings for it: for in these parts it is the custom to pay on the nail for everything set on the table; they won't take anything back. And if he sees there is a young chicken in the egg he will say you must pay for the fowl as well as the egg; and he will reckon it full-grown, however small it may be." So I swallowed the egg as quick as I could, chicken and all. Afterwards I remembered that it was a Friday: and I said to my companion, "You have made me commit a mortal sin, in eating meat on a Friday." "Oh, no," he replied, "it is not a mortal sin, or even a venial one. A young chicken like that is reckoned part of the egg, until it is hatched out." And he told me that it was the same with cheese that had maggots in it, or with insects in cherries, beans, and so on. They could all be eaten on Fridays, and even on Vigils of the Apostles.' And so the book goes on. It is of course a parody, and no fair account of the whole class attacked. But the evils were sufficiently serious —ignorance, superstition, loose living—and the attempt of the Church to reform these abuses is sufficient evidence that they existed.

For the third cause of the Reformation I should take the publication of the New Testament. This we have already mentioned when dealing with the Renaissance. The invention of printing enabled the Greek text of the New Testament (for scholars), and (for less educated people) translations of it in French, German, Italian, and other languages, to obtain quick and wide circulation. The prejudices to be overcome were at first immense. The Vulgate, the authorized Latin version of the Bible, had been used so long that every word of it had come to be thought sacred: and when in 1522 the Spanish University of Alcalá published an Old Testament with the Vulgate in the middle, and the original Hebrew and the old Greek Septuagint translation on either side of it, the editors compared this arrangement to Christ crucified between two thieves. But the greater the prejudice against first-hand knowledge of the Bible the greater its effects, if widely spread. This was the object of Erasmus's famous edition of the New Testament—in Greek, with a new Latin translation opposite—which appeared in 1516. 'I wish,' he says in his Preface, 'that even the weakest woman should read the Gospels, and the epistles of Paul; I wish that they were translated into all languages, so that they might be read and understood, not only by Scotchmen and Irishmen, but also by Saracens and Turks. I long for the farmer to sing portions of them to himself as he follows the plough, for the weaver to hum them to the tune of his shuttle, and for the traveller to beguile with their stories the tedium of his journey' [*Seebohm*]. Erasmus, however, was not content to let the Bible speak for itself. He introduced each Gospel and Epistle with a preface of his own; and added notes and paraphrases in which he pointed to the contrast between the teaching of Christ and the practices of the Church. This, for instances, is his comment on the passage in Matthew xxiii, dealing with the Scribes and Pharisees: 'You may find a bishop here and there who teaches the Gospel, though life and teaching have small agreement. But what shall we say of those who destroy the Gospel itself, make laws at their will, tyrannize over the laity, and measure right and wrong with rules constructed by themselves? Or those who entangle their flocks in the meshes of crafty canons, who sit not in the seat of the Gospel, but in the seat of Caiaphas and Simon Magus, prelates of evil, who bring disgrace and discredit on their worthier brethren?' Or, on Matt. xxiv, 23 ("Lo, Here is Christ"): 'I saw with mine own eyes Pope Julius II at Bologna, and afterwards at Rome, marching at the head of a triumphal procession, as if he were Pompey or Caesar. St. Peter subdued the world with faith, not with arms or soldiers or military engines. St. Peter's successors would win as many victories as St. Peter won if they had St. Peter's spirit.' This kind of commentary might not suit the 'Cambridge Bible for Schools.' But the case was urgent, and Erasmus was determined that new readers of the Gospel should not miss its modern application. Nor did they.

III

It is time now to leave the causes of the Reformation, and come to the man who actually began it. I will not stop to give an account of Luther's life, which is in all the books [e.g. *Smith*]. But I will pick out one or two points which may help to explain him, and then go on to the movement to which he gave origin and expression.

Before he became a Reformer, Luther was a peasant, a monk, and a scholar; he experienced conversion; and he went on a pilgrimage to Rome. His peasant origin explains his manliness, his lack of refinement, his simple way of dealing with complex problems. His monastic training left him devout, and rather superstitious, with a strong leaning towards orthodoxy outside those matters in which his conscience made him a rebel. Nor was he a mere agitator: all his life he was a great reader of books, and for many years a prolific writer. As a monk he had studied the Bible and the Fathers; as a lecturer at Wittenberg he read Lefèvre, Erasmus, and many other mystical or humanist writers. He was a self-educated man: his opinions might be crude; but he had formed them himself, and was prepared to stand by them.

Then he had suddenly discovered, like St. Paul, that though he could form his own mind, he could not save his own soul. He went through a vivid experience of conversion, and found salvation in the text, 'The just shall live by faith.' This conviction gave his life the centre it needed. Round it he built his theology: upon it he based his moral courage. He feared nothing but not to preach his faith. Finally, soon after his conversion, Luther visited Rome; and it was the shock of what he saw there—the crying contrast between the New Testament in his heart and the old Church before his eyes—that turned him into a Reformer.

The Reformation might have come about if Luther had done no more than challenge the sale of Indulgences. But it would not have taken the course it did unless he had also become a great and popular writer. We know something about the circulation of his books. The number of German works printed in 1518, including Luther's, was a hundred and fifty; three years later they were more than six times as numerous. It was in 1520 that Luther began publishing his chief theological works; and the rapid increase from that date is largely attributable to his own writings, and those to which they gave rise [Smith]. We have also a letter from Froben, Luther's publisher at Basle, dated 1519, in which he says that six hundred copies of his latest 'Lucubrationes' have been sent to France and Spain, as well as to all parts of Italy, to England, and to the Netherlands; that they are being sold in Paris, and read even by students of the orthodox Sorbonne. Practically the whole edition is sold out. 'I never knew a book,' says Froben, 'sell so well' [Kidd]. It was a favourable moment for publication. To be educated then was to know Latin; and any book published in Latin had an international circulation, like a cinema film nowadays. Luther and Erasmus must have had reading publics unrivalled until the eighteenth century, when French became what Latin had been, and made Voltaire and Rousseau international. It was an age, too, of translations, of national as well as European demand: and everywhere printing-presses were springing up to supply food for the new appetite. But it was not merely the demand for books, or the interest in theology, which secured Luther his circulation; but also his style. Michelet compared it to a mixture of Moses and Rabelais. As those two authors never collaborated, I cannot tell whether it is a good comparison. But that Luther's style is vigorous, eloquent, wordy, and rather vulgar, you can judge for yourselves, even from an English translation. It was a new way of treating theology, in the sixteenth century; and it made an immense appeal.

Let me mention three other points, closely connected with one another. Politically, Luther was a conservative, and stood for the rights of the German princes against their own subjects, as well as against the Pope. The discontented knights of 1523, the rebellious peasantry of 1524, got no sympathy from him. Unlike Calvinism, which became a disintegrating force in politics, Lutheranism played into the hands of the government, and became a State religion.

Again, as in politics Luther supported the Government, so in ecclesiastical matters he was what we should call a 'strong Churchman.' In 1519 he was willing to drop his attack on Indulgences, and to submit to the Pope. 'I testify,' he writes, 'before God and his whole Creation, that I have never wished, and do not wish today, in any way to impair or destroy the power of the Roman Church . . . I fully believe that the power of this Church is supreme' [*Kidd*]. And though later he threw over the Pope, Luther never surrendered the Catholic system. He bitterly opposed the innovations in Church order and customs introduced by more advanced 'Lutherans' than himself—Carlstadt, Munzer, or the Anabaptists. Like John Wesley, he was never really a member of the sect called by his name.

One more point. The upshot of Luther's teaching was to dethrone the Pope and to enthrone the Bible. Authority was not destroyed; it was only transferred. Orthodoxy was not impaired: it was refounded on the Scriptures. But on what Scriptures, and how interpreted? Those which Luther thought important, interpreted in Luther's way. For instance, Philip of Hesse quarrelled with his wife, and wanted to marry again. As a Catholic, he would have gone to the Pope, and paid for a divorce. As a Protestant, he went to Luther, who, without any payment, referred him to the example of Abraham, and allowed him to keep both wives at the same time. True, this caused something of a scandal. But no Protestant doubted that such matters must be settled by authority, or that the principle of authority which Luther set up was sound.

IV

Luther's great protest came about in this way. In 1514 Leo X needed money for the building fund of St. Peter's, and proposed to raise it, in his cynical way, by the sale of Indulgences. He accordingly entered into an agreement (and nothing shows better the character of papal finance) with Albert, Archbishop of Mayence, and with a big banking firm, the Fuggers of Augsburg. Albert owed the bank a large sum of money, which he had borrowed from them to pay the Pope when he received his archbishopric. The bank was now to undertake the sale of Indulgences. Half the receipts were to go to the bank in payment of the archbishop's debt, and half to the Pope, to build his new cathedral. The actual business of selling the Indulgences was put into the hands of one Tetzel, who carried out a kind of 'national mission' to advertise his wares. We have a contemporary account of Tetzel's methods: it comes from a mining village called St. Annaberg. 'It is incredible what the ignorant and impudent friar gave out. He said that if a Christian had committed incest, he had only to drop a coin into the Pope's Indulgence box, and the Pope had power in heaven and on earth to forgive the sin; and if he forgave it, God must do so too. Item, if they contributed readily, and bought grace and indulgence, all the hills of St. Annaberg would become pure solid silver. Item, as soon as the coin tinkled in the box, the soul for whom the money was paid would go straight to heaven. The Indulgence was so highly prized that, when Tetzel entered a city, the Papal Bull was borne on a satin or gold-embroidered cushion, and all the priests and monks, the Town Council, the schoolmaster and his scholars, men, women, maidens, and children, all went out to meet him with banners and tapers, with songs and processions. All the bells were rung, and all the organs struck up. He was conducted into the church, and a red cross was erected in the middle of the building, and the Pope's banner displayed. In fact, 'God himself could not have been welcomed and entertained with greater honour' [*Kidd*]. This was the kind of thing that roused Luther, and no wonder. His famous 'Theses,' nailed to the church door at Wittenberg in 1517, were in form no more than questions for discussion: they were in fact a comprehensive denunciation of Tetzel, the Papacy, and all their works.

Charles V was at this time in Spain, and had not yet been elected Emperor. How did he hear of Luther, and what did he think of him? In October, 1520—and the date shows how slowly news travelled in those days—*Peter Martyr*, writing from Spain, transcribes a long letter that he has received from his friend Valdes at Brussels about a fearful portent [prodigium horrendum] which has appeared in Germany. He goes on to quote a full account of Luther's 'Theses,' and the burning of the Pope's Bull. 'I am terribly afraid,' wrote Valdes, 'that this evil will spread too widely for us to be able to apply any remedy to it.' The next news, which is also from Spain, shows that Valdes was right. In April, 1521, Charles received a letter from his old tutor, now his Regent in Spain, Adrian of Utrecht. It ended as follows (but I have had to prune the Cardinal's style): 'A person named Martin Luther has been properly and justly condemned by the Holy See for a number of errors and heresies. Nevertheless he obstinately persists in diffusing and spreading the said errors and heresies by writing in districts subject to the Empire, to the great dishonour and disservice of God, and of our holy mother the Church: besides which it is a blemish and insult to your Majesty, since everyone knows your Majesty's fervent intention to oppose all who act contrary to our Lord Jesus Christ and our holy faith. And so I beg you, Sire, most humbly, to make the whole world understand that you are the enemy of the enemies of Christ, and of the holy faith . . . or at least to defend your own honour, by prohibiting and preventing this wicked and pestilent fellow from openly and publicly corrupting the said holy Catholic faith; and to send and transfer the same Martin Luther to his judge, our holy father the Pope, for just chastisement, and the punishment he deserves. Your very humble servant, A., Cardinal of Tortosa' [*Gachard*].

This letter did not reach Charles until he was already at the Diet of Worms (April, 1521). There he saw and heard the heretic for himself. Luther had come to the Diet more than half expecting to be made a martyr: but his safe conduct was respected, and he was allowed to go away into ignominious retirement. Honesty was the Emperor's best policy; and Luther's political position was stronger than that of John Huss. But Charles must also satisfy the Pope; so he made a declaration pledging himself to use all his power for the suppression of Lutheranism. 'My predecessors,' he said, 'the most Christian Emperors of the German race, the Austrian Archdukes, and Dukes of Burgundy, were until death the truest sons of the Catholic Church. They have left behind them the holy Catholic rites, that I should live and die therein; and so until now, with God's aid, I have lived, as becomes a Christian Emperor ... A single monk, led astray by private judgment, has set himself against the faith held by all Christians for a thousand years or more, and impudently concludes that all Christians up to now have erred. I am therefore resolved to stake upon this cause all my dominions, my friends, my body and my blood, my life and my soul' [Kidd].

Charles, I am sure, honestly hated the Lutheran heresy. He was known to be a devout Catholic. 'Every day in his life,' says the Venetian envoy, 'he has heard one, and often two, masses. At present (1557) he hears three ... He attends sermons at the great Church festivals. ... He reads the Bible every day, makes his confession and communion four times a year, and gives alms to the poor ... I have heard it related as a fact, and as a notable evidence of his religious zeal, that when he was at Ingolstadt, and near the Protestant army, he was seen at midnight in his tent, kneeling before a crucifix, with his hands clasped in prayer' [Badoaro]. To such a man it was a matter of conviction, as well as of policy, to declare war on Lutheranism.

V

But what could Charles do? His difficulties were immense. The only policy which his conscience allowed him—the extirpation of Protestantism—was rendered practically impossible by the political character of Germany, the popularity of Luther's appeal, and the uncertain relations between the Emperor and the Pope.

First, the political state of Germany. The minute and varied subdivision of the Empire made it as easy to propagate heresy there as it was difficult to eradicate it. There were always princes who would turn Protestant because their neighbours were Catholic, or remain Catholic because their neighbours were

Protestant. A preacher of heresy who was prosecuted in one state could always flee into another. A long apprenticeship in caballing had taught the princes how to form leagues in order to attack one another, or to defy the Emperor. Any strong policy that issued from Vienna was certain to be opposed at Nuremberg, at Dresden, or at Berlin. If it was to be imposed by force, that could only be by the use of foreign or mercenary troops. Indeed Charles himself visited Germany as a foreigner, and did not spend there more than eight or ten out of the thirty-seven years of his reign. Such conditions left him little chance of a successful religious policy.

Again, public support made Luther irrepressible. At the very moment when the Emperor and Diet (at Worms, 1521) were publishing their ban against him, and burning his books, the Venetian ambassador wrote home, 'I cannot tell you how much favour Luther enjoys here ... In truth, had this man been prudent, had he restricted himself to his first propositions and not entangled himself in manifest errors about the faith, he would have been ... adored by the whole of Germany' [*Contarini*]. And Valdes writes to Peter Martyr at the same time to say that Germany is as little likely to listen to the Emperor as to the Pope; and that, in spite of his prohibition, Luther's books are being sold with impunity in every village street [*Peter Martyr*]. In face of this passive resistance Charles was powerless. His decrees were as useless against paper and ink as the Pope's Bulls were against Protestants. He might and did attempt a theological compromise. The Colloquy of Ratisbon in 1541 was one step in this direction: the Interim of Augsburg in 1548 was another. But both attempts failed, owing to the bitterness of party feeling, not only between Catholics and Protestants, but also between one body of Protestants and another. The only settlement which could be reached, and that not till thirty-eight years after Luther's protest at Wittenberg, was a mere truce (the Peace of Augsburg, 1555), which left Germany divided into hostile camps, and arming for a thirty years' war.

Napoleon is reported to have said that Charles might have solved all his difficulties by becoming a Protestant. An easy solution for a realist of the eighteenth century, who was ready, if it would serve his turn, to profess Mohammedanism; but for

Charles an impossible one. He was a convinced Catholic, king of the most Catholic country in Europe, and secular partner of the Pope. How could he, or why should he sacrifice so much for the unification of Germany? And the country itself was half Catholic. Is there any likelihood that Charles would have united the whole of Germany, where Gustavus Adolphus failed to unite even the Protestant north?

A third and unexpected difficulty that Charles had to face was the attitude of the Popes. In 1521 he was on friendly terms with Leo X, and this is reflected in his declaration at Worms against the Protestants. The same year Leo died. His successor, Adrian VI, Charles's old tutor and viceroy, disappointed his patron by taking Francis' side in their quarrel, and listening to Francis' offer of help against the Turks. The Emperor grew less anxious to oblige such an ungrateful Pope, and the proceedings against the Lutherans languished. Clement VII, who succeeded to the Papacy in 1523, was at first friendly. But the victory of Pavia in 1525, which set Charles free to deal with the Protestants, also earned him the jealousy of the Pope. They took opposite sides in the League of Cognac (1526); and in 1527 came the fatal sack of Rome by a renegade Imperial army. The next year, indeed, they were reconciled, and in 1530 Charles went straight from his Coronation at Bologna to deal with the Lutherans at the Diet of Augsburg. But by this time the Protestant states of Germany were too strong for coercion, and too stubborn for compromise. I don't think that Charles ever gave up his intention to crush Lutheranism. But had he succeeded, it would have been regarded as a victory for the Church: and he did not feel inclined to do so much for an unfriendly or intriguing Pope. The Popes, for their part, disliked Charles's power in Italy, and distrusted his independent type of Churchmanship. But, if he failed to crush the Protestants, their jealousy was very largely to blame.

Taking all Charles's difficulties into account, I think we shall feel more surprise at his attempting so much than at his achieving so little. He fought a losing battle for Catholicism single-handed, not only against the Protestant Princes of Germany, but also against the official head of Catholic Christendom.

VI

Charles's failure secured the survival of Protestantism. But how did it emerge from the struggle?

Its virtues are best judged from what it did outside Germany, and in its later Calvinistic rather than its earlier Lutheran form—when it stimulated a great national revival in England, and a great national revolt in the Netherlands; when it helped to create new states in the old world, and to found a fresh civilization in the new. Wherever it went, it carried the Renaissance spirit of freedom into the deepest part of human nature—the desire for a religious and for a moral life.

You must not think, then, that I am belittling the Reformation if I call attention rather to other points, more noticeable in the Germany of the sixteenth century, and not so favourable; points in which Protestantism inherited faults from the old Church, or even acquired new failings of its own.

Notice, for instance, the political flavour of Protestantism. The Reformation broke up the medieval unity of Church and State into the State Churches of the modern world. Where there had been one Holy Roman Empire, there were now almost as many Churches as there were princes. In France or England, in Holland or Scandinavia, this was a healthy development. It canonized nationality. But in Germany the multiplication of small states, which had been a condition of the growth of Protestantism, was also a cause of its decay. Every Protestant prince was his own Pope. States went Catholic or Protestant by Local Veto. Religion became a matter of party politics. And so the way was prepared for the tragedy, half political and half religious, of the Thirty Years' War.

Notice, again, how Protestantism tends to split up. Catholicism had its divisions too; but they rarely reached the surface. Those of the reformed religion broke it into protesting fragments—Lutheranism, Zwinglianism, Calvinism, and Anabaptism—within quite a few years; and many other sub-divisions as time went on. To a world brought up under the medieval order, with its one social and religious system, its one code of conduct and belief, this tendency seemed simply to prove that Protestantism was the work of the devil. To a modern mind, which knows a whole class of fissiparous organisms that generate the new life by splitting up the old, it is rather a sign of health and progress. Moreover, the Renaissance had already split up the old society in one direction; and the Reformation was needed to resplit it in another. The development of national government and national spirit had divided Europe vertically, state from state, along the lines of its political frontiers. The Reformation divided it horizontally, Church from Church, on lines of doctrine and organization which tended to ignore national differences. Hence the wars of religion which followed the Reformation. Hence also, perhaps, the hope of ending war by the growth of a new Internationalism.

One other point, which we might not expect to be a fault of Protestantism—its intolerance. Luther, we saw, was very little behind the Pope in his belief in authority. He was no less zealous for orthodoxy, outside those matters in which he himself was a heretic. The authority of the Bible became a tyranny not unlike that of the Church. Meanwhile the splitting up of the old orthodoxy into a number of new orthodoxies hardly made for toleration. I doubt whether theological controversy was ever so bitter as in the sixteenth century.

Not long ago an enterprising American produced a film called 'Intolerance.' Part of the story passed in ancient Babylon, part in Palestine, part in sixteenth-century Paris, and part in Chicago at the present day. The moral of it all was a little difficult to make out; but it may well have been this—that intolerance is the most difficult of all vices to eradicate; that it never seems to die out, but only to reappear in fresh forms. The medieval Church, in common with medieval society, was fiercely intolerant—intolerant of witches, intolerant of criminals, intolerant of heretics. It was intolerant because it was afraid: the worst crimes are due to fear. The Reformation altered men's ideas of religious truth more quickly than the Renaissance banished men's fear of irreligion. Protestantism therefore inherited Catholic intolerance, and even added an intolerance of its own. It was not Germany and the Peace of Augsburg, but France and the Edict of Nantes, which first accustomed Europe to the idea of religious toleration. And the Edict of Nantes was the work of Henry of Navarre, who gave up the Protestant Church for the Catholic, but at heart belonged to neither.

LECTURE VI

THE COUNTER-REFORMATION

I

We have dealt with the Reformation: we must now deal with the movement of reaction and reform called the Counter-Reformation. Let me introduce it by returning for a moment to Oxford, which we have not visited since 1494.

At that time the Renaissance had already arrived here. Grocyn of New College was teaching Greek, and Colet of Magdalen was planning his lectures on St. Paul. It was Colet again who founded St. Paul's, the first humanistic school in England (1510): there is an attractive account of it in Erasmus's letters. In 1515 Corpus, the first humanistic college, was founded by Foxe of Magdalen. And in 1525 Wolsey, who had been Bursar of Magdalen, founded Cardinal College, afterwards Christ Church.

It was not until that year, apparently, that the Reformation reached Oxford; and then it was brought—I am making no reflexion on the movement—by some Lutherans from Cambridge. At first it made little progress. Perhaps a local outbreak of sweating sickness which happened about that time was attributed to its arrival. Perhaps Oxford was already a home of lost causes. Anyhow, ten years later, in 1535, a Visitation was found necessary, to enforce religious conformity, and to encourage the New Learning. Thirteen years later again, in 1548, the old Italian and Spanish humanist, Peter Martyr, now a fervent Protestant, was brought over to lecture here on St. Paul and the doctrine of the Mass. In 1549 he was followed by King Edward VI's Visitors, who commended the true religion by smashing the carvings in All Souls Chapel.

But the Reformation in Oxford ended almost as soon as it began. In 1553 came Queen Mary's Commissioners, to undo the work of Edward VI, and to inaugurate the Counter-Reformation. Their victims were not statues, but men. In 1555 Cranmer was tried for his life in St. Mary's, and Latimer and Ridley burnt. The next year Cranmer himself was burnt outside the city wall, probably in what is now the Broad, opposite Balliol, at a point marked by a stone cross on the ground: and he was fastened to the stake by an iron band which can still be seen in the Ashmolean.

There is a curious story belonging to this period which illustrates the changes through which Oxford was passing. The Dean of Christ Church from 1549 to 1553 was a certain Richard Cox. He was famous for his zeal against Popery, which led him, by some strange disconnexion of ideas, to destroy ancient MSS. in the local libraries. He was also famous (or should I say infamous?) as being the first Dean to introduce a wife into college. Encouraged by this example, when Peter Martyr was made Regius Professor of Divinity (1548) and Canon of Christ Church (1550), he also brought his wife with him—a German lady and a Protestant. She died in 1552, and was buried in the Cathedral. When Queen Mary's Commissioners arrived two years later, Peter fled, and the new Catholic Dean dug up Mrs. Martyr's body, and buried it in a dung-hill in his back garden. Then Elizabeth came to the throne. Mrs. Martyr's body was once more dug up, in order to be restored to the Cathedral. But about the same time they discovered there a bundle of old bones, believed to be those of St. Frideswide, the patron saint of Oxford, which only a few years before had been venerated as sacred relics at the shrine which you can still see in the Cathedral. The opportunity for combining economy with edification was too good to be missed. An elaborate funeral was arranged. The bones of the Catholic saint and the remains of the Protestant Canon's wife were mixed together, and buried in the same grave: and one Canon Calfhill, who tells the story, published a volume of Latin poems to draw the moral of the occasion:

> Vivite nobiscum concordes ergo, Papistae;
> Nunc coeunt pietas atque superstitio.

or:

> Papists and Protestants should now
>   In peace abide,
> As here religion true and false
>   Lie side by side.

But the Canon tactfully left it to his readers to infer which was which [*H. L. Thompson*].

II

That was how Oxford experienced the Counter-Reformation. On the Continent King Philip II of Spain was the husband and counterpart of Queen Mary of England. The year of Cranmer's trial (1555) was the year in which Cardinal Caraffa, the leading spirit of the Counter-Reformation, became Pope Paul IV, and in which the Peace of Augsburg divided Germany and Europe, beyond recall, between the Catholics and the Protestants.

The Counter-Reformation was Rome's reply to the Reformation. It may be dated from 1540, when Paul III granted a charter to the Jesuits, to the close of the Council of Trent in 1566—a momentous generation in the history of the Church. It took two shapes—reaction against attempts to reform the Church from without, and reform of the Church itself from within. Its three main agents were the Jesuits, the Inquisition, and the Council of Trent.

First, the Jesuits. 'All the great crises of Church history have resulted in a renewal of religious life, and a reformation or creation of monastic orders. In the eleventh century Gregory VII had the monks of Cluny to help him; in the thirteenth century Innocent III had the Franciscans and Dominicans. And now in the sixteenth century most of the old Orders reformed their Rules, or restored them to their primitive rigour—for instance, the Franciscans in 1528. At the same time, between 1524 and 1541 no less than fifteen new Orders were founded' [*Malet*]. Some of these, such as the Theatines and Barnabites, set the pattern for the most famous of all the new Orders—the 'Company of Jesus.'

Most religious movements, and most religious Orders, have been founded by one person, and regulated by another. Christianity was founded by the life and teaching of Christ: but the forms in which it invaded Italy and converted Europe—its creed, its ministry, and its system of sacraments—were the work of the Church in the centuries following his death. St. Francis founded the Franciscans, and gave them a simple rule of life: but by the time of his death everything was altered, and the Order became an example of the very things against which he had meant it to be a protest. The Jesuit Order, on the other hand, was not only founded, but given its constitution and its rule of life by one and the same man, Ignatius Loyola. He stamped himself upon it so indelibly, and yet so impersonally, that his death made no difference to its development. If it lost, by this, the power which Christianity has shown of adapting itself to new conditions, it gained no less by its faithfulness to the original spirit of its founder. Like the Salvation Army, it learnt almost all it had to learn, and became almost all it was capable of becoming, under the guidance of its founder, and within the lifetime of its original members.

Inigo de Recalde, called Loyola from the castle in which he was born (1491), came of a noble Basque family, and was brought up as a page at the court of King Ferdinand of Spain. His head was full of romantic adventures, as a boy's should be. He got them, as Don Quixote did, from the famous medieval romance, which everyone read in those days, called *Amadis of Gaul*. I cannot ask you to read it—it runs to twenty-five books, and the Bodleian edition contains two hundred pages to each volume, two columns to a page—so I will give you a specimen of it. This is how it begins in the English version of 1619. 'Soone after the passion of our Saviour Jesus Christ there reigned in little Brittaine a king named Garinter, enstructed in the lawe of veritie, and highly adorned with many laudable virtues, having a noble ladye to his wife, by whom he had two beautiful daughters.' The eldest, married to the King of Scots, was called the Lady of the Garland, because she had such beautiful golden hair that her husband would not let her wear anything on her head but 'a fair circle or chaplet of flowers.' The younger daughter was even more beautiful, and was called Elisena. She was wooed by many princes and great lords, but rejected them all, and lived a solitary and holy life: so she was called 'the Lost Virgin in Devotion.' At the opening of the story King Garinter is hunting in the forest, loses his escort, and comes upon a knight fighting two others. The two are vanquished and slain, and the victor reveals himself as 'King Perion of Gaule, who of a long time had been desirous to know' King Garinter. On their way to Garinter's city the two kings hunt a stag. The stag is leapt upon and killed by a lion. King Perion slays the lion single-handed. There is a great feast in King Garinter's palace. King Perion and the fair

Elisena fall in love at first sight. All that is in Chapter I: and I doubt whether any of our romantic novelists could do better.

With his head full of such ideas Loyola became an officer in the Spanish army under Charles V, but was so badly wounded at Pampeluna in 1520, or so badly doctored afterwards, that he limped for the rest of his life. Whilst in hospital he turned from *Amadis of Gaul* to Spanish translations of Voragine's *Legenda Aurea* (Anthology of Saints), and Ludolf of Saxony's *Life of Christ*; and soon resolved that, as he could no longer serve in the Spanish army, he would enlist in the army of the Church. As soon as he could get about again, he climbed that fantastic mountain which you can visit from Barcelona, Montserrat, and dedicated his arms, like a medieval knight, in the monastic church. Then, after a period of penance and fasting at Manresa, close by, he set out for Jerusalem, intending to convert the infidels. This, however, the Franciscan missionaries in Palestine, finding him too inexperienced, or too indiscreet, would not allow; so he came back, resolved to educate himself for his life-work. After a course of Spanish Universities, where he more than once got into trouble with the Inquisition for unauthorized preaching, he walked to Paris, and there ultimately took his degree (1528–1534). His contemporaries at the University included Calvin (his most dangerous enemy), Servetus (whom Calvin burnt for heresy), Rabelais (who makes characteristic fun of Loyola's *Spiritual Exercises*), and a Scotch teacher of Latin named Buchanan, whose account of his experiences (1529–1531) throws a curious light on the character of Renaissance education [*Sedgwick*]. But Loyola's immediate friends were six students, who fell under his influence, and took the first vows of the Jesuit Order at Montmartre in 1534—Francis Xavier (a Frenchman), Lefèvre (a Genevan), three Spaniards—Lainez, Salmeron, and Bobadilla—and Rodriguez (a Portuguese). The seven met again, by arrangement, at Venice; were again prevented (this time by difficulties of travel) from going to Palestine; and determined instead to offer their services to the Pope, for any use he would make of them. In 1540, with the help of the reforming Cardinal Contarini, they obtained a Charter from Paul III under the name of 'the Company of Jesus.'

Loyola's opinions 'had passed through three phases. In the

first he entertained elementary medieval notions of religion, picked up during childhood and youth in Guipuscoa and Navarre, which denounced somewhat vaguely the World, the Flesh, and the Devil, and very definitely Moors and Turks, as enemies of Christ. In the second, the period of his travels in Italy, he became acquainted with the evil spirit of the Renaissance, the spirit that questions. And in the third, that of his sojourn in Paris, he learned to believe that the demon of disobedience and private judgment was as harmful to the old ecclesiastical order as infidelity or doubt. Now (in 1540), with the forces of Satan, all visible, drawn up before his eyes in battle array, he girded himself to the task of recruiting and drilling a battalion of light horse that should, at the command of the general-in-chief, Christ's Vicar on Earth, be ready for service at all times, in any place, reckless of everything except the greater glory of God' [*Sedgwick*].

I have laid stress upon Loyola's life and opinions, because he stamped them so upon his Society—the romantic and crusading spirit of the Spaniard, the fanatical and medieval piety of the Catholic, the soldier's belief in discipline and organization. We find them all in the Constitution of the Order.

The aim of the Jesuit's life was 'to employ all his powers, with the help of divine grace, in saving and perfecting his neighbour'; and he was to do it by means of religious education, preaching, the hearing of confessions, works of charity, and the service of the sick and poor. So far there was nothing very original. But notice the new points that followed.

First, the Jesuits were a 'Company,' a military body, living under military discipline. The rule was enforced upon all alike —upon Loyola's own friends, the original members of the Order; upon its General, Loyola himself. And it was backed by a system of friendly *espionnage*, which left no place for privacy, and no man his own master. Again, the rules for recruiting and promotion had a military strictness. No infidels, schismatics, murderers, criminals, ex-monks, married men, slaves, or feeble-minded persons could be admitted to the Order. There was a hierarchy of ranks: no Jesuit could be admitted to full membership, or ordained priest, until he had gone through sixteen years' training, including a nine years' course of reading. The 'higher command' was organized in the same spirit. At its head was the 'General,' elected for life, and given autocratic powers. The Company was divided into Provinces, each under the command of a Provincial, nominated by and responsible to the General. As Loyola himself said, 'he had never left the army: he had only been seconded for the service of God.'

Secondly, all religious orders had a vow of obedience; but that of the Jesuits was specially strict. It was to be passive obedience. 'Let each member be fully persuaded that those who live under the vow of obedience ought to let themselves be directed and ruled by divine providence through their Superiors, just as though they were a dead body [perinde ac cadaver], which lets itself be moved in any direction, and drawn about for any reason; or like an old man's staff, which lends itself to the hand of him who uses it, wherever he wishes to go, or whatever use he wishes to make of it' [*Constitutions*]. Again, there must be obedience of the mind, as well as of the body. In his *Spiritual Exercises*, the devotional manual of the Order, Loyola himself wrote, 'If the Church defines anything that seems to us white to be black, we must at once assert that it is black.' Lastly, the Jesuits took a special vow of obedience to the Pope. This was embodied in the original Charter given by Paul III, 'Let all the associates know . . . that this entire Society and all its members became God's soldiers under the faithful obedience of the most sacred Lord the Pope, and the other Roman pontiffs his successors. And although we are taught in the Gospel, and in the orthodox faith acknowledge and firmly profess, that all Christ's faithful people are subject to the Roman pontiff as their head, and the Vicar of Christ; nevertheless, for the greater humility of our Society, and the perfect mortification of every member, and for the denial of our own wills, we have deemed it highly conducive that each one of us be bound by a special vow beyond that general obligation, so that whatsoever the present or other Roman pontiffs for the time being shall ordain, pertaining to the advancement of souls, and the propagation of the faith, and to whatever province he shall resolve to send us, we are straightway bound to obey, as far as in us lies, without any tergiversation or excuse (whether he send us among the Turks, or to any other unbelievers . . . even in those parts called India; or to any heretics or schismatics, or likewise to any believers).'

Notice, again, the stress laid by Loyola upon education. This was not a new thing for a religious Order to undertake; but it was undertaken in a new way. Colleges were founded in Italy, Spain, Portugal, south Germany, and elsewhere. They were placed in educational centres, where they were most likely to attract the sons of influential Catholics. The education was humanistic as well as theological; and it was given free. In this way the Society hoped first to capture the Renaissance, and then to counteract the Reformation.

The 'Company of Jesus' were not popular with the older Orders. Their disuse of monastic dress and monastic Offices, their preference of physical health to corporal penance, their refusal of ecclesiastical preferment, the special privileges granted them by the Papacy—indeed, the very name of their Society, became so many causes of offence. But nothing could stop the progress of the Order. Within sixteen years its original seven members had become 1,500. It had twelve provinces, of which one was in China, and another in Japan. Its sixty-eight houses and thirty-six colleges were educating 6,000 pupils. Everywhere it was consolidating the Catholic army, and challenging the divided forces of Protestantism.

I am not concerned either to defend or to attack the Jesuit system. But it is often misunderstood; and there is a good deal of force in the comparison drawn by the latest of Loyola's biographers between religious discipline in the sixteenth century and patriotic discipline in the twentieth. 'Protestants,' he suggests, 'have declaimed against what they call the iron constraint put upon the human soul. But if one stops to think, how does the Jesuit training differ, unless perhaps in conscientious intensity, from that at West Point or Saint Cyr? In a military academy the whole weight of authority comes down on the individual soul. Substitute the flag for the cross, country for church, famous generals and marshals for saints and martyrs, honour for grace, and you will find that the constraint in either case is very much the same. Obedience is of equal obligation, the word of the Superior as indisputable, the period of preparation about as long. As for liberty of thought, there is no more room for patriotic agnosticism in West Point than for religious agnosticism in a Jesuit college. In New York State men have been sent to prison for insults to the symbol of our patriotic faith. The difference is that we have lost our belief in supernatural religion, but not as yet our faith in nationality' [*Sedgwick*].

III

The second instrument of the Counter-Reformation was the Inquisition. This, like the Jesuit Order, was an old weapon used in a new way. Popular fear or hatred of Jews, witches, and heretics goes back almost behind European history: it only needed organization, secular or ecclesiastical, to turn it into something like an Inquisition. If Pope Innocent III was morally responsible for the Inquisition, if his successors in the thirteenth century formulated and legalized it, the modern revival of an outgrown medieval system came from Spain, where Ferdinand and Isabella gave a charter to the Dominicans in 1477. In 1481 the first 'Commission' was set up at Seville. Within a year three hundred heretics were burnt in the city itself, and over two thousand in the diocese. After this auspicious beginning the Spanish Inquisition never looked back. It became a weapon of the State as well as of the Church. It punished political liberalism as it punished unorthodoxy in religion: they were regarded as two sides of the same sin. It was turned less against Protestants than against Jews, Moors, and renegade Jewish Christians. It chose its victims from the classes best worth plundering. If they could not be burnt, at least their goods might be confiscated, or they might be frightened into purchasing their freedom cash down.

It was apparently the sight of this admirable system at work in Spain, followed by some experiments of his own at Venice, that led Cardinal Caraffa to propose the re-establishment of the Inquisition at Rome. Lutheranism had made more progress in Italy than in Spain, and the old policy of patronage had broken down. Contarini, the peace Cardinal, must give way to Caraffa, the Cardinal of war. In 1540 Paul III had granted their charter to the Jesuits: in 1542 he set up the 'Holy Office,' or Standing Committee of the Inquisition. Soon there were burnings at Rome, Ferrara, and elsewhere. When Caraffa became Pope in 1555 he presided at the Congregation of the Inquisition once a week, and stiffened the procedure—for instance, the use of torture was re-introduced. Pius IV massacred the Vaudois Protestants, and burnt Pasquale, the Italian translator of the New Testament. Persecution reached its maximum under Pius V, when (except for a few refugees at Florence or at Venice) Protestantism was successfully wiped out in Italy.

North of the Alps the Inquisition never succeeded. We shall meet it again in the Netherlands under Charles V and Philip II, and in France under Francis I and Henry II; there will be rumours of it in Germany. But everywhere it is a weapon that wounds those who use it. Everywhere it brings war, and the assertion of political and religious independence. This was not because it was cruel and intolerant—it was a cruel and intolerant age; but because it was essentially medieval, and there could be no truce between the medieval and the modern points of view. The Inquisition was not interested in morality, or in religion, as the northern nations understood them. It did not concern itself with the state of a man's character, but with the fate of a man's soul. Such an attitude might persist, and has persisted, in some forms of popular Protestantism. There might be, and there were, Catholic victims of Protestant persecution. But the spirit of reason and toleration at the heart of the Renaissance, and the spirit of freedom and personal responsibility at the heart of the Reformation, were bound to emancipate men, by degrees, from the fears and superstitions to which the Inquisition appealed. And so, even in countries whose criminal law was still cruel and bloodthirsty, even among peoples who were hardly less brutal and superstitious than the Spaniards, the Inquisition came to be regarded with horror.

I cannot pretend to like the Inquisition. But I do not want you to judge it unfairly; so I would end by correcting one or two common misconceptions about it. First, as we have seen, it was not invented in the sixteenth century, to deal with the Reformation: it grew up gradually. If it belonged to any one century more than another it was to the thirteenth; and its use in the sixteenth was a return to medievalism. Secondly, its cruelties were not invented by the Church, but borrowed from the State. For a long time the Church stood out against the death sentence, and would not allow the use of torture. It was only under pressure of what it thought necessity that the Church adopted the methods used by the best as well as by the worst governments of the time against traitors and criminals. Thirdly, the worst cruelties of the business, especially death by burning alive, were sparingly and unwillingly employed, particularly outside Spain. The Inquisition had a hundred methods of dealing with its victims. You may condemn them all, but you must distinguish between them.

Lastly, the chief aim of the Inquisition was not to punish Protestants, but to prevent heresy and backsliding among Catholics. It was not a pogrom, or a crusade, but a Reign of Terror, and it was set up for, and accepted by, the Catholic nations as a measure of public safety. In Spain it was a popular institution, administered till the nineteenth century. Wellington, who knew Spain well, thought Napoleon unwise to get rid of it in 1812; and it was, in fact, revived again for a few years before its final abolition in 1820.

IV

The third instrument of the Counter-Reformation was the Council of Trent. The demand for a General Council, or Pan-Catholic Congress, had been put forward by Luther, and supported by Charles V. The alternative was a purely German Synod, which might set the fashion for a number of national secessions from Rome. But their experiences at Pisa and Constance had not encouraged either Pope or reformer to hope much from another Council. Paul III, who became Pope in 1534, was at first ruled by the moderate Contarini, afterwards by the militant Caraffa. When the main points of the forward policy had been secured by the foundation of the Jesuits in 1540 and of the Holy Office in 1542; when the Colloquy of Ratisbon (1541) had broken down, and a preliminary meeting of Germans and Italians at Trent (1542) had shown that apparent concessions might be made without real compromise, Paul thought that he might safely summon the Council of Trent (1545). This was followed by a second session in 1551, and by a third in 1562.

The points at issue in the successive sessions of the Council were of four kinds. The first were questions of Church reform; for instance pluralism—the holding of a number of Church offices or benefices by one man; absenteeism—not residing in one's parish or diocese; or the sale of benefices, against which Luther had so much to say. On such points as these all parties were more or less agreed; and it was in the Pope's interest to allow discussion, and to promise concessions with regard to them, so as to postpone or avoid the treatment of more personal issues. In the second place there were the questions raised by the demands of the Protestants, or of the reforming Catholics, such as the marriage of the clergy, the translation of the Bible, or Communion in both kinds—that is, the old custom, only discontinued in the twelfth century, of administering the wine as well as the bread to the laity at Holy Communion. These concessions the Pope was not disposed to make generally as a matter of right; but he allowed some of them in certain cases, as a matter of privilege. To the third class of questions belonged the theological doctrines of Protestantism, especially with reference to the nature of the Mass, Original Sin, and Justification by Faith. Here the Pope was determined to obtain from the Council a final condemnation of the Protestant position. The last kind of question —which the Pope very much hoped would never be reached— affected the claims and privileges of the Papacy itself; for instance, the problem, which may seem to us academic, but which then had very practical bearings, whether the bishops derived their powers and exercised their functions by direct divine right, or by delegation from the Pope. The point was in fact debated at the third Council, when the papal position was defended with some difficulty by the Jesuit representatives against the bishops of Spain.

When the third Council of Trent finally dissolved in 1566, victory rested with the Pope. Just such a degree of Church reform had been granted, just such concessions had been made to lay demands, just such a condemnation of Protestant doctrines had been secured, as left the Church more than ever in the hands of the Papacy. It is not difficult to see how this came about. One reason was the extraordinary prestige of the papal system—a prestige much more likely (I think) to be enhanced by a good Pope than to be endangered by a bad one. Incidentally, the Popes of the Counter-Reformation—Paul III, Paul IV, Pius IV, and Pius V—were of a very different stamp from their predecessors of the Renaissance period—Alexander VI, Julius II, or Leo X.

Again, the Council was held at Trent, a place technically within the Emperor's jurisdiction, but in fact most easily accessible from Italy; and it was packed with Italian bishops, who voted consistently for the papal policy. To make more certain of his majority, the Pope ruled that the voting should be by head, not by the countries which the delegates represented; under this system the Italian representatives had an absolute majority. In any case, though the Spanish, French, and German bishops all brought with them to the Council programmes of reform, their programmes did not agree with one another. Nor indeed did the delegates. Feeling ran so high that they caballed together in private, and even fought together in public, with violence and bloodshed. It was thus easy for the Pope to play off one party of Reformers against another, and to carry his own policy against them all. Besides, it was not only a difficult and expensive business for these foreign bishops to attend at Trent; but they knew also that their rulers did not expect much of the Council, or intend to pay much attention to its decisions. Ferdinand of Austria, Catherine de Medici, and even Philip of Spain used the doctrinal decrees of Trent less to persecute the Protestants than to keep the Catholics in order; but in matters of Church government and Church discipline they intended to keep their independence, and to manage their own affairs in their own way. Lastly, it must be remembered that most of the work of the Council was done in its third session, which opened in 1562. This was seven years after the peace of Augsburg, when the last attempt to unite the Catholics and Protestants of Germany had failed, and they had agreed to go their different ways. The Reformation was now an accomplished fact. There was nothing to be hoped or gained by concessions to the Protestants. The only thing left to do was to reorganize the Catholic Church, and to re-define the Catholic faith for the benefit of its own adherents.

By its refusal to compromise with the Protestants, and by the rigid lines upon which its doctrine and practice were now set, the Roman Church ceased to be an all-inclusive communion, and became one denomination among many. As the Imperial policy was henceforth to mean little more than the interests of the Archduke of Austria, so the papal policy was henceforth to mean little more than the interests of the Bishop of Rome. This was the price of the success, such as it was, of the Counter-Reformation. The Roman cause was saved in northern Europe; but Rome itself became provincial. The change is embodied in the altered meaning of a word. 'Ultramontanism' before the Reformation meant the extremist zeal of Catholics north of the Alps. After the Reformation it meant the extremist claims of Rome itself, to which the scattered Catholics of northern Europe rather wistfully looked back.

V

There was one institution set up by the Council of Trent which may almost be called a fourth instrument of the Counter-Reformation—I mean, the Index. The Index, like the Jesuits and the Inquisition, was an old expedient used in a new way. In the days when a heretical work existed only in manuscript, it was practicable to burn the few existing copies, with or without their author. Even after printing made this policy futile, it survived as a ceremony: the burning of heretical books was common enough in France down to the eighteenth century; and even in 1915 a copy of a London paper containing an attack on Lord Kitchener was solemnly burnt in the Stock Exchange. But obviously it was now more practicable to prohibit the reading of books, than to destroy all the copies in circulation. The result was an Index—that is, a 'Black List' of books or authors not to be read by the faithful. In 1546 the Council of Trent prohibited the sale or possession of any anonymous books on religion (for heretical authors seldom dared publish in their own name) which had not been approved by the proper ecclesiastical authority. The first authoritative Roman Index was issued by Paul IV in 1557. It contained three lists—one of authors whose writings were wholly proscribed; another of proscribed books by known authors; and a third of anonymous works not to be read by the faithful. There was also general condemnation of all anonymous books published during the last forty years, and a list of sixty-two printers, all of whose publications were proscribed. Among the books at once condemned was Erasmus's commentary on the New Testament, and the Report of a Commission to which Caraffa himself had put his name. From 1564

THE INDEX

onwards a revised 'Index Librorum Prohibitorum' was continually reprinted and kept up to date: even so, it was as difficult to keep pace with the books published as to enforce the prohibitions. The Index (reorganized as recently as 1897) has outlived the Inquisition. It is still, I suppose, an effective means of discipline among Catholics; although in other quarters novelists have been suspected of getting their books 'banned' in order to increase their sale; and societies exist whose chief purpose is to produce on Sundays plays which the Censor considers unfit for presentation on week-days.

Anyhow, you may still see, on the front page of Roman Catholic books, the Latin formulae, 'Nil obstat' ('There is no objection to its being published') and 'Imprimatur' ('It may be printed'): and you may fairly take these words as the last relics of the Counter-Reformation.

LECTURE VII

THE NETHERLANDS REVOLT

I

Men had scarcely accustomed themselves to the idea of religious freedom, when they were forced to fight in its defence. The attempt to enforce the Counter-Reformation was followed by nearly a century of civil wars—the Revolt in the Netherlands, the Wars of Religion in France, and the Thirty Years' War in Germany. The motive of these wars was not wholly religious. The Counter-Reformation was not only the Church's attempt to recover the ground lost to Protestantism: it was also an attempt on the part of the absolute monarchies to enforce their government upon political minorities. The civil wars which followed were fought not only for the religious freedom of the Protestants, but also for the political and economic freedom of the middle classes. Nevertheless, the main cause of these troubles was religion. It was the Reformation which gave rise to the idea that a man's religion cannot be dictated to him either by the Church or by the State; that it is his right and duty to choose it according to his own mind and conscience; that he may then freely associate with others who share his choice and his beliefs; and that, as a political consequence of this, the various religious bodies must be allowed to live their own life within the protection of the State. This claim, in view of everything that the medieval world had been accustomed to, was revolutionary. It was this claim which gave rise, almost inevitably, to the wars of religion.

II

There was one King in Europe to whom the whole idea of freedom was anathema. Philip II of Spain was (you remember) the eldest son of the Emperor Charles V. He had been born at an unlucky moment. His birth festivities were turned into mourning at the news of the sack of Rome by an Imperial army—

an event that was thought at once disgraceful for Charles and disastrous for Christendom (1527). The death of his mother and brothers left him, while still young, to the influence of his father, who brought him up a prig, an autocrat, and a fanatic.

There are few people of his time whose appearance is better known. His light hair, blue eyes, and Hapsburg chin reappear in a series of portraits at all ages. At thirty-one a Venetian ambassador speaks of his short figure, broad forehead, big blue eyes, thick eyebrows nearly meeting, well-shaped nose, big mouth with heavy lower lip, short pointed beard, white skin and yellow Flemish hair. His manners are stiff and Spanish, but his nature modest and polite. Though phlegmatic and slow, he has a good head for business. He reads history, knows geography, and dabbles in sculpture and painting. His habitual language is Spanish; but he understands Italian also, and a little French, and speaks Latin well 'for a prince' [*Badoaro*]. At forty-one he is still pale and blond, very slow and dignified, a lover of solitude. He has had four wives, and his hair is turning grey. He retires for eight or ten months in the year to one of his country houses, with the members of his family and a few ministers. He still 'occupies himself unremittingly with business, and conducts it with extreme care, because he wants to know and see everything' for himself [*Priuli?*]. At sixty-six he is still described as phlegmatic, dignified, inscrutable; a regular recluse now, living a semi-monastic life at his gloomy Escurial, and not appearing in public as often as two or three times a year [*Contarini*].

You can visit the Escurial on the way from Burgos to Madrid. It is a huge oppressive building—a fit monument for the golden age of Spain. It is indeed as typical of Philip and Spain as Versailles is of France and Louis XIV. Versailles is just a huge palace, designed to house an enormous Court, and to provide a background for the most elaborate royal ritual in Europe. The Escurial is a monastery, and its centre is a mausoleum in which Philip and his dynasty were to be buried, and the monks were to say innumerable masses for their souls. One wing of the great square block was kept for the royal apartments, and one room for the royal study. Imagine Philip sitting there year after year (for forty years he never left Spain) reading, hour after hour, the endless reports of his ministers, and writing his laboured notes in the wide margins. That was how Spain was governed for nearly half a century, during the most critical and influential period of its history, by a man who was fanatical without enthusiasm, stubborn without resolution, and so slow that one of his viceroys said, 'If death came from Spain, I should be immortal.'

What was Philip's policy? It was to make Spain supreme in Europe, and to extirpate heresy from Christendom. He was quite clear about both aims, and nothing would turn him from them. Fortunately for civilization, the second purpose interfered with the first, and prevented its achievement.

It looked at first as though nothing could do so. Consider the extent of Spanish territory, which, disembarrassed of Germany, still included Spain, north and south Italy, much of the Rhine valley, and the Netherlands; besides Central and South America, and (for a time) Portugal. Consider the constant influx of Spanish gold—though at first much of it went to German and Italian bankers to pay for the wars of Charles V. Think of the Spanish army, the finest and best led in the world, with its gentleman-rankers, and generals such as Alva, Don John, and Alexander Farnese. Charles seemed to have left his son all the wealth of his own empire, and none of its weaknesses.

But there was one weakness—and for Spain it proved a fatal one—the strength of Philip's religious principles. His Catholic fanaticism made it impossible for him to rule over heretics. This is not an exaggeration. Here are his actual words, written to his ambassador at Rome in 1566, and meant for the Pope—the one person to whom Philip always told the truth. 'As to the pardons publicly announced in my name, whisper in the ear of his Holiness that I do not pretend to pardon in matters religious. Assure his Holiness that, rather than suffer the least thing in prejudice of religion, I will lose my states and a hundred lives; for I will not live to be a king of heretics. And if I must use force, I will carry out my intentions myself, and neither my own peril, nor the ruin of these provinces [the Netherlands], or even of all my dominions, shall stop me from fulfilling my duty as a Christian prince, to maintain the Catholic faith, and the Holy See, now filled by a Pope whom I love and revere' [*Harrison*].

Philip's charity began at home. The Inquisition was turned with fresh savagery against the few Protestants in Spain, so that within ten years not one of them was left. Another four years, and the Moriscoes, the descendants of half-Christianized Moors, were hunted from their homes, and the remnants of them scattered up and down the country. Granada, the market garden of Spain, was left a desert. But Philip slept more happily. Better an orthodox than a prosperous people.

Then he turned to the Netherlands, the one blot on his reputation for orthodoxy and absolutism.

III

The provinces at the mouth of the Rhine were at this time amongst the richest and most liberal in Europe. Since the death of the last Duke of Burgundy, and their transfer to Austrian rule, the manufacturing and trading cities of the Netherlands had recovered from an easy-going government liberties long overthrown. The 'Great Privilege' granted to Holland by Mary of Hungary (Regent for Charles V) provided that the Dutch cities might hold Diets whenever they wished; that they could not be taxed, or involved in war, or their coinage tampered with, without their own consent; that Dutch should be the official language; and that all their local privileges should be respected. Under Charles V, who had himself been brought up in Flanders, and had the good sense to entrust his government to women, the Netherlands were prosperous, and, on the whole, contented.

But there were already signs of coming trouble. The first was the growth of Protestantism. For various reasons—one was the commercial intelligence of the people, and another was the slackness of Church life so far from the centre of Catholicism—there had grown up in the Netherlands, ever since the thirteenth century, a temper and tradition of religious independence. It was Catholic, not Protestant; but it was mystical, moral, and therefore a little unorthodox. Its greatest product was the *De Imitatione Christi* of Thomas à Kempis in the fourteenth century. This was good soil in which to plant Protestantism—Protestantism carried down the Rhine, the great highway of western Europe, by merchants and scholars from Italy, Switzerland, and the German states. Wherever it came, having (as we saw) no political organization of its own, it adapted itself to the needs of the governing classes, and became a state religion. At Zürich Zwingli made it into municipal Humanism: at Geneva it inspired Calvin's Puritan Commonwealth. The Protestantism of the Netherlands was pre-Calvinistic, but of the same type. It easily allied itself with the ideals of the commercial cities, and the aims of the ruling burgher class. The merchants of Ghent and Bruges made common cause with the scholars of Leyden and Louvain. Religious and economic freedom kissed each other. Liberty looked down from heaven—and saw Philip and his Inquisition.

The second sign of trouble was a controversy about bishops. I said that religious independence gained ground in the Netherlands partly because of a breakdown in church life. There were few bishoprics in the country, and the only two archbishoprics were in foreign hands. This, of course, favoured the Reformation. 'In Ireland, in Italy, in Spain, and in France, where the dioceses were small and well organized, the Reformation made comparatively small way. In Germany, Switzerland, Scotland, England, and Scandinavia [and we may add the Netherlands], where bishops were few, and secular in their ideas, the Reformation made great way' [*Stubbs*]. Charles V had drawn up a scheme for rearranging the dioceses, and increasing their number: but he had not carried it out. Philip tried to do so, and made it one of the causes of the Revolt.

The third sign of trouble came from Charles's attempt to introduce the Spanish Inquisition into the Netherlands. He published edicts against heresy in such pitiless terms that they were said to be written not in ink but in blood. Some executions followed. But they roused such opposition that Charles acquiesced in the virtual suspension both of the edicts and of the Inquisition. A live tax-payer was, after all, better than a dead Protestant. It was left for Philip, who would not reign over heretics, to carry out Charles's policy to its logical and fatal conclusion.

Philip was in the Netherlands in 1559. His Spanish manners displeased the Flemings as much as he disliked their political and religious independence. Before he left for Spain, never to return, he instructed his Regent, Margaret of Parma, and her minister, Cardinal Granvella, to set up the new bishoprics, and to enforce the Inquisition. But for eight years more there was no serious departure from Charles's policy. The Regent was on good terms with the Netherland nobles. She respected their rights, and promised not to enforce the Inquisition, so long as they prevented any popular disorders such as might call Philip's attention to the country. For their part, as the Venetian ambassador informed his Government, 'the chief nobles never had any intention of rebelling against the King: their only object, in employing intimidation, was to prevent the Inquisition being set up in the country. They foresaw that, if this design were once realized, not only their own authority and position would be destroyed, but also that commerce, on which the prosperity of the country chiefly depends, would be ruined' [*Tiepolo*].

IV

In what follows I shall be relying mainly on the correspondence of the greatest of these nobles, who led the opposition against Spain, and became the hero of the War of Independence—William the Silent. William was not a Dutchman or a Fleming by birth, but a German, and his home was in Nassau, on the Lahn, a tributary of the lower Rhine. He inherited the family property of Orange, in the south of France, on condition of being brought up as a Catholic. From ten to eighteen he was a page at the Emperor's court, and for three years fought in the Imperial army against Henry II of France. Charles trusted him more than any of his younger men; and it was upon William's arm that he leant, a broken man, at the famous ceremony of abdication in 1556.

There is a fine portrait of William at this time—young-looking, clean shaven (later he has a beard), and in full armour: it is a strong, interesting, rather melancholy face. And there is a description by a contemporary writer, by no means his friend, which corresponds to the portrait. 'Never,' he says, 'did an arrogant or indiscreet word issue from his mouth, under the impulse of anger or other passion. If any of his servants committed a fault, he was satisfied to admonish them gently, without resorting to menace or abusive language. He was master of a sweet and winning power of persuasion, by means of which he gave form to the great ideas within him; and thus he succeeded in bending to his will the other lords about the Court as he chose; beloved and in high favour above all men with the people, by reason of a gracious manner that he had of saluting and addressing in a fascinating and familiar way all whom he met' [*Payen*, quoted by *Harrison*]. William was to need all these gifts, and more, in the struggle before him.

The first period in his political life, and in the history of the Netherlands Revolt, runs from 1556 (Philip's accession) to 1567, when he threw up his post under the Spanish Government. This period also coincides with the Regency of Margaret of Parma. During the whole of it William remained a king's man and a Catholic; and you can judge how bad Philip's policy must have been to turn the father's best friend into the son's bitterest enemy. True, in 1561 William took his second wife, for political reasons, from a German Lutheran family. But he writes in the same year that 'the King may rest assured that he will live and die a Catholic'; and at present he means it. Soon after this he joins Egmont and Horn, two other dissatisfied nobles, in writing to Philip to protest against the policy of Granvella. The Cardinal, they complain, is overriding the constitutional rights of the State Council, and setting the whole country by the ears. After long-drawn negotiations Granvella was recalled to Spain (1564), where his resentment did more harm to William's cause than was ever done by his bad government. For a time Philip masks his feelings by a complimentary correspondence, in which he only urges William to greater zeal for religion, and asks for the loan of a cook. (William 'the Silent' was not specially so except upon the occasion which earned him the nickname. Nor was he by preference a poor man, or a simple liver. At this time he was very rich, kept up a big establishment, entertained lavishly, and enjoyed a good dinner.)

It is in 1566 that the real trouble begins. After six years' meditation, Philip has made up his mind. The Duchess of Parma sends round a circular letter giving an outline of his religious policy for the Netherlands. There are three points. First, the decrees of the Council of Trent are to be enforced. This, says William, will cause no great difficulty. The decrees were unpopular, but they have been modified. The Catholics will grumble, but acquiesce. Secondly, the Inquisition. 'As to the Inquisition,' writes Philip to the Regent, 'my will is that it be enforced by the

Inquisitors as of old, and as is required by all law, human and divine. This lies very near my heart, and I require you to carry out my order. Let all prisoners be put to death, and suffer them no longer to escape through the neglect, weakness, and bad faith of the judges. If any are too timid to execute the Edicts, I will replace them by men who have more heart and zeal.' William could not miss the threat to himself and his friends contained in the last words. 'You know,' he comments to the Regent, 'that the chief objection to the new bishopric scheme lay in the fear that it was a step towards the Inquisition: besides, both you and your predecessor [Mary of Hungary] promised that it should not be introduced.' And on the third point, the enforcement of the Edicts against heresy, he adds, 'This means nothing but trouble for the King and misery for the country. I would rather resign than carry out the King's orders.'

For a few months more he carried on, trying in vain to pacify the people, and to stop the public preachments and the printing of seditious pamphlets which were everywhere rousing the country against Spain. At last, early in 1567, he could stand it no longer. He knew by this time that the King did not trust him, and would like to be rid of his services. Granvella, even before his dismissal, had written to Philip, 'The Prince of Orange is a dangerous man, sly, full of ruses; pretending to support the people, and to consider their interests even against your edicts; seeking only the favour of the populace; appearing sometimes Catholic, sometimes Calvinist, and sometimes Lutheran. He is capable of any underhand deed that might be inspired by an unlimited ambition. It would be a good thing to remove him from Flanders.' Philip's way of doing this was to require of all his magistrates in the Netherlands a new oath, which he knew William would not take. 'I, William of Nassau,' he was required to swear, 'declare by oath that I am ready to serve him [the King of Spain] and carry out his orders with regard to all persons without limitation or restriction.' When William read this, he replied to the Regent the same day that he could not sign it, and retired to Nassau.

V

The second act of the drama opens the same year (1567) with the arrival of a Spanish army, and ends with the withdrawal of its commander, the Duke of Alva, in 1573. Alva is described by the Venetian Ambassador as a tall, thin man, with a bilious complexion: he thinks him proud, avaricious, and fond of flattery [*Badoaro*]. His military reputation had been won, a generation before, in Tunis, and at the battle of Mühlberg. He was now a man of sixty, with little idea of government beyond a military tyranny, and no objection to the cruellest methods of the Inquisition. 'I have tamed men of iron,' he said to Philip, 'and shall I not be able to tame these men of butter?' He lost no time in getting to work. 'He is exiling preachers,' writes William, 'and confiscating their property: he is arresting many innocent and loyal citizens on accusations of heresy or rebellion: he has executed publicly and in prison many persons of means, both bourgeois merchants and nobles, on religious grounds— by strangling, burning, decapitation, and other horrible methods, besides letting many more die in prison.' In particular, he has executed two great nobles, William's friends, Egmont and Horn, who foolishly supposed that the King of Spain would be as loyal to them as they were to the King of Spain; and 'many thousands of persons,' including prominent Papists, have fled from the Netherlands before a persecution that makes no distinction between Catholic and Protestant. For it must be remembered that this was not only an attempt to crush out the Reformation, but also an attempt to force the Inquisition, and the Decrees of Trent, upon the Catholic majority of the country.

William is convinced, or pretends to be, that all this cruelty cannot express the real will of a King so 'good and debonnaire' as Philip. He himself is no rebel. Whatever his enemies may say, his only motive is the advancement of God's honour, the free exercise of religion, the prosperity and loyalty of the Netherlands, with its ancient privileges, under the King of Spain and his rightful successors, and the restoration of himself and other fugitives to their honour and to their homes. He is not fighting against the Church. He is not fighting against the King. He inscribes on his banners, 'Pro Rege, Grege, Lege'—'For King, for People, and for Law.' He has protested before against the arbitrary rule of Granvella. He is in arms now against the 'sanguinary and tyrannical government of the Duke of Alva.'

In 1568 Philip proclaimed William a rebel, a traitor and an

outlaw. He replied by a long 'Justification' of his actions, which he circulated all over Europe in German, Latin, Dutch, English, Spanish, and French—one of the earliest uses of the printing press for political propaganda. For the next ten years he was too busy fighting to write many letters.

I need not go into the details of the war. There were few pitched battles. It was a matter of sieges and counter-sieges, of rebellion and re-conquest, town by town. The Spanish troops were invincible in the open, but could be checked by manning the city walls, or drowned by opening the dykes. There was much scope for daring and endurance, but little room for strategy or generalship. There were all the horrors of war, without any of its scientific interest. It will be enough, therefore, to mention one or two points without which the course of events does not explain itself.

In 1569, not content with the Spanish Inquisition, Alva tried to introduce the Spanish taxes—a tax of 1 per cent on all property, a tax of 5 per cent on every transfer of real estate, and a tax of 10 per cent on every sale. It might be tolerable in Spain to penalize enterprise and industry. For a country that lived by commerce such taxes meant literal ruin. The threat of them united all classes against Spain.

But Philip seemed to be winning. 1569 was the worst year that William had to go through. His mercenary troops were on the edge of mutiny. He had to retreat from the Netherlands. Alva wrote to his master, 'Orange may be considered as a dead man. He is without influence or credit.' In an old print of this date the Belgian lion is being crushed to death in a kind of press. Don Frederick has a rope round the animal's paws, and is pulling it taut through an iron ring. Alva, Granvella, and Margaret are working the press with bars, like a capstan. Philip and the Pope stand looking on. The lion's crown lies broken on the ground, with a torn charter, and the damaged emblems of freedom [*Putnam*].

The next three years brought some relief. In '71 the 'Beggars,' as the rebels called themselves (adopting a term of abuse from their enemies), manned a few ships, and seized the port of Brill: the whole revolt is sometimes dated from this incident. In '73 William, whose religious colour had changed with his political loyalty, declared himself a Calvinist. He no longer fought for Philip and the Church against Alva, but for Dutch independence against the whole power of Spain. The same year Alva was recalled. His troops were out of hand. Everyone hated him. He was disheartened by his losses at the siege of Haarlem, and by his failure at Alkmaar. He felt Philip's growing discontent. But he remained a terrorist to the last. 'His parting advice to the King and to his successor was to burn down every place in the country not actually occupied by the royal troops, even if it were to need eight or ten years for the land to recover. It was idle to attack cities one after another. The only practical plan was one of general destruction' [*Harrison*]. This was not a mere threat. Alva had done his best to put it into practice during the seven years of his Governorship. The results had been terrible enough: but the policy had failed. Philip was now to try other means.

VI

The third period of the Revolt begins with the dismissal of Alva in 1573, and ends with the Union of Utrecht in 1579. This is the central and constructive period, when the results of the contending policies come to a head. Alva's withdrawal gave breathing space. Philip was meditating a new policy: the States could discuss new plans of resistance. William by this time knew his adopted country well. He was certain of the support of Holland and Zealand, but of nothing else. All kinds of difficulties lay between the union of the northern states, which he had practically accomplished, and what he still desired, the union of the north and south. There was the class enmity between nobles and burghers, burghers and common people. There was the bitterness of religion between the Protestants of the north and the Catholics of the south. There was the long-standing jealousy between state and state, and the suspicion of a military Dictatorship. Nothing had held such varied interests together, and nothing could hold them together, except the common cause against Spain. In 1574 one of the periodical mutinies of the Spanish army, followed by a brutal sack of Antwerp, drowned every feeling but hatred for Spain, and William was able to unite all the fifteen Provinces in the Pacification of Ghent (1576).

The terms of the agreement read more like those of a truce between enemies than of an alliance between friends. But there was some hope that, under Spanish pressure, it might develop into a real union.

Unfortunately for William's plans, Philip chose this moment to launch his new policy, under the command of Don John of Austria, whose military reputation was not inferior to that of Alva—he was the hero of the great victory of Lepanto over the Turks—whilst in every personal quality he was infinitely superior. Don John soon fascinated the Flemings, and saw his way to playing off the south against the north. He began with a great stroke of policy. He professed himself ready to make peace with William on the basis of the Pacification of Ghent. You may say, this was all that William ever hoped for, and he should have accepted such terms with delight. But by this time William utterly distrusted the Spaniards, not least when they brought gifts. He remembered how Philip had used Margaret's peaceful policy to cover his attack on the liberties of the country; how he had withdrawn Granvella, only to send Alva in his place; how he had rewarded the loyalty of Egmont and Horn by putting them to death. He knew that Philip might change his methods, but that he would never change his mind. He could guess, even without the hints sent him by his own spies in Spain, that Don John was Alva in disguise; and that the Pacification, in Spanish hands, would be transformed into a final attempt to crush the political and religious liberties of the north. So he stood out coldly against all the overtures of Don John; and for the sake of the right—it is the hardest thing a statesman can have to do—allowed himself to be put in the wrong.

It was the same when, in 1579, Philip sent his last and ablest viceroy, Alexander Farnese, son of Margaret of Parma. Don John's work was completed. The southern states were won from their allegiance to William, and forced into the Union of Arras under the Spanish crown. From that time onwards, until the early years of the eighteenth century, Flanders, Brabant, and Hainault constituted the Spanish Netherlands.

At the same time Philip, who had long been urging his agents to have William assassinated, took the direct road to this by putting him under a ban. 'We hereby declare,' runs the document, 'this head and chief author of all the troubles to be a traitor and a miscreant, an enemy of ourselves and of our country. We interdict all our subjects from holding converse with him, from supplying him with lodging, food, water, or fire, under pain of our royal indignation. And in execution of this declaration [here comes the practical part of the business] we empower all and every to seize the person and the goods of this William of Nassau, as an enemy of the human race; and hereby, on the word of a King, and as minister of God, we promise to anyone who has the heart to free us of this pest, and who will deliver him dead or alive, or take his life, the sum of 25,000 crowns in gold or in estates for himself and his heirs; we will pardon him any crime, if he have been guilty, and give him a patent of nobility, if he be not noble; and we will do the same for all his agents and accomplices' [*Harrison*].

William answered this elegant incitement to murder by publishing his 'Apology'—an elaborate defence of his life and policy, and sending it round in various languages to all the leading princes of Europe. And within a few months the seven Northern Provinces showed their loyalty to him and to one another by solemnly renouncing their allegiance to Spain, and forming themselves into the Union of Utrecht (1579). Two years later this became the Republic of the United Provinces.

The act of separation had become inevitable: but it was a serious step, with momentous consequences. 'To the traders it meant confiscation and outlawing in Spanish ports; to the Catholics [of whom there were a number in the northern provinces] it meant Protestant ascendancy; to the ordinary citizen it was a formidable defiance of all the traditions of loyalty and civil society. It was the first great example of a whole people officially renouncing allegiance to their hereditary and consecrated monarch; and it was by two generations in advance of the English Commonwealth, by two centuries in advance of the American and French Republics. It was destined to have a crucial influence over the cause of modern civilization' [*Harrison*].

With 1580 begins the fourth and last period of the Revolt, which may be said to have lasted until the Twelve Years' Truce in 1609—afterwards it was merged in the Thirty Years' War. By this time William had been long dead—assassinated in 1584, after several attempts, by a Catholic fanatic, whose reward was not a title of nobility from the 'minister of God,' but a painful death at the hands of indignant Dutchmen. It did not matter now. William's life-work was done. Every effort of Philip and of his two successors could do no more than detach the southern fringe of the United Provinces. The north stood firm; and its independence was notified to all Europe by the Peace of Westphalia in 1648.

The loss of the Netherlands was a fatal blow to Philip's credit, and hastened the close of the golden age of Spain. Philip's aims cannot be ours. But we must not refuse all homage to the crusading spirit, however misapplied. 'Let politicians and political economists laugh their fill' (I am quoting 'the most distinguished Spanish scholar of our times'); 'but if we are to choose between the maritime greatness of England under her Virgin Queen, and the slow martyrdom and impoverishment of our own nation, which during two centuries was the unselfish arm of the Church, no heart that beats with enthusiasm for the noble and the beautiful will hesitate to bestow the palm on us' [*Menendez y Pelayo* quoted by *Sedgwick*].

VII

It remains to estimate William's achievement, and its results. As to the man himself—the guiding conviction of his life was, I think, hatred of persecution. It was because he hated persecution that he championed the cause of the Netherlands. Like many national heroes, he was a foreigner. It was not patriotism, but pity, not love of what he was defending, but hatred of what he was attacking, that made him a liberator. 'I feel a Christian compassion,' he writes to the Emperor, 'towards the inhabitants of the Netherlands, who have been so hardly treated: I am moved by their tears, touched by their entreaties, and bound to them by my oath of allegiance, and by the extremity of distress in which I find myself and my followers.' The same conviction explains his slowness in aiming at political independence. To secure freedom from religious persecution, 'he would accept the suzerainty of France, or of England; he would accept incorporation in the Empire; he would accept partition of the provinces between France, England, and Germany. He sought for a royal Podesta from abroad. He would even advise submission to Spain, if adequate guarantees could be devised to secure the cessation of religious persecution, and the withdrawal of Spanish troops' [*Harrison*]. His lack of political squeamishness sprang from the same feeling. At one time he gets help from the French rebels, and fights against the French crown. At another he is in close alliance with Charles IX and Catherine de Medici. A champion of the Protestants, he is found, within a few months of St. Bartholomew, negotiating with the authors of the Huguenot massacre, and making friends with the murderers of his friend Coligny. It is all for the cause. Against religious persecution he will accept the aid even of the persecutors of religion. So too with his changes of creed. His religion was a matter of personal conviction: his church was a matter of policy. His hatred of persecution made him tolerate every sect. He saw no reason why they should not live peaceably side by side. The State existed for the safeguarding of free religion: the churches existed for the good order of the State.

William combined to a very unusual degree strong convictions with a broad mind, passion with prudence, and religion with common sense. He could not have started a religious movement, like Luther. He could not have organized, as Calvin and Cromwell did, a Puritan Commonwealth. He had less humanity than Henry of Navarre, and less statesmanship than Elizabeth of England. But for the rather dour burghers and Bible men of Holland he was an ideal leader. And for the world at large he is more than a national hero: he is one of the founders of that political and religious freedom which we now enjoy—seldom thinking at what cost it has been won.

Finally, what were the results of the Netherlands Revolt? It made of the United Provinces a great maritime and commercial power. Not directly or at once: it needed time to recover from the poverty of war, and to find new customers instead of Spain. But independence was the clue to progress. Now full advantage could be taken of the decay of Portuguese trade with the East Indies, and of the decline of the Hanseatic League. Now Spanish gold could be captured on the high seas, and Swedish timber be imported from the Baltic. Now the northern provinces could develop their agricultural wealth, and Holland its monopoly of the herring fisheries. Within a generation or two the Dutch became the world's carriers, and Holland the world's stores. The bank of Amsterdam became the bank of Europe, eighty years before London had a bank at all.

With freedom and prosperity came intellectual and artistic fame. The first half of the seventeenth century was the golden age of Holland, when Grotius wrote his *De jure belli ac pacis*, and Descartes (a French refugee) his *Discours de la Méthode*, when Elzevir published his lovely editions of the Classics, and Spinoza, polishing his lenses, meditated on the nature of God; and when the great Dutch school of painting was founded and developed by Van Dyck, Franz Hals, Ruysdael, Hobbema, and Rembrandt. Holland, too, was the earliest home of newspapers. The 'Leyden News' and the 'Holland Gazette' appeared in French two or three times a week. They were small enough, with only two columns to the page. But they were in touch with foreign correspondents all over the world; and they started the tradition that made Holland, right down to the nineteenth century, a country to which disillusioned but still hopeful diplomatists went to learn the truth.

Politically, the Revolt leaves all Europe in debt. The success of the northern states gave 'the right of citizenship to revolutionary principles.' For the first time since the organization of the New Monarchies a whole people had claimed and won its independence. The United Provinces stood during the seventeenth and eighteenth centuries as a warning to monarchs, and as a signpost to patriots. The finger, indeed, pointed to Revolution, not as yet to Republicanism. 'So far were the Dutch from desiring a republic that, while Holland and Zealand insisted upon placing themselves under William of Orange, the remaining provinces invited the Duke of Anjou to step into the place of the King of Spain. The sovereignty of the Dutch provinces was offered in turn to the Hapsburg, the Valois, and the Tudor houses; and in the institution of the Stadtholderate the Dutch found a means of gratifying something of that monarchical instinct which the tyranny of Spain had been unavailing to destroy' [*Fisher*].

Lastly, the Netherlands Revolt was a striking instance of the political results of the Reformation. It showed that Protestantism could give not only the desire for political freedom, but also the resolution to achieve it. Luther had not desired this. Germany had not discovered it. French Calvinism, as we shall see, obtained religious toleration, but at the cost of political independence. Only Holland in the Old World set the pattern of Protestant democracy which was to be copied on so big a scale in the New. Had there been no United Provinces in the Netherlands, there might have been (but I almost hesitate to suggest it) no United States of America.

LECTURE VIII
THE FRENCH WARS OF RELIGION

I

French historians have discovered that it was not a German, but a Frenchman, who started the Reformation. This was the humanist philosopher and mathematician, Lefèvre of Etaples. Born thirty years before Luther, it was not till late in life that Lefèvre turned his attention to theology, and published a Psalter, a Commentary on St. Paul, and a French translation of the Gospels—this last appearing about the same time as Luther's Reformation Tracts and German Bible (1521-23). Lefèvre was neither a Protestant nor a violent Reformer, but a Catholic of the type of Erasmus, who wished for a return to primitive Christianity. But Luther admired him, and read his books: and his influence prepared the way for Protestantism in Paris.

Luther's books might be burnt by the Parlement, and his doctrines condemned by the orthodox Sorbonne: but it was known that the new religion found favour at Court, and that Francis I was unwilling to persecute it. His sister, the Queen of Navarre, corresponded with Calvin, and entertained Protestant refugees. He himself, in a fit of coolness towards the Pope, asked Melanchthon to become head of the Collège de France. He needed the support of the Lutheran princes in Germany against his rival Charles V.

But when Francis invaded Italy in 1524, and thought it necessary to propitiate the Pope, the burning of Lutherans began: and it was continued by the Queen Regent, during his imprisonment after the battle of Pavia, in the hope of securing his release. When the news came in 1527 of the sack of Rome, it was attributed to Charles's Lutheran soldiery. The Catholics turned the baptism of two converted Turks into an anti-Protestant demonstration. The Protestants replied by defacing Catholic images, and placarding Paris with attacks on Catholic doctrines. This was in 1530, just after the Peace of Cambrai had set Francis free from any fears of Charles, or any obligation towards the German Lutherans. In 1533 he seems to have determined almost suddenly, in his inconsequent way, on a policy of persecution. In December of that year the King of France wrote to the Parlement of Paris, 'We are much annoyed and displeased because this cursed heretical sect of Lutherans flourishes in our good city of Paris, the head and capital of our realm, containing the principal University of Christendom, where many will be able to imitate it. This sect we intend to attack with all our power and authority, sparing nobody. We therefore will and intend that such and so heavy a punishment may fall upon it, as to correct the cursed heretics, and be an example to all others': and the letter goes on to outline the procedure to be followed [*Journal d'un Bourgeois*].

Within a few months forty Lutherans were burnt in Paris. The punishment became so common that it was confined to heresy, and it was ordered that in future brigands, and other such victims of the barbarous justice of those times, should not be burnt, but only broken on the wheel. We can tell, from the lists given by a contemporary writer, from what rank of life these poor Lutherans came. There were two shoemakers, a Franciscan friar, a law student, two beneficed scholars, a gentleman in the army, a boatman, a draper, a printer, a mason, a bookseller, a clerk in private service, a hatseller, a tax-collector, a fruiterer, a merchant, two jewellers, a painter, a mercer, a singer at the Chapel Royal (no Court protection for him now), two dyers, two lawyers, a tailor, a carpenter, and a manufacturer of silk ribbons and tissues. They belong mainly to the trading and lower professional classes—to those educated by their business, in touch with wider interests, or accustomed to the use of books. They do not come from the crowd. One of the victims was a woman; several were rich; most were young [*Journal d'un Bourgeois*].

Paris was shocked by these executions, and 'it was reported in June, 1535, that Pope Paul III [the organizer of the Inquisition], informed of the execrable and horrible justice that the King was executing on the Lutherans in his realm,' had written to say that 'though he was sure he was acting in good faith, and using the excellent claims he had to be called the Most Christian King, yet God the Creator, when He was Himself in this world, made more use of compassion than of rigorous justice; that one ought never to use severity; and that it is a cruel death to burn a man alive . . . Wherefore the Pope requested and required of the King by his letters to appease the fury and rigour of his justice, by giving pardon and reprieve to the Lutherans' [*Journal d'un Bourgeois*]. Whether or not for this reason, the persecution paused in 1535. But ten years later came the massacre of the Vaudois in the south of France; and with Henry II's accession in 1547 systematic persecution began again. In less than three years a special committee of the Parlement, fitly called the 'Chambre Ardente,' found 500 persons guilty of heresy, and put sixty to death. Two years later it was ordered that death should be the only penalty. So it went on.

II

Among the crowd of Paris students who watched the burning of Lutherans in 1534 was a young French Protestant named Jean Cauvin, or John Calvin. He fled from Paris, changed his name, and took refuge at Basle. There, at the age of 26, he wrote one of the great books of the world, the *Christianae religionis Institutio* (1536). King Francis himself received the first copy, with a dedication. 'When I first began this book,' wrote Calvin, 'nothing was further from my intention than to dedicate it to you. But when I saw the fury of certain wicked men go to such lengths in your kingdom that there was no place there for healthy doctrine, it seemed worth while to try to produce at the same time an "Institutio" for those whom I had undertaken to instruct and a "Confessio" from which you may learn what kind of doctrine it is against which those fanatics so furiously rage together, disturbing your realm with fire and sword.' No doubt it was good policy to exonerate Francis himself from the blame of persecution, and to suppose him anxious to learn the truth about Protestantism. Anyhow, Calvin's account of his purpose is quite clear. The book was a 'Confessio' or Apology, like those written by the Christian Fathers for the Emperors of Rome, intended to show that there was nothing in Protestantism which need alarm Princes: that it was an attack upon the Church, not upon the State: that it aimed at government of the Church by the Church, and of the State by a union of Church and

State [*Acton*]. It was also an 'Institutio,' an ordered system of theology and religion, completing in a logical way the work of Luther, and giving the Reformation a political and social programme.

In what way did Calvin carry Lutheranism to its logical conclusions? I will suggest only two points, and those not theological. First, the real failure of the medieval Church lay in the divorce which it tolerated between religion and morality. What was needed was not so much a new creed as a new code of conduct. Luther had been distracted from this problem by his doctrine of faith *versus* works. Calvin saw that what religious people really wanted was a moral discipline to take the place of the Confessional. And this need he supplied in the Puritan rule set up first at Geneva, and thence carried into France, the Netherlands, England, Scotland, and North America. The history of Calvin's ministry at Geneva is an extraordinary one; but I have no space for it here. The essence of it is that, acting in alliance with the City Council (for Geneva was a free city that had just won its independence both from the Duke of Savoy and from the Pope), and as President of a Church Council which had an almost absolute authority over faith and morals, he enforced a rigidly Puritanical system of morality and religion, which began by prohibiting dancing, or the ringing of church bells, and ended by putting the citizens in prison if they found fault with his own sermons. This Puritanism was an ugly and intolerant creed; but it gave the Calvinists some of the power which the early Christians had of bearing persecution and handing on their convictions. 'In the suppression of the liberties of Geneva was sown the seed of liberty in Europe' [*Pattison*].

Secondly, when Luther destroyed the ecclesiastical authority of the Pope, he could find nothing better to put in its place than the ecclesiastical authority of the Prince. His world was one in which every prince was his own Pope; and he made no provision for the ordering of Protestant congregations under other political conditions than those of Germany. Calvin saw that the natural unit of Protestantism was the self-made congregation; and that, whether (as at Geneva) the congregation included a whole city, or whether (as in France) it was one of a number of secret minorities scattered up and down the country, it must be its own Authority, live its own life, and organize itself for support and defence. That, on a small scale, means Congregationalism; on a larger scale, Disestablishment. It can be summed up in the formula, 'A free Church in a free State.'

Both these features of Calvinism made it specially fit for the part it was to play in France. Its Puritanism enabled it to bear persecution: its Congregationalism enabled it to organize victory.

III

From about 1560 onwards the French Protestants—'those of the so-called Reformed Religion,' as they are described in the State documents of the time—came to be called 'Huguenots.' Their name, like their creed, came from Geneva—from a party of Genevan patriots called 'Eidgenossen,' or Confederates. It was as Huguenots, and through the fresh impulse that Huguenotism gave, that the various dissident elements in France—the humanist followers of Lefèvre, the persecuted Lutherans, the disfranchised middle classes, and the discontented nobility, joined together against the weakening forces of the Church and the Crown.

Why did Huguenotism spread so readily in a Catholic country? The causes were only partly religious. Everywhere, no doubt, there was some degree of slackness in Church life, of absenteeism or immorality among the bishops and clergy. This had its effect in France, as elsewhere. But there were also political causes. Many parts of France, especially those furthest from Paris, were still half-hearted in their allegiance to the central government. In districts which, like Normandy, had political grievances, or thought themselves overtaxed, Protestant preachers got a good hearing, and attacks on Church and Government went together. The provinces, too, were controlled by the hostile interests of the great land-owning families. If the Guises carried their part of the country into one camp, the Montmorencys would carry theirs into the other. Huguenot agents were as sure of a home in Montpellier or La Rochelle as they were of a prison, or worse, in Paris or Toulouse. And it is noticeable that some of the frontier provinces of France, or those specially open to foreign influences, as well as Universities, trading cities, and other places frequented by foreigners, were specially favourable to the preaching of Protestantism.

How were the Huguenots organized? Here it is important to

distinguish two stages—the religious organization of the congregations, which from the first (as we have seen) followed Calvin's theory of church government; and the military organization superimposed upon it when, about 1560, the Huguenots came out into the open, and prepared to fight for their freedom. This military organization was not Calvin's: he always protested against the use of force. It was due to the nobles and country gentlemen who (for reasons more political than religious) made themselves patrons of the Huguenot congregations. Under these leaders the Protestants were divided into local commands, armed, drilled, and led to battle against the forces of the Crown. It was a radical change in the character of the movement [*Romier*].

How were the Huguenots distributed? They probably numbered from one and a quarter to one and a half million out of a total population of fifteen or twenty millions. Even with their political allies they were never more than a small minority. Had they been evenly distributed over the whole country, they would have found it impossible to combine. But, as we have seen, the Huguenot congregations tended to coagulate in certain districts—in the parts furthest from Paris, in the parts which had recently enjoyed political independence, or in the parts most open to foreign influence. In four districts—Dauphiné, Northern Provence, the Cevennes, and the Pyrenees—most of the population was Protestant. Geneva and Navarre were headquarters safe from attack. La Rochelle was a fortified seaport. As to social distribution, there were in most parts of France no Huguenots among the peasantry or the working classes. They had many sympathizers among the lesser nobility, the clergy, and the Religious Orders. The great majority of them came from the tradesmen and professional men of the lower middle classes.

Such was the material out of which Calvin and his preachers produced the Huguenot Church of France. There are not many references to the French Huguenots in *Calvin's* earlier letters. He is more concerned with the fate of Protestantism in Switzerland and Germany. He speaks of France in 1544 as having been 'hitherto the fortress and defence of our liberty and safety.' He sees clearly that the fortunes of Protestantism depend upon the issue of two political and military contests—that between Francis I and Charles V, and that between Christendom and the

Turks. He begins by fearing Charles, and having hopes of Francis. He ends by abominating them both. 'I hope,' he writes, 'that our Antiochus [Charles], who presses us at present, will be so hard pressed that he shall be regardless of the gout in his hands and feet, for he will have it over his whole body. As regards his companion Sardanapalus [Francis], may God have a like care of him: for they are both well worthy to have the same measure meted to them.' But this Balaam did not only come to curse. When serious persecution began in France, under Henry II, Calvin became the spiritual leader of the Huguenots, and Geneva their Intelligence Office, their Theological College, and their printing press.

IV

The premature death of Henry II in 1560 left the French crown to a family of children. But whether they would ever wear it depended upon the ability of their mother, Catherine de Medici, to defeat or evade the pretensions of several rival royal or semi-royal houses—the Bourbons, the Guises, and the Montmorencys. Of these the Guises were the most powerful and the most unpopular. Francis, the head of the family, had been Henry II's adviser, and his most successful general. Charles, Cardinal of Lorraine, its ablest member, was nicknamed (like a French statesman of more recent date) 'the Tiger.' And a popular ditty was sung to the effect that—

> King Francis, he knew very well
> The nature of the Guises,
> Who dress *their* babes in broidered clothes,
> Their tenants' in *chemises* [*Tilley*].

Catherine soon showed that she was well able to defend the rights of her children. She was an Italian, a niece of Pope Leo X, and inherited the family gift for diplomacy. Henry, her husband, had neglected her for years, going for love and advice to his mistress, Diane de Poitiers. She was now a widow at 41, experienced, cunning, and tenacious of power. The common view about her was neatly put by an English traveller, when he said that 'she had too much wit for a woman, and too little honesty for a Queen' [*Dallington*]. But I think that she has been ungenerously treated both by history and by art. When Brantôme calls her beautiful, and says that she has remained so all her life, he is, if there is any evidence in portraits, more gallant than truthful. But the rest of his description agrees with what others say of her —that she was fond of playing pall-mall, shooting with the crossbow, dancing, and hunting, in which she was the first lady 'to put the leg round the pommel, which was far more graceful and becoming than sitting with the feet upon a plank.' 'It was one of her greatest pleasures,' he says, 'to ride far and fast, though she fell many times with damage to her body, breaking her leg once, and wounding her head, which had to be trepanned.' And I like this picture: 'It was fine to see the Queen . . . going through the country on horseback attended by forty or fifty ladies and demoiselles mounted on handsome hackneys well caparisoned, and sitting their horses in such good grace that the men could not do better, either in equestrian style or apparel; their hats adorned with plumes which floated in the air, as if demanding either love or war' [*Brantôme*]. Catherine's Court, too, was famous for wit as well as for beauty. And if she was a schemer, and at times unscrupulous and cruel, it is only fair to remember the situation in which she was placed. The fairest verdict on her is that of a man who had little cause to love her, Henry of Navarre. When one of his courtiers suggested that his marriage with Mary de Medici would repair the harm done to France by Catherine de Medici—'But I ask you,' he replied, 'what could a poor woman do, left by the death of her husband with five little children on her hands, and two families in France who were thinking to grasp the crown—ours and the Guises? Was she not compelled to play strange parts, to deceive first one and then the other, in order to guard (as she has done) her sons, who have successively reigned by the wise conduct of that shrewd woman? I am surprised that she never did worse.'

In politics, then, Catherine's only hope of securing the succession for her sons lay in playing off one party of pretenders against another. And in religion she must adopt somewhat the same course. The King must be Catholic, but not a bigot. Protestantism must be fought, but not crushed. The Crown must be the arbitrator, not the persecutor of religion. Too weak to separate the combatants, and too wise to entrust herself to either, Catherine still hoped to profit by their mutual exhaustion.

The religious controversy was everywhere. It had invaded even the royal nursery. Catherine's daughter *Margaret*, a child of seven or eight at this time, and brought up a Catholic, remembered long afterwards 'the stand she made to keep her religion at the time of the Synod of Poissy (1561), when the whole Court was infected with heresy, against the imperious persuasions of a number of ladies and gentlemen of the Court, and even of her brother of Anjou, afterwards King [Henry III] of France: for his infancy (she writes) had not been able to escape the influence of that wretched 'Huguenoterie,' and he was always loudly demanding that I should change my religion, and frequently threw my book of Hours into the fire, and gave me Huguenot psalters and prayer-books instead, which he insisted on my carrying. But I gave them straight away to my governess, who, thank God, remained a Catholic; and she often took me to see that good man the Cardinal de Tournon, who gave me advice, and encouraged me to suffer anything in defence of my religion, and presented me with new books of Hours and Chaplets in place of those which my brother had burnt. My brother of Anjou, and the other souls who had undertaken to ruin mine, took to abusing me, saying it was mere childishness and silliness that made me act as I did; that evidently I had no intelligence; that all sensible people of both sexes and all ages, once they learnt the truth, gave up practising this bigotry of mine: but that I was as big a fool as my governess. My brother of Anjou said that my mother, the Queen, would have me whipped. But as a matter of fact she did not know the heresy he had fallen into; and as soon as she did, she took strong measures with his tutors, and had him instructed, and made him return to the true and holy and ancient religion of our ancestors, which she had never left. I answered my brother's threats by breaking into tears, for I was only seven or eight at the time, and it is an impressionable age: but I said he could have me whipped, or killed, if he liked: I would suffer anything they could do, rather than be damned.'

If the Court was divided as to religion, the country was divided as to many other matters as well. In 1560 things were so bad that it was decided to summon an assembly of Notables—an expedient tried again in an even worse crisis two hundred years later. The Notables in 1560, as in 1787, demanded the convocation of the

Estates General, which accordingly met at the end of the same year. The Estates were an Occasional Parliament, consisting of three Houses—Clergy, Nobility, and Commons. The three Orders deliberated apart, but voted together; so that the two privileged Orders could always outvote the one unprivileged. They could present petitions and make recommendations to the Crown: but they had no power to make laws, or to administer them. The Clergy and the Nobility represented their own class interests. The Commons, owing to their indirect method of election, did not represent the mass of the people—the peasantry and the working classes—but only the middle-class tradesmen and professional men. With this caution, it is worth while to look at the demands put forward by the Estates of 1560; for they show both how wide was the demand for religious toleration, and how far the country had already advanced towards the situation in which it found itself two hundred years afterwards. 'The nobles demanded liberty of worship for the Protestants, the suppression of such civil and feudal jurisdiction as was in the hands of the clergy, and the nationalization of Church property. [It was this anti-clericalism which made so many of the nobles join the Huguenots.] The clergy called for vigorous action against the heretics, for economy at Court, and for the suppression of useless and sinecure offices. [This was a hit at the nobles.] The Third Estate [the Commons] demanded a general reform of the administration, the cessation of persecution, "since it is unreasonable to compel men to do what in their hearts they consider wrong" [a remarkable sentiment in 1560], periodical meetings of the Estates, the abolition of internal Customs dues, a regular financial Audit, the meeting of a national Council of both clergy and laity to settle religious disputes; and they [too] suggested the appropriation of Church property to pay off the debt.' [*Atkinson*].

Catherine was in no position to deal with most of these suggestions. But she seized on the idea of a national Council to discuss the religious situation, and summoned the Synod of Poissy to meet the next year. It was what we should call a Round Table Conference between Catholics and Protestants, under the chairmanship of Catherine's moderate Chancellor, Michel de l'Hôpital. De l'Hôpital, a virtuous old idealist, who wrote

THE STATES GENERAL OF 1560

Memoirs in Latin hexameters, has left us his views on the situation in a memorandum 'On the necessity of bringing the civil war to an end.' He shows us the motives which underlay Catherine's policy. 'One by one he takes the arguments of his adversaries, and confutes them: he shows that there is no special reason to expect a complete or a speedy victory for the royal cause. The King may have more troops and more money, but the Huguenots are fighting for all they hold dear, and despair has given them strength and discipline; while the royal camp is rent with quarrels, envy, and rivalry. To introduce mercenaries is expensive and unpopular, and foreign help is nowadays a broken reed—the Swiss in particular, on whom the Catholics so much rely, are as a body unhealthy and corrupt, and cannot keep the field six months, owing to their dirty and careless way of living. The war is likely to be protracted, and the outcome is doubtful; the longer it lasts, the worse the condition into which the kingdom will fall. The Huguenots are warlike, and have many capable leaders and strong towns, so that neither the loss of one or two battles, nor the fall of some of their chiefs, is likely to finish the war; while, on the contrary, all those who always go with the strongest will desert the royal cause the moment fortune turns against it. Protestants alone form a quarter of the royal army, and they are not the only waverers: the loss of one battle would mean the loss of the whole State. He then goes on to show that in coming to terms with the rebels the King will be doing nothing unworthy or ignominious. The King's business is to rule his subjects, but not to enslave them. The Huguenots have no wish to throw off the royal yoke; they have been driven into rebellion by outrages and oppression . . . but if the cause of their revolt be removed, disloyalty and rebellion will disappear with it. . . . Peace must be restored, and the transgressors of the edicts punished. It will then be possible to separate the merely seditious from those who have risen for conscience sake, and to punish the guilty without injustice to the innocent' [*Atkinson*].

De l'Hôpital lived to see his policy apparently wrecked by the Massacre of St. Bartholomew. He was twenty-five years in his grave when it was vindicated by the Edict of Nantes. But that was after the fight was over, and tempers had cooled down. At the moment (1562) it was possible to grant an edict of toleration, but impossible to secure the observance of it. The Synod was followed by outrages and murders, in which the 'Massacre of Vassy' gave the palm to the Catholics: and the inevitable war broke out.

V

The fighting went on, with short intervals, for thirty years. It is generally divided into eight 'wars': but some of these were no longer than a summer campaign, and there were intermediate events that had more important results than the actual fighting: so that it seems best to divide the war into four periods, in each of which the situation of the parties changed, and their aims became rather different; and to lay more stress upon the political than upon the military happenings.

The first period covers eight years, and includes the first, second and third 'wars' (1562–1570). From the first we find both sides putting party before patriotism, and calling in foreign aid—the Catholics Philip of Spain, the Protestants Elizabeth of England. The fighting was indecisive, and the Edict of Amboise, which ended the first 'war,' was renewed at the close of the third (Treaty of St. Germain, 1570), when the Huguenots found themselves in a slightly less favourable position than at the beginning, but no more. The Catholics lost Francis of Guise, and the Protestants Condé—both assassinated.

During the interval between the first period and the second everything was changed by the Massacre of St. Bartholomew (1572). The responsibility for this crime has never been fixed beyond doubt; but most of the evidence points to Catherine de Medici; and motives were not wanting. Since the truce of 1570 many Protestants had come to court; a marriage had been planned between Catherine's daughter Margaret and the new Huguenot leader, Henry of Navarre; whilst Coligny, the most distinguished Huguenot statesman, had become chief adviser to Charles IX, and was urging the young King to intervene on behalf of the Protestants in the Netherlands. Catherine felt that her policy of toleration was carrying her too far, and that the control over the crown, which she had with difficulty saved from the Catholics, was in danger of being lost to the Huguenots. Her jealousy of Coligny was backed by the hatred of Henry of Guise, who believed him guilty of his father Francis' death. Together they planned to have Coligny murdered; and when the plot failed, in order to cover up their tracks, organized a greater crime, which could be attributed to the mob—a general massacre of the Huguenots in Paris. The crime, then, seems to have been extemporized. But if it had been long planned, the opportunity could not have been better chosen, for Paris was full of Protestants who had come to town for the royal wedding. The number of victims, in Paris and the provinces together, was probably about 8,000.

Whatever their complicity in the crime, the heads of Catholicism were delighted with its result. 'My Cousin,' wrote Catherine to the Duke of Tuscany, 'I know that you have always been so devoted to the service and glory of God, and particularly to the welfare of this [French] crown, that I am sure you will be exceedingly pleased to hear of the successful execution of the Admiral [Coligny] and his followers ... It is a matter from which the King, my son, derives very great satisfaction, seeing himself praised and encouraged by good and virtuous men in his holy and praiseworthy resolution. He hopes that God will give him grace to draw from it results necessary for the restoration of His Church and the general repose of Christianity' [*Lettres Royaux*]. Charles himself struck a medal to commemorate the massacre, with the mottoes, 'Virtus in rebelles' and 'Pietas excitavit justitiam.' But he died soon after, haunted (according to his enemies) by the phantoms of murdered Huguenots [*Sully*]. The Pope, too, had a medal struck, on which an angel was represented as carrying out 'Ugonottorum strages' with the help of a sword and a cross; and Rome was illuminated for three nights. But France disapproved—the attacks of the pamphleteers were diverted from the Guises to Catherine; and Ivan the Terrible of Russia wrote to protest.

There I might leave an event which has figured so often in fiction, and even on the films. But I should like you to hear one account of it, written by an eyewitness, and a central figure in the drama—the young princess Margaret, who had just been married to Henry of Navarre. I know few narratives more vivid or circumstantial. It is history at first-hand. *Margaret's* story begins with the preparations for the massacre. 'For my part,' she says, 'I was told nothing about all this. But I saw everybody agitated—the Huguenots in despair because of the attempt on Coligny, the Guises fearing they would have justice done, and all on the alert. The Huguenots suspected me as a Catholic, and the Catholics as the wife of the King of Navarre, who was a Huguenot: nobody told me anything.' (Now we come to the night of the massacre.) 'One evening, at my mother the Queen's evening reception, I was sitting on a chest near my sister of Lorraine, who was looking very depressed. The Queen, who was talking to some people, saw me, and told me to go to bed. When I had made my curtsey, my sister took me by the arm, and stopped me, bursting into tears, and said, "For God's sake, sister, don't go." This terrified me. The Queen noticed what had happened, and called my sister, and abused her, and told her she was not to say anything to me. My sister told her it was not right to send me off to sacrifice myself like that, and that, if "they" discovered anything, they would certainly avenge themselves on me. The Queen answered that "Please God, I should come to no harm: but that in any case I must go, for fear of rousing any suspicion that would spoil the plan"; I could see they were disputing, though I did not understand what they said. At last my mother told me again, roughly, to go to bed. My sister, in tears, said good night to me, but dared not add another word. For my part, I seemed to see everything changed and lost, without being able to imagine what there was to fear. Directly I reached my room I prayed God to take me under His protection, and to keep me safe, without knowing from what or from whom. Just then my husband the King, who had already gone to bed, sent for me to come to bed too. So I did, and found his bed surrounded by thirty or forty Huguenots whom I didn't yet know, having been married only a few days. All night they did nothing but talk of the attempt which had been made on the Admiral's life: they resolved that, as soon as it was day, they would ask justice from the King against M. de Guise, and that if he refused it they would execute it themselves. For my part, I couldn't forget my sister's tears, and couldn't sleep for fear of the warning she had given me, though I didn't know what it meant. So the night passed, without a wink of sleep. At daybreak the King said he was going to play tennis till King Charles was awake, when he would at once demand justice of him. He left my room, and all his gentlemen with him. Seeing that it was daylight, and thinking that the danger of which my sister had spoken was now past, and overcome with sleep, I told my nurse to shut the door, so that I could sleep quietly. An hour later, when I was fast asleep, there came a man beating on the door with his hands and feet, crying "Navarre! Navarre!" My nurse, thinking it was my husband the King, ran quickly to the door and opened it. It was a gentleman named M. de Léran, with a sword-wound on his elbow and another from a halberd on his arm; and he was still being pursued by four archers, who all came after him into my room. To save his life, he threw himself on my bed. Feeling him clutching me, I dragged myself into the space behind the bed, and him after me, holding me all the time in front of his body. I didn't know the man at all, and had no idea whether he had come to insult me, or whether the archers were attacking him or me. We both shrieked, and each was as frightened as the other. At last, thank God, M. de Nançay, the captain of the Guard, came up, and finding me in such a position, though he was sorry enough, couldn't help laughing. He abused the archers for their indiscretion, and got rid of them, and granted me the life of the poor man who was holding on to me. So I put him to bed, and nursed his wounds in my room, till he was completely recovered. I changed my nightgown, too, because the man had covered it with his blood: and M. de Nançay told me what had happened, and assured me that my husband was in the King's room, and would come to no harm. So I threw on a dressing gown, and he took me to my sister's room, where I arrived more dead than alive; for just as I reached the lobby, all the doors of which were open, a gentleman named Bourse, trying to escape from some archers who were pursuing him, was run through by a halberd-stroke three paces from me; I fell the opposite way, half fainting, into the arms of M. de Nançay, and thought that the blow had pierced us both. When I felt a little better, I went to my sister's bedroom. Whilst I was there, M. de Moissans, my husband's first gentleman, and Armagnac, his first footman, came to look for me, to beg me to save their lives. I went and threw myself on my knees before the King and my mother the Queen, to ask this favour, which at last they granted.'

VI

I said that the Massacre of St. Bartholomew changed everything. Its immediate result was the formation of Leagues—a Calvinist Union of defence on one side, a Catholic League on the other, and (a consequence not foreseen by the authors of the massacre) a party of Moderates, the 'Politiques,' who wished for a return to the conciliatory programme of de l'Hôpital and the Synod of Poissy.

The second period of the fighting, which broke out the same year, and lasted till 1580 (the 4th, 5th, 6th, and 7th 'wars'), went at first in favour of the Huguenots, who by the Peace of Monsieur (1576) won greater concessions than they ever got again—liberty of worship everywhere except in Paris, eight 'cities of refuge,' which they were allowed to garrison, and eight tribunals, in which half the judges were to be Calvinists. But the Estates General, summoned the same year, and alarmed at concessions which gave so much political power to religious minorities in the State, determined the Catholics to go on fighting; and at the Peace of Bergerac (1577) these concessions were partly withdrawn.

During this second period of war, Henry III came to the throne —the third and most unpopular of Catherine's degenerate sons (1574). 'I shall never forget,' says *Sully,* 'the fantastic and extravagant equipage and attitude in which I found this prince in his cabinet: he had a sword at his side, a Spanish hood hung down upon his shoulders, a little cap, such as collegians wear, upon his head, and a basket full of little dogs hung to a broad ribband about his neck.' Henry's natural unfitness to rule had not been corrected by his short experience as King of Poland, which seemed rather to add another touch to the foreign make-up of the Italian Court party. Only a French King could save France.

At this crisis (1584) the death of the Duke of Anjou made Henry of Navarre heir to the throne. Now Henry, Captain of the host of the Huguenots, was a great man and honourable; he was also a mighty man of valour; but he was a Protestant. The prospect of a Protestant succession was like leprosy to the Catholics. Henry of Guise was able to reorganize their League, to get a Bull from the Pope disinheriting Navarre, and to put up the old Cardinal de Bourbon as a rival candidate for the Crown. The League was soon strong enough to coerce the King. He consented to the exile of all Protestant ministers, and the exclusion of all Huguenots from public office: and he granted the Catholics eight 'cities of refuge,' to balance those already allowed to their opponents.

Thus the third period of fighting (the first part of what is generally reckoned as the 8th 'war'), which lasted from 1585 to 1588, was a contest between Henry III and the League on the one side and Henry of Navarre on the other. Spain and England were again called in, and the war seemed likely to involve all the Catholic and Protestant powers in Europe.

But soon all was changed again. In 1588 Henry III, jealous of the growing power of his namesake of Guise, had him assassinated, and joined Navarre against the League, which had seized Paris. Next year Henry himself was dead, and Navarre became rightful King of France (1589). He was a King without a kingdom. But whereas hitherto the Huguenots had borne the reproach of fighting against the Crown, now it was borne by the Catholics; and the Moderate party at once came round to the Protestant side. On the other hand, many of the Catholic nobles were irreconcilable; some of his Calvinist supporters suspected Henry of extending to their enemies the toleration they claimed for themselves; and Paris was in a state of revolt under a popular government which anticipated by two hundred years the Insurrectional Commune of 1792.

Under these circumstances Henry had to fight another four years for his kingdom—the last period of the war lasted from 1589 to 1593. He won two battles—Arques and Ivry—which have become famous in fiction. He only failed to reduce Paris because it was relieved by Alexander Farnese and a Spanish army from the Netherlands. Two obstacles still lay between him and Paris, between him and his crown—a foreign army and a heretical faith. He took the only possible way of ending the war, and declared himself a Catholic (1593).

VII

It was high time. Thirty years of war left France covered with ruins. The authority of the Crown was gone. Self-constituted

Governors raised troops, imposed taxes, and administered what seemed to them justice. Large tracts of the country were devastated and deserted. The peasantry had lost their crops, and the merchants had lost their trade. 'More than half the noblesse,' reported an English traveller, 'is perished, the people diminished, the treasure exhausted, the debts increased, good order overthrown, religion vanquished, manners debauched, justice corrupted, and the men divided' [*Dallington, 1598*].

Thus, at a moment when France seemed likely to become one of the strongest Powers in Europe, it became one of the weakest. The spirit of the Renaissance, of which no country in the world was so fit to be the interpreter, was overlaid by an alien influence which it was never able to assimilate—the spirit of the Reformation.

LECTURE IX

HENRY OF NAVARRE

I

Since Ferdinand the Catholic rounded off his north-west frontier by annexing Spanish Navarre (1512), the Kingdom of Navarre had been only a few square miles of France on the northern slopes of the Pyrenees. But it still kept its court, and its independence; and the D'Albret children made royal marriages. There Henry's mother lived, and there Henry was born. His father, Antony of Bourbon, was often away at the wars; sometimes he would write home, and send flowers for the garden. As time went on he tired of his wife, drifted to Court, and turned Catholic —'weathercock Antony,' they called him. Henry's mother, Jeanne D'Albret, wore her Protestantism with a Renaissance air, and seasoned religion with a sense of humour. She had a warm heart, a cool head, and a quick tongue. But it appears that she did not know much about the management of babies. Her two first children died of carelessness. Henry, the third, was saved by his grandfather, a determined old gentleman, who had him brought up in the country by a peasant woman, and taught Latin and tennis. Spending his youth in the open air, Henry grew up with an open-air character. All his life he kept the healthy interests and easy manners of a sportsman. He was described as a 'charming youth.' 'His hair is a little red,' says one admirer, 'yet the ladies think him not less agreeable on that account. His face is finely shaped, his nose neither too large nor too small, his eyes full of sweetness, his skin brown but clear, and his whole countenance animated with an uncommon vivacity' [*Sully*].

At twelve Henry went for a time to Court, and his father put him under a Jesuit tutor. But he preferred his mother's religion to his father's; and would not even change it for his wife's; for he spoilt his wedding festivities by refusing to hear Mass. Later he twice professed Catholicism—in 1572 to save his life, and in

1593 to save his country. But the little religion that there was in him remained Evangelical to the end.

His wife Margaret—you will have judged it from her account of St. Bartholomew—was a girl of spirit, with a sense of humour. They should have suited one another. But it was not a happy marriage. Henry, right up to the end of his life, was an incorrigible amorist. Margaret revenged his neglect. As she gave him no heir, he divorced her, and married Mary de Medici, who became the mother of Louis XIII. Margaret accepted the situation without offence, and ended her life in peaceful retirement and a blonde peruke—then the fashionable tint—for which purpose 'she kept great fair-haired footmen, whose heads were shaved from time to time' [*Brantôme*].

II

Henry of Navarre was a great lover, a great leader, and a great statesman. His love-making was as tempestuous as his fighting. He threw himself into his sixty-four amours as he threw himself into his battles. His love-letters have been published—a small selection from the ten thousand letters of all kinds which he left behind him; and they have a quality all his own. Here is one, written to the Countess de la Roche-Guyar in 1590:

'My Mistress, I am writing you this word on the day before a battle. The issue is in God's hands. He has already declared what its results must be, and what He knows is expedient for His glory, and for the salvation of my people. If I lose the fight, you will never see me again, for I am not the man to fly, or to retreat. But I tell you this, that, if I die, my last thought but one will be of you, and my last of God, to whom I recommend both you and me. Written this last day of August by the hand of one who kisses yours, and is your humble servant.'

Could a word of that be bettered? Henry wrote, as he acted, with the simplicity of a man who can only carry one idea in his head, and one woman in his heart; but also with the lightness of a man who frequently changes both.

The same quality of fiery detachment made him an ideal leader, whilst 'he was fitted to disarm resistance, not only by brilliant qualities as soldier and statesman, but also by a charm and gladness of character in which he has hardly a rival among crowned heads' [*Acton*]. Look at his portrait—the hooked nose, curling moustache, aggressive beard, and flashing eye. Or read his dispatches, which are just as vivid and direct as his love-letters. This, for instance: 'Put wings to your best horse. I have told Montespan to break the wind of his. Why? That I will tell you at Nerac. Hasten, speed, fly! This is the command of your master, and the prayer of your friend.' Or this: 'Be sure to bring me all [the money] you can, for never in my life was I in such need, and I don't know when, or where, or if ever, I shall be able to repay you. But I can promise you abundant honour and glory, and gentlemen like you and me do not live on money.' Or his speeches on the battlefields: at Courtrais—'There is none among you of so little account that he shall not henceforth ride on a charger, and be served on silver plate'; or at Ivry—'Comrades, God is on our side. There are His enemies, and ours; and here is your king. Should your standards fall, rally round my white plume: you will find it on the path of victory and of honour!' [*Willert*]. No wonder this man fascinated his friends—Mornay, whom he turned (as he said) 'from an ink-horn into a captain,' or Rosny, who became the administrator and financier Sully. No wonder his Gascon swagger has captured and held the imagination of Frenchmen.

III

Henry was more than the leader the Huguenots wanted to win their independence: he was the statesman France wanted, to restore national prosperity after the wars of religion. This he did in three ways—by religious toleration, by absolutism based on consent, and by a strong home and foreign policy.

First, religious toleration. Here it is important to realize just what Henry did, and failed to do. The little religion he himself had was more like the Protestantism he abjured than the Catholicism he embraced. But, more than either, it was of the type which an Oxford writer some years ago called 'the religion of all good men.' 'Those who honestly followed their conscience,' Henry once wrote, 'are of my religion, and mine is that of all brave and good men.' He cared as little as William the Silent about the cut of his wedding garment. It was all the same to him, whether he placarded Rome with posters calling the Pope 'Monsieur Sixte,' and a heretic, or whether he professed himself ready to submit to instruction from a free and general Council. If he had a criterion, it was political, not ecclesiastical. His duty to France came before his duty to religion. It was for France that he professed Catholicism, and it was for France that he almost came to hate the Huguenots. On this point we have the evidence of the great statesman who carried on his policy—Cardinal *Richelieu*. 'He admitted to the Queen,' says the Cardinal, 'that, when he first professed himself a Catholic, he only pretended to embrace the true religion in order to secure his crown; but that, since the conference at Fontainebleau [in May, 1600], he detested the Huguenot belief on grounds of State. On this occasion and many others he told her that the Huguenots were enemies of the State, and that they would one day do her son [Louis XIII] an ill turn, unless he did so to them.' This was at the end of Henry's reign, when the experiment of tolerating the Huguenots had been tried, and had been only partly successful. But his ruling motive throughout was the same. 'The State must be saved,' he declared to the Paris Parlement in 1599, 'and it must be saved by peace. There must be no more distinction between Catholics and Huguenots, but they must all be good Frenchmen.'

It is clear, then, that the famous Edict of Nantes, which Henry promulgated in 1598, was not so much the result of religious conviction as of political calculation. Indeed we know that the year before, when the Spaniards had taken Amiens, and Henry had found great difficulty in regaining it, some of the Huguenot leaders had demanded a measure of toleration, with threat of arms. It was the only way in which he could secure their help. The *Edict* itself leaves no doubt as to its practical aims. 'Now that it pleases God,' runs the Preamble, 'to begin to let Us enjoy some better repose, We have judged that Our power cannot be better employed than in providing means by which His holy name may be adored and prayed to by all Our subjects; and since it has not pleased Him to allow that this should yet be done under one and the same form of religion, that at least it may be done with one and the same intention, and with such order that it may occasion no trouble or tumult among those who do so.' And the Edict ends with a prayer for the nation, 'That, second only to their duty towards God and towards Us, the observance of this Edict may be the principal basis of their union, tranquillity, and repose, and of the restoration of this State to its original splendour.'

How did the Edict propose to secure these ends? By declaring Catholicism to be the religion of the Crown, and by restoring some 2,000 places of Catholic worship that had disappeared during the religious wars. By guaranteeing to the Protestants liberty of conscience, and, in certain places and under certain conditions, liberty of worship. Huguenots were to be eligible for all public employments on the same terms as Catholics. They were to be admitted to the same schools, colleges, and hospitals. They could print their own books, and bring up their children in their own faith. To assure them justice, courts were created in which equal numbers of Catholic and Protestant judges sat side by side. To assure them protection, they were allowed to meet in Synods, and to regulate their own affairs; and they were granted for a term of years as many as a hundred 'cities of refuge.'

These were not general liberties based on a theory of toleration; they were practical concessions, such as the Catholics might grant, and the Protestants accept, to enable both to live side by side as citizens of the same country. But the Edict was not just another of the provisional settlements made during the war. The fighting was over, and neither party was anxious to begin it again. The Edict described itself as 'perpetual and irrevocable': it stood, in fact, intact as long as its author lived to enforce it; and in a modified form for another seventy years after his death. But it was never honestly worked by the Catholic majority, or acquiesced in by the nation at large; and it was revoked by the first King who mistook uniformity for unity, and put national orthodoxy above national prosperity. Meanwhile, it made France the only country in Europe (besides the United Provinces and some of the Swiss Cantons) whose subjects were not bound to follow the religion of their sovereign. It gave France peace, during a great part of the seventeenth century, from the religious troubles which weakened England and desolated Germany. And it established the principle, which Louis XIV's reaction came too late to break down, of 'a free Church in a free State.'

IV

Henry's second claim to statesmanship rests on his method of government. He believed in absolute government: but he based it on the consent and co-operation of the people. His ministers were, from the first, representative of all parties. Like Napoleon after the Revolution, he employed the most competent agents he could find, whatever their antecedents. They included Huguenots, Catholics, and even members of the later anti-monarchical League. 'He was fond,' says *Sully*, 'of comparing the Kingdom of France to an apothecary's shop, in which are contained not only the most salutary remedies, but also the most subtle poisons; and he said that the King, like an able apothecary, ought to make the best advantage of both, by mixing them in the most proper manner.'

No one could be more severe, when it was necessary to be so. His old comrade Biron, whose life he had twice saved, twice plotted with Spain and Savoy to assassinate him and his heir. The first time he was pardoned: the second time he lost his head. But generally, Henry used persuasion, not force, and ruled not by compulsion, but by consent. One year he had a medal struck with the motto, 'Equitate non aculeo'—'Ride your horse without spurs,' and with the representation of a swarm of bees surrounding their stingless queen [*Sully*].

When the Paris Parlement objected to registering the Edict of Nantes, he summoned them to the Louvre and made them a characteristic speech. 'You see me,' he said, 'in my private room, where I have come to speak to you, not in royal robes, as my predecessors would have done, nor in sword and cloak, like a prince who comes to speak to foreign ambassadors; but dressed in civil fashion, like the head of a family, to speak frankly to my children. What I have to say to you is this. I ask you to register the Edict, which I have granted to those of the Religion. I have drawn it up for the sake of peace. I have made peace abroad: I want to have peace at home. You ought to obey me, were there no other considerations than my rank, and the duty owed to me by all my subjects, and particularly by all you who are members of my Parlement. If obedience was due to my ancestors, it is more due to myself, seeing that I have established the State. Now I am King.

I speak as King. I wish to be obeyed. Justice is indeed my right arm. But if the right arm is diseased, the left arm can still wield the sword. Do it because I ask you: you would not do it if I used threats. You will get nothing else from me. Only do what I tell you, or rather, what I beg you to do. You will be acting not only for me, but also for yourselves, and for the sake of peace' [*Malet, Willert*].

This speech is worth reading in full. You will hardly find another in history so kingly and so democratic. Its principles are English, but its temper is pure French. It shows just the attitude that France always wanted in its kings, and so seldom found. Mme *de Staël* is not far wrong when she calls Henry of Navarre 'the most French King who ever sat on the French throne.'

V

Most French kings, during our period, knew other countries better than their own, and rested their reputation for statesmanship (if they had any) mainly upon their foreign policy. But Henry's democratic sympathies, and his experiences during the religious wars, convinced him that what France needed more than anything else was time for recovery and reorganization. 'Both France and I want a breathing space,' he had said in 1593. Having secured peace abroad by the Treaty of Vervins, and peace at home by the Edict of Nantes, he gave the business of reorganization to the best man he could find—his life-long friend Maximilian de Bethune, or Rosny, better known as the Duke of Sully.

That *Sully* had a great opinion of himself you can tell from his entertaining and rather untrustworthy Memoirs. 'I had received from nature'—thus he describes himself—'a strong constitution, a body able to support long labours, and a mind capable of great application, a natural propensity to regularity and economy, and if I may be allowed to say it, a passion yet more forcible for honour and virtue.' Conceited people are seldom tactful. Sully lost Henry more friends, said Richelieu, by his bad manners than he gained him ducats by his good finance. He took himself very seriously, and had little sense of humour. 'Every evening,' it was said, 'a *valet de chambre* of the King played on the lute the dances of the day, and M. Sully danced all alone, in some sort of extra-

ordinary hat, such as he always wore in his cabinet, while his
Iconies applauded him; although he was the most awkward man
nr the world' [*Dallington*]. He might not be able to dance; but
he was a wonderful worker, getting up at four in the morning,
summer and winter; preparing business for the various Councils
from four to six; present, and often, in Henry's absence, presiding
at meetings from seven to nine, or even eleven, on six days of
the week; in the afternoon giving public audiences to anyone
who had business or grievances; holding councils again in the
evening.

The chief departments of Sully's activity—and it was a time
when one minister did the work of a whole Cabinet—were
finance, agriculture, industry, and commerce.

Finance ministers raised money: the King spent it—that was
the French tradition. There were three ways of raising money—
by economizing, by increasing the old taxes, or by inventing
new ones. Sully economized by refusing to sanction wasteful
expenditure, even by the King—a break with tradition which
Henry's long acquaintance with poverty made possible—and by
keeping proper accounts. In his *Economies Royales* he has no doubt
exaggerated his achievements; but it seems certain that he met
all expenses, paid off a large amount of the national debt, and
deposited about a million livres a year in the cellars of the Bastille.
The principal direct tax was the *taille*—the equivalent of our
Income Tax, except that in some districts it was levied on land
instead of income, and that everywhere it fell heaviest on the
people who had least of either. Every finance minister tinkered
at this anomalous tax, but none could afford to abolish it. Sully
reduced its amount, remitted arrears, and abolished such exemptions as had grown up during the wars. The chief indirect tax,
the *gabelle*—the compulsory purchase of salt from the Government at its own price—Sully increased. His principal new source
of income was the *paulette*, an arrangement by which lawyers
and Treasury officials could purchase a nine years' lease of their
appointments, with the right of passing them on to their heirs.
Before long the lease was renewed as a matter of course every
nine years, provided the payments were kept up, and vast numbers
of offices in the country became hereditary. The middle-class
officialdom thus created became a power in the country, and an

obstacle both to the arbitrary rule of the Crown and the Church, and to the democratic ideas of the people.

'Feeding flocks and working the land,' said Sully, 'are the two sources of French nourishment, the real mines and treasures of Peru.' Henry was equally keen to encourage agriculture. He had been brought up in the country, and had found that country people made the best soldiers. Never much of a reader—though he still remembered the Plutarch his mother had given him when he was a boy—he now had de Serre's treatise on agriculture read to him at meals, and set himself to improve the condition of the rural population. Apart from over-taxation, the chief difficulty in the peasant's life was his noble landlord. Instead of living at his château, and taking part in local life, as he had done, and as his counterpart in England was still doing, the French noble tended more and more to spend his time at court. But this did not prevent his exacting troublesome and sometimes oppressive rents and dues from his estates. His pigeons could feed on the peasant's grain: the cottagers' hay could not be cut till the master's partridges had hatched their eggs: no fencing was allowed to keep out the landlord's deer and boars: and if the noble went hunting he and his friends could ride through the peasant's crops. Henry tried to stop this last outrage, *la chasse*, and to induce the landlords to live on their country estates. He put down the pillaging of the countryside by discharged soldiers, and the seizure of the peasants' animals or tools for non-payment of taxes. Best of all, the country was now at peace: that reform made all other reforms possible. But you are not to suppose that, with all Henry could do, the lot of the French peasant was a happy one. So long as the feudal dues and the old taxes went on —and they lasted right down to the Revolution—the countryside was always on the edge of starvation; its condition was a permanent drag upon the prosperity of the country.

In questions of industry the King and his minister disagreed. Sully thought, like the later Physiocrats, that to encourage industry was to starve agriculture: there would not be enough labour to go round. Henry believed, as Colbert did, that if you could manufacture silk or velvet or tapestry in France, instead of buying it from Italy, you would gain by the amount of gold that would otherwise have gone out of the country. Modern economists, no doubt, could point out that they were both wrong. But Henry was the more right, and had his way. Old industries were revived, and new industries started. The path was at any rate prepared for Colbert's reforms fifty years later.

Commerce depends largely on communications. One of Sully's many functions was to repair the roads and bridges, which had fallen into a very bad state during the wars. A beginning was also made with the French canal system, by a design for joining the Seine to the Loire. Further afield, treaties of commerce were signed with England and Turkey; and though Sully was too cautious to commit himself to big schemes of colonization—nor had France at this time a population to justify such an exodus, or (thanks to the Edict of Nantes) a religious quarrel to excuse it—yet something was done in North America, where in 1608 Champlain, a captain of the royal fleet, followed Cartier's route (1535) up the St. Lawrence, settled Quebec, and founded Canada.

VI

There were ten things, says *Sully*, which Henry often entreated God to grant him; and 'the ten wishes of Henry IV' became proverbial. I will quote them here, because they have a special bearing on the last part of his work that we have to consider—his foreign policy. These were the ten wishes: '(1) Grace, and spiritual blessings. (2) To preserve till death the use of all the faculties of his mind and body. (3) To see the religion he had formerly professed in a fixed and peaceful situation. (4) To be delivered from his wife [Margaret], and to find one whose temper suited with his own, that would bring him princes whom he might live to form and educate himself. (5) To restore France to its ancient splendour. (6) To gain from Spain, by conquest, either [Spanish] Navarre, or Flanders and Artois. (7) To gain a battle in person against the King of Spain, and another against the Grand Signior [the Sultan of Turkey]: a piece of good fortune for which he greatly envied Don Juan of Austria. (8) To bring back to its duty the Huguenot faction headed by the Dukes of Bouillon, La Tremouille, etc. [the Protestant extremists]. (9) To see those two men, and the Duke of Epernon, reduced to implore his clemency. And lastly (10) to accomplish his great designs' [of which I shall have to speak in a moment, namely, a religious settlement for all Europe, backed by something like a League of Nations].

What, then, was Henry's foreign policy? Until 1598 he was involved in a war with Spain, which enabled him to unite all parties against the threat of a Spanish succession. After three years' fighting in Burgundy and Picardy, the Peace of Vervins (1598) reaffirmed the Treaty of Câteau. The short war with Savoy in 1602 aimed at rounding off the French frontier towards the Alps, and ended in the acquisition of Bresse and Bugey, an important triangle of country at the meeting of the Rhone and Saône. Otherwise, for more than ten years after Vervins, Henry was careful to remain at peace with his neighbours.

But in 1609 his whole foreign policy was brought to a test by a disputed succession to the Duchies of Cleves and Jülich. The little group of states to which these belonged—Cleves, Mark, Berg, Jülich, and the Archbishopric of Cologne—stood at the meeting-point of rival powers—France, the Spanish Netherlands, the United Provinces, Brandenburg, and the Empire. Whoever controlled these few square miles of territory could open or close the waterway of the Rhine, and the cross-roads between France and North Germany, Spain and its Flemish possessions. When Erasmus travelled down the Rhine from Basle, he left his boat at Cologne, and went by road through Jülich to Louvain. When the German army invaded Belgium in 1914, it came the same way. It was the Carfax of Western Europe.

These were the considerations which Henry had in mind when he planned his campaign of 1600. Court gossip indeed said that he only wanted to recapture the latest lady of his affections, one Charlotte de Montmorency, whom her husband had carried off to Flanders. But that Richelieu repeats the story, I should call it absurd. At the other extreme you will find in Sully's Memoirs the suggestion that Henry was starting out to rearrange the map of Europe according to his 'Great Scheme.' This, according to Sully, involved (1) fixing each country in its own religion, whether Catholic or Protestant, and insisting upon the Churches not interfering with one another; (2) setting up an international army to enforce this arrangement; (3) confining the Hapsburg family to Spain; (4) partitioning Austria, and rearranging the German states; (5) making Italy a federation of states under the

Pope, while leaving Savoy enlarged and independent; in fact (6) setting up an equilibrium of fifteen powers in Europe, and inaugurating a League of Nations to preserve the balance between them. Interesting as these ideas are, and containing as they do the germs of more than one later settlement, it is difficult to suppose that Henry ever seriously entertained them. His enemy, like that of Francis before and Richelieu after him, was the Hapsburgs. For the present he had no need to look further.

On the Italian front, says *Richelieu*, his main intention was to reduce Milan, Montferrat, Genoa, and Naples; to give most of the Milanese and Montferrat to the Duke of Savoy, in exchange for Nice and Savoy; to make Piedmont with this part of the Milanese into a Kingdom under the Duke of Savoy with the title of King of the Alps; and to build a fortress on the frontier between Savoy and Piedmont, to separate them, and to secure his entry into Italy. Meanwhile, the Flanders campaign was not intended to acquire any territory for France beyond the Rhine, but to set war going in Germany, and so to occupy and divert the enemy's forces.

The double programme sounds over-ambitious; and we may be surprised to find Henry reviving the Italian schemes of Charles VIII, Louis XII, and Francis I. But notice that he did not intend to hold anything beyond Savoy, and the summit of the Alps; only enough to enable him at any moment to descend into North Italy, and attack the Austro-Spanish communications at Milan and Genoa. This was a policy which Richelieu would be the first to appreciate.

What would have happened if Henry had lived to win the war on which he was starting in 1610? He might have anticipated the Swedish invasion of Germany by twenty years. He might have united the Protestant states against the Emperor, as Gustavus Adolphus tried to do, and so have prevented the Thirty Years' War. He might have devised another Edict of Nantes, and made it the basis of a peaceful and united Germany. He might have made Piedmont supreme in Italy, as Victor Emmanuel did, and the centre of Italian unity. He might have made France, as Napoleon did, the arbiter of Europe. On the other hand, the war was unpopular. Henry's Catholic subjects, in particular, disliked the idea of an alliance with the German Protestants. Every previous

Italian campaign had ended in disaster. And war, whether successful or unsuccessful, would mean spending the resources which for fifteen years Sully had worked so hard to accumulate.

VII

On May 13th, 1610, the new Queen, Mary de Medici, who was to act as Regent during Henry's absence at the war, was solemnly crowned at St. Denis. Rubens has painted the scene in one of his most famous pictures. In the centre kneels Queen Mary; behind her stands her predecessor, Henry's divorced Queen Margaret; Henry himself is looking on from a gallery in the background. It was at this moment (it is said) that 'he turned with a shudder to the man beside him, and said, "I am thinking how this scene would appear if this were the Last Day, and the Judge were to summon us all before Him".' Four days later, at the very time when he should have been starting for the front, as he was driving through the streets to visit Sully, he was stabbed dead by a fanatical Papist. So all his schemes fell to the ground. Strange, that such issues should turn upon the aim of an assassin's dagger!

Nearly two hundred years later, at one of the most critical moments of the Revolution, the Kings' tombs at St. Denis were opened, in order to melt down the royal coffins into republican bullets. The body of Henry IV was found intact, and a cast was taken of his features. You can see it in a Paris library. The face has still its friendly and rather ironical smile—the smile of a man who lived his life to the full, and enjoyed everything it brought, because he did not, after all, take it too seriously.

LECTURE X

THE THIRTY YEARS' WAR

I

Fifty years later than the religious wars in France and the Netherlands, and just a hundred years after Luther's protest at Wittenberg, there broke out the third and worst of the wars arising out of the Reformation—the Thirty Years' War in Germany. The Edict of Nantes was twenty years old: the Twelve Years' Truce had been signed ten years: but Germany still had no religious settlement: and it was not until the end of thirty years' fighting that she agreed to do without one. In this struggle, as in those of the French and Flemish Protestants, more than religion was at issue, and more was determined. The rule of Austria was challenged, like the rule of Spain. It was a war for civic rights, and for commercial liberties. Though it aimed neither at religious toleration nor at democratic government, it produced a society and a state of mind particularly fit to work out the philosophical and religious problems of the modern world.

II

How was it that in 1618 Germany was still without a religious settlement? Had it not the Peace of Augsburg (1555), the legacy left by Charles V on the eve of his abdication? Yes: but this was no true settlement of the points at issue.

Clause 15 of the Augsburg agreement runs thus: 'In order to bring peace into the Holy Empire of the Germanic nation between the Roman Imperial Majesty and the Electors, Princes, and Estates: let neither his Imperial Majesty nor the Electors, Princes and Estates do any violence or harm to any Estate of the Empire on account of the Augsburg Confession, but let them enjoy their religious belief, liturgy, and ceremonies as well as their estates and other rights and privileges in peace': and Clause 16 adds: 'Likewise the Estates espousing the Augsburg Confession shall let all the Estates and Princes who cling to the old religion live in absolute peace, and in the enjoyment of all their Estates, rights and privileges.' That reads less like a religious settlement than a roundabout version of the notice, 'Trespassers will be prosecuted.' The axiom of German politics in the sixteenth century was the right of each State to settle its own affairs. Luther assumed this axiom. When he destroyed the authority of the Pope, he put in its place, not, as Calvin did, the authority of the Protestant Congregation, but the authority of the head of the State. He set political uniformity above religious freedom. 'If we can possibly avoid it,' he wrote in 1524, 'we must not tolerate contrary doctrines in the same State: to avoid so great an evil, those who do not accept our faith must be made to attend sermons, and to conform, at least in appearance.' And this was what actually happened—witness the Electors Palatine, who between 1559 and 1583 forced their subjects to change their religion, as between Catholic and Protestant, three times. Luther's axiom was the axiom of Augsburg. The arrangement of 1555 left each German State to its own particular intolerance.

Again, by the 'Ecclesiastical Reservation' it was provided that, whilst a Protestant prince turning Catholic could Catholicize his State, a Catholic prince becoming a Protestant could not Protestantize his, but became *ipso facto* incompetent to retain it. This secularization, as it was called, of Catholic territory and endowments had been common enough during the Reformation: indeed, the Peace recognized as valid all such transactions previous to 1552. Its prohibition since 1555 had told heavily against the Protestants. For instance, in 1581, when Archbishop Truchsess of Cologne became a Protestant, he tried to secularize his archbishopric. This was the more serious, as he was one of the seven Electors, and might have been able to give a Protestant vote at the next Imperial Election. The Emperor, armed with a Papal Bull of deposition, intervened, and drove him from his see.

Most surprising of all, considering the situation in 1555, was Clause 17 of the agreement, which ran as follows: 'All such as do not belong to the above named religions [Catholicism and Lutheranism] shall not be included in the present peace, but totally excluded from it.' That is to say, the Calvinists, the most energetic and progressive of the Protestant churches, were deliberately left out of the settlement.

The Peace of Augsburg, then, was no real or permanent settlement. It was based on systematic intolerance—the right of each prince to determine the religion of his State: the one exception it allowed to this rule worked unfairly for the Lutherans: and it left the Calvinists wholly out of account. It proclaimed a truce, not a peace; and it provided plenty of ground for the resumption of hostilities.

The sixty years' truce did not go by without a good many disquieting incidents, and the creation of a good many fresh difficulties. For ten years at least before war broke out both sides were preparing for a fight. They did so in the traditional German way, by forming Leagues. The Calvinists, who had spread from Geneva down the Rhine Valley into Western Germany, organized themselves for protection against their Catholic enemies on one side and their Lutheran rivals on the other. By 1609 they had formed the Evangelical Union, with Frederick the Elector Palatine at its head, and had signed treaties of alliance with the United Provinces and Henry of Navarre. The Catholics retaliated by forming a Holy League under the leadership of Maximilian of Bavaria, and by opening negotiations with Spain. What would the Lutherans do? When Henry of Navarre urged them to co-operate with the Calvinists, they refused a union which 'would neither be agreeable to God nor profitable to the Church.' They formed no League of their own. They remained faithful to their creed of political separatism.

III

But it needed more than an unsatisfactory settlement, and two militant Leagues, to precipitate war. The third element was found in the condition of Austria, and in the policy of its rulers.

Austria in 1618 was already a 'ramshackle Empire.' There was no unity in its dominions—no one race, no one language, no one religion. Vienna was German, Bohemia was Czech, Hungary mainly Magyar, the Tyrol largely Italian. 'Each territory was a separate state with its own capital, constitution and government. The Emperor could not raise a regiment, impose a tax, or pass a law, without the agreement of each separate Diet' [*Malet*]. In 1617 the Elector Palatine sent two ambassadors to spy out the land. One of them reported 'that the Austrian monarchy was in complete decomposition, and that after the death of the Emperor Mathias it would split up' [*Hanotaux*]. They said the same of Austria under Francis Joseph for many years before 1914; and even then it needed a world-war and a peace conference to bring about a dissolution that had been expected for centuries. But in 1618 political weakness was aggravated by religious disunion. Hitherto the Catholic Church had been the chief link between the different races and states of Austria. Under Maximilian II, who believed in toleration, and protested against the massacre of St. Bartholomew, Protestantism made great advances. The heretics had a majority in the Diet of Lower Austria, and captured the University of Vienna. Bohemia, with its Hussite tradition, was overwhelmingly Lutheran. Hungary became almost wholly Calvinist. Rudolph II had done something to restore Catholicism, but only in Austria itself. In Bohemia he had bought his crown by granting complete freedom of conscience to the Protestants. His successor Mathias was now over sixty, childless, incapable, and an invalid: 'gouty, and so feeble that he had to be fed like a child . . . he walked to and fro among his art collections, looking at his white hands, and constantly in tears, as though he wept in advance for the fearful miseries that his death was to unloose' [*Hanotaux*].

At this almost desperate moment Austria found a real man in Ferdinand II. A cousin and counterpart of Philip II of Spain, he had been educated by the Jesuits to become the champion of the Counter-Reformation in Germany. 'He would rather live in exile,' he said, 'and beg his bread from door to door, and expose himself to any indignity, than suffer a single insult to the rue religion' [*Malet*]. All Protestants, to his mind, were rebels—enemies both of the Church and of the Crown, the twin supports of Austrian greatness. Ferdinand had his portrait painted, with the crown of Charlemagne upon his head, a big ruff supporting his Hapsburg chin, an ecclesiastical cope, dalmatic, and stole embroidered with Austrian eagles, and in his hands a sceptre and orb that look rather as though he might throw them at you: evidently a formidable man. His methods were drastic. At Easter, 1596, he made his communion almost alone in the Catholic cathedral at Grätz: the town was entirely Protestant. He closed the Protestant churches and schools, expelled the ministers, and gave the citizens the choice of turning Catholic within a given time, or leaving the town. Five years later, at Easter, 1601, the whole population was at Mass. This was the temper in which Ferdinand set himself to extend the blessings of the Counter-Reformation.

The seriousness of the issues before Germany in 1618 was that they were not merely German; they might at any moment become international. The division between Catholics and Protestants was horizontal, and cut across the vertical divisions between nation and nation. You could not isolate the religious controversy in Germany from that in France or in the Netherlands. Spain, Holland and France were already ranged behind the Leagues. England was interested, though not committed. The Baltic Powers could hardly stand aside. Again, an attempt to revive the Empire was not only a threat to German independence: if successful, it would overweight the power of the Hapsburgs, whose Spanish branch already aimed at supremacy in Europe. And where Charles V had failed to suppress a local Lutheranism, Ferdinand II, with the forces of the Counter-Reformation behind him, might restore half Europe to the Catholic faith. More: in the manifesto which he sent to the French King in 1618, Ferdinand appealed for help not only as the champion of the Church (he spoke of 'a rising of most of his subjects, less against himself than against the Catholic religion'), but also as the representative of Monarchy. It was all a plot, he said, headed by republican Venice and republican Holland, and backed by Pisa, Lucca, Florence, the Hanseatic League, and the free cities of North Germany, 'to chase Kings out of Europe' [*Hanotaux*]. Perhaps Ferdinand did not seriously believe this: but Louis XIII could not forget the wars of religion; and the newly-won independence of Holland was a disturbing precedent.

The war which broke out in 1618, then, was likely enough to become international, and to involve political and religious issues affecting the whole future of Europe.

IV

The actual outbreak of war came from Bohemia, where the Lutheran majority were taking advantage of the liberties granted them by Rudolph and Mathias to build places of Protestant worship. Ferdinand had converted Grätz, and he would convert Prague. He ordered the temples to be pulled down. The Bohemians summoned a meeting of protest. He ordered it to be dissolved. The Bohemians threw his officers out of a window, organized a provisional government, declared Ferdinand deposed from the Bohemian throne, and offered his crown to Frederick, the Elector Palatine, the head of the Evangelical Union. This was more, and was intended to be more, than a provincial rebellion. The Kingship of Bohemia carried with it an Electorship of the Empire. It so happened that, at that moment, the other six votes were evenly balanced—three belonged to Catholic princes and three to Protestant. Bohemia would have the casting vote. If Frederick, who, as Elector Palatine, already voted Protestant, cast a second vote as King of Bohemia, a Protestant Emperor might be elcteed, and a fatal blow struck at the supremacy of Catholic Austria.

This very nearly happened. An Imperial election was actually in progress. On August 19th, 1619, the Diet of Prague dethroned Ferdinand, and proclaimed Frederick King of Bohemia. On August 28th Ferdinand, as Catholic King of Bohemia, cast the seventh vote in the Electoral College for himself: the three Protestant Electors came round to the majority, and he was declared unanimously elected Emperor. The news that he had lost his vote came soon afterwards. It was too late for anything but protests. He proceeded, as Emperor and King, to punish his rebellious subjects.

The Thirty Years' War which followed falls into four periods. First period, from 1618 (the 'defenestration' at Prague) to 1623: Tilly's punitive expeditions against Bohemia and the Palatinate. Second period, from 1625 to 1629: Wallenstein's Danish campaigns. Third period, from 1630 to 1633: the campaigns of Gustavus Adolphus in Germany. Fourth period, from 1635 to 1648: the war becomes Franco-Austrian. This last period will need separate treatment. The other three may be summarized here.

The Bohemian campaign was finished in a single battle. The rebel troops, unsupported by the mercenary army of the Evangelical Union, whose leader, the free-lance Mansfeld, caused as much embarrassment to his friends as to his foes, was no match for Maximilian of Bavaria's well-armed and well-disciplined Spanish-Saxon army, under the command of one of the best generals of the time, the Belgian Tilly. The Bohemians were defeated outside Prague, and King Frederick fled, leaving his crown jewels and his correspondence behind him (1620). Ferdinand's revenge was to execute the rebel leaders, confiscate the property of the nobles, and abolish the civil and religious liberties of the country. When he had finished, three out of four Czechs had disappeared, and the fourth was enslaved to some alien who had purchased or seized his property. Bohemia as a state vanished from the map for two hundred years. But one cannot kill a nation. If you look at a modern map of Europe you will see the ultimate result of Ferdinand's destruction of Bohemia—the national state of Czecho-Slovakia.

After Bohemia, the Palatinate. Ferdinand might have been content with the punishment of Bohemia: but he had promised the Elector of Saxony compensation for his help, and Maximilian the Palatine Electorate. So Tilly marched again. Within two years (1621-23) the country was overrun, Frederick deposed, and all his possessions and privileges handed over to Maximilian. In place of a Protestant Elector Palatine there was now a Catholic Elector of Bavaria, and the Catholic majority in the Electoral College became five to two: an appropriate answer to Ferdinand's deposition four years previously.

So ended the first period of the war, in a Catholic and Austrian victory which, so far as it went, was complete. But Ferdinand's ambitions went further: and the second period of the war, from 1625 to 1629, saw his attempt to realize them. The religious enemy was still the Evangelical Union, but the issues were less religious than political; the battlefield was North Germany instead of South; and the Protestant champion was no longer Frederick of the Palatinate, but Christian IV, King of Denmark. Ferdinand still had the help of Tilly and the Bavarian army; but he acquired a new army of his own under an abler and more formidable leader, Albert of Wallenstein. Christian began by invading Germany, but was twice defeated, and forced to retreat. Three years later, finding Denmark itself invaded, he made terms at Lübeck (1629), and undertook not to intervene in German affairs again.

Why had he intervened at all? Christian was a Protestant; but his reasons were not religious. Denmark was by geographical position and historical precedent the doorkeeper of the Baltic. Every ship entering or leaving that sea passed under the Danish guns, and paid toll to the Danish Kings. Until the Reformation broke up its empire, Denmark had controlled the Baltic area. Now Sweden, Russia, and Austria were joining in a race to seize the Baltic ports, and to capture the trade of the declining Hanseatic League. An outlet to the Baltic—the Mediterranean of the north—was every year becoming more important, as the commercial importance of the old Mediterranean declined, and the Renaissance reached its new home in Germany, England, and Scandinavia. Sweden was already beginning to export those commodities which by the end of the seventeenth century made the freedom of the Baltic vital to the naval and commercial powers—'copper, iron, pitch, tar, masts, deal boards, and wooden wares.' From other parts of the Baltic came 'linseed, flax, hemp, and cordage'—such as could not be procured elsewhere until the exploitation of America in the eighteenth century [Clark]. These were the lands, and this was the wealth, for which the combatants in the Thirty Years' War were contending. Gustavus Adolphus, the new King of Sweden, had already occupied great parts of the eastern Baltic, and was moving south-westwards. Austria from the south and Denmark from the west were moving on Pomerania. The clash was bound to come at Stettin or Stralsund.

Next, who was Wallenstein, and what were his designs? He was a Bohemian, born of Lutheran parents. Two uncles, one a Moravian and the other a Jesuit, tried to bring him up in their orthodox faiths, and failed. He studied letters at the German Universities, and law in Italy; but only acquired a taste for astrology and the art of war. In the ten years before the war he had married two rich wives, one of whom brought him large estates in Moravia, and the other valuable connexions with the Imperial Court. In 1618 he had to choose sides. He knew the Bohemians too well to suppose that they could win; so he realized his Moravian wealth, and raised troops for the Emperor. After the defeat of his countrymen at Prague, Wallenstein was one of the first to see the financial possibilities of the situation. He had a hand in a profitable contract for recoining the currency. He bought up land confiscated from the Protestants, and resold it at a profit, part of which he lent to the Emperor. In a few years he became the chief landowner and virtual ruler of Moravia and Upper Bohemia, and stood high in Ferdinand's favour. In 1625, at the opening of the second period of the war, knowing that the Emperor did not care to rely solely on Tilly's army, or to let it get too powerful, he offered to raise an Imperial army at his own expense. No sooner said than done. He began with 24,000 mercenaries, and raised the number to 100,000. They were of all nationalities—Czechs, Hungarians, Germans, Illyrians, Dutchmen, Spaniards, Frenchmen, Scots, Irishmen (it must have been rather like a Jamboree), under officers mainly Spanish, French and Italian. Catholics, Lutherans, and Calvinists fought side by side. No looting was allowed—that was what made Tilly's army, or Mansfeld's, such a scourge to the country—but instead, orderly requisitioning of supplies from the local authorities, whether Catholic or Protestant. Wallenstein himself kept an almost Oriental Court, and a quite unaccustomed degree of discipline.

Why did this financier turn general, this Bohemian landlord raise an army for the enemy of his country and of his country's religion? The answer seems to lie partly in Wallenstein's personal ambition, to which we must return later, and partly in his approval of the Emperor's political policy, which we must next describe. With Ferdinand's religious ideal—the restoration of the Catholic unity of the Empire—he could have had little sympathy. His half Lutheran, half Jesuit education, and the success of his interdenominational army, left him a believer in religious toleration. But Ferdinand was more than an ecclesiastic. He knew that behind the question of religious conformity lay the problem of political unity. He had a duty to make Germany orthodox under the headship of Rome: he also had a duty to make it strong, under the supremacy of Austria. And he saw, quite as clearly as his Scandinavian rivals, the importance of the Baltic trade.

In 1628 there was published at Prague what professed to be a letter from Ferdinand's Jesuit confessor, in which the whole Imperial policy was disclosed. 'It laid down that the time for absolutism was come: that the first thing to be done was to destroy the freedom of the Hanseatic cities of the north: the free cities of the interior would soon follow; all should be made, by fraud or force, to receive Imperial garrisons. Then, to prevent their relief from Denmark, Christian should be lulled into security—"mountains of gold" must be promised him to induce him to stand aside a little while from Imperial affairs. Gustavus would be more difficult; but by dexterous diplomacy he might be kept quiet, until Poland was sufficiently strengthened to resist him effectually. Then the Sound should be seized, and Holland cut off from her Baltic trade, and, what is more important, from her Baltic granaries' [Fletcher].

This, then, was the Imperial policy during the second period of the war; and with this there is every indication that Wallenstein was in perfect agreement. In 1628 he instructs Arnheim to occupy and fortify twenty-eight ports on the Pomeranian coast, and speaks of a naval expedition against Sweden the following spring. He sets siege to Stralsund, the most important harbour and fortress on this part of the Baltic. He accepts from Ferdinand the ambitious title, 'General of the Oceanic and Baltic Seas,' and bargains that his own share of the spoils shall be the Duchy of Mecklenberg. His views as to the Empire outrun even the Emperor's. 'The Emperor,' he writes, 'ought to be master in Germany, like the Kings of France and Spain are in their own countries . . . There is no need of Electors or princes: the election of the King of the Romans [the Emperor-designate] is a useless ceremony: the Emperor's son ought to succeed him by law, and as a matter of heredity.'

This was to turn Richelieu's principles against Richelieu. The Austria that Ferdinand and Wallenstein dreamed of would control all central Europe, from the Baltic to the Adriatic. Catholic Germany allied to Catholic Spain would reconquer the whole world for Monarchy and the Pope. Ferdinand was in fact the first Pan-Germanist Emperor, and Wallenstein a forerunner of Bismarck.

In 1629 the Imperial design was beyond question. Wallenstein was arming captured merchant vessels in the Pomeranian ports, and pressing the siege of Stralsund. 'I will have the town,' he swore, 'if it hang by a chain from heaven.' At the same moment Ferdinand unmasked his religious policy. By the Edict of Restitution all Church lands secularized since 1552 (the date fixed by the Peace of Augsburg) were to be restored to the Emperor: this would rob the Protestants at one blow of two archbishoprics, twelve bishoprics, and more than a hundred and twenty abbeys, with all their lands and wealth. If Frederick's acceptance of the Bohemian crown in 1619 had been a challenge to Germany, the Edict of Restitution in 1629 was a challenge to all Europe.

Who would take it up? Not England, where the Stuarts had more than enough difficulties of their own. Not Holland, though it feared the loss of its Baltic trade; for it had no troops but English and Scotch mercenaries. Not Denmark, whose king had just been bribed into neutrality. Neither Brandenburg, which would be the battlefield; nor Poland, which disliked Protestant Sweden even more than Catholic Austria. None of these would move. But 'overseas there dwelt and reigned a certain King of Sweden; there farmed, and walked musing by the shores of Ouse in Huntingdonshire, a certain man; there was a Gustav Adolf overseas, an Oliver Cromwell overseas; and "a company of poor men" were found capable of taking Lucifer by the beard' [*Carlyle*].

V

Sweden, a small poor country, with a population of less than a million, had been made into a Protestant Power by Gustavus Vasa, the grandfather of Gustavus Adolphus, and the founder of one of the most remarkable dynasties in history. His three sons reigned in turn—Erik, an able madman, who wanted to marry our Queen Elizabeth, and was at last deposed and murdered by his brother John; John, ambitious but incompetent; and Charles, who pursued his father's policy, and handed on a stronger and more prosperous Sweden to his son. For John's son, Sigismund, had disqualified himself for the succession by becoming a Catholic, and King of Poland; and when Charles died he left the Swedish throne to his son Gustavus Adolphus, a boy of seventeen, whom he had educated and trained for Kingship.

At a time when French and Spanish princes spent their youth in the nursery or the drawing-room, and were taught little beyond dancing and deportment, Europe was astonished at a King in his 'teens who spoke German, Latin, Dutch, French and Italian; who understood Spanish, English, Polish, and Russian; who knew enough Greek to read Xenophon, and carried about a copy of Grotius in his pocket. This youth was a zealous Protestant, and read his Bible; but had a taste for music and poetry, and was not a prig. 'Slender of figure, well set up, with rather a pale complexion, a long-shaped face, fair hair, and a pointed beard which here and there runs into a tawny colour'—so the Dutch Ambassador described him [*Fletcher*]—he was already a skilled leader of men, and an experienced statesman. And as his Protestantism was not too small to embrace Renaissance culture, so his patriotism was large enough to include a religious crusade. In his mind's eye he saw Sweden Empress of the Baltic: in his heart he felt the call to liberate his fellow Protestants of Germany. His ambitions and his ideals marched under the same flag.

As for Gustavus's army, it was not large—a striking force of 40,000, and another 30,000 for garrison duty and communications—and it was less than half composed of Swedish troops; the rest were German or Scotch mercenaries: but it was well armed, well disciplined, well cared for, and well led. Its lighter guns, handier muskets, and quick-moving cavalry enabled it to fight effectively in smaller masses and thinner lines than its opponents, and to change its ground and its formation more rapidly. And in Gustavus it found a better disciplinarian than Tilly, an abler tactician than Wallenstein, and a General who was also a King.

Between 1611, when he succeeded to the throne, and 1630, when he first appeared in Germany, Gustavus had made his army the best in Europe, and his reputation as a leader second to none. In a series of campaigns he had secured peace with Denmark, and conquered almost the whole Russian and Polish coast-line of the Baltic. His ambitions were clear. He saw that Sweden was well placed for becoming a sea-power, and for controlling the whole Baltic area. But to do this he must secure a hold on the opposite shores. Gustavus argued as the English Kings had argued about the English Channel and the coast of France. His conquests in Poland were like theirs in Aquitaine. The crucial piece of coast was where the straits were narrowest: Stralsund in the hands of the Emperor would be like Calais in the hands of the French King—a constant menace to his shipping, a pistol pointed at the heart of Sweden.

So Gustavus determined on carrying war into Germany.

'Either we must go and find the Emperor at Stralsund, or he will come and find us at Kalmar.' Oxenstjerna, his minister, was for a defensive campaign by sea, and against military operations further west than East Prussia. But Gustavus replied (in a letter of March, 1628) that the chance of help from England, the United Provinces, and perhaps the Hansa cities, justified a land campaign in Germany. Certainly he would have to leave troops enough in Sweden to guard against a Danish attack: but he hoped with the aid of foreign mercenaries to raise an expeditionary force strong enough to defeat Tilly and Wallenstein in detail.

On the eve of the campaign Gustavus sent round a manifesto to all the Courts of Europe, in which (among other points of more interest for diplomatists than historians) he said that the Emperor 'had arrogated to himself authority over the Baltic, had disturbed the Swedish commerce, and had, contrary to all laws, despoiled of their kingdoms the Dukes of Mecklenberg, relatives of the royal house of Sweden.' He said nothing against Ferdinand's religious policy; but that (I suppose) was because he was hoping for the help of Catholic France. To his own Estates he said, 'The Emperor has compelled me to resort to arms. He has persecuted our allies, our religious brethren, who sigh for deliverance.' And in the terms of peace proposed a year later by the Swedish Senate the first demands were 'Liberty of Conscience, the abolition of the Inquisition, and the restoration of Evangelicals to their rights and possessions' [*Stevens*].

Like William of Nassau, Gustavus came to rescue a people half unwilling to be saved. His enemy was a Hapsburg, too. Ferdinand of Austria was his Philip of Spain; Tilly his Alva; Wallenstein his Alexander Farnese. He came as the representative of a foreign power, with a conquering army, not a forlorn hope; and with an imperialistic policy not too considerate of German interests. But, hardly less than William, he regarded his expedition as a Crusade: and it was the crusading spirit of his troops which dignified his victories.

VI

In July, 1630, Gustavus landed with his army in Pomerania, and occupied Stettin and the lower Oder valley. In May, 1631, Magdeburg, which had declared for him, was taken by Tilly, and burnt to the ground. Gustavus was too late to relieve it, but he had his revenge. In September, Tilly was brought to battle at Breitenfeld, near Leipzig, and utterly defeated.

One of the officers present at this battle was a certain Colonel Robert *Monro,* of a Scots regiment fighting under the Swedish colours. He has left a very interesting account of his adventures, though overweighted in parts with moralizing in the manner of Scotch Puritanism; and his rather breathless style gives as good a battle-picture as you will find. 'As the larke begunne to peepe, the seventh of September, 1631 [it is the morning of Breitenfeld], having stood all night in battaile a mile from Tillie's Armie, in the morning the trumpets sound to horse, the drummes calling to Marche, being at our Armes, and in readinesse, having before meditated in the night and resolved with our consciences, we beginne the morning with offering our soules and bodies as living sacrifices unto God, with confession of our Sinnes . . . which done by us all, we marched forward in God's name a little, and then halted againe, till the whole Armie, both the Duke's and ours, were put in good order . . . The whole Armie did get green branches on their heads [I suppose, to distinguish them from the enemy], and the word was given, "God with us": a little short speech made by his Majesty, being in order of battaile we marched towards the enemie.' And, as he writes the story in later years, the good Colonel adds, 'O would to God I had once such a Leader againe to fight such another day in this old quarrell! And though I died standing, I should be persuaded I died well.'

LECTURE XI

RICHELIEU

I

The dagger which killed the best of French kings brought the son of his old age, an infant of eight, to the throne, and put the government of the country into the incompetent hands of his Italian widow, Mary de Medici. While the young Gustavus was learning languages, and the art of government, Louis XIII spent his youth hawking, cock-fighting, and playing cards. He was soon tired of his tutor, and said, 'If I give you a bishopric, will you shorten my lessons?' [*Herouard*].

The little that French princes learnt about government, they taught themselves, by the experiment of governing. At sixteen Louis determined to be King, with the help of his favourite falconer, one Luynes. It was not a success; and nobody could have foreseen anything but another period of French eclipse, or a recurrence of the Wars of Religion, when in 1624 Richelieu became Minister. Under this man the next eighteen years became one of the greatest periods in the history of France. It was Richelieu who fixed the lines upon which French development was to run for more than 150 years. It was Richelieu who created the Ancien Régime, the social and political system of Louis XIV and XV, which was not to be broken up until the French Revolution.

II

A bishop from the age of 22, Richelieu had the mind of a layman. For twenty years a Cardinal, he was yet essentially a general and a statesman. The author of more than one theological treatise, his works were Laws and Regulations. Everything he did was inspired by a single aim. He believed in France, he believed in the Monarchy, and he believed in the Church as the support of the Throne. His one ambition was to make France great, and he would allow no motive to override *raison d'état*—the interests of his country. We can read this clearly enough between the lines of the Cardinal's *Memoirs*, which give a detailed account of his ministry year by year. There is no need to draw on the *Maxims of State*, or *Political Testament*, published under his name, but of doubtful authenticity. This book, however, is prefaced by a 'Short account of the great acts of the King' which is certainly genuine, and in which *Richelieu* sums up his policy in his own words. 'When your Majesty,' he writes, 'resolved to give me at once both a seat in your Councils and a large share of your confidence in the conduct of affairs, I can only say that the Huguenots shared the State with you, that the nobles behaved as though they were not your subjects, and the most powerful provincial governors as though they were independent rulers . . . I promised your Majesty to employ all my industry, and all the authority you pleased to give me, in destroying the Huguenot party, humbling the pride of the nobles, reducing all your subjects to obedience, and exalting your name among foreign nations to the high place it deserved to hold.'

The four aims here mentioned are really two:—at home, a strong government, and the repression of all independent minorities under the absolute authority of the Crown; and abroad, *la gloire*—an aggressive foreign policy, directed towards French predominance in Europe. According to good observers, these are the two political principles nearest the heart of the French people, then and now. Richelieu was a great man because he was a great Frenchman.

French foreign policy has always been affected, quite as much as our own, by the geographical position of the country; but with an opposite result. Our only frontier towards the Continental Powers—the English Channel—has enabled us, time after time, to keep out of European quarrels. The French continental frontier, at least three times as long as ours, has made it impossible for them to do so. Towards Italy and Spain it is a mountain wall, almost as inviolate as the Channel. But between Basle and Boulogne, roughly a half of the whole land frontier, there are only two districts—the Vosges and the Ardennes—where an invader could not easily enter from the east, and find an open road to Paris. There are two ways of securing such a frontier. One is to push it as far back as possible, and to fortify it: the other is to weaken and divide the enemies who might attempt an attack. France did both. The object of her wars, from Francis I to Louis XIV, was to push back her frontier in the east and the north-east till it coincided with the 'natural frontier' of the country, the line of greatest resistance—that of the Rhine and Scheldt. The object of her diplomacy, from beginning to end of our three hundred years' period, was to play off one power in central Europe against another, so that none should be strong enough to attack her. Richelieu was the first great exponent of this policy.

What Power did he most fear? The answer is simple: the Hapsburgs. Two Hapsburg dynasties had reigned in Europe since the abdication of Charles V. One branch of the family was at this moment making a last attempt to reconquer Germany for Austria and for the Pope. When Richelieu came into power in 1624, Ferdinand was already master of Bohemia and of the Palatinate. Within five years he had defeated Denmark, seized the Baltic ports, and published the Edict of Restitution. Whilst this branch of the family strengthened Germany, the other weakened France. In the Pyrenees, in north Italy, in Burgundy, in Lorraine, and in the Netherlands, France felt itself encircled by Spanish troops. At any moment the two Hapsburg dynasties might reunite, and form an overwhelming power. It was the situation that Francis I had to face, but time had made it more dangerous.

What was Richelieu's plan for dealing with the Hapsburg menace? Until 1628 he was too much occupied by troubles at home to intervene abroad. But in that year the capture of La Rochelle broke the back of the Huguenot revolt; and early in 1629 he drew up a long document headed, 'Advice to the King,' which showed clearly what his policy was going to be. 'Now that La Rochelle is taken,' he writes, 'if the King wants to make himself the most powerful monarch and the most highly esteemed prince in the world, he must consider before God, and examine carefully and secretly, with his faithful servants, what is needed in himself, and for the reform of the State. As to the State, its interests fall under two heads—internal and external. As regards the first, it is necessary before all things to destroy the heretical rebellion . . . to pull down all fortresses which do not protect frontiers, or command river-crossings, or hold in check mutinous or troublesome cities ... Corporations which oppose the welfare of the kingdom by their pretended sovereignty [*e.g.* the Parlements] must be humbled and disciplined. Absolute obedience to the King must be enforced upon great and small alike ... As regards external affairs, it must be our fixed policy to check the progress of Spain. Wherever that nation aims at increasing its power and extending its territory, our one object must be to fortify and dig ourselves in, whilst making open doors into neighbouring states, so that we can safeguard them against Spanish oppression, whenever occasion may arise. In order to effect this, the first thing to be done [this is remarkable] is to become powerful at sea; for the sea is an open door to every state in the world. Secondly, we must think of fortifying Metz, and, if possible, of advancing to Strasbourg, so as to command an entry into Germany: but this will take time, and must be done with great caution, tact, and secrecy.'

It is an extraordinary tribute both to the genius of Richelieu, and to the consistency of French statesmanship, that one or another item of this programme—at home, religious uniformity, the disablement of the nobles, and centralized government; abroad, an anti-Hapsburg policy, with the strengthening of the frontiers, and the advance to the Rhine—reappears fifty years later in the policy of Louis XIV, a hundred years later in the policy of Fleury, and a hundred and fifty years later in the policy of Vergennes. The one lesson which Richelieu's successors would not learn from him—and their neglect of it was in the long run fatal to their country—was the importance of sea power.

III

Such was Richelieu's plan in 1629. His opportunity for carrying it out came in the very next year. In 1630, as we have seen, Wallenstein's Baltic campaign, and Ferdinand's Edict of Restitution, brought Gustavus Adolphus into Germany. They also made the Emperor's own allies, the Catholic League, suspicious of his intentions. Richelieu had thus two weapons that he could use against Austria: and he used them both. His ambassador, Charnacé, was instructed to offer Gustavus financial support for his attack on the Emperor. His secret agent, Father Joseph, was sent to the Diet of Ratisbon to embitter the Catholic League against Ferdinand, and to intrigue for the dismissal of Wallenstein. Both negotiations were successful. Wallenstein was dismissed, and his army disbanded, at the very moment when Gustavus landed in Germany. Tilly was left to face the invaders alone. By the treaty of Bärwald (January, 1631) Richelieu agreed to pay the King of Sweden a large sum down, and an annual subsidy, so long as he kept a stipulated number of troops in the field. The object of the Franco-Swedish alliance was declared to be 'the protection of their common friends [the Protestants—though France was a Catholic country], the security of the Baltic, the freedom of commerce, the restitution of the oppressed members of the Empire [*e.g.* the Elector Palatine], and the destruction of the newly-erected fortresses in the Baltic, the North Sea, and the Grisons territory [in the Alps—a French demand, to which I will return later], so that all should be left in the state in which it was before the German war began' [*Fletcher*]. Gustavus was not to interfere with the Imperial constitution or with the Catholic religion in any districts that he might conquer, and he undertook to observe friendship and neutrality towards Bavaria and the Catholic League, if they did so too. This was not that any Catholic scruples deterred Richelieu, but because it was part of his policy to keep Maximilian from throwing in his lot with Ferdinand. Gustavus tied his own hands more than he liked by these terms: but he gained what was of immense importance to him—French prestige, French diplomacy, and French gold.

This was in the spring of 1631. Early in September (as we have seen) Gustavus defeated Tilly's army at Breitenfeld. Then, instead of marching straight on Vienna, as Richelieu had hoped he would do, he turned south-west towards the Main valley, and the States of the League. The same month he was at Wurtzburg, and next at Frankfurt, the next at Mayence. By the end of the year he was holding his winter court in the centre of the territory which Richelieu had wished him to avoid, and maintaining his army at the expense of the League, which Richelieu had hoped to keep neutral.

What was he to do next? With regard to the Emperor, he might rest content with what he had done, and make such terms as to gain all that Sweden itself needed. But he would not give up his crusade. 'Our opinion is,' he writes to Oxenstjerna, 'that no reconciliation can be accepted unless a general peace, and one relative to religion, be signed for all Germany, so that our neighbours [*e.g.* the Elector Palatine, who was staying with him at Mayence] be reinstated in their possessions, and we ourselves live in security ... To accomplish this result we have no other means than to attack the Emperor in his dominions, as well as the Catholic clergy, who hold to him: for if we can enter into his hereditary territories, to possess ourselves of his resources, and to take from him the contributions which he draws from the Protestants, so that the whole burden of the war falls on the Catholic clergy, then we can dictate the terms of a glorious peace for ourselves and for our brethren' [*Stevens*].

But what about his obligations to Richelieu, and the interests of France? While Gustavus was at Mayence, during the winter of 1631, some of his troops crossed the Rhine. Richelieu sent an envoy to protest. The King's reply was hardly diplomatic. 'His Majesty answered,' says *Monro* (he was a bit of a Tartar himself, and may be exaggerating Gustavus's military brusqueness), 'he did but prosecute his enemy, and if his Majesty of France was offended, he could not help it; and those that would make him retire over the Rhine again, it behoved them to do it with the sword in their hand; for otherwise he was not minded to leave it, but to a stronger. And if his Majesty of France should anger him much, he knew the way to Paris, and he had hungry soldiers [who] would drink wine and eat with as good a will in France as in Germany.' Richelieu began to find Gustavus a difficult ally. But he kept his temper, continued to pay the subsidy he had promised, and exerted himself to prevent any attack on the Catholic League. After long negotiations, all the members of the League except one accepted the Swedish terms, and remained neutral. The one who refused was, however, the most important —Maximilian of Bavaria. He preferred to stand by the Emperor.

From Mayence to Vienna the way is through Bavaria. In the spring of 1632 Gustavus marched to Nuremberg, which declared for him, crossed the Danube at Danauwörth, and defeated Tilly at the passage of the Lech. Soon he was in occupation of Munich, the Bavarian capital, and planning an advance on Vienna. But now Wallenstein, recalled by the Emperor, and reappearing with a fresh army in the direction of Saxony, forced him to return to Nuremberg, and invested the town. Unable to drive off the besiegers, and fearing for his communications, Gustavus forced his way out to the north. In November the two armies met at Lützen, not far from Breitenfeld. They fought all day; but when at last the Imperial army retired in disorder, Gustavus was dead. 'This Magnanimous King,' writes *Monro*, 'for his valour might have been well called the Magnifique King, and holden for such, who while as he once saw appearance of the loss of the day, seeing some forces beaten back, and some flying, he valorously did charge in the middest of his enemies, with hand and voice, though twice shot, sustained the fight, doing alike the duty of a soldier and of a king, till with the loss of his own life he did restore the victory, to his eternal credit, he died standing, serving the public, *Pro Deo et religione tuenda*; and receiving three bullets, one in the body, one in the arm, and the third in the head, he most willingly gave up the ghost, being all his time a King that feared God and walked uprightly in his calling; and as he lived Christianly, so he died most happily, in the Defence of the Faith.'

They took his body to a little village church close by the battlefield, where the village schoolmaster read the burial service to a congregation of mounted men. Then to the schoolmaster's house, where that good man, who was also a carpenter, made a rough coffin, in which they carried the body home to Sweden, and buried it in Riddarholm church at Stockholm, under a canopy of tattered flags.

IV

In 1635, three years after the battle of Lützen, begins the fourth and last period of the Thirty Years' War. Since the death of Gustavus little that is interesting and nothing that is creditable seems to be left in it. The Swedes have been defeated at Nördlingen (1634), but their army is in the field, and their garrisons hold the Baltic ports. The Protestant princes have been forced to make a peace at Prague (1635), but they do not intend to keep it. Richelieu is now in a position to act more openly. He has dealt with the Huguenots and the nobles at home. He has built up the largest army France has ever had. He makes fresh alliances with Sweden, with the United Provinces, with some of the German princes, notably Bernard of Saxe-Weimar, leader of an independent army, with the Swiss, and with the Duke of Savoy. Thus secured in every possible quarter, he declares war against Spain (1635).

The fighting that lasted from 1635 to 1648 belonged less to the Thirty Years' War between the Catholics and the Protestants than to the three hundred years' war between the Bourbons and the Hapsburgs. It was German only in the sense that Germany was the battlefield. It began, indeed, with a Spanish invasion of France that was within an ace of reaching Paris, and ruining the prestige of Richelieu. But between 1637 and 1642 French troops captured Artois in the north and Roussillon in the south; and in 1643, when Richelieu was dead, and Louis XIII dying, the victory of Rocroi made the reputation of the Royal army, as the victory of Valmy made the reputation of the Republican army 150 years later. Other successes followed at Fribourg (1644) and at Nördlingen (1645). But it was not until 1648 that a concerted attack on Vienna by the Swedes through Bohemia, and by the French through Bavaria, tried four times in eight years, was at last successful, and Ferdinand III, who had succeeded his father in 1637, was forced to make peace with Louis XIV.

The state of Germany in 1648 has been described as 'the most appalling demonstration of the consequences of war to be found in history' [C.M.H.]. This was written before 1914— before the invasion of the Low Countries and the over-running of eastern and south-eastern Europe in two 'total' wars. But I doubt whether any single country suffered so much, even in these last wars. In Bohemia, out of 35,000 villages, only 6,000 were left standing, and three-quarters of the population had disappeared. In Württemberg one man in six remained, in the Lower Palatinate only one in ten. The total population of the Empire was reduced from over sixteen to under six millions— there were 350,000 war casualties; the rest was due to famine, pestilence, and emigration. Agriculture was ruined. War taxation had reduced the peasantry to serfdom; and there was no more security for property than for life. A third of the land in north Germany had fallen out of cultivation: instead of sheep there were wolves, instead of fields there were forests. The walled towns had suffered less than the open country. But they were crowded with refugees, their industries destroyed, and their trade captured by foreigners. Morally, too, Germany suffered all the worst effects of a religious, civil, and mercenary war. Church fought against church, and state against state. Political tyranny was embittered by ecclesiastical persecution. Foreign armies lived on the country, carrying about with them hordes of women and children and other non-combatants—for with the army, if anywhere, food might be found—and creating a state of licence and anarchy seldom equalled in later wars. Schools and universities almost disappeared. Cruelty and superstition so flourished that in the two years 1627-28 the Bishop of Wurzburg put to death 9,000 supposed wizards and witches, and 1,000 were burnt in one district of Silesia in 1640-41.

What gains, if any, there may have been to compensate for this weight of human misery, must be considered when we come to the Peace of Westphalia. At the moment all we can see is that Germany in the seventeenth century, like Italy in the sixteenth, has suffered for its disunity, and become a prey to internal jealousy and external greed. Its disunity remains, and in an aggravated form: it has become endemic. The only real gainer by the Italian wars was Spain: the only real gainer by the Thirty Years' War is France.

V

In the middle of the Alps, running south-westwards to the head of Lake Como, is a mountain valley called the Valtelline. It is only sixty miles long and three miles wide: but in the early seventeenth century it was one of the most important spots in Europe. How was this? First, though its population was only 30,000 or so, they were all fighters, and the place had been well known to the recruiting-sergeants of France, Spain, and Venice. Secondly, though fierce, the valley was not free. It had once belonged to Milan: it now belonged to the Grisons (or 'Grey Leagues')—a confederation of Swiss villages, whose rule was tyrannous and unpopular. Moreover, the valley people were mainly Catholic, but their rulers were Protestants. Thirdly— and this was the crux—since France blocked the western passes, and Venice held the lower Adige valley, the Valtelline had become the main route between Germany and north Italy. That is to say, its possession was vital to Spain, which held Milan, and sent its troops by this route to the Rhine valley and the Netherlands. It was equally a point of French policy to close the pass, and break the enemy's line of communications. With so many interests crossing one another, the position of a ruler in the Valtelline must have been rather like that of a policeman on point duty at Carfax.

The religious quarrels had led to rioting and massacre in 1619. The international struggle for the pass had ended in the occupation of the valley by the Spaniards in 1620; and though they promised to evacuate it the next year, it was obvious that they would only do so under compulsion. When Richelieu became minister in 1624, negotiations were still going on. In July of that year a meeting of the State Council was held, at which he gave his views on the whole situation. The Memorandum was reprinted in his *Memoirs*, and it gives so good an idea of the scope and character of his diplomacy that I want to summarize it here.

First, he says, Spain has behaved very badly in the whole matter. In spite of its promise to evacuate the place, 'one of the Commissioners of the Duke of Feria and the Archduke Leopold had said, not long before, to persons worthy of belief, that, if they could get six months' grace, all the Kings in the world could not make them loosen their hold on the Valtelline.' Secondly, the Grisons are ancient allies of the King of France, and he has a perfect right to help them to defend their property—though the Swiss have only themselves to thank for their present troubles, since they have been intriguing with Spain and Venice against France. Next—this is so characteristic that I will quote *Richelieu's* own words—'The interest of France and of the whole of Europe is involved: the union of the separated states of the house of Austria outbalances the power of France, which secures the liberty of Christianity.' Fourthly, an argument for active intervention: 'if we do nothing, Spain will think us afraid, and our allies will desert us. Fifth, the worst maladies are those with complications. The Valtelline business is one of these. It involves questions in Switzerland, Flanders, Germany, and France itself—for we must not give an opening to the Huguenots or financiers for making troubles at home. So we must begin by sending the nobles back to their provinces, fortifying the frontiers, and raising enough troops to keep both nobles and Protestants quiet.

Then, sixthly, we must try to get the Pope to persuade the Spaniards to give up the Valtelline: if he won't, the Grisons must do their part, and the Swiss must help them. Next, to prevent Spanish troops being sent from Milan, or Spanish gold from Genoa, we must attack the Genoese in the name of Savoy (the Zucarel dispute will serve as a *casus belli*). Then we must keep Spain busy in Flanders by trying to relieve Breda [which the Spaniards were besieging], and by getting the United Provinces to make fresh efforts. Ninth, to keep the Catholic League in Germany employed, we must urge the King of England to finance the King of Denmark for the recovery of the Palatinate [which Tilly had just conquered for Ferdinand], and we must use Mansfeld's army for the same purpose. But we mustn't overdo this, or exasperate the League; so it will be best to hold Mansfeld back for six months (England paying his expenses), whilst we try to make Maximilian of Bavaria come to terms with James of England, and with his son-in-law, the Elector Palatine. In all this the Pope will be on our side, because he can see that our whole policy is in the interests of religion, and because his political position, like that of other princes, requires a balance of power between the Bourbons and the Hapsburgs. Finally, we must act with dexterity, to avoid an open break with Spain, which might be fatal to Christianity. But if the Spaniards take offence at our helping the Grisons, everyone will be against them, all Christendom will be on our side, and we can hope for a good and glorious success.'

I need not follow out Richelieu's attempts to put this policy into practice. We have seen some of them from a rather different angle in dealing with the last part of the Thirty Years' War. As to the Valtelline, France won it in 1635; in 1639 she lost it again; in the end the valley people gained religious toleration, but remained under Spanish rule. I have drawn attention to this bit of history mainly to illustrate Richelieu's grasp of international politics, and to show how his diplomacy followed out a central idea—that of breaking through the Hapsburg ring round France —into almost inconceivable ramifications. He is a master player at the game of statesmanship; studying his opponent's mind, and knowing his own; realizing just what use can be made of each piece on the board; calculating in advance the effect of each move, and of others that will follow from it; co-ordinating every means to the single end of winning the game.

VI

At the head of Richelieu's home policy we may put his own maxim, 'Il faut pourvoir au coeur'—'the health of a country depends upon its heart.' His aim at home was the counterpart of his aim abroad. His constructive mind, which saw how every situation in Europe might be made to serve the interests of French foreign policy, saw also how every class in France might be made to serve the interests of the French crown. Unity was his watchword: and in France as he knew it the only practicable centre of unity was the throne. So he set himself to destroy political independence at home, as a step towards destroying political rivalry abroad. We have seen how, from 1629 onwards, he carried out his policy against Spain and Austria. We must now see how we gained freedom to do so by destroying the political power of the Huguenots and of the French nobility between 1624 and 1629.

When Richelieu became Minister the position of the Huguenots was still regulated by the Edict of Nantes. This settlement bore clear marks both of the genius of its author, Henry IV, and of the difficult situation in which it had been drawn up. It gave the Huguenots not only a limited freedom of worship and citizenship, which was their due, but also a political and even military independence, which they had been strong enough to demand. Henry's own qualities as ruler, and the exhaustion of the country after thirty years of civil war, had made this arrangement workable. But since his death it had not been honestly carried out by either side. The Catholic majority used their superior position to practise indirect persecution of the Protestants: the Huguenot minority used their synods and cities of refuge to organize opposition, not merely against the Catholics, but against the crown. Richelieu was not a religious but a political persecutor. He could tolerate a church within a church, but he could not tolerate a state within a state. He determined to crush the political independence of the Huguenots.

In 1625, when France was engaged with Spain in the Valtelline, there were Protestant risings at La Rochelle, and in the Cevennes.

Richelieu was not strong enough to deal with two enemies at once, and came to terms. Two years later La Rochelle rose again, first helped and then abandoned by the incompetent Buckingham. It was a very strong place, with a population of 40,000 and a tradition of independence—the chief symbol of political Huguenotism; Richelieu determined to make an example of it. After nearly a year's siege, the repulse of two English fleets, and the death of 15,000 of its inhabitants, the city surrendered. Richelieu allowed no reprisals, but pulled down every stone of the fortifications. With them fell the resistance of the Huguenots. Next year was published the Grace of Alais—not a treaty such as had previously been made between the Catholics and the Protestants, but a concession on the part of the crown to its rebellious subjects. It left the Huguenots their liberty of worship, and their rights as citizens; but it took away from them their synods and their fortified cities. No doubt this left them more than ever at the mercy of the Catholics. Richelieu might claim that he was tolerant; but by withdrawing the political safeguards of toleration he prepared the way for Louis XIV's revocation of the Edict of Nantes. At the moment, however, and for his immediate purpose of national unity, the policy was effective. Richelieu had no further trouble with the Protestants. And it was noticed that, when the disorders of the Fronde broke out twenty years later, the Huguenots took no part in them.

Next the nobles. This was a longer struggle, and Richelieu's success was less final. He had to deal, not with an organized party, but with a series of plots. The centre of trouble was not in distant provinces, but in Paris, and at Court. Restive or ambitious nobles found support in Gaston of Orleans, the King's brother who, until the birth of Louis XIV in 1638, was heir to the throne; in the Spanish party round the Queen, Anne of Austria; and in Mary de Medici, the Queen Mother, who could never forgive Richelieu for superseding her in the government of the country. Mme *de Staël* says that the French are born revolutionaries, but bad plotters. Certainly every intrigue against Richelieu was a complete failure. The Cardinal's spies kept him well informed; and once a plotter was convicted, no rank or favour availed to save him from the King's gaoler, or the King's executioner Forty-seven sentences of death for high political offences were passed during Richelieu's Ministry, and twenty-six of them were carried out. The victims included five Dukes, four Counts, a Marshal of France, and the King's special favourite, Cinq Mars. The King's brother could not be punished. But he could be frightened. Almost the only extant sermon of Richelieu's, preached to the Court before the trial of a disloyal noble against whom Gaston had turned King's evidence, is an attempt to put the fear of Hell into his soul. It is eloquent enough; but the Cardinal must have felt handicapped by having to use such uncongenial methods.

Whilst disloyal nobles lost their liberty, or their lives, even loyal nobles might lose their homes. Castles, except where they were needed for the defence of the frontiers, were systematically pulled down. Duelling, one of the curses of the times, was forbidden, and rigorously punished. In every way the nobles were made to feel that there was only one power in the land, and that was the King's. It is impossible to feel much sympathy for them. Some were plotting against the government, and in face of a foreign enemy. Many more valued their class privileges above their duty to the country. But there is generally something wrong with the government of a state, as there is in the management of a school, or in the discipline of a regiment, when punishments are numerous or excessive. 'The despotism' of Cardinal Richelieu may not have 'entirely destroyed the originality of the French character—its loyalty, its frankness, its independence' [*de Staël*]; but it did much to destroy the political usefulness of the class which should have been the chief support of the Crown, and so to leave the monarchy isolated in face of a disfranchised and discontented middle class. As Richelieu's treatment of the Huguenots pointed to the revocation of the Edict of Nantes, so his treatment of the nobility led to the troubles of the Fronde, and prepared the way for the Revolution. At the moment it added another figure to his score of unpopularity. When he died, someone wrote this ironical epitaph for him:

>KIND RICHELIEU'S BODY HERE DOTH LIE,
>WHO NEVER HURT A SINGLE FLY—
>A VERY JUST AND PEACEFUL FELLOW:
>AS FOR HIS SOUL, IF GOD NO BETTER
>FORGIVES THAN HE FORGAVE HIS DEBTOR,
>I RATHER FEAR IT'S GONE TO HELL, OH! [*Roca.*]

VII

Something remains to be said about other sides of Richelieu's home government.

One of his first needs was an army and a navy. His 'Ordonnance' of 1619 set the pattern which, in many respects, the French army followed for a hundred years and more. When Louis XIII came to the throne he had 10,000 men; when he died, 164,000. A navy was created out of nothing. In 1626 it was necessary to borrow Dutch ships for the siege of La Rochelle. In 1642 there were two French fleets at sea, numbering eighty sail. Richelieu was one of the first modern statesmen to realize the importance of sea power. We have seen it in his Memorandum of 1624. We see it again in a paper published among his letters, in which he describes with great indignation how, when Sully sailed as ambassador to England, he was summoned to dip his flag to an English vessel in the Channel, and how, when he refused, the British skipper fired three shots, which 'pierced the hull of his ship, and the hearts of all good Frenchmen,' and compelled him to acknowledge our supremacy at sea [*Avenel*].

Richelieu gave the French monarchy a new impulse, but no new ideas. The traditional government by the King and the King's friends was now represented by the King, the King's Ministers, and the King's Council—the *Conseil du Roi*, or *d'Etat*. This last sat for different kinds of business—provincial, financial, legal, and so on—on different days; the Secretaries of State, who had been merely the Clerks of the Council, were beginning to become departmental Ministers. But they had as yet no independent responsibility, and Richelieu was careful to keep foreign diplomacy in his own hands.

In the government of the provinces increasing use was made of the Intendants, who, since the time of Francis I, had occasionally been employed to supersede the seigneurs. They were given summary jurisdiction, and executive authority in matters of police and finance. Nothing did more to centralize the government of France: but nothing did less to create (what was more needed) national French feeling. Meanwhile, the natural organs of public opinion—the provincial Estates—were discouraged almost out of existence; and the one body representing the nation, the one constitutional check on the power of the Crown—the

States General—was never allowed to meet. Richelieu thought himself better acquainted than they were with what France needed, and better able to carry it out alone. But by not consulting the people he rendered it unfit to be consulted. By being so strong himself he made his successors too weak. Richelieu created the French monarchy: the French nation was the work of the Revolution.

In financial administration Sully's good tradition was not preserved. The expenditure during Richelieu's ministry was more than quadrupled, and the taxes proportionately increased. The peasantry, forced to pay five times as much 'taille' as before, fell into a terrible state of poverty. But little more than 50 per cent of what was extorted reached the Treasury. Too much was embezzled, too much went in expenses of collection, too much was diverted for local expenditure. To raise more money, offices were sold wholesale: but out of the 500 million livres so raised, 150 millions could not be accounted for. There were peasant risings in 1634 and 1639, and the cruelty with which they were put down made Richelieu as much hated by the country population as he was by the Huguenots or by the nobility.

VIII

You may wonder how it was that, in face of such difficulties, the Cardinal could carry on. The answer lies partly in his army and in his spies, partly in the success of his foreign policy; but mostly in the support given him by the King. Richelieu's enemies said that he terrorized Louis; that he exaggerated the dangers of rebellion, in order to make the King dependent on him; and that during his last illness Louis was heard to declare that the Cardinal had been the death of him. It was at least commonly supposed that the rôles of Minister and King were reversed. A popular epitaph on Louis ran:

> THIS KING WAS VALET TO A PRIEST,
> AND PLAYED HIS PART WITHOUT DISASTER;
> HE'D ALL THE VIRTUES OF A MAN,
> BUT NEVER ONE THAT FITS A MASTER. [*Roca.*]

But Louis was in fact more than a brave man and a good soldier: he was a sensible, hard-working sovereign, and jealous of his authority. He generally left matters of policy to Richelieu; but insisted on being kept informed of what was done: and when he took the initiative, as he often did, in military affairs, he expected Richelieu to carry out his orders. The Cardinal himself once said that 'it was more difficult to conquer the four foot square of the King's study than all the battlefields of Europe' [*Malet*]. Louis, for his part, admired the Minister, defended him against every attack, and carried on his policy during the short time that he outlived his death. It was a real partnership, and I think that Louis' share in it has been understated. He was not a king who naturally caught attention. In character more English than French, he had neither the geniality of Henry IV nor the grand manner of Louis XIV. His reputation has suffered both from Richelieu's unpopularity among the memoir-writers of his own day, and from his popularity with the historians of later times [cf. *Topin*].

Of Richelieu himself we may say what Wellington said of Napoleon, that he was not a person but a principle. His virtues were dedicated to the service of the State: his crimes, he would have urged, were excused by it. His two great designs—the unity of his country at home, and its supremacy abroad—if not (as Cardinal de Retz suggested) as great as those of Caesar or Alexander, were sufficiently ambitious; and their success created the France of Louis XIV—a society which set the fashion to all Europe, and a government which was the last word in unenlightened despotism. We shall soon see the limitations of that society, and the disasters to which that government led. We may blame Richelieu for not trusting the nation more, for not educating it in self-government. But we can hardly blame him for not being a prophet. He achieved the most that is generally asked of a statesman—a policy suited to the nation as he knew it, and the power to carry it out. With that, he was no self-seeker, but a genuine patriot. It is said that on his death-bed he refused to be spared the questions from which high ecclesiastics were usually exempt. 'Treat me,' he said to his confessor, 'as an ordinary Christian.' 'Well then, do you believe the articles of the Faith?' 'Absolutely; and I would that God would grant me a thousand lives, so that I might give them all to the Faith, and to the Church.' 'Do you forgive your enemies?' 'With all my heart; and I pray God to forgive me if I have ever had any other intention than the good of the State and of the Church' [*Topin*].

LECTURE XII

THE MINORITY OF LOUIS XIV

I

When Richelieu died, it seemed possible that all his work might be undone. But on the Cardinal's own recommendation the King appointed as his successor his understudy, the Italian Mazzarini, whom the French called Mazarin. Seven months later Louis himself was dead, leaving as his heir a boy of five. The Queen Mother, Anne of Austria, became Regent for Louis XIV. She had hated the French Cardinal: she loved (and, some say, married) the Italian, and kept him as her minister. And so, partly by a statesman's foresight, and partly by the accident of a woman's affection, the old policy ran on for another eighteen years, and Richelieu's France passed almost without a break into the France of Louis XIV.

Of one part of Richelieu's policy there is nothing more to be said. The Huguenots had learnt their lesson, and gave no further trouble. On the other hand, the repression of the nobles proved to be incomplete, and they contributed as much as the discontented middle class to the disorders of the Fronde. But the new power and prestige that Richelieu had given to the Crown enabled the Government to survive this bad time. Abroad Mazarin had only to carry the Cardinal's programme to its logical conclusions—the humbling of Austria at the Treaty of Westphalia, and of Spain at the Peace of the Pyrenees. The first five years of Mazarin's eighteen (1643-48) were peaceful; the next five (1648-53) were the years of the Fronde; the last eight (1653-61) saw the end of the war with Spain, and set the European stage for the entry of Louis XIV.

II

Mazarin was an Italian of humble birth, once an officer in the Papal Guard, and educated in all the refinements of Rome and Madrid. Richelieu had picked him out for his knowledge of European politics, and rewarded him with a Cardinal's hat. But no one was ever less ecclesiastical. A big, handsome, insinuating man, he looked less like a cardinal than a cavalier, and lived less like a priest (if he was one) than an aesthete. Louis XIV's earliest memories were of hours spent in the Cardinal's perfumed rooms, with their wonderful furniture and statues; of the Cardinal's tame monkeys, and of his ingenious lift [*Bertrand*]. It was at Mazarin's house that he met and fell in love with Marie Mancini, the Cardinal's niece. But Paris disapproved of the Cardinal and all his works. Ever since Charles VIII's invasion of Lombardy, France had seen and suffered from Italians at Court —Catherine de Medici, Mary de Medici, Concini and his wife; and now, people complained, there was to be another, and—to make matters worse—a protégé of the tyrant they had so long hated. But Mazarin made good, and became an exception to the rule that France is best governed by Frenchmen.

In character and methods he was quite different from Richelieu. Neither violent nor vindictive, he would sooner forgive an enemy than destroy him. With plenty of moral courage, he had little physical bravery, or aptitude for war. His manners were simple and easy-going, where Richelieu's had been stiff and overbearing. Richelieu never moved about without a crowd of attendants: Mazarin was easy to approach, and took off his hat to everyone he met. If this disarmed his enemies, it also misled them. They thought they could do what they liked with him. It took them five years to discover their mistake.

Meanwhile the country was slowly recovering from the shock of Richelieu's ministry. The Cardinal, said *de Retz*, had never realized how discontented the people were: he had taken silence for consent. He 'set about treating the country, like an amateur doctor, with violent remedies, which seemed to restore its strength, but really only stimulated it, and ended by exhausting it, body and limbs. Cardinal Mazarin was too inexperienced a physician to realize how low the country had been brought. He did not keep up its strength by his predecessor's private prescription: he made it still weaker by bleeding it, till it fell into a lethargy; and he was so stupid as to mistake this artificial repose for a healthy sleep. The provinces, which had been abandoned to the plundering methods of the Superintendents, remained crushed and depressed under the weight of their misfortunes . . . The parlements, which had so recently groaned under Richelieu's tyranny, were rendered insensible to present measures by their lively and recent memory of the past. The nobles, most of whom had been chased out of the country, were now lazily asleep, delighted to be back in bed. If this general state of indolence had been carefully attended to, the lethargy might perhaps have been maintained for some time longer. But, as the doctor took it for healthy sleep, he prescribed no remedy for it. The illness got worse, and went to the patient's head. Paris woke up, came to itself, groaned . . . and went into a fit.'

III

This fit was the Fronde. A *frondeur* was a 'slinger'—of something more serious than mud or stones. Who started slinging, and why?

It began with the Paris Parlement. France at this time kept two relics of popular and constitutional government. The Estates General was the relic of a parliament without whose consent the King had not been able to raise taxes or impose laws. The Paris Parlement was the relic of a Privy Council without whose sanction the King's decrees could not have the force of law. The Estates General had last met in 1614, and was not to meet again for 170 years. The only body in the country which could in any sense stand up for the people against the Crown was the Paris Parlement. Its original character had been lost long ago. Instead of a Privy Council it had become a Court of Law. But circumstances, if not its constitution, gave it political power. Its function of registering the royal edicts, in practice a mere formality, could be represented as equivalent to our 'Consent of Parliament'. The purchasable and hereditary nature of its membership made it a middle-class House of Lords, at a time when the historical House of Lords—the Clergy and Nobility of the Estates—had ceased to function. And during an interregnum, such as had occurred on the death of Louis XIII, the Parlement was the only body which could conveniently be called in to vary a royal will, or to regulate a Regency.

The Parlement was for the people, but not of the people. It did not even represent the middle class as a whole, but only the upper middle class—the magistrates, financiers, and government officials. The lower middle class, the *petite bourgeoisie*—the soundest and most enterprising part of the nation—was unprivileged and unrepresented. Its day was still to come—in 1789. In 1648 it was still the day of the 'haute bourgeoisie,' a class in some respects more selfish and corrupt than the nobility. It was Louis XIII's favourite distraction (they said) to sit at the window with one of his ministers, and to look out for unregistered coats of arms on passing carriages. 'Do you recognize that device?' he would ask the minister. If he didn't, so much the worse for the owner of the carriage. The Parlement of 1648 was full of such men, whose money cut them off both from the middle class which they had deserted and from the aristocracy into which they were trying to force their way.

This Parlement fought primarily for its own rights, not for those of the people. It refused, for instance, to register new taxes unless its own members were exempted from them. But it also drew up 27 Articles, demanding, among other reforms, the abolition of the Intendants, the submission of all proposals for taxation to its deliberation and consent, and the right of every person arrested to be brought to trial within 24 hours. This was a kind of Petition of Rights, expressing the bitterest grievances of the country, and attacking the privileges of the Crown in some of their most vital points. One has only to remember what was happening in England at this moment to see the significance of it. The English Petition of Rights had been accepted by Charles I just twenty years before. The Long Parliament was eight years old. The year before the Fronde broke out (1648) the Civil War came to an end, and the English King was a prisoner in the hands of his Parliament. In January, 1649, Charles was put on his trial. Before the month was out he was beheaded.

These things were well known in Paris. Since the Thirty Years' War prevented any travelling in Germany, and the Inquisition made Italy unhealthy for Protestants, Englishmen came to finish their education—an education of manners rather than of books—in France. There was also a French colony in England; for in 1650 appeared the first number of a French paper printed in London, the *Nouvelles Ordinaires de Londres,* and a French version of the *London Gazette* continued to be published throughout the reigns of Charles II and James II [*Bastide*].

There was, indeed, no question of the French Fronde going to the lengths of the English Revolution. It was not an attack upon the Monarchy. Richelieu, indeed, represents de Retz as an organizer of Republican propaganda, and at heart a regicide. But in any case de Retz had little following. And in his own account of the rioting in Paris he says that he met a man carrying about an image of the monk who killed Henry III, with the inscription, 'Vive St. Jacques Clément!' 'This,' he says, 'I ordered to be broken, amid shouts of "A bas Mazarin!" and "Vive le Roi!"' Though there might, then, be a French Westminster, there would be no Whitehall. The Paris Parlement would confine itself to the spoken part of the Long Parliament, as the champion of vested interests against absolutism. But one can imagine how, with their minds full of the wars of religion, and their eyes fixed on the catastrophe of Charles I, Mazarin and the Court party were decidedly nervous.

Their safety lay in the army. Two months after the Parlement made its challenge, Condé beat the Spaniards at Lens: within four months the German war ended in the Peace of Westphalia (October, 1648). In January, 1649, the Regent, Mazarin, and the young King retired from Paris, which was by now in the hands of a revolutionary mob, and set Condé to besiege it. Two months later the city surrendered, and the Parliamentary Fronde was at an end.

But meanwhile the trouble had spread beyond Paris, and become more serious than barricades. There was one class in the country —the nobility—who were always ready for rebellion; who never forgot the independence they had enjoyed during the Wars of Religion, and never forgave the punishment they had received at the hands of Richelieu. 'For the last 25 years,' wrote *Mazarin* ironically, 'it has been their daily despair to see France so badly governed, and yet to have failed in all their remedies—revolts, plots, parties, seizures of towns, and corrupting the minds of princes and intelligent men with the Spanish gold that they have brought into the country . . . Time after time they have left the country, either from fear of punishment, when their crimes were discovered, or because they hadn't the heart to remain in a kingdom so unhappy and so ill-managed. When the warlike spirit has come uncomfortably near them, they have gone to look for fighting elsewhere.' Some of these men, notably Condé's brother Conti, had already joined in the Parliamentary Fronde:

they now started a fresh revolt, which may be called the Fronde of the Princes (1650-52). Mazarin, their special enemy, was forced to retire to Germany, whence he kept up a cipher correspondence with the Queen Regent, discussing every change in the situation, and scheming for his return. Soon there was civil war between Condé (now for the Fronde) and a royalist army under Turenne, and the unedifying sight was seen of the two greatest French generals of the day fighting against one another. Nor was Turenne's patriotism proof: but fortunately the two could not agree to betray their country at the same time. And when Condé, worsted at Paris, proposed to call in Spanish aid from Flanders, every decent *frondeur* felt that the matter was going too far. The revolt collapsed. Louis XIV made a triumphant entry into Paris (October, 1652). Mazarin followed a few months later.

IV

What were the results of the Fronde? Its immediate effects were seen in the character and policy of the young King, Louis XIV. It is just possible that, if he had succeeded peacefully to his father's throne, if he had felt that all classes in the kingdom were doing their best to forget their private differences, and to support the Crown, he would have reigned in a more liberal spirit. If there had been no unconstitutional reaction against Richelieu's system, it might have been modified by constitutional means. But Louis could never forget his flight from Paris in the winter of '48-9, or the years he spent, from eleven to thirteen, as an exile in the provinces. He could never forgive the Parlement for its pretensions, or the nobles for their intrigues, or the Paris mob for its disloyalty. He set himself, from the moment he regained power, to reinforce order and obedience. His panacea, like Richelieu's, was the absolutism of the monarchy, which had hardly been challenged even by the Fronde. And the very weakness to which the revolt had reduced France made it tempting and possible to apply it.

But the Fronde had an importance beyond its influence upon the policy of Louis XIV. It was a foretaste of the French Revolution. It was not, as we have seen, anti-monarchical—indeed, it did not take shape in any theory of government—and it ended by tightening the chains which it had attempted to shake off.

But the French nation has always had a dual personality. In one state of mind it is constitutional, and likes strong government: in another it is revolutionary, and likes anarchy. With one voice it talks the language of monarchy, with another the language of Republicanism. The interest of the Fronde lies in the emergence, for a few years, of this second self, which hardly reappears until the Revolution.

There was one curious half-way stage. The Memoirs in which de Retz described his part in the Fronde were not published till 1717, just after the death of Louis XIV, and the end of his fifty-five years' tyranny. Their effect was not, as the publishers expected, to show Frenchmen the dangers of anarchy, but rather to put them in love with revolution; and their appearance was followed by a plot against the Regency, in which Paris ladies and Spanish diplomatists intrigued together in the best style of the Fronde. There were too many interregna in French history. Perhaps if there had been no Regencies there would have been no Revolution.

V

I need not say much about the last eight years of Mazarin's ministry (1653-61). There being less need now to conciliate opposition than to intimidate it, he out-Richelieus Richelieu; goes about with a hundred mounted men, and keeps a bodyguard of three hundred foot; fills his palace (now the Bibliothèque Nationale) with pictures and objects of art, and marries his nieces to dukes and princes. Unlike Richelieu, he set the bad example, which was only too readily followed by other officials, of using his public position to make a private fortune. 'The King sometimes demanded money of Fouquet (the Superintendent of Finance), whose answer was this: "Sire, there is none in your Majesty's coffers: but the Cardinal will lend you some" ' [*Voltaire*]. France suffered more, in the long run, from self-seeking, complaisant Mazarins than from severe but incorruptible Richelieus.

But Mazarin's main work for France was, after all, his foreign policy, with its two great achievements—the Austrian settlement, and the end of the war with Spain·

The Peace of Westphalia (1648) did not merely end the Thirty Years' War, both as a civil war in Germany and as part of the struggle between the Bourbons and the Hapsburgs: it was also a settlement of all the outstanding quarrels in Europe, except those between France and Spain (the Peace of the Pyrenees, 1659), and between the Baltic Powers (the Peace of Oliva, 1660). The map of Europe in 1648 was the first which showed the political results of the Renaissance and Reformation. In its main outlines, it remained fixed until the time of Napoleon.

The Thirty Years' War had begun as a religious war, and the Peace of Westphalia was primarily a religious settlement. One of the failings of the Peace of Augsburg in 1555, and one of the causes of war in 1618, had been the non-recognition of the Calvinists. The treaty of 1648 gave them legal status within the Empire. Another ancient difficulty had been the 'secularization' of Catholic estates. This was now met, partly by arranging that each state should in future remain Catholic or Protestant according to its condition in 1624; and partly by stipulating that any citizen who dissented from the established religion of his state might emigrate to another without forfeiture of his property. To enforce this settlement the Imperial Court was reconstituted so as to consist of an equal number of Catholic and Protestant members. Such was the rather crude arrangement arrived at after thirty years of internecine war. The old intolerant principle, 'cujus regio ejus religio,' must still be the basis of everything. You may limit the princes' power of persecution: but you must not touch their rights, as owners of property, over the 'dead souls' of their subjects. There was more hope for religious freedom, after all, in a single country, large and strong enough to stand the strain of religious toleration, than in a federation of small states, each of which was too weak to be anything but intolerant.

On the other hand, if the Thirty Years' War had given Germany no Edict of Nantes, it had defeated once and for all the policy represented by the Edict of Restitution. Ferdinand's scheme to Catholicize Germany had definitely failed. The Protestant north remained divided from the Catholic south very much as it is today.

Such was the religious settlement. On the political side the Peace of Westphalia was equally decisive against Ferdinand's designs, and left the semblance of Imperial powers even more shadowy than before. One article of the treaty reaffirmed the political liberties of the separate states in all matters of individual interest: another article reaffirmed their right to be consulted in everything concerning their common welfare. And, as a final precaution against Austrian ambition, the Constitution of the Empire was guaranteed by the signatory Powers.

At the same time Austria lost much of its superiority over the other German states in point of territory and population. In the south, Bavaria kept the Upper Palatinate: in the north, Brandenburg gained Eastern Pomerania, Magdeburg, Halberstadt, and Minden. Bavaria, as the protégé of France, and guardian of the Upper Danube, was to become the chief obstacle to Austria in southern Germany. Brandenburg was to become its rival, and ultimately its supplanter, in the north.

That was not all. Sweden, as the reward of its intervention, kept Bremen, Werden, and Western Pomerania, controlling the mouths of the Elbe, Weser, and Oder—the chief outlets of German trade; and France retained the greater part of Alsace. To complete the dismemberment of the Empire, the independence of Switzerland and of the United Provinces was finally recognized.

As a result of this set-back in Central Europe, coinciding (as it happened) with a revival of the Turkish power, we find Austria during the next century looking more and more eastwards for territorial compensation, and an outlet for its trade. Hence the Turkish wars of the eighteenth, the Balkan wars of the nineteenth and twentieth centuries, and in 1914-18 the question of Salonica.

Summarily, the Peace of Westphalia recognized for the first time, and fixed for a considerable period, the Balance of Power in Europe. For more than a century past—ever since the accession of Charles V—France had been afraid of encirclement by the Austro-Spanish Hapsburgs. After 1648 (with its sequel in 1659) that danger was definitely averted. Austria was paralysed by the failure of its scheme for German unity, by the growth of rival powers within the Empire, by Swedish supremacy in the Baltic, and by French influence on the Rhine. The Spanish power was broken, and the Spanish Hapsburgs became 'poor relations' of the Kings of France. The centre of gravity in Germany was shifting from south to north. The centre of gravity in Europe was moving westwards across the Rhine. During the succeeding half-century the danger was not of Hapsburg but of Bourbon supremacy. At the next settlement (1713) it might be necessary to readjust the balance in favour of Austria.

VI

The Peace of Westphalia was followed eleven years later by its corollary, the Peace of the Pyrenees (1659). From 1648 to 1653 Philip IV of Spain had taken advantage of the Fronde to carry on war in Flanders; and for five years the north-eastern parts of France suffered what Germany had suffered for thirty. It was not till 1658 that Mazarin found a way of ending the war, by making an alliance with the foreign hero of his enemy de Retz. In return for the cession of Dunkirk to England, Cromwell sent over 6,000 of his invincible Ironsides. The Spaniards were defeated at the battle of the Dunes, and Philip, at the end of his resources, signed peace the next year. The terms were hard. Spain ceded to France Roussillon and Cerdagne in the Pyrenees, in the north Artois, and certain places in Luxembourg and Flanders. But the indignity of the surrender was softened by the marriage of Louis XIV to Marie Thérèse, the Infanta of Spain—the beginning of a family alliance which was the source of more than half a century's ambitions, intrigues, and war.

We have seen why Austria failed in the Thirty Years' War. It will be well to end by asking what were the causes of the collapse of Spain. For it was nothing less: at the end of the sixteenth century Spain, under Philip II, was still the most powerful country in Europe: by the middle of the seventeenth century it was reduced to the second rank; and it has never recovered the position which it then lost. Why was this?

There were some permanent reasons in the character of the country and of the people which we discovered in our first survey of Spain, and upon which I need not now go back—geographical isolation, economic backwardness, religious fanaticism, and a quixotic pride which unfitted the Spaniard either to rule or to be ruled. Even in the middle of the seventeenth century these causes were having their effects, and Spain was failing to keep pace with civilization: a century later it seemed to have dropped out of the race. 'Spain,' wrote *Lord Chesterfield* in 1752, 'is surely the only country in Europe that has been barbarizing itself every day more and more, as all other countries have been civilizing themselves. Since the conquest of that people by the Romans, their most shining period is without question the time of the Moors; and ever since their expulsion, civil and ecclesiastical tyranny has acted in concert, and successfully, in scattering [*i.e.* spreading] that general darkness and ignorance which are necessary for their views.'

The national ills of Spain might have been remedied by good rulers. But the blight which affected the country seems to have fallen with special severity upon its kings. Philip II was prepared to ruin his kingdom for the sake of religion; and this was the only one of his crusades which was at all successful. The expulsion of the Moriscoes, the enforcement of the Inquisition, and the war against the United Provinces, were carried out with fatal conscientiousness. Philip III (1598-1621) had no idea of a king's duties. His time was divided between hunting, dancing, and the practices of devotion, between bouts of gaiety and fits of religious melancholia. The misgovernment of the country was carried on by a favourite named Lerma, who at last retired with a large fortune and a Cardinal's hat. The court expenses, more than trebled since Philip II's death, were met by ruinous taxation.

The reign of Philip IV (1621-65) was a time of political decadence, but also (as often happens, by some unexplained law of compensation) a golden age of literature and art. He came to the throne at an unhappy time, and he had no illusions either about his own incompetence, or about the desperate state of the country. Soon after his accession he wrote a report for his Council, describing the low state to which Spain had been reduced—its finances exhausted, its currency debased, its fleet non-existent, its army discredited, its prestige gone—all 'because God Almighty decreed that it should be so; and [notice this conclusion] I myself experience this every day; for no matter how adequate may be the remedies that I adopt, our sins suffice to condemn all our affairs to the most miserable state imaginable' [*C.M.H.*].

I said that Philip had no illusions. I was wrong. He suffered from the worst of all illusions—religious fatalism. His grandfather, believing it was God's will that the country should be ruined for religion, had ruined it. He, believing it was God's will that the country should remain ruined, left it so. For some twenty years, indeed, the providential fall of Spain was arrested by the government of Olivares, an able statesman, hard-working, ambitious, and masterful; save for lack of opportunity, a Spanish Richelieu. But during the second half of his reign Philip's fatalism met with the disaster it deserved. The costly and unsuccessful fighting in Italy and Flanders, the Catalonian revolt (1640), the independence of Portugal (1640), the rebellion of Naples (1647), and finally the Peace of the Pyrenees (1659), hastened the break-up of the Spanish Empire. Meanwhile Philip, who was too lazy to sign his name on State documents (he used a stamp instead), wrote plays for the theatres at Madrid, and patronized the group of writers and artists—Calderon, Velasquez, Zurbaran, Murillo—who made Spain great in its fall. He was a bad king and a bad man: the famous portrait of him by Velasquez is a chapter on the causes of the decay of Spain.

The curse that rested upon the Spanish Hapsburgs came to its climax in Charles II (1665-1700). He was a wretched relic of his race—a chronic invalid, almost a monstrosity. His conversation, says the English ambassador, who knew him well, consisted of 'I dare say' and 'I can well believe it.' When well, he was greedy. 'He has a ravenous stomach, and swallows all he eats whole; for his nether jaw stands out so much that his two rows of teeth cannot meet; to compensate which, he has a prodigious wide throat, so that a gizzard or liver of a hen passes down whole.' When ill, he was a pitiable object. 'The King is so very weak, he can scarcely lift his hand to his head to feed himself; and so extremely melancholy, that neither his buffoons nor puppet-shows can in the least divert him from fancying everything that is said or done to be a temptation of the devil; and never thinking himself safe but with his Confessor and two friars by his side, whom he makes lie in his chamber every night' [*Stanhope*].

VII

So ended the Spanish Hapsburgs, and the power of Spain. By the end of the seventeneth century Spain had no king worth the name, no government, no army, no navy, no trade, no money in the treasury. Only one institution flourished. The frequent and successful burning of heretics showed that there still presided over the providential ruin of the country a rich, orthodox, and efficient Church.

LECTURE XIII

LOUIS XIV: HOME AFFAIRS

I

On the seventh of September, 1652, two famous Englishmen—John Evelyn, the diarist, and John Hobbes, the philosopher—sat in a window at Paris, and saw Louis XIV ride through the streets on his public entry into the capital after the troubles of the Fronde. 'The King himself,' says *Evelyn*, 'like a young Apollo, was in a suit so covered with rich embroidery, that one could perceive nothing of the stuff under it; he went almost the whole way with his hat in hand, saluting the ladies and acclamators, who had filled the windows with their beauty, and the air with "Vive le Roi!" He seemed a prince of grave yet sweet countenance.'

Eight years later Mazarin died 'as gracefully as he had lived, and handed on Richelieu's mantle to the new King. Louis, now 22, determined to rule for himself. He sent for the Secretaries of State, and said to them, 'Gentlemen, hitherto I have been content to let my affairs be managed for me. In future I shall be my own Prime Minister. You will help me with your advice, when I ask for it. I order you to seal no documents without my orders, to sign nothing without my consent' [*Malet*]. From that day of March, 1661, till the day of his death in September, 1715—a period of nearly fifty-five years—Louis and Louis alone was the real and personal ruler of France.

II

Louis had been little better educated, in the ordinary sense of the word, than other French princes. He had a whole staff of tutors, but paid no attention to them, and preferred an open-air life. He had been taught the usual dancing, drawing, and riding. He had picked up a little French history. He liked poetry and romances (says *Voltaire*), 'which by pictures of gallantry and heroism secretly flattered his own character. He read the tragedies of Corneille,' and modelled his manners on the Spanish taste of the day, which his mother Anne of Austria had introduced into Court circles. From Marie Mancini, at an impressionable age, he learnt the poetry and the art of love. 'The King made a greater progress in this school of pleasure, from his first to his twentieth year, than he had done in that of the sciences under his preceptors,' from whom 'he had learnt hardly anything.' A translation of the first book of Caesar's *Commentaries* was, indeed, published under his name when he was only thirteen: but it would not be uncharitable to suppose that his Latin tutor had more than a little to do with it.

Badly educated in many respects, Louis had been well grounded in what a French King needed more than Classics—the art of government, and the art of war. Mazarin had been his tutor in the first, Turenne in the second; and he had been forced by circumstances, from an early age, to put their lessons into practice. He showed a great aptitude for the business of kingship. *Mazarin* once said 'that he had in him the makings of four Kings, and of one honest man.' In 1661 he was a 'Prince Charming'— brave, handsome, and courteous: a social favourite, yet never forgetting, or letting others forget, that he was a King. He never lost his personal charm; but as he played his part of King day after day, and year after year, there came a time when he could not become himself again, but must always be on the stage. How to be a king was the question which filled his mind day and night: being a king absorbed all his energies, employed all his faculties, and moulded his whole character. Many princes you can just label 'good' or 'bad,' like the Kings of Israel and Judah. Louis XIV you cannot judge at all, unless you know what kind of part he was trying to play. The important question about him is this: what was his idea of kingship?

Fortunately we have the best possible evidence on this point —Louis' own *Memoirs*. They only cover a few years of his reign; but the historical sections generally end with political or moral reflexions, intended for the Dauphin, and written (this was partly due to Louis' editors) rather in the style of the Book of Proverbs; and in these we are given a portrait gallery of Louis himself, taken from various points of view, and a collection of his *obiter dicta* on the subject of kingship.

First, it is clear, as we have already guessed, that Louis might have been a different kind of king—better in some ways, much worse in others—if it had not been for the Fronde. 'You must picture,' he writes, 'the state of affairs: dreadful convulsions all over the kingdom both before and after I came of age, and a foreign war, in which the troubles at home had made France lose a thousand opportunities: a prince of my own blood, the bearer of a noble name [Condé], at the head of the enemy: the State full of party feeling: the Parlements still holding and enjoying an usurped authority: at court, very little disinterested loyalty, and those of my subjects who seemed the most obedient often turning out to be the most rebellious; a Minister [Mazarin] re-established in power in spite of all these factions, who was very clever and very adroit, who loved me, and I him, and who had done me great services, but whose ideas and ways were naturally very different from mine, and whom (nevertheless) I could not contradict or discredit without danger of raising afresh against him, even by a false impression that he was in disgrace, the very storm which it had been so difficult to calm: myself still quite young . . . and not at the age at which men in private life begin to have full control over their affairs: knowing only too well the weight of the burden I had to bear, but not the extent of my capacity to bear it: in my heart of hearts, I will admit, putting the hope of fame before everything, even before life itself: but realizing at the same time that if my first moves did not lay the foundations of fame, they might deprive me for ever of the hope of achieving it; so that my plans seemed to be almost as much hindered as helped by my one and only desire for glory.'

This is a confession that would do anybody credit. It shows a healthy ambition, good sense, and moral courage—all of them great qualities in a King. You feel that Louis has learnt Mazarin's lesson, and is not likely to make the usual mistakes of a young man in a big position. And contrast his attitude towards the troubles of the Fronde with that of Philip IV towards the misfortunes of Spain. There is no talk of the miseries of the country being a punishment for its sins; no fatalistic acquiescence in bad government. The worse things are, the more there is for a King to do. The more helpless the situation, the greater the opportunity for glory. To the very end of his reign, when he was overwhelmed with public and private misfortunes, Louis never failed in moral courage. We shall have occasion to find how much of his success depended upon the accidents of his position, and the externals of royalty. It is well to realize from the first that these helps would have been useless to a smaller man; that Louis had in his own character the qualities which made him a great King.

Next, Louis shared the common belief of his age in the Divine Right of Kings. His earliest attempt at writing is the sentence, 'Homage is due to Kings, and they do whatever they like'— not a good lesson for a young prince, according to our notions, but a mere copybook maxim in the seventeenth century. Remember our James I's sentiments on the subject, fifty years earlier. Remember how in England as well as in France sick people thought they could be cured by a touch of the King's hand. One of Louis XIII's councillors, in a treatise on sovereignty, had said that 'Kings are instituted by God. Royalty is a supreme power entrusted to a single person. It is no more divisible than a point in geometry' [*Le Bret,* 1632]. Richelieu regarded kings as 'the living images of Divinity'; and Bossuet, in a treatise drawn up for the son of Louis XIV, wrote, 'The royal throne is not the throne of a man, but the throne of God himself. Princes act as ministers of God, and as His lieutenants on earth.' [*Malet*].

No one was more soaked in this assumption than Louis himself. But—this is the remarkable point—he always balances the Divine Right with what I may call the Divine Duty of Kings. Here, for instance, is a passage from his *Memoirs,* apropos of the question of rebellion. 'It must certainly be agreed,' he writes, 'that, however bad a prince may be, it is always a heinous crime for his subjects to rebel against him. He who gave men kings willed that they should be respected as His lieutenants, and reserved to Himself the right to question their conduct. It is His will that everyone who is born a subject should obey without discrimination. This law, as clear as it is universal, was not made only for the sake of princes: it is also for the good of the people themselves, on whom it is imposed, and who can never break it without exposing themselves to much worse evils than those against which they think to guard themselves by rebellion.' This is also, he goes on to argue, the doctrine of Christianity: and pagan states have suffered most from rebellions (he found it convenient to forget the history of Spain during the last fifty years). 'It is therefore,' he concludes, 'the duty of Kings to sustain by their own example the religion upon which they rely; and they must realize that, if their subjects see them plunged in vice or violence, they can hardly render to their person the respect due to their office, or recognize in them the living image of Him who is all-holy as well as almighty.' People born as we are (he continues), with inclinations towards virtue, never of course go to scandalous extremes: but our smallest faults have bad results: everyone is watching us. And he ends thus: 'This, my son, is the conclusion of the whole matter. A sovereign can never live too wisely, or too innocently. To have a happy and glorious reign, it is not enough to manage public affairs efficiently: we must also regulate our own conduct. The only means by which we can be really independent of and superior to other men is by doing nothing, whether publicly or in private, which they can legitimately blame.'

That was, quite definitely, Louis' ideal. He did not always live up to it: he persuaded himself (as we all do) that certain exceptions prove the rule; and he was surrounded by people who regarded every indulgence as his right. Further, his ideal was unprogressive: he was a man of routine in morals and religion, as he was in business: he hated new ideas. But, so far as it went, and so far as he lived up to it, Louis' ideal of Kingship raised his rule from a personal tyranny into a kind of delegated theocracy.

I might quote other passages of equal interest from the *Memoirs*. But I will add instead one extract from a manuscript which was found among Louis' papers after his death, and which shows how much trouble he took to live up to his ideal of kingship. 'One must be on one's guard,' he writes, 'against oneself, one's inclinations, one's natural tendencies. It is a fine thing, a noble and enjoyable thing, to be a King, when one feels fit to carry out properly all the duties of the office. But it is not without its pains, its fatigues, and its troubles. Sometimes one is in a state of desperate uncertainty, and, after spending a reasonable time going into the matter, one must settle it somehow, and take whichever seems to be the best line of solution.' And he ends with

M

a paraphrase of the famous '*L'Etat, c'est moi*'; 'In working for the State, a King is working for himself. The good of the one is the glory of the other. When the State is prosperous, famous, and powerful, the King who is the cause of it is glorious; and he ought in consequence to have a larger share than others do of all that is most agreeable in life.'

Louis certainly earned his reward. 'One must work hard to reign,' was one of his maxims; and he was himself the hardest-working man in the country. Colbert, his Minister, gives a specimen day: 'Finance Council from 10 till 1.30, another Council in the afternoon, two hours' study of Latin (in order to read Papal dispatches), and a third Council in the evening, lasting till 10 o'clock.' Every day was mapped out. 'Given an almanac and a watch, one could always tell what the King would be doing' [*Saint-Simon*]. And this was not a mere formal attendance at meetings. The King, said his Foreign Secretary, 'sees everything, hears everything, makes every decision, gives every order.' He was not a political genius, like Richelieu, but he was a shrewd business man, a skilful diplomatist, and an ideal chairman, who knew everything that was going on, and kept the initiative in his own hands.

To complete the centralization of government, Louis got rid of the crowd of nobles and ecclesiastics who encumbered the Councils, and substituted middle-class officials nominated and paid by himself. His Secretaries of State came from the same class. And in spite of what he owed to Richelieu and Mazarin, he determined never to have an ecclesiastic for a Minister, least of all a Cardinal.

Working so hard himself, Louis could inspire others to work for him. One of the greatest tributes to his character is the admiration and affection that some of these men felt for him. Here, for instance, is a letter written by Vauban, the famous military engineer, who spent all his life in Louis' service. 'After having spoken of the King's business, I dare to presume that I may be allowed to speak about myself. It is the first time in my life that I have done so. I am now in my seventy-third year. I have been fifty-two years in the Service. I have superintended fifty important sieges. For nearly forty years I have been travelling continuously, to visit places on the frontier . . . alike in summer and in winter. [He feels he is growing ill and old, but]. In spite of all this, if I absolutely must carry on, I shall do so, without regard to anything which might be said, or anything which may happen. After God, the King is all in all to me. I shall always joyfully carry out anything he pleases to order me, even though I know it means the sacrifice of my life: and he can count upon it that I shall never lose my feeling of gratitude for all his kindness to me. The only favour I ask of him is to consider my reputation' [*Halévy*].

Judge a man by his friends, and a master by his servants. If that is a good rule, Louis must have been one of the best of kings.

III

The stage which Louis chose for the pageant of royalty was not Paris, but Versailles. He knew Paris to be crowded and unhealthy: he suspected it (since the Fronde) of disloyalty and republicanism. He wanted a quieter and more dignified setting. The French throne should not be stumbled on round a street corner, but approached by an avenue of magnificence, and be the climax of the view. Yet, if he had lived in Paris, his reign might have had happier results. Versailles meant at first only the detachment that seemed necessary for good government, and a stage big enough for the effects that royalty required. It came to stand for pride, extravagance, and ignorance of public opinion. Those few miles from Paris to Versailles seemed to grow longer every year, the mind of the Court to grow more and more remote from the mind of the people. Within little more than a century they were bridged again—but by revolution.

I need not describe Versailles, for you can see it today, much as Louis left it. But to realize all that it meant in his time, you must imagine yourselves back in an age when the art of manners was (indeed) studied more than it is now, but when the science of living was understood much less perfectly. You must picture the huge palace, overcrowded with royal and noble families, their clients and their domestics, from attic to basement, like a London flat; but with such cold in the rooms that in winter the wine froze on the King's table, and such dirt and smell in the passages as would hardly be tolerated in a city slum. Remember the habitual use of scents, the constant fear of small-pox; and the idleness, dullness, and pettiness of mind which can be felt behind the picture of the Court given by Saint-Simon or the Princess Palatine [*Bradby*].

Yet it was a splendid place, after all, and the pageant that Louis played there was a spectacle we should all have liked to see. The town of Versailles had a population as large as pre-war Oxford, and they all lived for the King or on the King. There were streetfuls of functionaries. There were acres of stables, kennels, coach-houses, and menageries. There were special buildings for the King's falcons and the King's boarhounds. In the centre, surrounded by terraces and gardens, at once in the town and in the country, stood the palace itself, a vast structure in the Italian style, which had employed 30,000 workmen, and cost fifteen millions sterling. It needed to be large. The Queen's household consisted of some five hundred persons; Monsieur, the King's brother, had over six hundred retainers; even Madame Royale, a baby of one month, had nearly eighty. As for the King's establishment, it included 9,000 guards, 200 carriages, 1,800 horses, 1,400 grooms, nearly 300 waiters and other officials of the table, a personal domestic staff of 200; in all, what with religious, literary, dramatic, musical, medical, and other staffs, some 15,000 dependants, whose salaries cost a tenth of the whole revenue of the country. About £170,000 a year was spent in hunting. There were meets every day: from 900 to 1,000 dogs were kept in the royal kennels: the wolf-hounds ran twice a week, and killed forty wolves a year. Louis XV used to kill stags at the rate of 500 a month: killing animals was the one healthy recreation of French kings.

But the one thing that mattered at Versailles, whether it was the time for politics, or for hunting, for receiving an embassy, or for going to chapel, was the King. He was *Le Roi Soleil*, the 'Sun King,' round whose light the planetary Court revolved. Every moment of his life had its audience and its etiquette—I should rather say its congregation and its ritual. When Louis got up in the morning, 100 favoured mortals were admitted to the function in six successive parties, each a shade less select than the one before. The most favoured saw him get out of bed and put on his dressing-gown: the least privileged watched him wipe his hands on an oiled napkin—the usual extent of his ablutions—

and finish putting on his clothes. When he went to Mass the
ladies of the Court knelt devoutly at their prayer-desks: if they
thought he would not be there to see them (*Saint-Simon* has a
story to this effect) they would shut their books and go away.
The King lunched alone, but every dish was brought in by a
gentleman, preceded by an usher and a butler, and accompanied
by three armed soldiers of the guard. On great days he still ate
alone, but was surrounded by some thirty functionaries, including
an armed guard of sixteen men; and the general public was
admitted to the spectacle. When he went hunting he was followed
by a crowd of attendants. When he changed his clothes there
were rules for the handling of every garment. He dined with his
family no less elaborately than he lunched: and his going to bed
at night, like his getting up in the morning, was a semi-religious
ceremony to which it was a privilege to be admitted. The Court
entertainments—there were balls, concerts, theatricals, or card
parties nearly every night—became, at least in later years, infinitely boring; and the standard of politeness set by Louis
himself made it such bad form to express one's real feelings that
everything in life became stilted and unnatural. 'A genuine
sentiment is so rare,' said one visitor to the Court, 'that when I
leave Versailles I sometimes stand still in the street to see a dog
gnaw a bone.'

With all its grossness, it was Versailles which prescribed—
what we hardly have now—an international code of good manners.
A young man going to Court in 1679 would have found it
advisable to study 'a New Treatise on Good Manners as practised
in France among Gentlemen,' in order to find out how he
should behave in the presence of 'persons of quality.' Customs
change, the author tells him. It used to be good manners to dip
your bread in the gravy at dinner, provided you hadn't already
bitten it. It was once allowable to yawn in company, so long as
you did not speak at the same time. At Versailles they would
be shocked at such behaviour. You used to be allowed to spit
on the floor, provided you put your foot over it. But nowadays
(he discovers), when speaking to a person of quality, you must
not even yawn, or scratch yourself, or blow your nose. If a
person of quality sneezes, there is no need to say out aloud 'God
bless you': you need only take off your hat, and make a low bow,

expressing the prayer internally. It is bad manners to knock loudly, or more than once, at the door of a prince, or of a great lord. Indoors, you must never knock, but only scratch. If no one answers, you must wait, or perhaps scratch softly: if no one comes then, you must go away. And—this is admittedly a refinement of good manners—you must never sit down with your back towards the portrait of any eminent personage.

The reader would find so much in this strain that he might be pardoned for thinking that French society existed for the sake of the persons of quality who inhabited Versailles. It nearly did. But he would discover one chapter in the book (true, a very short one) which showed that Louis XIV's courtiers, like their King, recognized the maxim 'Noblesse oblige.' 'This would be the natural place,' writes our author, 'to say something more precise about the politeness due from a superior to his inferiors. But this would look like dictating laws to those who make them; and so I think I will dispense with it. I will only take the liberty of reminding young lords . . . that if they are not sensible enough to realize that poor and insignificant people are men like themselves, and have often as much merit as themselves, and sometimes more . . . yet they ought for their own interest to be kind to their servants, and polite and gentlemanly towards those who are dependent on them. A great lord without good manners is nothing less than a monster . . . He is in the world, but not of the world: for you cannot be that unless someone loves you' [*Courtin*].

Such was the perfect gentleman, as you would have met him at Versailles. It was part of Louis' policy to domesticate this nobility, to employ its members as supers on the royal stage. They enhanced his importance, they were under his eye; and if they were ruined by gambling, or by the expenses of Court life, a loan or a sinecure made them more than ever dependent upon himself. This uprooting of a large part of the French landed gentry, and its replanting at Versailles, had serious effects on the history of the country. During the golden age of the French *noblesse,* from the end of the fifteenth to the end of the sixteenth century, they lived, as their English neighbours did, on their country estates, were on good terms with their tenants, and played a considerable part in local government. It was the disorders of the Wars of Religion, the rise in the standard and cost of living, and the concentration of the Government and Court in Paris, which started the change. Louis XIV and Versailles made the fashion permanent, and opened a breach between the Court nobility and the county families which, in the long run, was fatal to both.

So, year after year, Versailles went on. There has been nothing quite like it before or since. You may think it unimportant, or mere stage-play. But it left its mark on France. It caught the attention of Europe. It supplied just the setting that Louis needed to make his moderate gifts look like genius, his military adventures like world-conquests, and his extravagance like a proof of illimitable wealth. If there were other illusions, Louis himself was the chief victim of them.

IV

Meanwhile the one man who made all this possible—who found money for Versailles, men for the royal army, ships for the fleet, and trade for the merchants—was sitting sourly in his office from half-past five every morning, posting up his innumerable ledgers. His name was Colbert. If he was not (as some say) of Scotch descent, he had at least a Scotch character. He saw through Louis' play-acting. But he liked power, he was grateful for being trusted, and he was interested in his work. Intendant and Financial Secretary under Mazarin, he had made himself useful to Louis by denouncing Mazarin's dishonest Finance Minister, Fouquet: now he made himself indispensable as Controller-General, by carrying on for twenty years the work of nine modern Ministries. He controlled what we should call the Treasury, the Home Office, the Board of Trade, the Board of Agriculture, the Office of Works, the Admiralty, and the Colonial Office; and he also did the work of the Lord Chancellor, and of the Minister of Education.

What was the policy of 'Pooh-Bah' Colbert? He believed, as a financier should, that wealth is power, and national prosperity dependent upon trade and commerce. He thought, as most economists did in those days, that commerce was to be captured, not created. There was a limited number of ships to carry a limited bulk of goods. The total amount of wealth could not be increased, but it could be transferred from one owner to another.

There must be a *guerre d'argent,* or money war, in which the armies are trading companies, the weapons are tariffs, and the plan of campaign is to make the 'balance of trade' in every commodity favourable to France.

How could this be done? Partly, Colbert believed, by making the most of the existing wealth of the country; partly by developing industries at home, so that there would be no need to spend French money in buying from abroad; and partly by manufacturing and exporting commodities for which the foreigner would have to hand over his gold.

The first part of this policy meant putting the collection of taxes on a business-like footing, as Sully had done sixty years before, and budgeting for the annual expenses. This Colbert did most effectively. For the first time in French history State finance was controlled by annual estimates of revenue and expenditure. For the last time in the history of the French monarchy (except for one year in the middle of the next century) the national accounts showed a balance on the right side.

It was, however, the commercial rather than the financial side of Colbert's policy which caused most stir in the world. 'M. Colbert,' the Venetian ambassador wrote home, 'aims at making the country superior to every other in wealth, plentiful in merchandise, rich in arts, abundant in goods of all kinds; needing nothing, and distributing everything to other States. He leaves no stone unturned to acclimatize in France the industries of other countries. He has taken pains to import into the kingdom the special manufactures of England, and the rare natural products of that country. For certain lines of production he has gone so far as to bring workmen from England, and to give up to them the Spanish royal residence, turning a palace into a workshop. He tries to get French hides tanned in the English manner, so that they may serve the same purposes as English leather, and replace their use. He has taken over from Holland the Dutch method of weaving, as well as Dutch cheese and butter, and other specialities. From Germany he has imported the manufacture of hats, of tin-plate, and many other industries; from our own country [Venice] lace and looking-glasses. Five or six thousand women, scattered over most of the provinces, are working at these things, and a number of forewomen have come from

Venice ... Tapestry work has been taken from Persia, and most beautiful and elegant tapestry is being produced at Paris. The rarest products of the Indies are imported and sold, and Africa has been despoiled of most of its manufacturing processes. All the finest products of every part of the world are being manufactured at Paris nowadays, and there is such a demand for them that orders are flowing in from every side ... To avoid the difficulties of exchange, the purchaser must send his cash to France, to the complete satisfaction of M. Colbert, whose only desire is to despoil other States for the aggrandisement of France.' [*Lavisse*].

It would be natural to suppose that, with his well-known dislike for *Messieurs les marchands,* Louis felt little sympathy for Colbert's commercialism. It is, therefore, interesting to find at any rate one passage in his *Memoirs* where he expresses Colbert's programme in the clearest terms, and calmly makes it his own. 'I knew,' he writes, 'the huge sums which individuals were paying, and which were going out of the country, through the trade in lace, and other foreign manufactures. I saw that the French had no lack either of industry, or of the materials requisite for manufacturing these articles themselves; and I had no doubt that, if they were made on the spot, they could be sold at a lower price than those imported from a distance. On these considerations I resolved to establish factories for those things in my country. The effect would be that the nobles would find their expenses reduced, the middle classes would profit by the whole expenditure of the rich, and the huge sums which at present went out of the country would be kept here, and would insensibly produce extraordinary abundance and wealth—not to mention that this plan would furnish an occupation to many of my subjects, who had hitherto been obliged either to be corrupted by unemployment, or to look for work in neighbouring countries.'

In accordance with this policy, whilst foreign industries were imported, home industries were subsidized and controlled. The factory system was introduced, and France underwent, a century before England, some of the experiences of an Industrial Revolution. Elaborate instructions were issued for the manufacture of just such articles as would command a sale abroad. Every product had to bear the maker's mark; and if anything was reported as defective by Colbert's inspectors, the manufacturer might find himself in the pillory, with the offending article hung round his neck. Under such encouragements Gobelins tapestry and Sèvres china became known all over the world; and English satirists complained that London ladies preferred Blois gloves to British kid, wore ribbons 'à la Maintenon,' and gave up home-made lace for 'French point and Colbertine' [*A Satyr*].

This mobilization of French industry involved Colbert in further activities. Communications had to be improved, roads made, bridges built, canals cut. Commerce had to be encouraged. Colbert tried to break down the aristocratic prejudice against a business profession. He founded trading companies on the Dutch model, and urged municipal and other bodies to subscribe for shares. This led a step further. If there was to be a colonial trade, there must be a mercantile marine; and if there was to be a mercantile marine there must also be a French navy. Richelieu had begun to form a fleet; in 1636 he had raised it to 36 capital ships, of which the biggest was 1,000 tons, with 52 guns, and a crew of 345: and before his death he had launched *La Couronne*, a ship 200 feet long, with 72 guns, and a crew of 500. But Mazarin had done nothing, and Colbert had to start afresh. In 1660 the fleet consisted of 18 ships in bad condition; when Colbert died it numbered 276, including ships of the line carrying 120 guns and 600 men—these were, I suppose, about the size of our third-class cruisers; but they could be built in six months, and cost no more than a modern torpedo-boat. For his crews Colbert abolished the press-gang (still practised in England), and started a system of conscription in the sea-coast provinces. It is hardly too much to call him the creator of French commercial and maritime power.

But it may be objected that Colbert's whole system was founded upon an economic fallacy, and could not be sound. The merest beginner in political economy nowadays knows that wealth is not a commodity, like butter: that it cannot be created by making a country self-supporting, or captured by building up an export trade without corresponding imports. National wealth depends on mutual credit, and the interchange of services between one country and another. Quite true. But we argue as people to whom peace is more natural than war: the economists of the seventeenth century argued as people to whom war was more natural than peace. A country at war, they thought (and we thought so in 1914), ought to be self-supporting, and build up a large gold reserve. Colbert's ideal, indeed, was a tariff-war: even in 1672 he was not for the capture of territory, but of trade; whereas Louis, with his ambitions fixed on *la gloire,* would never be satisfied short of military conquest and territorial aggrandisement. Sooner or later the pull between the two ideals was sure to come. But for some years, at any rate, the King and his minister could work harmoniously together. Military and commercial expansion, the pursuit of wealth and the pursuit of fame, could go on side by side.

There were other parts of Colbert's activities in which he could be sure of Louis' support. He organized a Censorship of the Press—a censorship so rigorous that little was left except his own 'Journal des Savants' (a kind of 'Athenaeum'), and the official 'Gazette'; and no one could publish a book without permission to do so. He codified the Laws. A special committee, with Louis himself as chairman, produced in rapid succession a Civil Code, a Criminal Code, a Commercial Code, a Naval Code, and a *Code Noir* dealing with the negro population in the French colonies. Soon France had the best laws in the world—though, owing to the negligence, ignorance, and venality of the magistrates, they were possibly the worst administered. Colbert also took Paris itself in hand. In 1661 the city had sixty policemen to deal with a population of half a million, including forty or fifty thousand beggars, thieves, and professional assassins; it was dark, dirty, and disorderly. Colbert lit the streets, and tried to keep them clean; set up an adequate police force; and dealt with beggary and brigandage, so far as he could, all over the country.

Finally, as Minister of Fine Arts, he 'governed the intellectual life of the country by the same methods as its finance, industry, and commerce' [*Lavisse*]. Richelieu's Académie Française was supplemented by Academies of Inscriptions, of Sciences, of Music, of Painting, of Sculpture, and of Architecture. Pensions and prizes were distributed to learned men. Literature and Art became, under the personal patronage of Louis XIV, the public services that modern Communists have dreamed of making them. But they suffered the inevitable consequence. They had to conform to the taste of the times, with its love of classical models, its artificiality, its fear of being natural. They had to reconcile the pursuit of truth and beauty with a proper respect for Louis and Versailles. It must have been very difficult sometimes; and most of us do not find it easy to admire the products of that age. Nevertheless few reigns can show a more famous list of writers than Molière, Boileau, Racine, La Fontaine, Bossuet, La Bruyère, Pascal, Saint-Simon, and Mme de Sévigné.

V

Such, in merest outline, was the policy by which Louis XIV and Colbert hoped to make France the leader of commerce and the pattern of taste in Europe. To a great extent they succeeded. Versailles was not a mere veneer. Paris did become what it has never quite ceased to be—a world-factory for the newest extravagances of intellect and the latest luxuries of social fashion.

But where is national prosperity to be found? Louis himself, though he backed Colbert's means, did not at heart believe in his ends. As time went on a gap widened between the minister's desire for commercial supremacy and the King's ambition for military glory. And behind both ideals lay a finer test of success which (we shall probably feel) neither of them fully recognized —the good relations of class and class in the community, and the happiness of the people taken as a whole. *Vauban,* the military engineer, who (as we have seen) had spent forty years travelling up and down the country, and was in far closer touch with the life of the people than either the King or his minister, felt moved in his old age to write a book, the *Dîme Royale,* which is the bitterest possible commentary on the glorious age of Louis XIV. In it he pictures the country under-populated, over-taxed, and poverty-stricken: and he calls for a complete revision of the taxation system. The magnificence of Louis' court and the culture of Versailles did, in fact, rest upon the oppression of the French people, as surely as the intellect and art of Athens rested upon a more literal slavery. That was the price France paid for its Kings. 'Monarchy exerted a charm over the imagination, so unlike the unceremonious spirit of the Middle Ages, that, on learning the execution of Charles I, men died of the shock; and the same thing occurred at the death of Louis XVI, and the Duke of

Enghien. The classic land of absolute monarchy was France. Richelieu held that it would be impossible to keep the people down, if they were suffered to be well off. The Chancellor affirmed that France could not be governed without the right of arbitrary arrest and exile; and that in case of danger to the State it may be well that a hundred innocent men should perish. There is nothing in the possession of their subjects which they (kings) may not lawfully take from them. In obedience to this principle, when Marshal Vauban, appalled by the misery of the people, proposed that all existing imposts should be repealed for a single tax that would be less onerous, the King took his advice, but retained all the old taxes, while he imposed the new. With half the present population, he maintained an army of 450,000, nearly twice as large as that which the late Emperor Napoleon [in 1870] assembled to attack Germany. Meanwhile the people starved on grass. France, said Fénelon, is one enormous hospital. French historians believe that in a single generation six millions of people died of want. It would be easy to find tyrants more violent, more malignant, more odious than Louis XIV; but there was not one who ever used his power to inflict greater suffering or greater wrong; and the admiration with which he inspired the most illustrious men of his time denotes the lowest depth to which the turpitude of absolutism has ever degraded the conscience of Europe' [*Acton*].

Such was the considered verdict of a great historian, who believed that all history was the history of freedom. We shall hardly arrive at any different conclusion if we judge Louis' reign by the other criterion that I suggested—the good relationship of class and class in the community. Here is *Louis'* own version of the matter. 'Each profession contributes in its own way,' he writes, 'to the support of the monarchy. The labourer by his toil provides nourishment for the whole of this huge body. The artisan by his industry produces everything needed for the convenience of the public. The merchant assembles from a thousand different places everything the world produces that is useful or agreeable, so as to furnish it to each individual at the moment he needs it. Financiers work for the support of the State by collecting public money. Judges, by executing the laws, maintain public security. And ecclesiastics, by instructing the people in religion, draw down the blessing of heaven, and preserve peace upon earth.' There is a complacency about all this which the last sentence renders odious. Was this how France appeared from the windows of Versailles? The labourer certainly toiled—from morning to night; and his reward was beggary and starvation. The artisan produced, and the merchant imported —but what? Largely the luxuries of an idle aristocracy. Financiers collected public money—they usually do; but in France they spared the rich and fleeced the poor. Judges executed the laws: every day men were tortured and imprisoned, chained in the galleys, or broken on the wheel. As for the ecclesiastics, they were far too busy persecuting their Christian opponents to preach the brotherhood of Christ. Above all, that happy co-operation of class and class in the service of the country, in which Louis professed to believe, simply did not exist. Clergy, nobility, and commoners were all bitterly divided within themselves, and against each other.

If Louis realized this, he must have been a very unhappy man. But I don't think he did. There was one blind spot in his political retina. Although he travelled about France more than any French king since Francis I, he knew almost nothing about the mass of the people he governed. The Kings of France 'never looked the facts of life in the face. They were provided with an imaginary world, in which they lived, from one end of the year to the other' [de Staël]. Hence the overthrow of the French monarchy. It did not reach its end till the inglorious reign of Louis XVI: but its fall began in the glorious days of Louis Quatorze.

LECTURE XIV

LOUIS XIV—CHURCH AND FOREIGN POLICY

I

Louis XIV was a shrewd man, but not a clever one. He avoided a new idea as he avoided a man with the small-pox. He accepted his Church policy as he accepted his theory of the monarchy, ready-made; from the tutors of his childhood, from his Jesuit confessor, or from his flatterers at court. And he showed the same competence and ruthlessness in working it out.

He assumed that as 'the Most Christian King' he must be the first champion of Catholicism north of the Alps. He assumed, at the same time, that he must preserve the independent traditions of the French Church. And he assumed the right of a sovereign to impose his religion upon all his subjects. The first assumption had been vindicated when Henry of Navarre violated his conscience to keep his crown; the second when Francis I used the victory of Marignano to extract his Concordat from the Pope; and the third when the diplomatists assembled at Munster made it the basis of the religious settlement of 1648. In fixing his Church policy on these principles Louis was sufficiently out of date to be sure of popular support. Religious toleration, even of the kind embodied in the Edict of Nantes, was a new idea: France and Louis would have none of it.

Starting from these principles, Louis' ecclesiastical policy took three forms—Gallicanism, the persecution of the Jansenists, and the revocation of the Edict of Nantes.

II

Gallicanism was the French equivalent to Anglicanism. It meant Catholicism adapted for French uses—orthodox in creed, catholic in worship, and acknowledging the Pope; but organized as a French Church, not as a Roman Church within a French State.

Louis himself was not likely to understate his claims. 'Kings,' he says in his *Memoirs,* 'are absolute sovereigns, and have full and free disposition of all goods, whether secular or ecclesiastical, to use them as wise economists—that is, in accordance with the needs of the State.' Louis could therefore, if he chose, confiscate all Church property. 'The so-called rights and liberties of the Church (he continues) are common rights of all churchmen, exercisable only subject to the sovereign.' For instance, no title-deeds or charters can exempt ecclesiastical foundations from taxation or other duties owed to the State. It is only by permission, not by right, that the Church Assembly assesses its own contributions to the Treasury. Lastly, the royal right of presenting to benefices must be maintained, for it secures a loyal and submissive body of ecclesiastics.

It was on this last point that Louis came into conflict with the Pope. By the Concordat of 1516, which was still in force, the French King had the right, in most of the dioceses of north and central France, to annex the revenues of a vacant see (*régale temporelle*), and to exercise episcopal patronage during the vacancy (*régale spirituelle*). In 1673 Louis revived a claim which had been made by Henry IV as far back as 1608, but which had never been pressed, to extend these rights to all the bishoprics in the country. Innocent IX, appealed to by some of the bishops, rejected this claim. Louis, who had found cause to complain of Innocent's predecessor, on the occasion of an attempt on the life of the French ambassador at Rome, was not likely to give way without a struggle. He engaged Bossuet to draw up, and induced most of the bishops to accept, a declaration of Gallicanism called the Four Articles (1682). The first Article declared that the Pope's jurisdiction was purely spiritual, and that the King was independent in temporal matters. The second said that even in spiritual matters a General Council was superior to the Pope. The third declared the rules and customs of the Gallican church to be binding. The fourth maintained that even in matters of faith papal decisions need the assent of the Church. Louis published these provocative statements broadcast, had them taught to all candidates for ordination, and refused to appoint bishops who did not accept them. Innocent retaliated by refusing to institute bishops who did; and at the time of his death, eleven years later, as many as thirty sees were thus left bishopless.

The Most Christian King had not intended to carry his quarrel with the Head of Christendom quite so far. As he could not get all he wanted, he compromised on a part. The Four Articles were discarded, and in return Louis was allowed to exercise the *régale temporelle* (but not *spirituelle*) over the whole of his domains. This was a considerable step towards complete control over the property and appointments of the Church. The sole ruler of the French State might soon become the sole ruler of the French Church.

But this was not enough. Louis was not the man to be satisfied with external conformity, if he could secure real obedience. He could dispose of the bodies and of the estates of his subjects: he wanted to dispose of their souls. The uniformity of a Catholic country, and the credit of its Most Christian King, would not be secured until every Frenchman shared the King's religion, as he shared the King's politics. As time went on the Spanish strain in Louis' nature became more dominant. He began to think it intolerable that any of his subjects should be heretics.

III

Somewhere deep under the ruins of Ypres Cathedral (1918) there lay a gravestone bearing the name Cornelius Jansen. He was bishop there, and died in 1638. His life-work, a great folio on St. Augustine, was published two years after his death. It was an attempt to reintroduce into Catholicism the leading doctrines of St. Augustine—the importance of spiritual experience, man's helplessness apart from faith, personal conversion, and pre-destination. The year Jansen died, some French admirers of his doctrines formed a religious settlement at the Abbey of Port Royal, about twenty miles south-west of Paris; and here 'Jansenism' developed, in ominous proximity to Versailles.

'The Port Royalists were the Calvinists of Catholicism. Their attempt at reconstruction embraced exactly those parts of the medieval religion which the Jesuits had neglected' [*Bridges*]. The Jesuits had laid most stress upon the social and institutional side of Catholicism: the Jansenists, no less Catholic than they, insisted upon its personal and devotional aspect. The Jesuits shared the usual Catholic dislike for the elements of predestinarianism in St.

Paul and St. Augustine; besides, these beliefs were associated with Calvinism and political revolution. The Jansenists, like the Calvinists, made predestination the basis of a Puritan protest against the vices of society. The Jesuits thought they could save souls, if not reform society, by making themselves 'all things to all men': their Casuistry became a system of 'religion made easy,' by which, if a man would not live as a Christian, he might at any rate die as a Catholic. The Jansenists, by their austerity, made religion difficult, and drove half-hearted Christians out of the Church. It was a new form of a very old difference, between the religion which expects much of men, and the religion which expects little; between the appeal to the individual and the appeal to the crowd.

If Louis had been a more charitable or a less stupid man, he might have appreciated (as Mme de Sévigné did) the harmless and indeed useful life led by the recluses of Port Royal. If he had been gifted with a sense of humour, he might have laughed over Pascal's *Provincial Letters* as Leo X laughed over Erasmus's *Praise of Folly*. If he had possessed more political insight, he might have realized that, whilst Calvinism 'necessarily produced civil wars, and shook the foundations of States, Jansenism could only raise theological disputes, and wars on paper' [*Voltaire*]. But he could not forget that during the Fronde the Jansenists had been in league with the democrat de Retz. He suspected every association of ulterior political motives. There were, indeed, Jansenists whom he patronized on other grounds, such as Racine and Boileau. But Jansenism itself was a new idea, and he disliked it. And so in the name of religious uniformity (which he mistook for unity) he declared war against a sect whose real offence was that they had attacked the Jesuit supporters of the throne.

In 1653 the Pope published a Bull condemning various heretical propositions said to have been found in Jansen's *Augustinus*. In 1660 Pascal's *Provincial Letters* were burnt by the common hangman, and everybody began reading them. In the following years many Port Royalists were imprisoned, or driven into exile. But persecution had its usual effect, and in 1709 the work had to be done again. Twenty-two pious old ladies were expelled from their nunnery at Port Royal by 300 soldiers under the Lieutenant-General of Police; and the buildings were pulled down. The

THE JANSENISTS

scanty ruins, and a walnut tree said to have been planted by Pascal, have become a place of Protestant pilgrimage.

Still Louis was not content. In 1713 a fresh Papal Bull, called the *Unigenitus*, condemned Quesnel's *Réflexions*, a Jansenist publication, as heretical. There was another outbreak of persecution; and when the King died, two years later, he left more than 2,000 Jansenists in prison.

We must reserve the later history of Jansenism for another time. Here I will only point out that Louis' policy had the effect which he most feared: it turned the Jansenists from a small body of religious enthusiasts into a formidable party with a political programme. The people sympathized with the persecuted Port Royalists, and found a new cause for disliking their Jesuit persecutors. The liberal party at Court, the self-seeking *Parlementaires*, and the discontented middle classes, joined hands with these new moralists and *Illuminati*. The *frondeur* spirit was reborn, and ready to receive instruction at the hands of the Enlightenment. The movement did not end till the Jesuits were driven from France and the Bourbons from the French throne.

IV

The Revocation of the Edict of Nantes was a worse blunder than the destruction of Port Royal, and its consequences were even more disastrous. There could be no question of the Huguenots being a political danger to the country. The privileges that might have made them so had been taken away by Cardinal Richelieu half a century ago. Their loyalty, or at least their impotence, had been tested during the troubles of the Fronde. Louis himself had declared, in 1666, 'Those who profess the so-called reformed religion are no less faithful to me than my other subjects, and must be treated with no less kindness and consideration': and he must have learnt from Colbert that they were the thriftiest, most hardworking, and most intelligent of his citizens. Nor had he any personal feeling against the Protestants. 'My grandfather,' he once said, 'loved the Huguenots, and did not fear them: my father feared them, but did not love them; as for me, I neither love nor fear them' [*Voltaire*]. He even believed in toleration—for Catholics. In 1661 he wrote to the King of Denmark, the Queen of Sweden, and the authorities of Hamburg, asking for liberty of conscience for French Catholics in the Baltic lands. There is a letter of his (dated April, 1663) to our King Charles II, protesting against the intolerant treatment of Catholics in England, and saying, 'You know with what leniency and moderation Catholic princes treat those of their subjects who profess other beliefs.' And when, as late as 1684, Louis had seized Strasbourg, and it suited his policy to pose as a tolerant ruler, he guaranteed the liberty of local Lutheranism.

But he was incapable of consistency, or even of common sense, where his ruling passion was concerned. There must be religious as well as political uniformity. The French King's religion must be the religion of all Frenchmen. If the Protestants do not accept it, they must be persuaded or compelled to do so. Encouraged by his Gallican clergy, who at every Church Congress passed resolutions against the Huguenots, and backed by the approval of almost every class of French society, which had never given the Edict of Nantes a fair trial, he embarked on a policy of state-aided conversion. In the very year in which he demanded toleration for Catholics in north Germany, he withdrew it from the Protestants of the Pays de Gex near Geneva. In 1666 he published an Edict recognizing or prescribing many forms of indirect persecution: Protestants were not to bury their dead, except at night: not more than twelve of them might meet together for a marriage or a baptism: they were not to teach anything in their schools except reading and writing: and so on. In 1677 Louis tried bribery. A fund was formed called the 'Treasury of Conversion,' and had great success. No less than 58,000 Huguenots declared themselves converted in the course of the next five years. Many were so poor that their conversion cost no more than six livres a head. Soon, Protestants were excluded from all positions at Court, all government posts, all liberal professions, almost from the trades by which they earned their living. By this time most of the Huguenots' churches had been closed, as well as their colleges and schools. There only remained the last and most brutal method of all—the Dragonnades (1681). This meant quartering troops (of whom the dragoons were the worst disciplined, and committed the greatest excesses) upon Protestant families. 'They took possession of the Protestants' houses,' says a contemporary account; 'destroyed all that they could not consume or carry away; turned the parlours into stables for their horses; treated the owners of the houses with every species of cruelty, starving them, beating them, torturing them'—you can imagine the rest from what happened in Belgium in 1914. A contemporary print represents a heretic signing his conversion-paper on a drum-head labelled 'An evangelical appeal,' while an armed dragoon threatens him with 'an irresistible argument'—a musket loaded with a crucifix [*Malet*].

The Dragonnades completed the work which the Treasury of Conversion had left unfinished. The number of Huguenots still unconverted was reported to be negligible. Louis prepared for the last step, which now seemed almost superfluous, but which was needed to advertise his orthodoxy to all Europe—the Revocation of the Edict of Nantes. We are fortunate in possessing first-hand information as to his state of mind at this time. It is an account of an interview with him given in Bishop Burnet's *History of My Own Times*. 'Old Rouvigny,' he writes, 'who was the Deputy-General of the Huguenot churches, told me that he was long deceived in his opinion of the King. He knew he was not naturally bloody. He saw his gross ignorance in those matters [of religion]. His bigotry could not rise from any inward principle. So for many years he flattered himself with the hope that the design [to destroy Huguenotism] would go on so slowly that some unlooked for accident might defeat it. But after the Peace of Nimuegen [1678] he saw such steps made with so much precipitation, that he told the King he must beg a full audience of him upon that subject. He gave him one that lasted some hours. He [Rouvigny] came well prepared. He told him what the state of France was during the wars of his father's reign, and how happy France had been now for fifty years, occasioned chiefly by the quiet it was in with relation to those matters. He gave him an account of their [the Huguenots] numbers, their industry and wealth, their constant readiness to advance the revenue, and that all the quiet he had with the Court of Rome was chiefly owing to them: if they were rooted out, the Court of Rome would govern absolutely in France, as it did in Spain. He desired leave to undeceive him, if he was made to believe they would all change, as soon as he engaged his authority in the matter: many would go out of the kingdom, and carry their wealth and industry into other countries. And by a scheme of particulars [statistics] he reckoned how far that would go. In fine, he said, it would come to the shedding of much blood: many would suffer, and others would be precipitated into desperate courses. So that the most glorious of all reigns would be in conclusion disfigured and defaced, and become a scene of blood and horror. He told me, as he went through these matters, the King seemed to hearken to him very attentively. But he perceived they made no impression: for the King never asked any particulars, or any explanation, but let him go on. And, when he had ended, the King said he took his freedom well, since it flowed from his zeal to his service. He believed all he had told him, of the prejudice it might do him in his affairs: only he thought it would not go to the shedding of blood. But he said he considered himself as indispensably bound to endeavour the conversion of all his subjects, and the extirpation of heresy, that if the doing of it should require that with one hand he should cut off the other, he would submit to it. After this, Rouvigny gave all his friends hints of what they were to look for.'

The consequences of the Revocation of the Edict of Nantes were so serious that it is sometimes questioned whether Louis realized what he was doing. This interview seems to prove that he did—that he had been warned of what the results would be by those in the best position to know, but that his bigotry deafened him to these warnings, and that he went into the affair deliberately and with his eyes open.

This same year (1685) the Edict was solemnly renounced. All the Protestant churches were to be demolished; all their ministers were to leave France within a fortnight, or be sent to the galleys. Those of their followers who were not yet 'converted' must stay in the country, and put up with what might happen to them; if they tried to emigrate, they too would be sent to the galleys (two years later the punishment was death); their children would be brought up as Catholics. The result of these measures might have been foreseen. Thousands of Protestants, seeing it had come to the extinction of their Church, adjured their forced conversions, and tried to escape from the country. In spite of every attempt made to stop them, the refugees crossed the

Swiss frontier (at Geneva, in 1687) at the rate of 3,000 a week: many fled to Holland, and many to England. It is thought that, in all, 300,000 fled the country, perhaps more, including some of the best elements in the industrial population, and that a potential force of many thousands of soldiers and sailors was lost to the French army and navy. It was more than mere loss. The emigrants strengthened the agricultural and industrial population of France's rivals. Colbert's weavers and leather workers settled in London and Amsterdam. The Great Elector gave 20,000 refugees free land and religious toleration in the neighbourhood of Berlin. French soldiers reinforced the armies that were already gathering to check the supremacy of France. Frenchmen served under Peter the Great in Russia. Frenchmen fought against Frenchmen at the Battle of the Boyne. Above all, it was the Revocation of the Edict which finally induced the Protestant Powers to make common cause against Louis: the League of Augsburg was signed the next year (1686).

Such was the price that Louis paid for national orthodoxy. With less excuse, and in a more enlightened age, he committed the same blunder as Philip II of Spain: he ruined his country in the name of religion. At the time the Revocation seemed to be the most glorious exploit of a glorious reign. A contemporary history of France, written in the form of question and answer, thus represented it: 'Q.: What have you to say (about Louis XIV) under the head of religion? A.: That is the point in which he has distinguished himself most of all: for he had all the Huguenot churches demolished, and utterly destroyed Calvinism throughout his States. He began by depriving the Huguenots of certain important offices; then, by a series of decrees, he prevented their holding any appointment; he gave allowances to those who became converted; and, after using gentle means to induce them to re-enter the pale of the Church, he finally employed force so effectively that, without causing any rebellion, he brought back to their religious duties an infinite number of heretics.' That was what they thought in 1685. When, however, the same history came to be re-edited in the following century, the passage I have quoted was struck out, and the following question and answer substituted: 'Q.: Was the Revocation of the Edict of Nantes profitable to the kingdom? A.: No. Its results were fatal to our manufactures, because of the protection given by Protestant rulers to the workmen and artisans forced to leave their country' [*Aulard*]. Commercial success is not everything, and a country should know when to sacrifice it for finer ends. But Louis' religious policy was more than a blow to trade: it was an offence against political good faith, an outrage to the decencies of society.

There is one fact which helps to explain his conduct, though not to excuse it. In 1680 Louis came under the influence of the last and most remarkable of the mistresses with whom he consoled himself for the dullness of his wife; and in 1683, on the death of Marie Thérèse, he secretly married her. Mme de Maintenon was not a politician; and if she had been, Louis would never have allowed her to interfere in politics. But she was something more dangerous than a politician: she was an educationalist: and the King, who had never been properly educated, could not resist the influence of an ex-governess. The new mistress had herself been a Calvinist, and was for that reason, as so often happens, an unusually stiff Catholic. She believed that her mission at court was to save Louis' soul, to reform Versailles, and to convert the Huguenots. Outwardly she succeeded. Louis became a *dévot*; the immorality of the court was driven underground; and Protestantism was 'converted' out of existence. Her indirect influence was seconded by the more brutal suggestions of Louvois, now Minister of War, and the more urgent demands of Le Tellier, the King's Jesuit Confessor—'a gloomy, fiery, vehement, and inflexible mortal' [*Voltaire*]. But Louis was persuaded because he wished to be, and because his whole policy of absolutism demanded, as its logical conclusion, the abolition of liberty in religion.

V

There remains Louis XIV's foreign policy. It was a habit of the French nation to demand a strong foreign policy, and a custom of the French kings, however incompetent in other ways, to supply it. Louis was far from incompetent, except in his lack of ideas; and that deficiency hardly mattered in a disciple of Richelieu and Mazarin—he had only to carry on their policy. He inherited an interest in foreign affairs, and a talent for diplomacy. He acquired a capacity for hard work. And if he understood anything in the actor's art of kingship, it was how to get his effects across the political footlights.

What was the position of foreign affairs in 1661? First, it was certain that there would be war. War had become a natural function of royalty, and a more normal state of society than peace. Even Colbert's commercial programme, as we have seen, presupposed a state of war; and Louis' first campaign was both a 'guerre d'argent' and a land-grabbing expedition.

But it was more. Louis inherited from Henry IV and Richelieu the classical tradition of French foreign policy: he aimed at extending the frontiers of France to the limits of ancient Gaul— the line of the Pyrenees, the Alps, and the Rhine. The Thirty Years' War, which he just remembered, and the Spanish war, in which he had served as a boy, had carried the country far towards this end. France had gained so much by the Treaties of Westphalia and of the Pyrenees that it seemed to be within sight of the whole. What remained to be done? The French frontier was at the Pyrenees: but Roussillon was a centre of Spanish intrigue. The Franche Comté remained a Spanish province almost in the heart of France. Southern Alsace had been transferred to the French crown by every formula known to international lawyers: yet its landlords professed feudal allegiance to the Emperor. Northern Alsace was still German: so was the greater part of Lorraine, in which the 'three bishoprics' of Metz, Toul, and Verdun were French islands surrounded by an Imperial sea. The Flanders frontier was still undefended, and the Spanish troops behind it were perilously near to Paris. There were thus five separate fronts on which an aggressive policy might be covered by a plea of consolidation, and a war of conquest be termed a war of national defence.

Again, it was a favourable moment for such a policy. In 1661, and for nearly thirty years afterwards, Louis had no serious rival to fear in the whole of Europe. England, from 1660 to 1688, was under Charles II and James II: the first may have outwitted and the second compromised him; but neither could afford to oppose his designs. After the Treaty of the Pyrenees (1659) Spain, under Philip IV and Charles II, went from bad to worse. Austria, under Leopold I, was doubly incapacitated by the results of the Thirty Years' War, and by a fresh advance of the Turks, culminating in the second siege of Vienna in 1683. The fall of Sweden and the rise of Prussia during the second half of the seventeenth century were both dependent on French patronage. The power of Russia did not begin until the personal rule of Peter the Great in 1689. Louis might be proud of his motto, *Seul Contre Tous*; but the supremacy of France lasted just so long as no power in Europe was in a position to challenge it. Holland always defied him; and with the accession of William of Orange to the English throne in 1688 the humbling of his pride began.

There was a special motif which ran through the whole of Louis' foreign policy—that of the Spanish Succession. Mazarin had married him to the Spanish Infanta, Marie Thérèse, in the hope that her dowry might include the Franche Comté and the Spanish Netherlands. But Philip IV, whose pride and niggardliness offended the French at every turn of the negotiations, made it a condition of the marriage that the Infanta should renounce all claims of succession to Spanish lands, and then failed to pay the sum of money which he had promised as her dowry. When Philip died, Louis made the non-payment of the dowry an excuse for ignoring the renunciation, and claimed large parts of the Spanish Netherlands in the name of his wife: it was this which led to his first war. It was the childlessness of Philip's successor, Charles II, and the expectation of his speedy death, which prompted the Spanish Partition Treaties of 1668, 1698, and 1700. And it was Charles II's disposal of his dominions by will to a French prince which brought on the Spanish Succession War with which Louis' reign closed. Spain was, in fact, the obsession of Louis' life. It was the Spanish passion in his policy which took him beyond the recovery of territories to which France had some natural right, and prompted him to seize a power which was unnatural and dangerous in the hands of a French prince. It was the Spanish frenzy in his blood which took him beyond the reasonable suppression of political minorities, and prompted his fanatical persecution of the Huguenots.

There was one other ambition behind Louis' foreign policy—this, too, derived from Mazarin, and pursued till the end of his life. He had been brought up to believe himself the successor of Clovis, the conqueror of Germany, and of St. Louis, the crusader against the Turk. 'The German Emperors,' he wrote in his *Memoirs,* 'are neither the heirs of the Romans, nor the successors of Charlemagne. They are only the elected heads of a German republic [and we know how poorly Louis thought of republics]. They cannot claim any superiority over the other Kings of Europe, of whom the most ancient and the most powerful are the Kings of France. None but France and the French King could claim any such right.' It was in this temper that Louis sent French troops to fight against the Turks at St. Gotthard in 1664. And throughout his reign he was only waiting for Leopold I to die, in order to get himself elected Holy Roman Emperor, and to make Versailles, instead of Vienna, a secular Rome, a centre of international Gallicanism.

VI

Directly Louis began to govern for himself, he asserted the French claim to seniority among the Powers of Europe. He forced the Pope to apologize for an attack on the French envoy at Rome. He compelled Philip IV, by a threat of war, to acknowledge the precedence of the French ambassador at London over the ambassador of Spain. And when our Charles II tried to enforce the old custom by which French ships in the Channel saluted the British flag, Louis wrote him such a threatening letter that he at once gave way.

After that, for thirty years out of the fifty-five of Louis' personal rule, there followed a series of wars, in which he was either pursuing the policy I have already described, or defending his acquisitions against the armed resentment of Europe. There were four of these wars: the War of Devolution, 1667-1668, ending with the Treaty of Aix: the Dutch War, 1672-1678, ending with the Treaty of Nimuegen: the Nine Years' War, or the War of the League of Augsburg, 1688-1697, ending with the Treaty of Ryswick: and the Spanish Succession War, 1700-1713, ending with the Treaty of Utrecht.

The first of these wars got its name from the Brabant law of Devolution, on the strength of which Louis claimed the succession to Philip IV's Flemish territory for his wife Marie Thérèse, the daughter of Philip's first marriage, as against the son of his second marriage, the reigning King Charles II. To enforce this claim Louis invaded not only Flanders, but also the Franche

Comté (1667). Spain was powerless to resist. But a French occupation of the Netherlands was resented by the Dutch, and by ourselves, no less in the seventeenth century than in the eighteenth or twentieth. England, Holland, and (for an inducement) Sweden formed a Triple Alliance—the first of a series of International Leagues against Louis XIV. The same year Spain gave way, and ceded part of Flanders to recover the Franche Comté. This was the Treaty of Aix, which ended the war (1668).

Four years later, after elaborate military preparations, Louis invaded Holland, and the Dutch War began (1672). Louis disliked the Dutch because they were Protestants, Republicans, and merchants: he wished to punish them for organizing the Triple Alliance, and for putting a tariff on French goods; and he believed that to defeat Holland was the shortest way to secure possession of Flanders. The burgher government of the United Provinces, under the Pensionary John de Witt, had trusted too much to diplomacy and sea power. It had no forces to stop an invasion by land. In the panic caused by Louis' advance de Witt, 'a downe right predestinarian Calvinist' [*Pepys*], was murdered, and William of Orange called to the defence of the country. At a critical moment Louis delayed. The dykes were opened; the land became sea; and Holland was saved. The first William of Orange had broken the power of Spain: the third was to break the power of France. But not yet. Louis, checked in the Netherlands, once more seized the Franche Comté. After six years of war, the Treaty of Nimuegen (1678) left this important province, and a fresh slice of Flanders, in French hands.

During the next ten years Louis pursued his old policy by a new method. The treaties of Westphalia and Nimuegen had ceded to France various territories along its eastern frontiers, with their dependencies. To a soldier this would seem to mean such districts as belonged to those territories at the date of annexation. But to a lawyer it presented richer possibilities. Under a special clause of the treaty of Nimuegen Louis set up 'Chambers of Reunion,' which proceeded to assign to France all dependencies which had at any time belonged to the ceded territories. When Louis' lawyers had made out a claim, Louis' generals marched in their troops. The climax of this procedure was the occupation of Strasbourg in 1681. Strasbourg had always been treated, even by Louis, as a free and neutral city: it commanded one of the few bridges across the Rhine: and its possession gave France an open gate into Germany. Louis' designs upon the Empire were now openly discussed. France was becoming a menace to Europe.

The year 1681 was the zenith of Louis' career. In twenty years he had made France the greatest power in Europe. He had won all the territory he was likely to be allowed to keep. The world's appetite for French goods was not yet sated. French art and French taste had not yet outstayed their welcome in the Courts of Europe. Louis himself was at the height of his capacity. If he had been assassinated in 1682 there can be no question that he would share, perhaps surpass, the reputation of Henry IV as the greatest of French kings. But he lived to lose, during the last thirty years of his reign, not indeed territory, or reputation, not the power to inspire fear, or even admiration; but all personal attractiveness, and all claim on the affections of mankind.

The seizure of Strasbourg (1681) and the Revocation of the Edict of Nantes (1685) were answered by the formation of the League of Augsburg (1686), into which William of Orange, working with new prestige as William III of England, was able to bring almost every power in Europe. The war which broke out in 1689 lasted till 1697; and fighting went on on five fronts—in the Pyrenees, Savoy, the Rhine valley, the Netherlands, and Ireland. Louis' main effort was to keep what he had gained in Flanders, and to restore James II to the English throne. His chief exploit on the Rhine was the devastation of the Palatinate (1689), which the Germans of that district have not forgotten to this day. The Irish expedition came to grief at the Battle of the Boyne (1690), and the French bid for naval supremacy in the naval fight off La Hogue (1692). But France won a number of lesser successes, and Louis claimed to have dictated the Treaty of Ryswick, which ended the war (1697). He kept what he had gained at Nimuegen, and, of what he had gained since, Strasbourg, but little else.

The crisis of Louis' policy was then past. The catastrophe was close at hand. Charles II of Spain was at last on his deathbed, and all Europe was discussing the succession to his crown. The Spanish hope was to find a successor strong enough to hold together Charles's scattered and weakened dominions. The French fear was that such a successor might be found in Austria, and that the old Austro-Spanish supremacy of Charles V, which during the last century and a half had gradually broken down, might be renewed. The general feeling of Europe was that a close alliance between Spain and Austria was less to be feared than a close alliance between Spain and France. It was on that side, now, not on the other, that the Balance of Power was likely to be upset. Louis himself had two strings to his bow. As King of France he had negotiated a series of Partition Treaties (the first with Leopold I of Austria, the second and third with William III of England, whom he thus hoped to conciliate) by which a German prince was to be allowed to hold Spain, provided that France might compensate herself in Italy. As head of the Bourbon dynasty he secretly hoped that he might see his own grandson, Philip of Anjou, whose claims were exactly parallel to those of the Austrian candidate, on the Spanish throne. Charles, dreading partition, and reckoning that his inheritance was more likely to be kept intact in French hands, ultimately drew his will in favour of Philip. All Louis' life was in the question, should he carry out the Partition Treaty, or accept the will? Charles had been shrewdly advised. Louis' natural caution, and genuine wish to do the best for his country, were overborne by the temptation to crown his lifelong anti-Spanish policy by the acquisition of the throne of Spain. The will was accepted, and the French king's grandson became Philip V of Spain (1700). The Pyrenees were erased from the map.

Austria was indignant, and Europe apprehensive. But the position might have been accepted: there need have been no war. Unfortunately Louis could not leave well alone. In 1701, by three separate blunders (in which it is not too fanciful to trace a new Spanish pride), he enabled William to rouse Europe against him. First, he declared that, by his succession to Spain, Philip had not sacrificed his claim to the French throne: next, he occupied the so-called Barrier fortresses in the Spanish Netherlands with French troops, turning out their Dutch garrisons: and lastly he recognized the 'Old Pretender' as James III of England. The first act was a menace to Europe, the second a threat to Holland, and the third an insult to England. This meant war.

SPANISH SUCCESSION

The War of Spanish Succession lasted for eleven years (1702-1713). It was fought in Spain, Italy, Germany, the Netherlands, and the East and North of France. The first period of the war consisted of a French offensive (1702-1704). Louis' plan was to hold the English and Dutch army, under Marlborough, in the Netherlands, whilst using Bavaria as a base to attack the Austrian army under Eugene, and to march on Vienna. But Marlborough refused to be held. He marched from the lower Rhine to the upper Danube, joined Eugene, and utterly defeated the French at Blenheim (1704).

During the second part of the war (1704-1713) France was on the defensive. In Spain Philip was twice driven from Madrid by an English advance from Portugal (which joined us in 1703), and by Anglo-Austrian advances from Catalonia. But, as Napoleon discovered a century later, Spain is almost impossible to conquer; and by 1710 Philip was safely back in his capital. In Flanders Marlborough won a series of victories at Ramillies (1706), Oudenarde (1708), and Malplaquet (1709). By 1712 Vauban's line of forts was pierced, and there was nothing to prevent the Allies from marching on Paris. France was barely saved by Louis' refusal to accept the terms unwisely proposed to him at the Hague (1709) and Gertruydenberg (1710); by the succession of the Archduke Charles (the Allies' candidate for Spain) to the Austrian throne (1711); by the fall of the Whig Government in England (1710); and by the eleventh hour victory of Denain (1712), which decided the Dutch to retire from the struggle.

Peace was at last signed at Utrecht and (with the Emperor) at Rastadt, in 1713-1714. Philip kept Spain, but renounced the right of succession in France; whilst he ceded to England Gibraltar, Minorca, and trading rights in his South American colonies. Austria took the Spanish Netherlands, Milan, Sardinia, and Naples. Sicily went to Savoy. France kept its frontiers intact, but demolished the defences of Dunkirk, and ceded to England Newfoundland and Acadia at the mouth of the St. Lawrence. Louis had to recognize the Hanoverian succession in England, and to renounce his championship of the Stuarts.

By dragging out the war a few more years Louis had got better terms than he was offered in 1709 or 1710. But France was exhausted of men and money. And if it had lost little territory, its rivals had gained much at the expense of its partner Spain. Worst of all, it had lost its European leadership, and shaken its world-wide prestige. Louis had so accustomed his country to victory that a defensive war, however well sustained, felt like a defeat. He had so adapted it to leadership that its worst humiliation was to accept a dictated peace.

On the heels of national disappointment came dynastic disaster —the death of every direct heir to the throne except Louis' great-grandson, a child of five. No wonder the reign ended in gloom and disillusionment.

VII

As Louis lay dying, a year after the Peace of Utrecht, he realized the results of his policy. For the first time in his life he saw himself as he really was: and for the first time we feel sorry for him. 'I have always heard it said,' he tells Mme de Maintenon, 'that it is difficult to die: I assure you that I find it quite easy.' And for the boy who was to succeed him he wrote his last advice, which is also his own best epitaph: 'My son, put all your trust in God. Live first as a Christian, secondly as a King. Do not by any moral transgression draw His punishment upon you. Give thanks to His Divine Providence, which so visibly protects this realm. Set your subjects an example that a Christian father sets his family. Think of them as your children: make them happy, if you would be happy yourself. Relieve them as soon as you can of the extra taxes laid on them by the necessity of a long war: taxes which their fidelity has enabled them to bear obediently. Enable them to enjoy a long peace: nothing else can re-establish the state of your realm. Always place peace before the doubtful issues of war; and remember, my son, that the most brilliant victory costs too dear, when purchased by the blood of one's subjects. Never shed that blood, if it be possible, save for the glory of God. Such conduct will draw God's blessing upon you throughout the course of your reign. Receive my blessing, whilst I embrace you for the last time' [*Bertrand*].

LECTURE XV

THE REGENCY

I

The Treaty of Utrecht and the death of Louis XIV were the end of an age that had done its work. The eighteenth century, before it was many years older, showed that it had a mind of its own, and was going to develop along new lines. This is our opportunity, then, to sum up the results of the first two hundred years of modern history. And we shall do it best by considering the position in which each country stood in 1715—by making a survey of Europe similar to that with which we began in 1494.

First, France. Here a clearly defined crown policy, consistently pursued, had brought a newly united country to the supremacy of Europe. But the romantic tyranny of Francis I, the chivalrous tyranny of Henry IV, and the just tyranny of Richelieu had been overlaid by the conscientious and unimaginative tyranny of Louis XIV. Everything had been sacrificed to what was, after all, a wrong idea of national greatness. Mazarin left France victorious and at peace, the unquestioned arbiter of Europe. Colbert made her the greatest commercial power in the world. Louvois' army and Colbert's navy set the fashion for Europe. Vauban's forts made the French frontiers impregnable. Louis was the ideal King to combine these legitimate elements of greatness, and to add the necessary ingredient of personal brilliancy. But national defence was sacrificed to dynastic aggression. French commerce, French sea power, and French colonies were thrown away for unsubstantial gains on the land frontier. French wealth was dissipated in private as well as public extravagance. No national needs were allowed to stop the waterworks of Marly, or the building of Versailles. During the campaigns of 1672-75, when the war expenditure already exceeded the revenue of the country by £4,000,000 a year, Louis wrote constantly to Colbert, urging him to press on the work at St. Germain's, where orange-trees were being planted, and cages and fountains constructed for Mme de Montespan's pet birds. Every class of society was dwarfed to exaggerate the King's stature: the nobles became court flunkeys, the clergy propagandists of divine right, the lower orders tax-paying animals. If Louis could get big results by inspiring public respect, he saw no advantage in inspiring public affection. France enslaved was great: he did not see that France free might have been greater.

This wrong idea of greatness vitiated even that department in which Louis showed most originality and achieved most success —his patronage of literature and art. There is a famous passage in Voltaire's *Age of Louis XIV* which raises the issue. 'Heroes and politicians are the product of all ages: all nations have suffered revolutions: and all histories are equal to him who reads only to store his memory with facts. But whoever thinks, and (what is yet more uncommon) whoever has taste, will regard only four ages in the history of the world. These four happy ages are those wherein all the arts have been perfected, and which, serving as a climax of the grandeur of the human understanding, are an example to all posterity. The first of these ages, to which true glory is annexed, is that of Philip and Alexander; or of Pericles, Demosthenes, Aristotle, Plato, Apelles, Phidias, and Praxiteles . . . The second age is that of Cæsar and Augustus; which is also distinguished by the names of Lucretius, Cicero, Virgil, Horace, Ovid, Varro, and Vitruvius. The third is that which followed the taking of Constantinople by Mahomet II . . . The Medici drew to Florence the arts which the Turks banished out of Greece . . . All the sciences recovered new life . . . Everything tended towards perfection: Michael Angelo, Raphael, Titian, Tasso flourished. Beautiful architecture again appeared . . . Gothic barbarity, which in all things had disfigured Europe, was banished from all parts of Italy, and a better taste succeeded. Finally the fourth is that which is called the Age of Louis XIV, and it is perhaps, of the four, that which approaches the nearest to perfection . . . True philosophy was discovered only in this age; and it may with truth be said that, from the last years of Cardinal Richelieu to the death of Louis XIV, there happened a general revolution, not only in our government, but in our arts, mind, and manners . . . And this happy influence was not confined to France, but extended into England, where it excited the emulation which that sensible and thinking nation then wanted.

It carried taste into Germany, and the sciences into Muscovy: it even reanimated the languishing state of Italy: and Europe in general owes its politeness (*politesse et l'esprit de société*) to the court of Louis XIV.' *Politesse*—that is just the word. Even Voltaire does not venture to name the great men of the age of Louis XIV in the same breath as those of Athens or Rome. He knew that Louis' France had neither the liberty of the Greek age, nor the laws of the Roman. French artists and literary men lived under a tyranny, and their greatness depended upon the taste of their tyrant. But Louis XIV did succeed in making France the centre of European culture, as Richelieu had made it the centre of European diplomacy. France handed on to the new nations, which came to the front in the eighteenth century, the Renaissance that it had learnt from Italy in the sixteenth. What Voltaire was pleased to call 'Gothic barbarity' went out of fashion for 150 years. For the first time since the days of Erasmus the educated classes of all countries were drawn together by the use of a single language and the study of a single literature—then Latin, now French. Voltaire himself was the Erasmus of this new Renaissance, which did not reach its height until fifty years after Louis' death. But it was Louis who planted it out, and made its later growth possible. In politics he left France the tradition of an efficient despotism: in society, class-ignorance and class-hatred: in commerce and finance, bankruptcy: in religion, persecution and scepticism. But as Philip II ruined Spain for orthodoxy, so Louis XIV ruined France for—politeness.

II

Spain was the chief loser by the Treaty of Utrecht. The Spanish Netherlands became Austrian. Milan, Sardinia, and Naples went to the Emperor, Sicily to Savoy, Gibraltar and Minorca to England. Spain ceased to be an empire: it became an unusually backward and burdensome province of France.

Italy became nominally Austrian. Large parts of its uninterested population were handed over to new governments. But little was really changed except the colours on the map. The city—not the state, still less the country—closed the horizon of the average Italian. There was still no Italy; no national unity; no patriotism. Only one sign pointed that way. The aggrandizement of Savoy-Piedmont, the consolidation of the Kingdom of Sardinia, suggested that there was one state in Italy capable of uniting the country. It was from Piedmont that there came, 150 years later, Victor Emmanuel, the first King of liberated Italy: it was in Sardinia that the Liberator, Garibaldi, found a home.

Austria was fully compensated for its loss of the Spanish throne. But Charles VI, an ardent pursuer of political will-o'-the-wisps, quite failed to profit by his real gains, or to understand who were his real enemies. The rise of Prussia found Austria unprepared to defend its most valuable possessions.

The Treaty of Utrecht was dictated by England, and written in Holland. The real victors, in 1715, were the maritime nations; and the greatest fact which Louis' land wars demonstrated was the importance of sea power. Richelieu's prophecy had come true. The sea was an open door to every country in Europe. The nation which ruled the sea would ultimately rule the land also. The removal of the French menace to Antwerp, the demolition of Dunkirk, the alliance with Portugal, and the occupation of Gibraltar and Port Mahon, gave a free passage to English ships from the North Sea to the Mediterranean. Our fleets could blockade the coast of France and Spain, whilst behind this screen our merchantmen were extending their trade with South America, or carrying negro slaves from Africa to the West Indies—a rich but discreditable traffic, in which Bristol, London and Liverpool led the way throughout the eighteenth century. Such was the outcome of Louis XIV's foreign policy. In the sixteenth century the French preoccupation with continental warfare enabled Portugal and Spain to found their colonial empires: in the seventeenth it enabled England and Holland to exploit sources of wealth that Spain and Portugal could no longer use; in the eighteenth it enabled England to found a new empire in India and North America.

By strengthening Austria apart from Spain, and by setting up Savoy in the south and the Dutch Barrier forts in the north to separate it from France, the Treaty of Utrecht tried to abolish what had been the chief cause of war in Europe for two hundred years—rivalry between the Bourbons and the Hapsburgs. Louis XIV himself instructed his Austrian ambassador in 1714 that the traditional anti-Hapsburg policy must now be changed: this was the first step towards the Diplomatic Revolution of 1756. But you cannot make nations friendly by an Entente any more than you can make men virtuous by an Act of Parliament. There was still an anti-Austrian tradition, and an anti-Austrian party in French politics, which were to drag the country into new and more disastrous wars.

One last remark about the Treaty of Utrecht. It was the first international settlement that recognized what we now call the principle of self-determination. I am not forgetting the Treaty of Westphalia. That, of course, by guaranteeing the independence of Switzerland and of the United Provinces, recognized the right of a subject population to renounce its allegiance to an external sovereign power. But it was different when whole nations claimed the right to depose their legitimate King, and to elect another out of the direct line of succession. This was what England had done in 1688, and this was what Louis XIV had refused to admit when he called the Old Pretender James III. By the Treaty of Utrecht he was obliged to throw over the Stuarts, and to recognize the Hanoverian succession. He had also to renounce Philip V's claim to the throne of France—again on the ground that dynastic rights could not stand against the needs of a nation. I suspect that these concessions hurt Louis more than anything else in the Treaty. He could bear the loss of a province more easily than the injury of his self-respect. Self-determination reminded him of the Fronde, which he had been trying to forget for over fifty years. It seemed to contain a threat of Revolution. Louis was partly right. The Treaty of Utrecht did legalize and internationalize the principles of the English Revolution of 1688. It was a step towards the League of Nations and the Treaty of Versailles.

III

If 1715 ends an old epoch, it also begins a new one. The eighteenth century has a character of its own—perhaps a more distinct character than any other century of modern times.

It is the twilight of the old régime. The old kings, as in France and Spain, are living on a reputation for absolutism which is degenerating into anarchy. The new kings—the 'enlightened despots' of the second half of the century—bring in a political

Counter-Reformation, which gives the principle of Monarchy another hundred years' uneasy life. The nobles are living on their past, and on their privileges. The Church exists beautifully. The state of the common people is neither privileged nor beautiful, but it is ominously silent. Eighteenth century life is like a sleeping village you may stumble on in a quiet corner of the hills—smoke rising from the chimneys, the scent of flowers in the air, but no movement or sound to show who dwells there, or what forces of life or death may be at work.

What did the eighteenth century produce? 'It is a barbarous age,' says Bartholo in the 'Barber of Seville'; 'It has produced liberty of thought, magnetism, electricity, toleration, vaccination, quinine, the Encyclopaedia, a few plays—in fact every kind of foolishness' [*Beaumarchais*]. There is a grain of seriousness in the satire. In the eighteenth century, when society was in chains, thought became free: when government was chaotic, thought became constructive. The idea of a better order of society spread from the philosophers to the Kings, and from the politicians to the peoples. What, then, did the century produce? 'To me.' writes *Carlyle*, 'the eighteenth century has nothing grand in it [this was before he wrote his *Frederick the Great*] except that grand universal Suicide, named French Revolution, by which it terminated its otherwise most worthless existence with at least one worthy act.' This is to put a truth rather hysterically. The eighteenth century was neither destitute of grandeur nor of worthy acts. Its suicide, like most suicides, was a crime as well as a release. But more. The French Revolution was not a detached event, a breach in the continuity of the eighteenth century: it was a natural and necessary outcome of it. Revolutions do not so much destroy an old order of things as re-establish it in a new form. The revolution of the fifteenth and sixteenth centuries—the Renaissance and Reformation—did not destroy the medieval tyranny of Church and State, but re-established it in the form of royal absolutism and ecclesiastical intolerance. Thus where there had been one Emperor there were now many Kings; and where there had been one Pope there were now many national churches: and it was the rivalry of these new authorities which came to a head in the eighteenth century. The eighteenth century Revolution—it began long before 1789, it was continued in 1848 and

1917, and we are still living under its influence—this revolution has altered the frontiers and the constitutions of almost every Power in Europe; but their national character and essential needs remain very much what they were before.

The interest of the years between 1715 and 1789 lies in their sequel. The unity of the century is dramatic. The play is the working-out of the character of the old order of society towards the catastrophe that perpetuates it in the new.

IV

The eighteenth century and the Regency began together at the death-bed of Louis XIV. When he had made his last speeches to the Court, and spoken his last farewell to the five-year-old child who was to be his successor, he sent for the Duke of Orleans, and said to him, 'My nephew, you see here one King in his grave and another in his cradle. I hope that you will take great care of this young prince, your nephew and your King. I entrust him to you, and I die in peace, leaving him in your hands ... Govern the State well during the minority of this prince. If he dies, you are the master. If he lives, try above all to turn him into a Christian King: make him love his people, and his people love him'.

Orleans thus became Regent. But when Louis' will came to be read, it was found that the position was almost nominal. His power consisted of a casting vote in a Council of Regency. He was neither the King's guardian, nor the King's tutor, nor the commander of the Household Troops. How was this situation met? Much as Louis himself, in his franker moments, had anticipated. 'I have made my will,' he once said, 'but perhaps it will be treated as my father's was. Whilst we live, we Kings can do what we like. Once dead, we have less power than common individuals' [*Duclos*]. The liberals who were for Orleans, and the legitimists who were against Maine and Toulouse, the King's bastards, joined together to defeat Louis' intentions. The Paris Parlement was only too glad to strengthen its constitutional position by annulling Louis XIV's will, as it had annulled that of Louis XIII. The famous session that Saint-Simon describes made Orleans the real and effective Regent. And the nation raised no objection. Whilst the lawyers reversed Louis' will, the undertakers carried his body to burial amidst a crowd that danced, sang, drank, and made merry: some even shouted insults as the hearse went by.

Orleans, who remained Regent until his death in 1723, was a considerable figure in his time, though more noted for his social vices than for his political virtues. He had played a part in the respectable court of Louis XIV's later years rather like that of the royal uncles in the early life of Queen Victoria [*Strachey*]. As Regent, we expect to find him carousing with his *roués* at the Palais Royale, or flirting in a box at the Opera. We picture him as he is described, the night before his sudden death, in a thick red overcoat, coughing a great deal, with short neck, puffy face, bloodshot eyes, and hesitating speech [*D'Argenson*]. His mother, the Princess *Palatine*—a large gruff sentimental German lady, whose letters about the French Court (where she hated everything except Louis XIV) are almost as racy as the *Memoirs of Saint-Simon*—says of him, 'My son has enough education to keep him from ever being bored: he has a good knowledge of music, and does not compose badly: he paints very prettily, understands several languages, and is fond of reading: knows a lot about chemistry, and can easily master difficult subjects. And yet all this does not prevent his being bored with everything.' Boredom is the chief source of vice in princes. In a society which did what it liked and said what it liked, Orleans became as notorious for his vicous living as for his liberal opinions. When he died, they made (among others) this epitaph for him:

They libel Orleans, who say he disbelieved in the Divine:
His Godhead was the Trinity of wealth, of women, and of wine'
[*Buvat*].

At the same time he was an able man, a good soldier, a clever administrator. He resembled his ancestor Henry IV, says Voltaire (and Saint-Simon agrees) in his courage, his kindness, his gaiety, his freedom—and in face as well as character. But he lacked, or had lost, Henry's resolution. At his birth, they used to say, the fairies had given him every gift; but the last fairy had said, 'He will possess all the talents, except the talent for making use of them' [*Duclos*].

Being what he was, it was a disaster that Orleans should have fallen into the hands of such an able rascal as his tutor and minister

Dubois. This man had been a friend of Fénelon, and Mme de Maintenon had trusted him. But, quite apart from the so-called *Memoirs* of Dubois, which are too damning to have been written by himself, it is difficult to disbelieve the general testimony of his contemporaries. 'He is a capable man,' writes the Princess *Palatine*, 'he talks well, and is good company; but he is false and selfish as the devil: he looks like a fox, his deceitfulness can be read in his eyes.' He intrigued for a Cardinal's hat, and was so proud of having got it that he died without the last sacrament, rather than receive it without the rites prescribed for cardinals [*Buvat*].

The state of French society under the Regency was very like that of English society under the Restoration fifty years before. It was a time of unhealthy licence following a period of unnatural repression. But its more scandalous aspects were confined to a small class, and unduly advertised in the literature of the age. The normal life of Paris and of the provinces went on as usual. The evidence for this is in the journals of Buvat and Barbier, the Evelyn and Pepys of Paris. Buvat, in particular, is full of interest. He gives the police news, and the cases in the courts; notes on the weather; accounts of public and social functions; church gossip; a regular Court Circular; and occasional foreign news. He is one of a succession of middle-class diarists who tell us more about the real life of the times than either the memoir-writers or the official historians.

V

The aspects of the Regency with which I want to deal are the character of its government; its financial situation; and its foreign policy.

The first is soon done with; Louis XIV's method of government had been to exclude the nobles from any share in public affairs, and to manage everything himself, with the help of a middle-class Controller-General of Finance, and four middle-class Secretaries of State. Because they were powerful, Saint-Simon called these ministers the 'Five Kings of France': because they were commoners, he hated them and the policy for which they stood. During Louis' later years there had grown up an Opposition at Court, part of whose policy it was to restore the rule of the nobles. Its figure-head was the Dauphin, Louis' grandson; its text-book was Fénelon's *Télémaque*; and Saint-Simon was one of its keenest partisans. But the Liberal Dauphin died three years before the Conservative King; and the reformers had to wait for the Regency. Orleans knew and shared their ideas. One of the first things he did, on coming into power, was to abolish the Controller-General and the four Secretaries, and to set up a system of Government by Committee, sometimes called 'Polysynody.' There were seven Committees, dealing with Home affairs, Foreign affairs, War, the Navy, Finance, Religion, and Commerce. Each included ten nobles, and elected its own chairman. The experiment had been tried in Spain, and had failed. It was not likely to succeed in France, where even *Saint-Simon* had to admit that their 'ignorance, frivolity, and lack of application' made the nobles quite unfit for the business of government. The Committees lasted three years: then the 'Five Kings' were restored to their thrones. Committee government was not tried again until the French Revolution.

VI

The financial condition of France in 1715 was as bad as it could be. The debt accumulated during the wars of Louis XIV was, in proportional value, seven times as great as the national debt of France in 1914. The annual revenue of the country was $12\frac{1}{2}$ millions sterling, the annual expenditure nearly $23\frac{1}{2}$. What was to be done? The traditional remedies—forced conversion of government stock, inflation of the currency, punishment of profiteers—were first tried, and failed. In despair, Orleans accepted the proposals of an ingenious Scotchman to restore the national finances by a system of credit. This man's name was John Law; but the French generally called him 'Jean Lass.' Law had studied banking, and knew that English and Dutch commerce was conducted, not on a cash basis, but on a deferred payment and credit system. He believed that this system could be made general. All that was needed was a bank like the old bank of Amsterdam or the new bank of England (it was twenty years old at this time) sufficiently strong to command credit. This bank would discount bills of exchange, issuing bank notes, which would circulate as paper money, stimulate trade, and be available for paying off the national debt. The operations of the bank and the opportunities for public investment were to be increased by buying out the existing Trading Companies in the East Indies, and by creating new Companies to exploit the West Indies and the Mississippi valley. The scheme was completed by acquiring control of three great monopolies—the coining, or rather printing, of money, the sale of salt and tobacco, and the collection of indirect taxes.

Law's scheme caught on. The fever for speculation which was raging in England (1720 was the year of the 'South Sea Bubble') spread to France. There was a rush to Paris like the rush to Klondyke. In two months, it is said, the population was increased by 30,000 people. Seats in the *diligences* for Paris had to be booked months in advance. The meat supplies of the city gave out, because so many of the visitors were Protestants, and did not observe the Catholic days of fasting [*Buvat*]. Law himself became Controller-General of Finance, and his bank the Banque Royale. 'Soon,' says *Voltaire*, 'you could see the Scotchman turn French by naturalization: instead of Protestant, he became a Catholic; instead of an adventurer, a landed gentleman; instead of a banker, a minister of State. I have seen him arrive at the rooms of the Palais Royale surrounded by dukes and peers, by bishops and marshals of France.' 'He is so pursued,' writes the Princess *Palatine*, 'that he has no peace, day or night. He is tormented like a lost soul.' A duchess kissed his hands in the sight of everybody, and a great lady arranged to have her carriage upset outside the bank, so that she might get an interview with him [*Buvat*].

Then the crash came. The shares in Law's Companies had risen to forty times their face value, and the dividends gave hardly 1 per cent on the purchase money. Shareholders began to sell out: the shares depreciated, and a panic began. When the demand for payment came, it was found that the face value of the bank notes in circulation was six times as great as that of all the cash in the country. Law had overlooked the necessity for a strong cash reserve. It was no use making the bank notes forced currency: nobody would have them. It was no use to forbid the hoarding of gold and silver: the Duke of Bourbon withdrew three carriage-loads of gold from the bank in a single morning. In May, 1720, the bank suspended payment. By December bank notes had depreciated 90 per cent, and the price of shares had dropped from £3,000 to £30. In the rush on the bank many people were crushed to death. The crowd wrecked Law's carriage, and nearly killed his coachman. The banker himself only just escaped. In January, 1719, he had been put in control of all the resources of France: in December, 1720, he fled from Paris in a borrowed carriage, and with £300 in his pocket. He lived on charity in London, and died in poverty at Venice, where the philosopher Montesquieu found him, still working at his system, and maintaining that it was sound.

And so, I suppose, it was. But he had made three fatal mistakes. He had expanded his business too rapidly; he had inflated his paper currency out of all proportion to his cash reserve; and he had forgotten the difference between the French character and that of the hard-headed Scotchmen and placid Hollanders from whom he had learnt his credit system. To this day the French peasant has a weakness for keeping money in a coffee-pot rather than in a bank; and French financiers seem to prefer German cash to German credit.

What were the results of Law's scheme? The craze for speculation, and the handiness of paper money, led to a considerable increase in such crimes as robbery and murder. *Buvat* mentions an ingenious gentleman who slipped an open bag into the letter-box at the Paris Post Office, and got away with all the letters that dropped into it. More than 5,000 rogues and vagabonds were arrested in Paris in a single week. It was in 1721 that the super-criminal Cartouche was captured and executed. But if Law's scheme filled the prisons, it also provided a means of emptying them. The criminal population, young as well as old, was shipped off to the Mississippi. One day 180 boys and girls from the prisons are married and emigrated. Another day thirty carriages drove through the streets full of 'moderately virtuous young ladies,' with their hair tied up in yellow ribbons, accompanied by as many 'lads with cockades of the same colour,' singing and calling to their friends to go with them. When the authorities in America wrote home to complain of the character of some of these colonists, children from the hospitals and orphanages were sent instead [*Duclos*].

The social results of Law's scheme did not end with crime and emigration. The craze for speculation, the inflation of currency, and the rise in prices produced economic effects very like those to which we have grown accustomed during recent years. People with fixed incomes were ruined. Fortunes were suddenly made by persons unaccustomed to wealth. A 'nouveau riche' class came into existence, conscious of its power, and sensitive about its lack of privileges. Moralists complained that the redistribution of wealth increased the spirit of avarice. 'I have seen a distinct change in morality,' says a contemporary writer. 'In the last century the nobility and army were inspired by love and honour; the magistrates desired a good reputation; the men of letters and talent aimed at fame; the merchant was proud of his fortune because it was a proof of intelligence, watchfulness, order, and hard work; the clergy, even if they were not virtuous, at least had to appear so. Nowadays every class in the State has one object, and one only—the making of money' [*Duclos*].

But lastly, although at the time Law's scheme seemed to have ended in disaster, it was judged in later days to have done much to improve the financial conditions of the country. A new impulse was given to French industry and commerce, which had been languishing since the days of Colbert. Money was better used. Business men became more enterprising. Law's system sharpened men's minds as a civil war sharpens their courage [*Voltaire*].

The balance of good and bad results was not easy to strike. As a popular ditty put it:

> The present aspect of the state of France
> Makes one man smile, another cry, Alas!
> Is it a God who orders our finance,
> Or Mephistopheles disguised as Lass? [*Buvat*].

VII

There remains the foreign policy of the Regency. International diplomacy had new problems to face from 1715 onwards. There was now no preponderant power in Europe. Under Louis XIV France had always made the first move. The Treaty of Utrecht left France, England, Spain, Austria, Prussia, and Russia—six more or less equal powers—face to face; and it was still uncertain who would take the lead. Again, the rise of Russia and Prussia widened the field and increased the complexity of international politics. Poland, Turkey and the Baltic were brought into the diplomatic account: Europe began to face the problem of the Nearer East. And to the old quarrel of England and France, the old rivalry of France and Austria, was added the new struggle for supremacy in Germany between the Hapsburgs and the Hohenzollerns. Lastly, national interests were no longer just dynastic and continental; they were complicated by the commercial needs of the middle classes, and by the possession of colonies overseas.

Two points stand out clearly in the confusing history of the Regency period—the Anglo-French alliance, and the final settlement of the Spanish Succession.

There were several good reasons in 1715 why England and France should stand together. First, they were both heavily in debt after the recent wars, and needed time to recover themselves. Secondly, the terms of Utrecht, so far as concerned the Spanish Succession, had been accepted neither by Austrian or by Spain, and could only be enforced, or revised, by the combined action of France and England. Thirdly, both George I and Orleans (representing Louis XV) were faced by claimants to the Crown. James Stuart, the 'Old Pretender,' had been allowed to start from France, in violation of the terms of Utrecht, for his attempt on the British throne in 1715; and as late as February, 1716, the Regent was intriguing with Charles XII of Sweden for an invasion of Scotland in the Jacobite interest [*Besenval*]. Orleans, for his part, knew that Philip V regarded his renunciation of the French succession as a 'scrap of paper,' and that the Spanish ambassador was intriguing with the Duchess of Maine, and other discontented parties, to raise provincial revolts, and overthrow the Regency. Philip's temporary abdication in 1724 freed him for the call to France which he still expected. When Louis XV nearly died of small-pox in 1728, it was rumoured that Philip was already packing up his trunks for the journey to Paris. Nothing but Louis' marriage, and the birth of a Dauphin (1729), could extinguish his hopes. This identity of dangers drew England and France together. Dubois, disguised as a curio-dealer, met Stanhope, George I's minister (and 'after myself, the ablest diplomatist of his time' [*Dubois*]), in Holland and Hanover.

Heinsius, the Dutch Pensionary, was won over, and England, Holland, and France joined in the Triple Alliance of 1717.

The 'rapprochement' thus begun lasted for a generation, and gave both England and France peace, and a secure succession. The alliance was indeed unpopular at the time, and some historians still say that it sacrificed the national interests of France to England, or to the Bourbons. But it was probably best for France to break off its embarrassing union with Spain, and to enter into a commercial partnership, which might become a commercial rivalry, with England. If only the opportunity had been better used, France might have made a reputation at sea instead of losing one on land, and the whole course of European history might have been changed.

VIII

At the moment, the chief use of the Anglo-French alliance seemed to be the hope it gave of a general pacification, by forcing Austria to acquiesce in Philip's accession, and Spain in the loss of its Italian possessions.

When Charles II on his deathbed left his crown to Philip of Anjou he might have hoped to rid his country of the curse which hung over the Spanish Hapsburgs. But it was no use. After a promising start, Philip V went the way of his predecessors. His portrait at the time of his accession shows him as a cheerful and effeminate-looking boy of seventeen, in a large yellow wig. His first wife, Marie Louise of Savoy, was only fourteen, but proved a brave and capable Regent during his absence in Italy. Unhappily she died in 1714, and Philip, always a very uxorious man, moped himself into a state of physical weakness and religious mania from which he never wholly recovered. The obvious remedy was another wife; and the Spanish minister Alberoni found one the same year in an Italian princess, Elizabeth Farnese, of Parma, his own native town. Elizabeth's beauty had been spoilt, like that of so many ladies in those days, by small-pox; but she carried herself well, had blue eyes, very sparkling and expressive, charming manners, and an extremely strong will. Within a week of her arrival at Madrid Philip was her slave; and from that time onwards she became to all intents and purposes the sole ruler of Spain.

The price she paid for power would have been beyond the means of any lesser woman. For nearly thirty years, day in and day out, she was hardly ever away from Philip's side. They breakfasted in bed together, they heard Mass together, they went hunting together, they did public business together. She was his wife, his sick-nurse, and his private secretary. After 1727 Philip's brain is affected. He takes to his bed, and refuses to be shaved for months at a time. He has supper at three in the morning, and sleeps till three in the afternoon. There is another relapse in 1732. First he refuses to go to bed for three years, or to change his clothes: then goes to bed, and refuses to get up again; suffers from acute melancholia; and from feverishness, because his hair has not been cut for several years. He is partially cured by a course of music and theatricals; and towards the end of his life, though grown almost too fat to walk, has a good memory, and enjoys talking about old times. But whether he is sick or well, mad or sane, Elizabeth is always by his side, and no official business can be conducted without her knowledge.

Thus it came about that what we may call the natural and material policy of Spain (which Philip himself was inclined to favour)—the recovery of territory and trading rights lost by the Treaty of Utrecht—was more and more overruled by Elizabeth's personal ambitions. What was her policy? In a word, it was not Spanish, but Italian—Italian, because, as a Farnese, she hated the Austrian rule in Italy; Italian, because her children were excluded from the Spanish succession by the sons of Philip's first wife, and she wanted to secure for them, as compensation, her own Duchy of Parma; Italian, because in this way she hoped to provide a home for her old age in Italy—she had no liking for the fate which ultimately overtook her, a neglected widowhood in Spain.

Elizabeth's first agent in this policy was Alberoni—like herself. an Italian, but with wider views (looking beyond the claims of Elizabeth's children to the freedom and unity of Italy), and with ability that, in happier circumstances, might have done Spain great service. Dubois called him 'a parody, a pale copy' of himself, but he was much more. Dubois was a diplomatist, Alberoni a statesman; Dubois worked for his career, Alberoni for his country: He hoped, given five years' peace, and a free hand, to do for Spain what Colbert had done for France; and Stanhope, who knew the country and the man well, said that he might have succeeded. Unfortunately he allowed himself to be hurried into war. In 1717, when only three years of his five were up, he revenged an outrage on a Spanish ambassador by seizing Austrian Sardinia, and followed this up the next year by an invasion of Sicily, which belonged to Savoy. When England and France protested, he tried to embarrass the one by stirring up Charles XII of Sweden, and the Old Pretender; and the other by encouraging the Cellamare plot. Austria, however, joined the Triple Alliance (which thus became Quadruple), hoping to secure a revision of the Treaty of Utrecht in her own interests. Admiral Byng destroyed the Spanish fleet off Sicily. The Scotch expedition came to grief. Charles XII was killed, fighting in Norway. The Cellamare plot failed. French armies crossed the Pyrenees. In 1720 Philip dismissed Alberoni, and came to terms with the Quadruple Alliance.

The unfriendly action (as he thought it) of England and France in this affair, and his failure to recover Gibraltar, induced Philip to follow Elizabeth's next move, and to propose an alliance with his old enemy, Charles VI—an alliance to be sealed by a double marriage between Elizabeth's sons, Don Carlos and Don Philip, and two Austrian archduchesses; though which of his daughters, Charles was long unwilling to say. The negotiations were carried through by Ripperda, another foreigner who had taken service with the Spanish court, and ended in temporary success at the treaty of Vienna (1725). But Charles VI never liked the arrangement, to which he only consented in the hope of gaining support for his Pragmatic Sanction, and his Ostend Company. It only lasted a year or two, and was finally shelved by the Treaty of Seville (1729).

From these negotiations Spain gained nothing; but the first part of Elizabeth's aims was achieved: Don Carlos was promised the succession of Parma and Tuscany on the death of the present occupants of those Duchies. To carry out the second part of her designs, and find a throne for her second son Don Philip, she would have to wait, and look for other opportunities. But she was not easily discouraged. As *Frederick the Great* said, she combined 'the pride of a Spartan and the stubbornness of an Englishman with Italian finesse and French vivacity . . . She marched boldly

P

towards the accomplishment of her designs. Nothing could surprise her, nothing could stop her.'

In 1731 Don Carlos succeeded to the Duchy of Parma. When the Polish Succession War broke out in 1733 the price of Spanish help against Austria was that he should be given the throne of Naples and Sicily. And so he was, Parma going back for a time to Austria, and Tuscany to the dispossessed Francis, Duke of Lorraine (1738). Two years later the War of Austrian Succession gave Elizabeth another opportunity: and by the settlement of 1748 Parma, ten years after its vacation by Don Carlos, was given to Don Philip. Elizabeth's ambition for her sons was now fully satisfied.

But not her plans for herself. When Philip V died of an apoplectic stroke in 1746, she followed his corpse to the gloomy palace of San Ildefonso, and there lived in solitude for another twenty years. An English traveller describes how he found her, not long before her death, helpless and half-blind, but still full of spirit, and keeping up, at the age of seventy, the eccentric hours and habits of life of the mad king [*Armstrong*]. A strange end to her thirty years' predominance! Philip proved the stronger after all.

LECTURE XVI

LOUIS XV

I

The reign of Louis XV was, after that of Louis XIV, the longest in French history. Excluding the eight years of the Regency, it lasted from 1723 to 1774. During these fifty years France threw away almost every opportunity either of military glory or of colonial empire. She was untrue both to the ideals of Colbert and of Louis XIV. The French army came to be despised; French diplomacy to be ignored; and French culture, the school of kings, became a school of regicides: abroad it might inspire the rule of the Enlightened Despots, at home it produced the Revolution.

The explanation of this break-up of a national tradition lies partly in the exhaustion and reaction following the fever of Louis XIV's later years, and partly in the mood of disillusionment which everywhere accompanied the free thinking of the eighteenth century. In any case it was the outcome of causes which were almost as old as French history, and which we have already discovered, more than once, working below the surface. But in other countries—England, Austria, Prussia, Russia—kings, however sceptical, were making history. Only France seemed unable to frame a policy or carry out an undertaking. And much of the blame for this must rest upon the character and conduct of Louis XV.

II

Make any allowance you like. Remember that he was an orphan and a king at the age of five: that he was flattered and spoilt by everyone who had to do with him—all the more because for years he was in very feeble health: and that he was married at fifteen to a girl seven years older than himself, without the charm or character to influence him for good. Remember his guardian, old Marshal Villeroi, showing him the cheering crowd in the garden of the Tuileries, and saying, 'Look, my master!

Do you see that crowd, do you see that people? All that is yours, it all belongs to you, you are its master' [*Saint-Simon*].

But when every allowance is made, there is no getting over the witness of those people who knew him best, and the evidence of his own acts, that he was one of the most evil men who ever occupied a throne. Here is a considered account of him by the *Duc de Choiseul,* who was for some years his minister, and always in close touch with the Court. 'When I became minister,' he writes, 'I set myself to understand the King, with whom circumstances obliged me to be on intimate terms. I had heard it said that nobody had known him well. Mme de Pompadour, who had studied him and thought about him [she was his mistress for nearly twenty years], had often told me that he was past comprehension [*inconcevable*]; and I remember that during the last days of her life, she told me repeatedly that he was indefinable [*indéfinissable*], and that I should see after her death that he was capable of going to the most extravagant lengths in any direction. I must say that I never found the King past comprehension, any more than I found it inconceivable that a lump of clay in the hands of a sculptor should represent either a hero or a villain ... After studying him steadily, and without any distraction, I have come to see that the King was a man without a heart and without a soul [*sans âme et sans esprit*]; a man who loved evil as children love hurting animals; a man who had all the defects of the vilest and most degraded character, but who lacked the power proper to his age of giving vent to his vicious desires as often as his nature prompted him to do so. It would have charmed him to watch Paris burning from Belle-Vue, as Nero did Rome; but he would never have had the courage to give the necessary orders. No spectacle would have delighted him so much as the public executions; but he was too cowardly to attend them. If anyone had offered to break a man on the wheel, for his benefit, in the marble court at Versailles, I am sure that he would have left his mistress's bed to stand at the window, and watch every detail of the execution. He treated himself as often as he could to spectacles so much to his taste, by gazing greedily at every funeral he could ... He was always talking of burials, of illnesses, of surgical operations. He showed how pleased he was, whenever an acquaintance died: when they did not die, he predicted that they would soon. I am convinced that what attracted him in hunting was the mere killing.' Choiseul goes on to speak of Louis' selfishness, his inconsequence, his studied indifference: and he ends with an anecdote which suggests that, in Louis' perverted nature, even the doctrine of divine right was debauched. 'One day, after speaking to me of the various indulgences which we allowed ourselves, and of the state of sin into which we had fallen through our taste for dissipation, he told me that I should be damned. I protested that this was too severe a judgment; and apart from not admitting it in my own case, I said it made me tremble for him; for, on his own admission, he offended the Deity still more than I did, by committing the same faults, and at the same time causing a far greater scandal and wrong than I could ever do. He answered that our situations were quite different. He gave me to understand that he was the Lord's Anointed, and that God would not allow him to be damned, so long as he carried out his mission as a King, namely to protect the Catholic religion of his realm. Holding the opinion that he was an emissary of God to sustain the Catholic religion, and believing that he had in his heart the resolution to do so, he was persuaded that he could give free rein to all his weaknesses, without sin and without remorse.'

This, remember, is an account—and I believe a substantially true account—of Louis the man. Louis the King, as the public knew him, was a handsome easygoing person, with 'a good head for places, persons, and things,' who 'listens to details, has tact and sensibility, understands men, and likes them honest.' The same witness speaks elsewhere, rather vividly, of Louis' 'lazy timid eyes, though accurate and kind' [*d'Argenson*]. To the world at large he was 'on the whole a very mild and merciful prince, wholly free from arrogance or ambition' [*Annual Register*]. Even Frederick the Great, writing to Voltaire, called him 'an honest man, whose only fault was that he was a King.' He had virtues, then: but I think that, as is so often the case with weak or lazy men, they were his vices turned inside out.

III

How was France governed, during Louis' half-century of nominal kingship? Partly by ministers, and partly by mistresses.

The reign falls into three periods, two of twenty years, and one of ten.

The first period begins in 1723, when Louis (at the age of thirteen) reached his majority, and both Orleans and Dubois died: it ends with the death of Fleury in 1743. During the first three years of his majority Louis' nominal minister was the Duc de Bourbon; but the real authority rested with his tutor, Cardinal Fleury, who made a point of being present at their interviews. It was Fleury and Bourbon who, to secure the succession, broke off Louis' engagement to the Spanish Infanta (still quite a child), and married him to Maria Leczinski, daughter of the ex-King of Poland.

In 1726 Fleury felt strong enough to dismiss Bourbon, and to take his place. He was already a man of 73—somewhat old, even for a tutor—and he lived to be a Minister at ninety. He was a shrewd amiable old gentleman, who made himself indispensable to the King, and outwitted his enemies at Court by an appearance of feebleness and simplicity. *Frederick the Great* contrasts the old mitred Machiavelli with his Cardinal predecessors. 'Richelieu and Mazarin,' he writes, 'had exhausted all the possibilities of pomp and pride. Fleury, by way of contrast, made his greatness consist in simplicity. . . . As first Minister he preferred negotiations to war, because his strength lay in intrigue, and he did not know how to command an army. He posed as a pacifist, so as to become the umpire rather than the conqueror of Kings. His plans were bold, his execution of them timid. He economized the State revenues, and had a methodical spirit—qualities which made him useful to France, whose finances were exhausted by the war of [Spanish] succession, and a vicious administration.' He had two great qualities in a minister, says another witness—economy and patience [*Hénault*]. He ruled France as securely as Richelieu or Mazarin, but without Mazarin's intrigues or Richelieu's decapitations [*Duclos*].

Above all, peace was secured from 1725 to 1733, though with some difficulty, by Fleury's co-operation with Walpole's Government in England. It was not seriously interrupted by the War of Polish Succession (1733-1735, though peace was not signed till 1738). When it was finally broken by the War of Austrian Succession, in 1740, Fleury was a very old man, and could no longer make headway against the militarist party. During the years of peace, under a nicely calculated régime of economy and *laissez-faire*, the social and economic condition of the country improved out of all knowledge. An English traveller in France in 1718 wrote that 'While the post-horses are changed, the whole town comes out to beg, with such miserable starved faces, and thin tattered clothes, [that] they need no other eloquence to persuade [one of] the wretchedness of their condition.' The same traveller writes again in 1739, 'France is so much improved, [that] it is not to be known to be the same country we passed through twenty years ago. Everything I see speaks in praise of Cardinal Fleury; the roads are all mended, and the greatest part of them paved as well as the streets of Paris, planted on both sides like the roads in Holland; and such good care taken against robbers, that you may cross the country with your purse in your hand . . . The French are more changed than their roads; instead of pale, yellow faces, wrapped up in blankets, as we saw them, the villages are all filled with fresh-coloured lusty peasants, in good cloth and clean linen. It is incredible the air of plenty and content that is over the whole country' [*Montagu*]. In 1738, for the first time since Colbert's budget of 1672, and actually for the last time before the financial reforms of Napoleon, the revenue of the country equalled its expenditure. Fleury's ministry proved, if proof were needed, that there was a practicable alternative to the policy of the Bourbon Kings; that France might become greater in peace than she had ever shown herself in war.

But Fleury was too old, and too remote, to form a powerful peace party. True, 'he enjoyed excellent health; and by means of a little rouge dipped in water, with which he rubbed his face, and a set of false teeth, he cheated himself, and made his enemies despair' [*Bernis*]. He outlived his seniors; he outwitted his juniors; he got the better of every court cabal against him. But he could not crush the younger militarist leaders; and it was they who led him into the fatal war of 1740, which undid all the good effects of his ministry.

The second twenty years of Louis XV's reign run from Fleury's death in 1743 to that of Madame de Pompadour in 1764. During the first twenty years Fleury's influence had done something to keep Louis a decent man, though it never succeeded in making him a good king. During the second twenty years he practically abdicated the throne in favour of the most famous of his mistresses, Madame de Pompadour. It was she who made and unmade his ministers and his generals. It was she who decided his policy at home and abroad—she had much to do with the expulsion of the Jesuits in 1761, and was mainly responsible for the Austrian alliance of 1756. The scandal of her position, according to the ideas of the time, did not consist in her being installed at Versailles, side by side with the Queen: it did not even consist in her playing a political role—with a king like Louis, that was inevitable. The real scandal, in that aristocratic Court, was that she was a 'bourgeoise,' educated to be a king's mistress, and brought to Court just in order to catch the king's eye. There were, besides, causes of jealousy in Madame de Pompadour's position that were not present in Louis XIV's mésalliance with Madame de Maintenon. She was young, handsome, talented, and very ambitious. La Tour's portrait shows her turning over a piece of music; on one side is a guitar, at her feet an album of etchings, and on a table beside her the plans for a Military School that she is founding, Besides dabbling in art and music, she patronized the Encyclopaedists, and they in turn advertised her gifts. Indeed, Louis might have been, and frequently was, in worse hands. 'She looked at all State questions,' said a Minister who worked with her, 'like a child'; yet she could on occasion 'tell the King the truth with energy and eloquence' [*Bernis*]. Better, in some ways, a French mistress than a foreign wife.

At Compiègne the Pompadour's rooms were over the King's, and all the Ambassadors, except the Papal Nuncio, went upstairs from his receptions to hers. The whole town and Court were there, and she knew how to make people of every rank feel at home with one another. She had, indeed, many of the qualities of a queen, and some of those of a lady. Her death makes one for the moment almost sorry for Louis. It was not etiquette for him to attend the funeral: but he watched it pass from a balcony at Versailles, following it with his eyes till it was at last out of sight; and then turned back into the room with tears on his cheeks, and said to his footman, 'And that was the only homage I could render her!' [*Cheverny*].

During the last ten years of his reign, Louis was less than ever a King. At a time when other Continental Powers were governed by hard-working and enlightened sovereigns—Frederick II in Prussia, Maria Theresa and Joseph II in Austria, Catherine II in Russia—the government of France was left to look after itself, whilst Louis was out hunting, or weaving tapestry, or making coffee for his lady friends. The Court had been scandalized by the régime of a bourgeoise mistress: it was shocked almost to protest when forced to honour as her successor Madame Du Barry—known to be dressmaker's assistant, and almost a common prostitute.

When Louis was a boy he was the idol of the people: when he went to the front at Metz in 1744, they called him *Bien Aimé*, the 'Well-beloved'; but by 1750 he had so thrown away his popularity, that there was talk of marching from Paris, and burning down Versailles; in '54, and again in '71, there was nearly a revolution. It was said that in Notre-Dame 6,000 Masses were offered for Louis' safety during his illness in '44: when the attempt was made on his life by Damiens in '57, the number sank to 600: and during his last illness in '74 only three Masses were said for his recovery. When at last he died, they dared not take his body through Paris by day. It was hurried off under cover of night through the suburbs; and those who saw the coffin pass shouted after it *Tiaout! Tiaout!*—the cry with which the royal huntsmen threw a broken stag to the hounds.

IV

Many things happened during Louis' fifty years' sleep. Some of them, such as the diplomatic entanglements of 1740 and 1756, or the wars of Frederick the Great, I must keep for separate treatment. But there are two questions which it seems best to mention here, because they run through the whole of the reign, and lead up to the French Revolution—I mean, the religious controversy, and the troubles with the Paris Parlement.

We have seen how Louis XIV used the Papal Bull *Unigenitus* (1713) as an opportunity for renewing his attack on the Jansenists; and how the effect of this persecution was to turn a religious sect into a semi-political party of opposition to the Crown. Under the Regency the French Church found itself divided into two camps—the 'Constitutionals,' who accepted the *Unigenitus*, and the Jansenists, who rejected it. Orleans, in his reaction against Louis XIV's policy, at first favoured the Jansenists, and made the Jansenist Archbishop of Paris, Cardinal de Noailles, President of his new Council of Religion (1715). But a few years later, when he was planning his daughter's marriage with the Catholic Infant of Spain, and his minister Dubois was canvassing for a Cardinal's hat, the Parlement was forced to register a declaration embodying the *Unigenitus*. Bishops, clergy, and people combined in growing numbers against this intolerance: there were anti-Constitutional riots in the provinces: the nation, said Voltaire, was on the side of the Jansenists: and when Louis married, his bride was nicknamed 'Unigenita.'

Fleury thought the Jansenists a little worse than the Ultramontanes. 'God has been good enough,' he said, 'to make me neither a Thomist, nor a Jansenist, nor a Molinist, nor a Scotist: I think there is no need for a bishop to be anything but a good Catholic.' He was against indiscipline—he allowed the condemnation of the bishop of Senez for publicly criticizing the *Unigenitus* (1726): and he discouraged 'enthusiasm' as heartily as any English bishop of the 18th century. When the anti-Constitutionalists tried to make capital out of miracles of healing alleged to have been performed at the tomb of a Jansenist deacon named Paris, he closed the cemetery. His enemies retaliated by putting up the ironical notice:

> *De par le Roi, défense à Dieu*
> *De faire miracle en ce lieu.*

Or in English:

> 'Notice to God. You mayn't do anything
> Miraculous here. By order of the King.'

In 1749 the controversy was given a fresh start by Archbishop Beaumont of Paris, who instructed the clergy of his diocese to refuse the sacraments, even in the case of a dying man, to all who could not produce a *billet de confession*—a religious ration-card signed by their confessor, certifying their acceptance of the *Unigenitus*. This outraged public feeling, and led to a number of incidents, the ultimate end of which was the downfall of the orthodox party. The Parlement punished the clergy for carrying

THE UNIGENITUS CONTROVERSY

out the orders of the Archbishop. The people backed the Parlement. The King and Court were officially on the side of the Jesuits and the 'Constitution.' But Louis himself cared little one way or the other. He listened unmoved to the Lenten sermons in which the Jesuit preachers annually denounced his immoral life. He allowed d'Argenson to write him long memoranda urging a conciliatory policy; and tried to enforce silence upon the whole controversy. He had the support of Pope Benedict XIV, who saw that Beaumont's zeal for orthodoxy was doing the Church more harm than good.

In 1761, when the *Unigenitus* controversy seemed at last to be dying down, the Jesuit Order was expelled from France. This was part of a general movement throughout Europe. As early as 1715 the Duke of Savoy, on grounds of sedition, had expelled all Jesuits from Sicily. Pombal exiled them from Portugal, on account of an attempt on the life of the King, in 1759. They were expelled from Spain in '66 and from Naples and Parma in '68. Their expulsion from France was a result of the *Unigenitus* controversy; but it came about in a curious way. In 1755 a commercial house in the Antilles, managed by a French Jesuit named La Valette, went bankrupt, and its creditors sued the Order. The Jesuits incautiously appealed to their Constitution, to prove that they had no responsibility for La Valette's debts. The Paris Parlement, before whom the case came, examined the Constitution —not very sympathetically, one imagines—and reported that it put the authority of the Pope above that of the King. Appealed to by Louis to modify this seditious principle, the General of the Order replied, in Latin which even the King could understand, *Sint ut sunt, aut non sint*—'Take it or leave it.' Louis found it impossible to shelter the Order any longer. Madame de Pompadour hated the Jesuits because they would not admit her to Communion; Choiseul hated them because he was a 'philosopher'; and the Calas case in 1761, when an unfortunate Protestant was put to death by the Catholic Parlement of Toulouse for a murder that he had never committed, enabled Voltaire to work up popular feeling against them. In '63 the Order was expelled from France, and ten years later it was formally dissolved by Pope Clement XIV. Its only friends in Europe were the heretic Frederick of Prussia, and the schismatic Catherine of Russia. It was in the latter country that the Society came to life again at the beginning of the nineteenth century.

What was the seriousness of this religious controversy? First, Jansenism had come to mean sedition; as in the days of the Fronde, the Parlement was against the Crown, the Paris people and the Press were behind the Parlement; and the suppression of the Jesuits took away one of the traditional supports of the throne. Secondly, the only point upon which the Jesuits and the Jansenists had been agreed was their hatred of the philosophers. The suppression of the Jesuits and the secularization of the Jansenists left the field clear for the philosophers. It soon became as fashionable to be irreligious as to be revolutionary; though the unfashionable crowd, especially the country people, knew nothing about the philosophers, and remained, as before, Catholic and Royalist.

V

Religion was not the only issue upon which Louis XV found himself opposed by the Parlements. Another was finance. The scandal of Louis' court life was embittered by its colossal and still growing extravagance. The Court cost the country about £11,000,000 a year, at a time when the whole national revenue was scarcely £25,000,000. Madame de Pompadour's pin-money came to about £300,000 a year. Madame du Barry spent £3,000,000 in three years. £300,000 is said to have been wasted on a single display of fireworks. Every time the King moved across the park from Versailles to the Trianon, which he was constantly doing, it cost £16,000. If you talked to him of economy, says *d'Argenson,* he would turn his back upon you. Meanwhile there was no money for the army, or for the fleet. The servants' wages at Versailles were sometimes three years overdue. The court 'had become the tomb of the nation.' And if Louis would not economize, neither would the privileged classes consent to bear their proper share of taxation. Machault's *vingtième* (5 per cent income-tax) of 1749 was avoided or compounded for by the clergy and nobles, and became an added percentage to the *taille* paid by the middle and lower classes. At last no remedy seemed left but the disgraceful one proposed by Terray in 1770—a declaration of national bankruptcy.

Both the religious and the financial quarrels came to a head in a more serious controversy between the Parlements and the Crown concerning the constitutional veto. We have seen how, during the Fronde, and after the deaths of Louis XIII and Louis XIV, the Paris Parlement, originally a Court of Appeal, used its duty of registering the royal edicts as a means of claiming constitutional privileges. Instructed by the philosophers, and emboldened by popular support, it now began to develop these claims. It told Louis that he was King *par la loi,* and could only govern lawfully. It maintained that its function of registering his decrees was not a mere formality, but a deliberate act of consent in the name of the people, without which they were invalid. If it refused to register, that was a real and constitutional veto, which could not be overridden by the traditional expedient of a *lit de justice.* Five times between 1750 and 1770 the Parlements (not only in Paris, but in the provinces) went on strike to enforce this protest; five times Louis punished them by exile; and five times, owing to popular clamour, they were recalled. 'The Regent made a great mistake,' complained Louis, 'when he gave back to the Parlement their right of remonstrance. They will end by destroying the State. . . . They are an assembly of Republicans. However,' he added, with characteristic indifference, 'there is no more to be said. Things will go on as they are: they will last out my time' [*Hausset*].

The d'Aiguillon case in 1771 brought matters to an impasse. Maupeou, who was Chancellor at the time, took his courage in both hands, and simply abolished the Parlements. Their place was taken by new Courts of Appeal whose members were no longer hereditary, but appointed by the Crown. The change was, in point of fact, a much-needed reform. But coming when and as it did, it only increased popular feeling against the King, and brought the country a stage nearer to revolution.

Three Latin words, it was afterwards said, destroyed France —Deficit, Veto, and Unigenitus. It was precisely on these three issues—financial, constitutional, and religious—that the contest between Louis XV and the Parlements was fought out.

VI

What part did Louis himself play in these matters? We shall be doing him no injustice if we regard it as almost negligible.

There were some things that he could do as well as anybody: for instance, he was noted for his skill in cutting off the top of a boiled egg with one blow of his fork; and he made a point of being served with boiled eggs on the days when he dined in public. There were some things, too, that he took trouble about: for instance, the royal kennels. He arranged exactly what each hound was to be doing from beginning to end of the year. He knew their names and judged their points better than any of his huntsmen. But if he took any part in public affairs, he cultivated indifference, and let himself be guided by the influence of the moment—the advice of his oldest minister, or the whim of his newest mistress.

There were, however, two odd corners of government in which he persuaded himself that he was doing serious work. One was the Censorship of the Post. 'It is the dishonest custom of every court,' writes *Choiseul,* 'to send Ministers and Sovereigns copies of letters which pass through the post. Obviously one can't take copies of all the letters delivered or dispatched in Paris. But copies are made of all the correspondence of persons whose names the King has given to the postal authorities, and the list is a very long one. The letters are taken to the King, who reads them. It is almost the only reading in which he indulges, apart from the Gazette, and the list of his hounds: and it is the only bit of work which he allows himself, by way of contributing to the government of his realm. After he has read these letters, Louis sends them on to his mistress, from whom he conceals no secrets, either his own or those of his subjects.' It is easy to imagine the unhealthy atmosphere of suspicion and scandal which this system of *espionnage* brought about.

But Choiseul is not quite fair in calling this amusement Louis' only contribution to government. He had another and more serious affair on hand, from about 1750 onwards—what is generally called 'the King's Secret.' This was a kind of private Foreign Office, with its own permanent secretary, its own ambassadors and spies, and its own secret correspondence, carried on by the King, without the help, and generally without the knowledge, of his ministers: and its policy was often different from that of the official Foreign Office; so that sometimes there were two French representatives working on opposite sides in the same diplomatic question, and sometimes (which must have been very embarrassing for the poor man) one ambassador with two contradictory sets of instructions. Such was the use made by Louis (who perverted everything he touched) of the Bourbon talent for diplomacy.

The countries in which Louis interested himself most were Russia and Poland: we shall come across some of the results of the secret diplomacy in those parts later on. England was also involved, from 1764 onwards, when that strange adventurer, the Chevalier d'Eon de Beaumont, who spent half his life masquerading as a woman, was attached to the French Embassy in London, with secret instructions to prepare the ground for an invasion of England. This was really the end of the whole business; for d'Eon quarrelled with his ambassador, refused to be recalled, and used Louis' secret correspondence as a means of blackmailing the King and the Government. When Louis XVI came to the throne, he pensioned off the staff of this sham Foreign Office, and closed it down.

VII

Can we sum up the half-century of Louis XV's reign? Just as it would be unfair to represent the King as doing absolutely nothing, so it would be a mistake to suppose that the country was in a state of absolute decay. You have only to compare the discontent and disillusionment at the end of Louis XIV's reign with the hopefulness, and the talk of a coming golden age, at the end of Louis XV's, to see how much France progressed, while the Court and the Government stood still.

This progress was partly economic, and partly intellectual. As regards economics, the country had needed time to benefit by Colbert's system under Louis XIV and Law's system under the Regency. Both were meant to encourage trade. But Colbert harassed the goose by prescribing the exact conditions under which its golden eggs should be laid; and Law nearly killed it by encouraging it to lay too many. Both extremes were corrected under Louis XV. This was partly due to the policy of *laissez faire et laissez passer*, practised by Fleury in the '30s, and formulated by Gournay in the '50s and '60s: and partly to the new school of economists called Physiocrats, whose apostle was

Quesnay, and whose followers included Louis XVI's great minister, Turgot. Both movements were working towards the Free Trade doctrines of Adam Smith. Under their influence there was a real improvement in the commercial and social prosperity of the people. One of its results—not so paradoxical as it seems—was to make the misgovernment and overtaxation of the country seem more than ever unbearable.

As regards the intellectual progress of France during Louis XV's reign, that involves a problem to which we shall have to return: I mean, the part played by the French 'philosophers' in bringing about the Revolution. Here it must be enough to point out one or two signs of progress.

First, from the time of the publication of Voltaire's *English Letters* (1734), English political ideas, English philosophy, and English manners became increasingly popular in Paris society. Secondly, although the burning of books by the common hangman, and the throwing of their authors into the Bastille, were still commonly practised, yet all effective censorship of literature disappeared during Louis XV's reign, and the Press became a powerful political agent. Thirdly, during the greater part of this period the Paris *salons,* run by rich or intellectual ladies, and frequented by poor philosophers and poets, were the centre of an elaborate and artificial culture; towards the end of the reign they became increasingly political, and were rivalled by the new clubs and cafés, that excluded ladies, and were managed on more English lines. Lastly, the stage comes to play a larger and more political part than it ever could under the patronage of Louis XIV. And you can trace an advance of natural taste and historical truthfulness when, towards the middle of the century, Cæsar and Alexander no longer appear on the stage in wigs and knee-breeches, when Andromache ceases to wear paniers, or to powder her hair, and rustic shepherdesses discard their white kid gloves and fans.

In fact, whatever way we look at it, we shall probably agree that the French people were very much alive during the latter half of the eighteenth century. But it was a kind of aliveness that threatened disaster to their rulers. Behind the prosperity of the bourgeoisie, and of a part of the working classes, lay a mass of misery and discontent. The diaries of the times are full of crimes of robbery and violence. The cruelty and bloodshed of the Revolution had its origin in the Paris slums and the public executions of the old régime. The Jacquerie of '89 was the result of half a century's bad landlordism, and more. d'Argenson's diary describes from year to year the terrible poverty of the country-people in his own province of Touraine.

The King was hunting one day in the forest of Sénard, during a time when bread was very dear. He met a man on horseback, carrying a coffin. Always interested in morbid subjects, he asked the man where he was taking the coffin. 'To the village of X,' he replied. 'Is it for a man or for a woman?' 'For a man.' 'What did he die of?' 'Hunger.' Louis spurred on his horse and asked no more questions [*Campan*].

Maupeou made Madame du Barry buy a portrait of King Charles I, and hang it up in her room, so that Louis might always have before his eyes a warning of the fatal results of royal weakness [*de Ligne*]. But the King was shrewd enough to know that 'the machine would last out his days.' The deluge would come, but after his time. A King would lose his head: but not the one who deserved to do so—only his harmless grandson and victim, Louis XVI.

LECTURE XVII

NORTHERN EUROPE, 1640–1740

I

The year 1740 is the most important date in European history between 1714 and 1789. The war of Austrian Succession, which broke out in that year, showed that France had ceased to lead Europe, and that two new Powers, Russia and Prussia, were making a bid for recognition, if not for supremacy, in the world of diplomacy and war.

We have followed the fortunes of the old Powers—France, Spain and Austria—up to, and even beyond, this date. We must now trace the rise of the new Powers, and see with what claims or prospects they came forward in the middle of the eighteenth century.

Russia and Prussia rose out of the ashes of Sweden and Poland. The dissolution of Poland may be dealt with separately: but the break-up of the Swedish Empire, and the change in the balance of power in the Baltic which took place between 1648 and 1721, is an integral part of our present subject.

I have chosen the dates 1640–1740, because that century exactly covers the reigns of the three Hohenzollerns—the Great Elector, Frederick I, and Frederick William I—who created the Prussia of Frederick the Great. Within these hundred years fall two shorter periods—that of the decline and break-up of the Swedish Empire, from 1648 (the Treaty of Westphalia) to 1721 (the Treaty of Nystadt); and that of the rise of Russia, from the personal rule of Peter the Great in 1689 to the end of the Northern War in 1721.

It will be best to begin by carrying on the history of Sweden from the point where we left it during the Thirty Years' War.

II

Gustavus Adolphus was succeeded (1633) by his daughter Christina, a young lady of a type less familiar then than now, who read Thucydides and Polybius in the originals, and discussed philosophy with Descartes; who disliked the routine of society, could not keep accounts, and refused marriage on the ground that it was a form of slavery. Wishing, after twenty-two years' rule of a Protestant country, to become a Catholic, she did what many kings have done under compulsion, but few of their own will—she abdicated her throne; then scandalized Brussels and Paris for some years by 'living her own life,' and finally died as an ornament of Catholic society at Rome.

Christina's throne was taken by one of her cousins, Charles X, and disputed by another, John Casimir, King of Poland. Charles was a great fighter, even for a King of Sweden, and astonished Europe by capturing Warsaw, and marching his army over the frozen Sound to attack the walls of Copenhagen. The peace of Oliva (1660) confirmed these successes. John Casimir gave up Livonia, and his claims to the Swedish throne. The King of Denmark surrendered (what was more vital to Sweden) Scania, and the eastern shore of the Sound.

Something like two-thirds of the Baltic shore were now in Swedish hands. Gustavus's dream had come true: the Baltic had become a Swedish lake. The Treaty of Oliva was as much a corollary of the Peace of Westphalia as was the Treaty of the Pyrenees, drawn up in the previous year. That made France supreme in the west, this made Sweden supreme in the north.

But there were reasons, and they were already appearing, why the Swedish Empire could not last. Sweden was a small and poor country, whose strength depended upon the weakness of its neighbours, and the ability of its Kings. There was no unity of race, language, or interests to hold together the Finns, Russians, Lithuanians, Poles, and Germans whom she had annexed. The conquered territory was a mere coastline, impossible to retain, if seriously attacked by the inland powers whom its loss had cut off from the sea. Sweden's main hope lay in the rivalry of other powers. She had won her empire by the help of Richelieu: she might keep it by the leave of Louis XIV. But though France would prevent her spoliation, she did not wish Sweden to be too strong. Holland was jealous of her control over the Baltic. Russia and Prussia were only waiting for an opportunity to drive her back into the sea. It is hardly surprising, then, that within sixty years of the Treaty of Oliva the Swedish empire had ceased to exist. The wonder is that it lasted so long.

It was the long reign of Charles XI (1660-97) which postponed the inevitable fall. It seemed, indeed, to have come in 1675, when the Swedish troops were defeated by the new Prussian army at Fehrbellin. But at this point Louis XIV stepped in, and prevented the Great Elector from seizing Swedish Pomerania. Afterwards, under French protection, Charles XI did a great deal to restore the military and economic power of the country. He was a queer, silent, strenuous man, who lived a rough country life, visited his capital at night-time, and was hardly ever seen except on parade. He played the same part in Swedish history as Frederick William I in the history of Prussia.

But his successor was not a Frederick the Great. Charles XII combined the generalship of Gustavus Adolphus with the recklessness of Charles X. He seemed to be a throw-back to the days of medieval knighthood. His contempt for pleasure, his cult of physical fitness, and his love of dangerous adventures appeared so strange to the self-indulgent and artificial culture of the age, that Voltaire made him the hero of one of his most famous works. The *Life of Charles XII* is still worth reading as a piece of romantic biography: and that its hero has appealed to men of very different traditions, you can guess from an enthusiastic preface to the *Everyman* edition written by John Burns.

Charles was only fifteen when he succeeded to the throne (1697), and found himself attacked by Russia, Poland, and Denmark, his hereditary enemies. In 1700 he forced Denmark to make peace, and at Narva utterly defeated a Russian army four times the size of his own. It is often said that, if he had pressed home his attack on Russia at this moment, he would have prevented his later disasters. But I think Russia would have proved as impossible to conquer in 1700 as in 1709 or 1812: and Charles was dealing with Peter the Great, an enemy no less determined than himself. Anyhow, he turned back, and spent an unprofitable six years (1701-6) chasing Augustus of Saxony from the throne of Poland, and setting up in his place Stanislas Leczinski, afterwards the father-in-law of Louis XV. Peter made better use of this interval, by organizing a new Russian army, occupying Swedish territory in the Eastern Baltic, and building there his new fort of Kronstadt, and his new capital of St. Petersburg.

In 1708 Charles returned to the attack—too late, and marched on Moscow with 30,000 men. He followed the same route as Napoleon, a century later, and came to grief in the same way. It was one of the coldest winters of modern times; and instead of fighting, Peter retreated, destroying or carrying off supplies. Finding it impossible to reach Moscow, Charles turned south from the neighbourhood of Smolensk, intending to join hands with Mazeppa, a friendly Cossack leader, and to revictual his army in the Ukraine. But Mazeppa brought him no troops, his relief column was defeated, his convoy captured; thousands of his men fell sick, and his ammunition gave out. The remnants of his army were surrounded and almost annihilated by Peter at Poltawa in 1709. Charles barely escaped to Turkey. After five years' captivity he rode home across Europe, to find Peter completing the conquest of the Eastern Baltic, and Prussia in occupation of Swedish Pomerania. He died, as he had lived, fighting—in an attack on Norway, in 1718. Sweden was left bankrupt, and so depopulated that practically all the work in the fields, and in public services, had to be carried on by women and girls [*Duclos*]. The battle of Poltawa is generally classed among the decisive battles of the world. The Treaty of Nystadt in 1721 gave diplomatic form to the fall of Sweden and the rise of Russia—a complete reversal of ownership in the Baltic, and a shifting of the whole balance of power in Northern Europe.

III

Russia was practically unknown to Western Europe before the time of Peter the Great. The embassies that occasionally appeared at London or Paris in the seventeenth century (you will find lively descriptions of them in Evelyn and Pepys) were stared at like deputations from Zululand or Patagonia. The few travellers who had been to Russia described it as 'a sad place,' with a sparse population, and 'poor, sorry houses, the Emperor himself living in a wooden house: his only sport hawking, or flying pigeons; all the winter spent within doors, some few playing chess, but most drinking their time away . . . Little learning among them of any sort. Not a man that speaks Latin, unless the Secretary of State by chance' [*Pepys*]. Yet the Russian people at that time were at least ten centuries old, and Tsars had ruled at Moscow for the last three hundred years. If we are to understand Russia's contribution to the eighteenth century, we must form some idea of the country and civilization which were then first thrown open to western eyes.

First, not only the size of Russia, but also its geographical unity, fits it to be the seat of a great empire. It is a huge, flat, triangular plain, with its base on the Urals and its apex at Warsaw. This shape gives it a special strength in defence: you may attack the apex, but the further east you go, the more the country opens out, and the more formidable your task becomes. The flatness of Russia is the flatness of the great northern plain of Europe. It is said that if you look eastwards from the top of Shotover there is no higher ground to prevent your having a clear view of the Urals. The only eminence in west Russia is the Valdai hills, south of Petrograd; and from these rise three rivers, which flow, after incredibly long and slow journeys, into the Baltic, the Black Sea, and the Caspian, covering the whole country with a system of water-roads. These three river-valleys were the homes of the three periods of Russian culture, and on them were built the three capitals of Russia. On the Neva, flowing north into the Baltic, was built Novgorod, where in the eighth century the Russian Slavs intermingled with the Varangians, or Normans, from Scandinavia, and developed a native civilization. On the Dnieper, flowing south into the Black Sea, rose Kiev, which became the capital in the tenth century, and derived its religion and culture from Christian Byzantium, and the dying Roman Empire. On a tributary of the Volga, which flows east, and then south right across Russia to the Caspian, and in the very middle of the country, lay Moscow, its religious and political centre since the fourteenth century—turning its back on Europe, and recalling Russia to its Oriental past.

The mass of the Russian population has always been agricultural, and the chief political question that of the ownership of the land. The size of the country has encouraged large estates; its featurelessness, communal rather than individual forms of peasant proprietorship, where such existed; and its emptiness, a nomadic tendency, for which the landlord's remedy was serfdom. For the Russian is by nature a nomad, a pioneer, a colonizer. 'With his crucifix [round his neck], his axe in his belt, and his boots slung behind his back, he will go to the end of the world' [*Rambaud*].

Russia is not encumbered, as so many nations are, by a political past. With no visible ruins, no relics of an earlier civilization, and no ancient literature, it has been free to extemporize whatever government seemed to suit it best. The centre of the Russian State is the family, and the union of families in the village community: the type of government this favours is a paternal despotism. Hence landlordism and Tsarism—the peasant becoming a serf and the citizen a child in the hands of tyrants whom he trusts, even when they slay him. Finally, a form of Christianity, learnt at the deathbed of the Roman Empire, and stiffened by centuries of isolation, ruled everything in the peasant's life, except his nomad conscience and his mystical turn of mind.

Such was the country which Peter the Great determined to add to Europe. There was one great fact in its favour: it was not an old nation gone to sleep, but a young nation not yet fully awake. Nor was Peter's attempt quite without precedent. In the fifteenth century Ivan the Great had patronized Renaissance scholars, and married a niece of the last Roman Emperor in the East. In the sixteenth century Ivan the Terrible made a commercial treaty with our Queen Elizabeth, and an Anglo-Russian Company kept up trade by sea between London and Archangel. Michael Romanoff, a contemporary of Charles I, had reorganized his army under foreign officers, some of them Irish. Alexis, the father of Peter the Great, was a man of liberal ideas. His minister married a Scotch wife, who scandalized the ladies of the Moscow *terems* by driving about in an open carriage; and built a theatre, in which German plays were performed. It was a ward of his wife, named Natalia, of Tartar descent, but western training, who became the Tsar's second wife, and the mother of Peter the Great.

IV

After some troubles about the succession, as was usually the case in Russia, Peter found himself Tsar in the same year as William III was acknowledged King of England, 1689.

Fortunately for Russia, Peter had not been brought up in the traditional way for a prince, in the dark little rooms (which you can still see) of the old palace at Moscow, but had been allowed to play truant in the foreign quarter of the city, where he made many friends—a Dutch architect, who taught him a little science, a Dutch carpenter, who built him a model sailing ship, a Scotch ex-colonel of the Austrian army, ending his life as a Russian general, and one Lefort, son of a Genevan chemist, who had taken service in the Russian army, married a rich wife, and made a home to which Peter was always welcome. It was his friendship with these foreigners, at an impressionable age, which europeanized Peter, and set him on the task of europeanizing his country.

Peter's portraits show a broad, thickly-moulded face, with fine eyes set wide, level eyebrows, and curly hair—suggesting much energy and some brutality. 'He was a very big man,' says *Saint-Simon*, 'well-built, a bit thin, with a rather round face, a fine forehead, good eyebrows; the nose rather short, but not too much so, biggish at the end; lips inclined to thickness; a ruddy-brown colour; fine dark eyes, big, lively, piercing, well set in his head; his look majestic and gracious when he wished it to be so, at other times severe and savage, with an occasional twitch that threw his eyes and whole face out of gear, and frightened one . . . It only lasted a moment, this wild, terrible look, and was gone at once.' As to his dress, 'he wore a linen collar, a round wig, brown and unpowdered, which fell short of his shoulders; a brown coat with gold buttons down to his knees, a waistcoat, breeches, stockings, but no gloves, no lace on his cuffs; on his coat the star of his order, with the ribbon below. His coat was often all unbuttoned, his hat on a table—even when he went out, never on his head. In this simple attire, however poor his carriage and his suite, one could not miss the air of greatness which was natural to him.'

Add to this picture a constitution which defied fatigue and excess. He could drink (it was said) for two days on end, and set himself right by three or four hours' sleep: and he was constantly at work—'dictating decrees, drilling troops, piloting ships, planning towns, ship-building, house-building, dissecting dead bodies, operating on live ones, extracting teeth (he made a collection of them), shaving off his subjects' beards, or clipping their coats (if they were worn too long for the European fashion), torturing his own criminals if need be, administering the knout or the stappado, cutting off heads' [*Malet*]. He was, in fact, part hero, part savage, and part madman.

When he was at Paris in 1717 he was particularly anxious to visit Madame de Maintenon: but the lady refused to see him, shut herself in her room, and went to bed. Peter was not to be out-manœuvred in this way. He forced his way into her room, pulled back the bed curtains, had a good look at her, and went out again without saying a word [*Duclos*].

At Paris and Berlin he was an expensive as well as an unmannerly guest, smashing the furniture in the royal apartments, damaging the pictures, and carrying off anything to which he took a fancy. In England he occupied *Evelyn's* house, Sayes Court. 'There is a houseful of people,' reported the steward, 'and right nasty.' The repairs cost £150.

Peter's talents, like his failings, were those of a noble savage. He was an admirer of Richelieu, and believed as strongly as any Bourbon in absolute government: but he anticipated the New Kings, the 'Enlightened Despots' of the eighteenth century, in considering himself the servant of his people. He gave up the greater part of his income to the State, and refused to spend public money on his private pleasures. He dressed like a tramp, and entertained at the expense of his friends. He travelled incognito in Germany and Holland to study the science of government, and worked as a carpenter in an English dockyard to master the art of ship-building. He lived for the good of his people, as he understood it, and died from the effects of plunging into the Neva in mid-winter to rescue some soldiers from drowning.

Peter had made up his mind that what Russia needed was europeanization, and that the way to bring this about was by opening windows (as he put it) in the wall that shut off Russia from the rest of Europe—Sweden, Poland, and Turkey. Most of all, his country must have an outlet to the sea. To get a port free from ice all the year round was impossible in the White Sea, barely possible on the north coast of the Black Sea, and difficult in the Eastern Baltic. But the last offered the freest and quickest route to Europe; accordingly Peter's main effort was put into the Swedish war, and his most symbolical act was the building of his new capital, St. Petersburg, at the head of the Baltic.

By europeanization Peter meant the externals, the institutions, the material products of civilization: he had no scales for immaterial values. He set himself to borrow 'military organization from Austria, manners from France, clothes from England, and administration from Germany': he had no use for that 'interior improvement of mind which makes a gentleman' [*Acton*].

Peter was an unsystematic reformer, making a stroke here and a stroke there, as the fancy took him: now abolishing the national dress, and the wearing of beards, or legislating against the seclusion of women; now encouraging agriculture, mining, or manufactures: at one moment founding a Naval College, an Engineering Institute, or a School of Surgery; at another importing foreign workmen and artisans to teach their trades—engineers, architects, officers, doctors, sailors, printers, five hundred of them from Holland alone. He organized a central and a provincial Government; and, in order to carry them on, turned his civil servants into nobles, and his nobles (on pain of loss of property, or compulsory celibacy) into civil servants. To secure respect abroad he raised (on paper) the largest army in Europe, and built a big shoddy fleet. To secure obedience at home he placed the police above the law, and the clergy beneath a Holy Synod, whose Procurator was his own nominee. He was once flattered on reading a comparison between himself and Louis XIV. 'All the same,' he remarked, 'Louis obeyed his clergy: I make mine obey me' [*Duclos*].

What were the results of Peter's reign? Territorially, Russia began to expand in every direction. The capture of Azof (though it was temporarily surrendered again by the Treaty of the Pruth) prepared the way for later conquests at the expense of Turkey: the Treaty of Nystadt transferred most of the eastern Baltic coast-land from Sweden to Russia: and during the last years of his reign, by occupying Baku, and placing envoys in Ispahan (and even Peking), Peter founded the Russian Empire in Central Asia.

The political results of Peter's reign were not at first realized. Russia no doubt became, almost suddenly, one of the great Powers, but chiefly in connexion with the Baltic, and for the nations concerned in the Baltic trade. Peter's Court was considered (not without reason) barbarous, and his daughter Elizabeth no fit wife for Louis XV. It was not until Russian armies intervened in the Wars of Succession towards the middle of the eighteenth century that the importance of Peter's work was understood.

Socially, Peter's reforms acted, as Frederick the Great said, like an acid on metal: they bit into the surface, and left marks which could never be effaced—permanent changes in the manners and institutions of the country: but below the surface the conservative character and outlook of the people remained much as before.

Peter left his work unfinished, and his country more than half uncivilized. But if the time had come for Russia to claim European citizenship, it was at least best that she should do so under a genius and a patriot, and in circumstances which gave some hope of her development on national lines. We can forgive Peter his many faults, if without him the world might never have known Russian literature, Russian music, and Russian mysticism.

V

Peter's only son, Alexis, had been disinherited, and cruelly put to death. His widow, Catherine, a rough camp-woman, 'small, thick-set, very tanned, without dignity or gracefulness' [*Wilhelmina*], and with manners more fit for a barracks than a palace, plotted with Menchikoff, his chief minister, to buy the support of the Guard, and declare herself Empress (1725). This way of settling the succession became the rule in Russia for the next thirty-seven years. As the French ambassador put it, 'Anyone can be master here, who has enough bayonets, and a cellar full of vodka and gold.'

For the sixteen months of Catherine's reign Menchikoff was the real ruler. When she died there was a succession of infants and intrigues until the reign of Anne (1730-40). The personal accounts of this lady are not complimentary. She is said to have been of a melancholy disposition, and addicted to drink. The French ambassador, after a rather detailed account of her looks, adds, with the gallantry of his nation, 'She looked best from behind' [*Hodgetts*]. But Russia was well governed by the German ministers whom she brought with her from Courland. She gave Poland a King, and sent an army to fight for Austria on the banks of the Rhine; waged a successful war against the Turks, and dispatched learned men to Kamchatka to find a shorter trade route between Moscow and Peking.

But Anne was more German than Russian; and it was the

unpopularity of this foreign régime which in 1741 enabled Elizabeth, the daughter of Peter and Catherine, to carry out her coup d'état, and make herself Empress.

Elizabeth had been born on the day of the great Tsar's triumphal return from the victory of Poltawa. Petrovna they called her, and she was in many ways a true daughter of Peter—'one of the handsomest women in Europe,' strong, sensual, sensible, a good judge of men, an almost fanatical patriot; yet without Peter's violence and Peter's energy. As time went on, she spent less of it on the business of government, and more on dissipation, dressing up, and superstitious devotions, 'passing from excesses that ruined her health to religious exaltations which injured her intellect.' She had a passion for frocks, and the means of indulging it—they found fifteen thousand in her wardrobes when she died. Her favourite luxury was to lie in bed, and have her feet scratched by her ladies-in-waiting [*Waliszewski*].

Elizabeth's government was a reaction against the German influences of Anne's reign. It was mainly in the hands of Bestujef, one of Peter's men, an able Russian with English blood in him, and a taste for amateur chemistry (he gave his name to a nerve tonic famous in the eighteenth century); and its policy was inspired by hostility to Prussia and to Frederick the Great, whether in alliance with England (the aim of Bestujef's diplomacy from 1745 to 1756), or as the partner of France and Austria in the Seven Years' War (1756 to 1763). Elizabeth made French the language of Russian society, and French culture the standard of good taste. Yet her best biographer calls her 'the last of the Romanoffs,' and regards her government and culture as genuinely Russian, a great national achievement on the lines laid down by Peter the Great.

VI

We must now go back to the last of the three northern Powers, and trace the rise of Prussia during the hundred years from the accession of the Great Elector (1640) to that of Frederick the Great (1740).

There is a remarkable sameness about this century of growth. From first to last, it was the Hohenzollerns who made Prussia. Their original home was a great castle, half palace and half fort, standing on the top of a wooded hill in the Suabian Alps, between the Neckar and the Danube. It dominates the whole country round, and the motto on its walls is 'From the mountains to the sea'—a good prophecy of the ambitions of its owners. In the thirteenth century a Hohenzollern who had helped the Emperor to his throne was rewarded with the Landgravate of Nuremberg. There the family made money. In the fifteenth century another Hohenzollern lent some of it to another Emperor, and received by way of mortgage the Electorate of Brandenburg, one of the barrenest districts of north Germany. In the sixteenth century Albert of Brandenburg, Grand Master of the Teutonic Knights, who held territory in East Prussia as a vassal of the King of Poland, became a Lutheran, 'secularized' the property of the Order, and turned it into the Duchy of Prussia. In the seventeenth century both this dynasty, and that of Cleves on the lower Rhine, came by inheritance into the hands of the Hohenzollerns. These family estates were the nucleus of modern Prussia.

Though Brandenburg was a poor land, with no natural frontiers, it was splendidly situated for unifying and controlling northern Germany. Lying between the Oder and the Elbe, the two chief waterways of the country, it was the meeting-place of the main routes both from east to west and from north to south. It inherited the goodwill of the Hanseatic League, and became the natural outlet of the commerce of central Europe. But the outlying estates were completely cut off from one another. Each governed itself, and valued its independence. The only link between them was their Hohenzollern landlord, and such central control as he could enforce. The Prussian problem was always of this kind—how to join estate to estate, by purchase, by marriage, by inheritance, or (ultimately) by war; how to keep these estates in the family—here the Hohenzollern law of inheritance and a fortunate line of succession contributed much; and how to colonize, cultivate, and organize them into a single state, able to defend its frontiers and pay its way. It was not a problem of government so much as of estate management on a large scale. And for this the Hohenzollerns showed themselves admirably qualified.

The history of Prussia, so far as it concerns us here, begins in the tragedy of the Thirty Years' War. Brandenburg, with an army of two hundred men, was at the mercy of any belligerent who chose to come there. It lost nearly half its population, and was left a desert. A century later, said Frederick the Great, its provinces were still poor and backward owing to the sufferings of that time. It might never have recovered, had it not been for Frederick William, justly called the Great Elector, whose rule began in the last years of the war, and lasted nearly half a century (1640–88).

Here is a characteristic sketch of him by *Carlyle*: 'Collectors of Dutch prints know him: here a gallant eagle-featured little gentleman, brisk in the smiles of youth, with plumes, with truncheon, caprioling on his war-charger, view of tents in the distance: here a sedate, ponderous, wrinkly old man, eyes slightly puckered (eyes *busier* than mouth); a face well-ploughed by Time, and not found unfruitful; one of the largest, most laborious, potent faces (in an ocean of circumambient periwig) to be met with in that century.'

Frederick William laid down lines of policy which were followed, with the family thoroughness and lack of originality, by his successors; he was the real founder of modern Prussia. The scattered estates were unified by a common system of taxation, including a land tax, and a tax on beer. The money thus raised was used to set on foot a standing army of twenty-four thousand men, the largest force of its kind in Germany. It was this army which beat the Swedes at Fehrbellin in 1675, and warned Europe of what was coming. To populate his empty estates, Frederick William imported religious refugees from other parts of Germany, from Holland, and from France. A year before the Revocation of the Edict of Nantes, France was placarded with notices in the Great Elector's name, offering the Huguenots land, houses, and employment in his country, a contribution towards the cost of the journey, and ten years' exemption from taxes. About twenty thousand French Protestants found refuge and religious toleration in this Hohenzollern haven. Frenchmen built Berlin; Frenchmen helped to create Prussian industry, Prussian culture, and the Prussian army.

The Great Elector died in the same year that his wife's nephew, William of Orange, became King of England (1688). Sixty years later his body was moved to the new cathedral at Berlin. Frederick the Great made them open the coffin, 'gazed in silence at the features for some time, which were perfectly recognizable; laid his hand on the hand long dead, and said *Messieurs, celui-ci a fait de grandes choses*—this one did a great work' [*Carlyle*].

The Great Elector's son Frederick, who succeeded him, is generally credited with one achievement, and no more. By financing the Emperor Leopold in the War of Spanish Succession he got the right to call himself a King. Not King of Brandenburg within the Empire, but King of Prussia outside it: as, a few years later, the Elector of Hanover became King of England. In 1701, at Königsberg, he placed a royal crown on his head, with ceremonies of a suitably vulgar and expensive kind, and called himself King Frederick I; and he left to his successors an elaborate establishment of Court officials, and a string of subsidiary titles as long as that of any monarch in Europe. But it would be a mistake to suppose that he neglected the family tradition of good government. Travellers in Germany reported a notable improvement in the roads, the inns, and other decencies of life, as soon as they entered the territories of the King of Prussia; whilst at Berlin elegant buildings were being erected, which combined practical usefulness with refined taste: in one of them the upper floor was an Academy of Science, and the lower floor a livery-stable [*Toland*].

VII

The second King of Prussia, Frederick William I (1714–1740) was one of the oddest figures even in the eighteenth century. Superficially regarded, he was a coarse, brutal, suspicious, ill-tempered tyrant, whose days were spent in bullying his family and his subordinates, and whose nights were given up to drinking and smoking.

The domestic life of the royal family almost passes belief. The King, who despised culture, was in constant antagonism with the French taste for music and literature which the Queen encouraged in his son Frederick and his daughter Wilhelmina. When he was irritated, or had a touch of the gout, Frederick William behaved like a madman, and his family went in fear of their lives. Here is one of many scenes described by *Wilhelmina*, who fully revenged herself by writing her *Memoirs*. It took place at Potsdam, where Frederick William was laid up with the gout. 'This ailment ... made his temper intolerable. We suffered more than the pains of Purgatory. We were obliged to appear in his room at nine in the morning; we had our lunch there and dared not leave it, for whatever reason. Day after day passed in nothing but invectives against my brother and myself. The King never called me anything but "that English gutter-snipe" [*la canaille Anglaise*] and my brother was "that rascal Fritz." He forced us to eat and drink things we hated, or which revolted our stomachs. . . . Every day was marked by some sinister incident, and one couldn't raise one's eyes without seeing some poor wretch tormented in one way or another. The King was too impatient to stay in bed; he had himself put into a wheeled chair, and so dragged about all over the palace: and we followed this triumphal car the whole time, like captives undergoing punishment. . . . One morning, when we came into his room to pay our respects, he drove us away. "Out you go!" he cried to the Queen, like one beside himself, "you and your damned brats [*maudits enfants*]: I want to be alone." The Queen tried to reply, but he silenced her, and ordered lunch to be served in her room ... We had scarcely sat down, when one of the King's footmen rushed in all out of breath, crying "For God's sake, Madam, come as quick as you can! The King is trying to strangle himself." The Queen ran at once, terrified, and found that the King had put a cord round his neck, and would have been suffocated, if she hadn't come to his assistance. His mental derangement [*transports du cerveau*] lasted till the evening.'

Those who got behind this unpleasant exterior found in Frederick William a blunt common sense, and a grim turn of humour. His motto was 'stick to reality,' and he hated unpractical theorizing. The only music he could listen to was Handel's: the only ritual he could tolerate was that of the hunting field. 'God never made Kings,' he would say, 'to pass their time in enjoyment, but to govern their country. Kings are made for work, and if they want to reign with honour they must look after their affairs for themselves.' Work was his hobby, organization the passion of his life.

The centre of his Government was a 'Directorium,' or War Cabinet, over which he himself presided, and which controlled every department of the State. His policy was that of the Great Elector—to encourage foreign immigration, to develop agriculture and commerce, to build up a gold reserve, and to organize a national army. The Prussian troops had an unusually large proportion of citizen soldiers: they were drilled to a mechanical perfection, and officered by a military caste of nobles under a King whom George II used to call 'my brother the Corporal.' The surest way of propitiating Frederick William was to find him a tall enough recruit for his giant guards, the crack regiment of this army. The Great Elector's policy was followed even in the matter of religion. Toleration was enforced as a corollary of immigration. Pietism was encouraged in Prussia at a time when Wesleyan enthusiasm was being snubbed by the English Church; and Catholics found themselves well treated by the Calvinist ruler of a Lutheran state.

When Frederick William lay on his deathbed, surrounded by the members of his family, he asked the minister who was attending him, 'In order to go to Paradise, must I forgive all my enemies?' 'Yes,' was the answer, 'without that it is impossible.' 'Oh, well then, Dorothea,' he said, turning to the Queen, 'write to your brother [George II], and tell him that I forgive him all the evil he has done me. Yes, tell him that I forgive him': then, after a moment's thought, he added, 'but wait till I am dead' [*Harris*].

LECTURE XVIII

THE WARS OF POLISH AND AUSTRIAN SUCCESSION

I

In our account of Northern Europe during the century ending in 1740 we have hitherto said nothing of one country which was a greater source of trouble than them all—I mean Poland.

A few years ago there was no such place on the map. Now that it appears so often in the news, you will realize what an important part it must have played in the eighteenth century. At the beginning of the seventeenth century (to go no further back) Poland was a very large state. It consisted of the Kingdom of Poland (i.e. the country of the Vistula, with Warsaw as its capital); the Grand Duchy of Lithuania (eastwards, with its capital at Vilna); to the south, Little Russia and the Ukraine, including the old Russian capital of Kiev: to the east again, White Russia, including Smolensk; and on the north it exercised a suzerainty over the 'secularized' possessions of the Teutonic Knights—the Duchies of Courland and East Prussia. During the seventeenth century first Sweden and then (as we have seen) Russia occupied Livonia (the northern end of Lithuania), Kiev and Smolensk were lost to Russia, East Prussia gained its independence, and the Turks conquered part of the Ukraine: the partition of Poland had already begun. But it still stretched right across Central Europe from the Baltic almost to the Black Sea; its Russian frontier ran a little east of the Dvina and the Dnieper, its German frontier a little west of the Vistula and the Dniester. With its large area and central position Poland might have become one of the new Powers of the eighteenth century. Why did it fail, and disappear?

II

The first weakness of Poland was geographical. Its central position was no advantage, because its frontiers (except the short section of the Carpathians) were impossible to defend. Austria could fight with its back to the Alps; Prussia had nothing to fear on the side of Holland and the North Sea; but Poland had open frontiers towards two rising Powers, Russia and Prussia, to its east and west, and two falling Powers, Sweden and Turkey, both centres of international intrigue, to its north and south.

To a country so placed the first necessity was a strong government. But the government of Poland was the weakest in Europe. First, ever since the end of the Jagellon dynasty in 1572, the Kings of Poland had been elected, and elected conditionally. On the occurrence of a vacancy, candidates for the throne, whether native nobles or foreign princes, sent in their names, and stated their terms. The electorate of Polish landlords considered which candidate would interfere least with their lands and liberties. A bargain was struck, called the 'pacta conventa.' The highest bidder became King. Again, though there was a Polish Diet, its proceedings had been rendered farcical, since the middle of the seventeenth century, by the rule that its decisions must be unanimous. A single deputy, by the use of his 'liberum veto,' could throw out not only the measure he voted against, but also all previous measures passed during the session. Lastly, the only remedy for this absurdity was another. If the Diet broke down, as under such conditions it almost invariably did, any body of nobles that thought itself strong enough might form a 'confederation' to carry its will by an appeal to arms. These three institutions—the pacta conventa, the liberum veto, and the right of confederation—might have been suited to a wandering tribe of savages. In the fixed and civilized society of Europe they meant sheer anarchy and dissolution.

Nor was there any remedy for this political weakness in the social condition of the country. European travellers in Poland regarded it rather as we regard Siberia. They described it as a wilderness of forest-land with occasional oases of cultivation: the country population poor and slavish, living in savage huts: here and there a rich and crowded city, or the castle of a turbulent and extravagant baron [*Ségur*]. 'By the side of the poor gentleman, whose only possessions were a suit of coarse fur, his horse, his sword, and his titles of nobility, who knew neither how to read nor how to write, and for whom the world was bounded by the limits of his low-lying horizon, might be seen the great noble, clad in sable, his plumed cap glittering with jewels, his elegant sledge drawn by blood-horses of great price—the great noble, who had been initiated into all the refinements of luxury at Paris, or at Constantinople into all the pleasures of the East.' There were similar contrasts among the clergy: some held state office, and travelled on embassies all over Europe: others lived in poverty, and 'preached in the highways the superstition and fanaticism of the Middle Ages.' But 'these widely opposed characters, instead of being separated by the artificial barriers of etiquette [as in France], were brought together, and elbowed each other at every moment, in public life, in the camps, in the tribunals, and in the Diets . . . In the midst of the smoky huts of the peasants stood splendid palaces' in pseudo-European or Byzantine style, where 'lovely and graceful women, magnificently gowned, held receptions, and talked the prettiest French in the world . . . At the same time the courts and markets would be thronged with future voters and future combatants, making the roofs resound with their patriotic songs and clash of arms, and passing the hours of the night in interminable repasts, at which quarters of beef roasted whole were washed down by floods of Hungarian wine' [*Broglie*].

Frederick the Great gave a characteristically unchivalrous explanation of the misfortunes of Poland. 'The human mind in this kingdom,' he said, 'is become feminine: the women are the supporters of all factions, and dispose of everything, while their husbands are getting drunk.' But the sneer was superfluous. Poland was just a relic of medievalism in Northern Europe, as Spain was in the South; but without a Spanish throne and a Spanish Church to hold it together—'an incredible mixture of ancient and modern, of monarchism and Republicanism, of feudal pride and democratic equality, of poverty and wealth, where wise debates in the Diet were closured by the drawing of swords, and no patriot was ashamed to raise a faction, or to call in a foreign power' [*Ségur*].

A government at the mercy of factions, a country without the means of defending itself, and party strife based on a system of bribery, were a constant temptation to foreign intrigue. At a time when royalty seemed almost divine, and the populousness of a state was taken to be a proof of its greatness, the annexation of Polish territory or the possession of the Polish Crown seemed highly desirable to such of its neighbours as had too few citizens, or too many princes. Brandenburg coveted the Poles who separated East Pomerania from East Prussia: Russia claimed the eastern Lithuanians as its own by title of race and religion: Austria in the south-west would 'compensate' itself, acre for acre, town for town, for anything taken by the other Powers. Again, Poland had economic possibilities. Even in the seventeenth century a considerable trade was being carried on there by travelling merchants from Scotland. A certain Sir John Denham was sent by our King Charles II to the King and Diet of Poland to extract taxes from these gentlemen. He came back with £10,000, and was so pleased with his success that he wrote a poem about it.

But why should France concern itself with the distant affairs of Poland? As long ago as the sixteenth century Henry of Anjou had been King of Poland for a few days, before he became Henry III of France. In the seventeenth century the Prince de Conti had been sent on a similar errand by Louis XIV, but had found it safer to return home before the coronation. Since the marriage of Louis XV to a Polish princess, a Polish policy had become a recognized part of Bourbon diplomacy. Poland could be used against the Hapsburgs. Sweden, Poland, and Turkey (a belt of states crossing Europe from north to south) played much the same part in the seventeenth and eighteenth centuries as the Balkan States played in the nineteenth. Before the rise of Prussia this belt was the 'Nearer East,' and could be used to embarrass its western neighbours. At the end of the seventeenth century the defeat of Sweden by Prussia and the driving back of the Turks by Austria left Poland as the one hope of this traditional French policy; but left it so at a moment when the rising rivalry of Russia and Prussia was to make Poland 'the centre of all contending interests, and the road of all the armies.' This is the clue to the tangled history of Poland from 1733 to 1772. France, carrying on (till 1756) its traditional anti-Hapsburg policy, failed to realize how the situation had been changed by the rise of Russia. Russia and Prussia combined to initiate a new Polish policy—a policy of peaceful penetration followed by partition—which disregarded and cut across the old lines of French diplomacy.

III

Under all these circumstances it was not unnatural that a disputed succession in Poland should bring about a European war. In 1733 Augustus II of Saxony and Poland died, hoping to be succeeded on both thrones by his son Augustus III. But the Powers had other views. Russia and Austria put forward a Portuguese prince. France nominated Stanislas Leczinski, a Polish noble, who had been given the throne by Charles XII, and deprived of it by Peter the Great, thirty years ago, and who had recently surprised himself and all Europe by marrying his daughter to Louis XV. The royal election was held in the usual fashion by an armed gathering of 64,000 nobles at Warsaw. The vast majority voted for Leczinski. But this did not suit the plans of Russia and Austria. They transferred their support to the Saxon candidate. Stanislas, driven from Warsaw, and besieged in Dantzig, disguised himself as a cattle-drover, and escaped home again. Augustus III became King of Poland.

Fleury had never liked the Polish adventure. France could only support Stanislas by sending a fleet to the Baltic, or by attacking the Austrian Netherlands, either of which courses England might well resent. But if the jingoes insisted upon war, he would at least see that France gained by it. If he could not annex the Netherlands, he might secure the cession of a province even more essential to France—Lorraine. It was the more necessary to attempt this, as Francis, heir to the Dukedom of Lorraine, had recently been married to Maria Theresa, the daughter and heiress of Charles VI, and designated as his successor to the Empire. If nothing were done to defeat this plan, the head of the Hapsburgs might at any moment be domiciled within striking distance of Paris.

The Polish Succession War broke out in 1733, and lasted two years; the principal fighting was in Italy and the Rhine valley. The Emperor was worsted, though a Russian army marched right across Europe to help him. By the Second Treaty of Vienna (1735) Stanislas gave up his claim to Poland, but was allowed as compensation the title of King, and the Duchy of Lorraine: he kept a model Court at Nancy, founded hospitals and public libraries, constructed a mechanical waterfall, carried on a controversy with Rousseau, and smoked a pipe six feet long. At his death his Duchy was to revert to France. Choiseul was credited with this policy, which matured during his ministry. It was in reality a triumph for Fleury, whose enemies discovered that a diplomat might not be too old at 85.

IV

Five years later Europe was again at war. This struggle, like the last two, was not national, but dynastic. But the War of Austrian Succession, which broke out in 1740, showed a new scene in the state of Europe, and brought new Powers upon the stage. It is more than usually important to understand how it came about. Its principal causes were the weakness of Austria, the French anti-Austrian policy, and the ambition of Frederick the Great.

By the weakness of Austria I mean chiefly three things—her failure and loss of territory in the War of Polish Succession; her defeat in the Turkish war into which she was dragged by Russia in 1736, and which ended with the disgraceful Treaty of Belgrade (1739); and the Emperor's failure to provide for an undisputed succession. This last is a complicated story. All that concerns us here is that in 1713 Charles VI had published a document called the Pragmatic Sanction, securing the succession for his daughter Maria Theresa, and, with a belief in the value of diplomatic promises quite pathetic in the eighteenth century, had spent the rest of his reign in bribing the other Powers to agree to this arrangement. When he died in 1740, of gout and a surfeit of stewed mushrooms, he left his daughter whole bundles of treaties guaranteeing her succession, but no means of enforcing them except a defeated army and an empty Treasury.

This might have mattered less, had not a formidable enemy been already arming against Austria. When Charles VI died, Frederick the Great had been five months on the Prussian throne. He had inherited from his careful and eccentric father a large gold reserve, and the most efficient army in Europe; and he was ambitious to use them. He believed '... that a monarch ought to make himself, and particularly his nation, respected; that moderation is a virtue which statesmen ought not to practise too rigorously, because of the corruption of the age; and that at the commencement of a reign it was better to give marks of determination than of mildness' [*Frederick*]. He knew also (he had studied history and geography) just what Prussia needed, to round off her territory—eastwards, West Prussia; southwards, Silesia. Silesia meant the upper Oder valley: the lower was already in his hands. Silesia was the high road to Vienna, and the back door to Bohemia. Silesia divided Saxony from Poland, and he had designs on both. Silesia could be made into a great agricultural and industrial district. True, it belonged to Austria, and he had no quarrel with Maria Theresa. But Austria was weak, and Maria Theresa was a woman. Chivalry might have prevented Frederick's taking advantage of such facts: but his home and training had left him anything rather than a gentleman; and he marched his armies into Silesia.

France might have prevented him: but French policy, where Austria was concerned, was even more unscrupulous than his own. Frederick need not, perhaps, feel himself bound by his father's adherence to the Pragmatic Sanction: Louis XV had guaranteed it himself. But Louis, in 1740, has already given up the attempt to reign. He gets up at eleven o'clock, and does one hour's work a day. He is like a card-player with an impossible partner, waiting for the end of the game. The partner is Fleury, still young enough at 87 to be a candidate for the Papacy—'more mischievous than wicked,' his enemies describe him, 'very old, and very popeable'; and they hint that 'the air of Italy is soft and excellent for old people.' Chauvelin, the jingo leader, was dismissed three years ago, but the militant anti-Austrian party has found a new leader in Marshal Belleisle, 'one of the greatest geniuses of the little century in which we live,' and is very strong in the country, and at Court [*d'Argenson*]. Fleury is as much opposed to war as he was in 1733. But he is still less able to prevent it. He salves his conscience, with regard to the Pragmatic Sanction, by joining in the war indirectly, and by putting in no French claim for Austrian territory. Whilst Frederick seized Silesia, Maria Theresa's succession was disputed by Charles Albert the Elector of Bavaria, Philip V of Spain, and Charles Emmanuel of Sardinia, all of whom could produce ancient

THE SITUATION IN 1740

claims overridden by the Pragmatic Sanction. Fleury, still nervous about Lorraine, would have preferred any Emperor to Francis, the husband of Maria Theresa: and the relationship between Louis XV and Philip V gave him an easy excuse for intervening on the side of Spain, and its ally Bavaria. So here was France, regarded in 1738 as the arbiter of Europe, going back on its solemn engagement to Charles VI, and joining in a quite unjustified attack on Maria Theresa, in which any advantages that were won would go, not to itself, but to Prussia (Silesia), Bavaria (Bohemia), or Spain (an Italian Duchy for Don Philip, the younger son of Elizabeth Farnese). We cannot feel much surprise or sympathy, if such an adventure ended in disaster.

V

Meanwhile, what of the victim of all this treachery, Maria Theresa? She was twenty-three, newly crowned and newly married, in love with her husband and in love with her people: handsome on a rather large scale, with dark blue eyes, golden hair, and a good complexion: with the look of a Queen, and accustomed to public business: brave, patriotic, and stubborn in defending her rights: at the same time with a charm and simplicity that appealed to the common people—'a great woman,' said *Frederick,* her constant enemy, 'who did honour to her sex and to her throne'; and 'her designs were worthy of a great man.'

She needed all these qualities. She had hardly ascended the throne when Frederick's armies were in Silesia. The banners under which they marched were to have been inscribed 'Pro Deo et Patria'; but Frederick deleted the 'Pro Deo,' saying that there was no need to involve God in the quarrels of men [*Voltaire*]. He had plenty of other allies—Bavaria, France, Saxony, Spain; and he knew that Austria was isolated and unprepared. So he quickly overran Silesia, and occupied it almost unopposed. Then in the autumn of '41 (without any declaration of war) a French army marched down the Danube valley, and captured Prague for Charles of Bavaria: and in January, '42, owing to French influence, he was elected Emperor.

Meanwhile Maria Theresa, though unable to resist this double invasion, was preparing for a return attack. She had allies, but they could not help her much. England, the only country with nothing to gain by the dismemberment of Austria, was the only Power to stand by the Pragmatic Sanction. She was already at war with Spain (over the matter of Jenkins' ear) in 1739. The long entente with France was near its close—Fleury died and Walpole resigned in the same year, '42. But England could give Maria no help beyond money and good advice; and it was not easy to make her accept either. Again, Russia under Anne had fought for Charles VI against the French. But in 1740 Anne died—it was one of the considerations which timed Frederick's attack—and it was not until Elizabeth was firm on the throne (1741) that Russian influence began to tell on the Austrian side. The King of Sardinia, though (as we have seen) himself a claimant to the Hapsburg domains, was more afraid of French designs on Savoy than of Austrian designs on Italy, and sold Maria Theresa his neutrality, if not his support, for a slice of Milanese territory. Lastly Holland, which 'followed after England as a pinnace follows the track of a ship of war behind which she is being towed' [*Frederick*], and which was always nervous of French designs in the Netherlands, could be counted an ally.

But, in the main, Maria Theresa must rely upon her own people: and it was just here that she proved her charm as a woman and her capacity as a Queen. As Queen of Hungary—eligible, but not yet elect—she appealed to the Hungarian nobles, and in return for unusual concessions to their liberties secured the grant of an army of 100,000 men. *Voltaire,* with an historical licence which you may admire, but which (I hope) you will not imitate, compresses the three months' negotiations into a single meeting of the Hungarian Diet, at which (he says) the Empress appeared, holding in her arms her eldest son, still almost a baby, and used the following words: 'Forsaken by my friends, persecuted by my enemies, attacked by my nearest relatives, I have no resources left but your faithfulness, your courage, and my own constancy. I place in your hands the daughter and the son of Kings. We look to you for our safety.' Whereupon all the barons, touched and inspired, drew their swords, and cried, 'Moriamur pro rege nostra Maria Theresa!' (They said 'rege' instead of 'regina,' although she was a queen, because it was their custom to call all their sovereigns kings: they said 'nostra' instead of 'nostro' because, after all, she was a woman. It was a clever solution of a grammatical difficulty, and their unanimity did them credit.)

The day of Hungarian heroism was to come. At the moment (the autumn of 1741) the only thing to do was to make terms with Frederick. A secret meeting was arranged at Schnellendorf, and the British Minister, Lord Hyndford, acted as intermediary. By the Treaty of Breslau (published in June, 1742) Maria Theresa ceded Silesia—planning all the time to recover it, and never doubting that she would succeed in doing so.

The immediate effect of this Treaty, which Frederick carried through without consulting his French allies, was to leave the latter exposed to the whole force of the Austrian counter-attack. *Frederick* himself explains unblushingly that he needed French help to gain Silesia, but that he had no wish to see Austria further weakened, or the French power established east of the Rhine. 'Prudence seemed to require that he should hold a middle line of conduct, by which he might establish an equilibrium between the houses of Hapsburg and Bourbon.' When the terms of Breslau were published, France naturally felt itself betrayed. Fleury, now 'at his last gasp, emaciated and withered as a mummy' [*d'Argenson*] wrote to Maria Theresa, disclaiming responsibility for the French war policy. He hoped to disarm her hostility: her publication of his letter was an open humiliation for France and for himself. It was followed by the advance of the Austrian army. The French troops in Bohemia and Upper Austria had the greatest difficulty in extricating themselves. The retreat from Prague in 1742 was as brilliant an operation as the capture of Prague in 1741, though Frederick, who was the cause of it, made it the subject of ungenerous satire. By the end of the following year Austria had not only recovered her lost territory, but also occupied Bavaria, and reached the Rhine.

So ended the First Silesian War, being the first part of the War of Austrian Succession. Frederick had gained Silesia, and lost his own soul. Maria Theresa had lost Silesia, and gained the admiration of Europe. France had been fooled.

VI

After a short breathing space, fighting began again. It was certain that Maria Theresa would not reconcile herself to the loss of Silesia. It was obvious that Frederick's policy of holding a balance between France and Austria would involve him in war, if either power seemed too strong. It was evident that France, now definitely at war with England at the side of Spain, would rather be fooled again by Frederick than risk having him for an enemy—France, which for some years after the death of Fleury had as many governments as there were royal mistresses, and as many policies as there were parties at Court.

Frederick began the Second Silesian War by invading Bohemia and seizing Prague (1744). Next year he conquered Saxony, now an ally of Austria, and forced Maria Theresa to confirm the terms of Breslau by the Treaty of Dresden (1745). The same year the Emperor Charles VII, the French nominee, died; and his son, the new Elector of Bavaria, came to terms with Maria Theresa, renouncing all claims either to the Empire or to the Hapsburg succession. So the chief reason for the war ceased to exist. But it is easier to begin fighting than to end it. In Italy, the Rhine valley, and the Netherlands, the war dragged on till '48, when it was closed by the Treaty of Aix.

It was mainly a trench war, in which open battles were fought only to cover or to drive away armies engaged in besieging fortified towns. Open fighting was still conducted on medieval principles. At Fontenoy (1745) an English and a French force, advancing up opposite sides of the same hill, met unexpectedly at the top. Both sides had their muskets loaded; but they knew that after the first volley it would take nearly a minute to reload, during which time they would be at the mercy of a bayonet charge; the French infantry had therefore orders always to let the enemy fire first. The English officers saluted the French, raising their hats. The French officers returned the courtesy. The officer in command of the English Guards called out, 'Gentlemen of the French Guards, fire!' The French commander answered, 'Gentlemen, we never fire first: please fire yourselves.' So they did. Nineteen officers of the French Guard fell at the first volley, 95 men were killed, 285 wounded: the other regiments lost as heavily. The front line being almost annihilated, the back ranks wavered, and fled: the English marched on [*Voltaire*].

During the last years of the war the French government and army retrieved some of the ground they had lost during the first.

Fleury's death, and the establishment of Mme de Pompadour at Versailles, brought the rich and able Paris brothers into power. It was Paris Duverney who ordered the finances, provisioned the army, and drew up plans of campaign. But any advantages that France won by the war, she lost by the peace. Severin, her representative at Aix, was outwitted by Kaunitz of Austria and Lord Sandwich of England. Whilst Austria surrendered Silesia to Prussia, and Parma to Spain, Louis XV, 'preferring (as he said) to make peace not as a tradesman, but as a prince,' gave up his conquests in Italy and the Netherlands, and agreed to leave Dunkirk unfortified, and to expel the Young Pretender from France. This fine gesture lost Louis the popularity he had enjoyed at Metz in '44. 'France,' said Maurice of Saxony, her most successful general, 'by giving up her conquests, has made war on herself. Her enemies are as strong as they ever were. Only she is weaker. She has lost a million of her population, and has hardly a penny left' [*Malet*]. Public opinion was summed up by the fishwife who, when she had exhausted every known term of abuse, called her friend 'as big a fool as the Peace' [*Rocquain*]. Far-sighted men saw in the state of the country omens of the catastrophe which came nearly half a century later. 'A revolution,' wrote *d'Argenson*, Louis' Foreign Minister from '44 to '47, 'is certain in this country. It is crumbling at its foundations. It is without King, without Ministers, almost without generals; without troops, without officers; without courage, without discipline, without money, without men in the kingdom . . . without reputation for good faith, ability, or power.'

LECTURE XIX

FREDERICK THE GREAT, AND THE SEVEN YEARS' WAR

I

The prime mover in all the events of the half century from 1740 to 1785 was Frederick the Great; and I must try to give some account of him. It is not easy. So much was written about him, and he wrote and talked so much about himself, that there is almost too much material. Yet all the time you have the uneasy feeling that you are interviewing an actor in the green room, and that perhaps you have never seen the real Frederick at all.

Frederick was the son of Frederick William I; and, by a trick which nature has played on many fathers, he was born utterly unlike him in tastes, if not in character. The son had a natural liking for everything which the father hated—books, music, and French philosophy. He hated everything that the other loved—eating and drinking, hunting, drilling, and making money. 'An effeminate fellow,' his father calls him to his face, 'who has no manly inclinations, who, to his shame, can neither ride nor shoot, and at the same time is uncleanly in his person, wears his hair long and curled like a fool': and again, 'the scoundrel declines to be shaved . . . he walks on the tips of his toes . . . he never looks an honest man straight in the face.' We know something of this type at school and University. We call it a 'phase'—it is often no more: and we have methods of our own for dealing with it. Frederick William (I suspect) was shrewd enough to guess that, concealed in 'this amiable youth, with the aspirations and vanity of a minor poet, was the most consummate practical genius that in modern times has inherited a throne' [*Acton*]. He thought (knowing no other method) that he could bully the boy out of his affections: he only succeeded in bullying him into hypocrisy and cynicism. When his father's cruelty became unbearable, Frederick tried to run away. Frederick William, who had dared him to do so, had him court-martialled as a deserter; and was only prevented by the protests of certain foreign representatives from putting him to death. Thrown into prison, the boy was forced to watch the execution of his fellow-deserter, Katt. The shock threw him into a fever, and he attempted to commit suicide. After a year's probation, during which he was confined to the town of Cüstrin, and kept to a routine of office work and estate management, Frederick was given a wife and an establishment at Ruppin. Near there, at Rheinsberg, he spent the four happiest years of his life—the last before he became King. He filled the place with literary men. He studied science, philosophy, art, and languages. He composed bad French poetry, and played cleverly on the flute. He corresponded and quarrelled with Voltaire. He wrote a refutation of Machiavelli, and modelled himself on 'the Prince.' But all the time he was studying history and politics with an eye to the future, and working out the ideas of conquest and government which he was soon to put into practice. Unintentionally, perhaps unconsciously, he was reverting to type. He never ceased to be a French aesthete: but he also began to be a Prussian, with the Hohenzollern genius for aggrandizement and organization.

We saw Louis XIV beginning his reign with a romantic and rather attractive passion for *la gloire*. Frederick in 1740 had an equal ambition, but it was of a hard, cynical, and self-centred type. And there was always a touch of grimness, a slight smell of brimstone, about his most amiable accomplishments. He was a brilliant talker, and he knew it. 'His encyclopaedical conversation,' says an interviewer, 'completely charmed me. Fine arts, war, medicine, literature, religion, philosophy, morals, history, and legislation, passed one after another in review. The grand ages of Augustus and Louis XIV, the good company of the Romans, Greeks, and Franks, the chivalry of Francis I, the frankness and valour of Henry IV, the renaissance of letters and their revolutions from the time of Leo X . . . in short, everything that was most amusing, varied, and poignant came from his mouth in the sweetest tone of voice, rather low, and as charming as the movement of his lips, in which there was a graciousness quite inexpressible' [*Ligne*]. Yet no one could speak more bitterly or cruelly: men almost died of his sneers. As to his writings—Dr. Johnson thought his prose 'poor stuff,' and said 'he writes just as you may suppose Voltaire's footboy to do, who has been his amanuensis.' When *Boswell* repeated this remark to Voltaire (at that time at daggers drawn with Frederick), the latter, who had previously characterized Johnson as 'a superstitious dog,' exclaimed, 'An honest fellow!' Boswell himself thought Frederick's poetry 'animated' and 'pathetick,' but 'fraught with the pernicious ravings of infidelity.' The poetry, so far as I can judge, is certainly poor stuff: but the *Memoirs* are well worth reading, both for what Frederick thought about his contemporaries, and for what he wished his contemporaries to think about himself. From this and from some other sources we may complete our portrait of Frederick in a few important respects.

Frederick's idea of kingship was absolute despotism. He did not say, *L'Etat, c'est moi*: but he might have said *Moi, c'est l'Etat*. Louis XIV thought the State served by service done to himself: Frederick thought himself served by service done to the State. But he was not a patriot, who ruled for the sake of his country: he was a political artist, who ruled for the sake of ruling; and who governed despotically because he could not trust anyone else to do his work, or because he feared that his subordinates 'would in time assume a will of their own' [*Harris*]. 'His generals,' said *Fleury*, 'were always adjutants, his councillors clerks, his finance ministers tax-gatherers, his German allies slaves.'

But if Frederick was a tyrant, he was a tyrant of a new kind —the first and greatest of the 'Enlightened Despots,' who made the old age of Absolutism respectable, and inoculated Europe against the infection of the French Revolution. He regarded himself as the servant as well as the master of the State; and his aim was to govern his subjects for their own good, whether they liked it or not, according to the latest principles of political and economic science. In pursuit of this aim he worked, and made others work, from morning to night. He was up at three in summer, at four or five in winter. He dictated to four secretaries till they were tired, and answered private letters personally by return of post. He saw everybody, decided everything, was his own chairman and committee for the work of a dozen departments; his own Prime Minister and Commander-in-Chief: and with it all found time to write French verses on the battlefield, or to entertain foreign diplomatists with solos on the flute. His life was as simple as it was strenuous. Sightseers at Potsdam, after admiring the magnificence of the palace, found with surprise that the King's bedroom was a mean, bare little place, with a small bed behind a screen; no slippers, no dressing gown [*Casanova*]. Privileged visitors were shown the royal wardrobe, which contained nothing but 'two blue coats faced with red, the lining of one a little torn, two yellow waistcoats, a good deal soiled with Spanish snuff [which Frederick took in such quantities that you could hardly go near him without sneezing], three pairs of yellow breeches, and a suit of blue velvet, embroidered with silver, for grand occasions'—this last was ten years old, and the King wore it so seldom that it was likely to last his lifetime [*Moore*].

Frederick was as ruthless as Richelieu in putting *raison d'état* above any other consideration in the world. 'The interests of the State,' he writes, 'ought to serve as the rule to monarchs': and he goes on to explain under what conditions an alliance may be broken, or a treaty regarded as a 'scrap of paper.' A private person, he thinks, should keep his promises: if he is cheated, he has the protection of the laws. 'But where is the tribunal that can redress a monarch's wrongs, should another monarch forfeit his engagement? The word of an individual can only involve an individual in misfortune, while that of a sovereign may draw down calamities on a nation. The question then will be reduced to this:—must the people perish, or must the prince infringe a treaty? And where is the man weak enough to hesitate a moment concerning his answer?'

Frederick, who always had a reason for what he did, justified war, as he justified treachery, by the principles of enlightened philosophy. He had been talking one day with his secretary de Catt (knowing that the latter would record what he said) about the sufferings of war. 'And do you believe, sir, in good faith,' he concluded, 'that [Providence] troubles about the quarrels, the squabbles, and the slaughter which scamps like us make? Do you believe that, if, when walking in my garden at Sans Souci, I tread on an ant-hill, I even think that there in my road are little beings who are running about worrying themselves? Would it not be ridiculous of those creatures to think—if, by the way, they are endowed with thought—that I know that they exist, and that I should take some account of their

S

existence? No, my friend, unburden yourself of this self-esteem, which misleads you by presenting Heaven to you as being ceaselessly occupied with your preservation; and get this well into your head, that Nature does not concern itself about individuals, but only about the species. The *latter* must not perish.' When de Catt raised the obvious objection that the species is composed of individuals, Frederick broke off the argument, and wished him good night [*de Catt*]. He would have agreed with Mirabeau's dictum, which put the same fallacy in another way— *La petite tue la grande morale,* or 'Moral scruples are the death of morality.'

Such a philosophy made Frederick, when he was not sentimental, inhumane. 'In order to persevere in this system it was necessary for him to divest himself of compassion and remorse, of course of religion and morality. In the room of the first he has substituted superstition, and in the place of the latter what is called in France 'sentiment'; and from hence we may in some measure account for that motley composition of barbarity and humanity which so strongly marks his character. I have seen him weep at a tragedy; known him pay as much care to a sick greyhound as a fond mother could to a favourite child; and yet the next day he has given orders for the devastating of a province, or by a wanton increase of taxes made a whole district miserable . . . Again, he is so far from being sanguinary that he scarce ever suffers a criminal to be punished capitally, unless for a most notorious offence; yet, the last war, he gave secret orders to several of his army surgeons, rather to run the risk of a wounded soldier's dying, than, by the amputation of a limb, to increase the number and expense of his invalids' [*Harris*].

And here I must leave Frederick, except for his acts, with which we have still much to do, and which are, after all, the best guide to his character.

II

We left France at the Treaty of Aix (1748) still allied with Prussia (in spite of Frederick's double treachery) against England and Austria. Eight years later, when the Seven Years' War breaks out, France is the ally of Austria, and England of Prussia. This Diplomatic Revolution (1756) had such important results that we must inquire how it came about.

Rumour (on Prussian wings) represented it as a hostile coalition against Frederick on the part of persons whom he had offended. 'Prince Kaunitz (the Austrian Minister) wanted revenge for Frederick's ridicule of his toilet: Madame de Pompadour for his treating with her through his ministers, and for certain remarks upon her health; the Empress Elizabeth of Russia for comments on her behaviour: the Count de Brühl (the Saxon Minister) for sneers at his wardrobe; the Empire, for sneers at the poverty of its means; Sweden, for sneers at its impotence, and its failure to produce another Charles XII' [*Ligne*]. Frederick had a sharp tongue: but there were more important interests at work, even in the diplomacy of the eighteenth century, than the offended vanity of ministers and mistresses.

Ever since the Treaty of Utrecht (1713) there had been people in France who realized that the old grounds for antagonism with Austria no longer existed. The anti-Austrian party was, no doubt, still strong enough to throw France on to the Prussian side in 1733 and 1740. But the experience of those adventures had not been happy; and now that the succession to Lorraine had been secured, France had nothing to fear from her old enemy.

But it was Austria which made the first advances. Already in 1738, acting on the advice of his Minister Bartenstein, Charles VI had sounded Fleury as to the possibility of a defensive treaty. In 1748 Kaunitz, sent as Austrian Ambassador to Paris, reopened the discussion—first, unsuccessfully, with Puysieux, the Foreign Minister, and then, with more success (for he knew how to flatter a lady) with Madame de Pompadour. In 1754-55 the situation was complicated by the intervention of England, which was anxious to provide for the security of Hanover, in case war broke out again, and which for this purpose came to a temporary arrangement with Elizabeth of Russia. It did not at all suit Frederick's plans that Russia should have an excuse for landing troops in north-west Germany: accordingly he offered his services to England instead of those of Russia, and they were accepted. In return for a large subsidy he would guarantee the integrity of Hanover; and would keep his continental enemies fully engaged, whilst England pursued her maritime and colonial designs undisturbed. These Anglo-Prussian negotiations, issuing in the Treaty of Westminster (1755), were known to

Kaunitz, now (since 1753) chief Minister at Vienna. He saw how he could use them to clinch the negotiations with France: for Frederick was still (until June, 1756) nominally an ally of Louis XV; and his alliance with England would be regarded in France as a third and final act of treachery. Stahremberg, Kaunitz's successor at Paris, divulged the Treaty of Westminster. Madame de Pompadour, advised by Seychelles, the Controller-General, and by her friend Cardinal de Bernis (who in his *Memoirs* claims the whole credit for it), agreed to the Austrian proposals, and carried through the first Treaty of Versailles. Russia, equally offended at the Anglo-Prussian alliance, also joined Austria. Thus the Diplomatic Revolution was complete.

The Austrian alliance was so unpopular in France, and has been so much blamed by French historians, that it is worth while to ask what there was to say for it. In the first place it was merely a defensive alliance: it was the Second Treaty of Versailles in the following year which made it offensive, and committed France to the Seven Years' War. Secondly, Austria had done France a service by divulging Frederick's double dealing: it would be ungrateful to refuse the proffered alliance, and impossible (in any case) to violate the Austrian Netherlands in the course of war with England. But the chief feeling of the French negotiators was that Frederick's treachery left France isolated, and in danger of a combined attack by England and Prussia, in which Austria might be unwilling to come to her aid, unless bound by treaty to do so. To these reasons we may add the ties of sentiment and religion that were bringing together, half unconsciously, Bourbons and Hapsburgs, the last two dynasties of the old Catholic tradition, in face of parvenu and Protestant Kings such as George the Second and Frederick the Great. Twenty years afterwards, in a letter to her daughter Marie Antoinette, whose unlucky marriage to Louis XVI was the pledge of this alliance, Maria Theresa speaks of it as 'the one alliance natural and useful to our countries, cemented as it is by such tender relations, and by our common way of thinking, so necessary for the religion, the welfare, and the prosperity of thousands of people: indeed it is very near my heart' [*Arneth*].

On the other hand—and French historians are never tired of urging this point—whilst the Diplomatic Revolution gave

England the security of Hanover, and freedom at sea, whilst Frederick gained English gold to fight Austria, and Maria Theresa French troops to fight Prussia, France was committed to a continental war, in which victory could only bring gain to Austria, and defeat gain to Prussia; whilst she herself was rendered quite incapable of resisting the victorious progress of England, her real enemy, in the colonies and upon the sea.

III

When Maria Theresa signed the Treaty of Aix in 1748, her enemy Frederick had been in possession of Silesia for seven years, and this was the fourth time that she had acknowledged his ownership. But she was not in the least reconciled to its loss. It was said that she could not see a Silesian without weeping. She regarded this peace, like the rest, as a truce, and she would use it to prepare for another war of reconquest. Everybody knew this: and while the diplomatists spent the eight years' interval from '48 to '56 in regrouping their alliances, the generals and ministers of war spent them in reorganizing their armies.

Austria created an almost new army of 130,000 men, and trained it on the Prussian frontier, where Frederick came to acknowledge its skilful use of the ground. Its soldiers were patriotic, its officers well trained. Its weakness lay in the slowness and caution which paralysed the higher command.

Frederick raised his army to 147,000 men—a number quite disproportionate to the size of his country—and made it the more formidable by brutal discipline, perfect drill, iron ramrods, and unity of command. 'The backbone of his army,' wrote *Voltaire* to a friend in 1758, 'has been drilled for over forty years. Think of what fighting you ought to get out of a set of regular, vigorous, and warlike machines, who see their King every day, whilst he knows them all, and exhorts them, hat in hand, to do their duty. Remember how these poor fools wheel and double on parade, how they empty their spent cartridges as they charge, how they fire as many as six or seven shots a minute.' An official report, written soon after the Seven Years' War by our own General Burgoyne, brings out some points which are less familiar. A third of the Prussian army, he says, consists of 'strangers, deserters, prisoners, and enemies, of various countries, languages, and religions: they have neither national spirit, nor attachment to their prince, nor enthusiasm, nor hopes of fortune, nor even prospect of comfortable old age to inspire them': the policy is 'to reduce the man as nearly as possible to mere machinery' —and 'as nature has formed the bulk of the King of Prussia's subjects, that is not very difficult. . . . The vigour of the army is in the subalterns, and non-commissioned officers, who undoubtedly are the best in the world': intelligence diminishes as ranks ascend. 'The army is more harassed with precautionary guards against their own soldiers than against the enemy . . . Desertion in peace is supposed to equal a fifth: after defeat the number missing usually trebles the number to be accounted for by death or capture' [*Temperley*]. Thackeray's *Barry Lyndon*, which is not all fiction, explains why this was so. It describes the life of a private soldier in Frederick's army as 'a frightful one to any but men of iron courage and endurance. There was a corporal (says his hero) to every three men, marching behind them, and pitilessly using the cane . . . The punishment was incessant. Every officer had the liberty to inflict it, and in peace it was more cruel than in war . . . I have seen the bravest men of the army cry like children at the cut of the cane. I have seen a little ensign of fifteen call out a man of fifty from the ranks, a man who had been in a hundred battles, and he has stood presenting arms, and sobbing and howling like a baby, while the young wretch lashed him over the arms and thighs with the stick.'

As to the Russian army, its nominal strength in 1756 was 360,000 men: but the numbers available for fighting in Europe were not more than 130,000. The men were serfs, who fought unwillingly but well, with their traditional obstinacy and endurance. They were handicapped by bad officers, scanty cavalry, and an enormous train of baggage.

The peace footing of the French army was 180,000; but it was frittered away on garrison duty, and little provision had been made for the emergencies of war, which found its drill and tactics in a state of transition. The officers generally owed their position to birth, wealth, or Court influence. St. Germain, who was in command of the rear-guard at Rosbach, called them ignorant, frivolous, negligent, and cowardly: and of his men he says, 'I am leading a band of robbers, of assassins fit to be broken on the wheel, who will show their heels without firing a shot, and who are always on the edge of mutiny . . . The King has the worst infantry in the world, and the most undisciplined . . . Our nation has no military spirit left. The feeling of honour is dead in us' [*Aubertin*]. The strongest part of the French army was the engineers, whose officers were of the middle class, and could not expect promotion to the highest ranks. With them the traditions of Vauban were still alive.

IV

In 1755 civilized society was shocked by an event which seemed to be an omen of fresh troubles—the destruction of Lisbon by a great earthquake and tidal wave. The same year there was fighting at sea between France and England: and in 1756 all Europe was again at war.

The first move on the Continent came from Frederick. He anticipated any possible attack, in the spring of 1756, by invading Saxony, and occupying Dresden, whence he published 'proofs' of the hostile intention of the Franco-Austro-Russian Coalition. Podewils, his Foreign Secretary, was snubbed for suggesting that there might be no such plot after all, and that it was rash to plunge into war with three great Powers. Frederick dismissed him with the remark, 'Good-bye, Mr. Timid Statesman.' But it was generally thought that, though Prussia might win an advantage by striking first, as she had done in 1740, she would not be able to draw back again, or to shift the war on to other shoulders. And so it proved.

The course that the war took was determined by the geographical position of Prussia. It was fought on three fronts. The occupation of Hanover (in the name of England, and with English help) and the seizure of Saxony (which was completed within a few weeks of the outbreak of war) enabled Frederick to keep his French enemies at arm's length on the short Western frontier. Southwards, again, the possession of Saxony was the key to Bohemia, which outflanked Silesia, and threatened the plain of Berlin. Silesia remained open to Austrian attack: and on this front most of Frederick's battles were fought. Eastwards lay the long open frontier towards Poland, where at any moment a

Russian army might appear. Thus Frederick had the advantage of fighting on inner lines, and it was difficult for his three enemies to combine effectively. But it was only by constant and rapid movement that he could hope to deal with them one by one.

There is not much to be said about the fighting on the Western front. In 1757 a French army under the Duc de Richelieu occupied Hanover, and forced an English army under the Duke of Cumberland to capitulate at Kloster-Zevern. But nothing was done about disarmament; and when the British Government refused to ratify the terms of capitulation, our troops returned to the field, and drove the French back again: it is not easy to say how much stupidity there was on the one side, or dishonesty on the other. From 1758 to 1762 desultory fighting went on, Cassel in the south and Minden in the north being the places principally disputed. The object of this part of the war was attained: Hanover was secured, the French were kept employed, and Frederick was left free to concentrate on his southern and eastern fronts.

Here the war went through three stages. During the first (1756–57) Frederick for a short time took the offensive: he invaded Saxony, forced the Saxon army to capitulate and join his own service, and overran Bohemia. But during the second year's campaign he was defeated by the Austrians at Kollin, near Prague, and forced to evacuate Bohemia; and though he won two subsequent victories—over the French at Rosbach, near Leipzig, and over the Austrians at Leuthen, near Breslau, he had lost the advantages of attack, and during the rest of the war remained on the defensive. The second period of the war (1758–59) nearly proved fatal to Prussia. Frederick was only saved from complete defeat, as he himself admitted, 'by the faults of his enemies, by their slowness contrasted with his rapidity of movement, and by their indolence in never taking advantage of their opportunities.' His most dangerous enemy was Russia. He had barely defeated an Austro-Russian army, after heavy losses, at Zorndorf, in 1758. At Kunersdorf, near Frankfurt on the Oder, in 1759, he attacked a larger force than his own, mainly of Russian troops, and was utterly routed. Frederick had more than once talked of suicide, and shown de Catt a box of opium pills which he carried round his neck. He talked of suicide now. 'It is a cruel reverse,' he wrote home. 'I will not survive it. The consequences of the affair will be worse than the affair itself. I have no further resources, and, not to lie to you, I consider that all is lost. I will not survive the loss of my country. Farewell for ever!' But the pill-box remained unopened. The Austrians, instead of marching on Berlin, turned off into Silesia and Saxony. The Russians, after sending a few Cossacks to the capital, retired into Poland, and left Frederick to reorganize his army. In the third period of the war (1760-61) he was able to defeat the Austrians at Liegnitz in Silesia and at Torgau in Saxony. But he was now at the end of his resources. 'If you saw me,' he wrote to Voltaire, 'you would scarcely recognize me: I am old, broken, grey, wrinkled: I am losing my teeth and gaiety . . . I have endured all the griefs which can afflict humanity.' France, too, was as tired of defeat as Frederick was of victory. Elizabeth of Russia had been succeeded by Peter III, a fanatical admirer of Frederick, who had already betrayed to him the plans of the Russian command [*Dashkoff*], and now offered him the services of the Russian army. Austria was unable to go on fighting without her allies. So in '63 peace was signed at Hubertsburg. Frederick kept Silesia, and was generally considered to have won the war.

V

How had he done so? In his own Memoirs Frederick gives three reasons—lack of agreement among his enemies, especially the Austrians and Russians; Austria's policy of making her allies bear the brunt of the fighting, whilst keeping her own army intact; and the accession of Peter III. To these causes we may add that Russia and Austria were not so anxious to destroy Frederick as to secure their own possessions; that Frederick's own qualities as a general—not his tactical inventions, like the famous advance *en échelon* at Leuthen (which was never repeated except on the parade-ground at Potsdam), but his quickness of decision and movement, his belief in disabling rather than out-manœuvring an enemy—were as valuable as an extra army; and lastly that the English subsidy (£670,000 a year) paid between a quarter and a third of his war charges, whilst we also bore the whole cost of the 'army of observation' on the western front, another million a year.

What were the results of the Seven Years' War? It turned the King of Prussia from 'Old Fritz' into Frederick the Great. Englishmen, seeing him fight so stubbornly with his back to the wall, forgot his robbery of Silesia, his violation of the neutrality of Saxony, and called him a sportsman and a Protestant hero. May I quote *Barry Lyndon* again? 'All I know is that, after His Majesty's love of his Hanoverian dominions had rendered him most unpopular in this English kingdom, with Mr. Pitt at the head of the anti-German party, all of a sudden, Mr. Pitt becoming Minister, the rest of the Empire applauded the war as much as they had hated it before. The victories of Dettingen and Crefeld were in everybody's mouths, and "the Protestant hero," as we used to call the godless old Frederick of Prussia, was adored by us as a saint, a very short time after we had been about to make war against him in alliance with the Empress-Queen. Now, somehow, we were on Frederick's side: the Empress, the French, the Swedes, and the Russians were leagued against us: and I remember, when the news of the battle of Lissa came even to our remote quarter of Ireland, we considered it as a triumph for the cause of Protestantism, and illuminated, and bonfired, and had a sermon at church, and kept the Prussian King's birthday; on which my uncle would get drunk—as indeed on any other occasion.'

Frederick's military exploits had more important effects than these. The peaceful organization of his father and great-grandfather had made Prussia efficient: his wars, though they left it in ruins, made it formidable; and thus enrolled it among Powers, which were reckoned great in proportion as they were feared. In Germany Prussia now definitely outbalanced Austria: in Europe it was to outbalance France. And the Prussia which triumphed was Frederick's Prussia, imbued (all the more because it had succeeded) with the belief that might is right, and with the notion that *raison d'état* overrides the distinction between good and evil. Prussian historians are right in tracing the beginnings of their national greatness to the Machiavellian author of *Anti-Machiavel*.

Lastly, the disasters which France experienced during the Seven Years' War, and the bankruptcy of honour in which it ended, were among the causes of the French Revolution. Great numbers of lives and incredible sums of money had been sacrificed in a contest in which France had nothing to gain, and which was carried on without either spirit or efficiency. Court intrigues and the quarrels of generals ruined the higher command, as surely as the lower ranks were demoralized by indiscipline. It was St. Germain, the leader of 'robbers and assassins,' who pointed to the tent of his commander-in-chief, and said 'There is the enemy!' The defeat and disgrace of the army in the field was paid for at home by constant and crushing taxation. The peasant and the workman did not talk yet, but they began to think. One of the last entries in *d'Argenson's Memoirs* (dated 1757) speaks of 'ideas of resistance passing into the popular mind,' of 'a dumb displeasure at Court, a fury, not disguised, against the greed of financiers, open revolt against the Intendants, envy, poverty, and hunger.'

France was not far from Revolution.

VI

When Frederick the Great invaded Saxony in 1756, England was already at war with France. During the next seven years there went on, in the background of the continental war for Silesia, a maritime and colonial war for Canada and India. In both, France was the victim: and the Peace of Paris was even more disastrous than the Treaty of Hubertsburg.

Both colonial Empires—English and French—had been founded much at the same time, in the same places, and in the same way—the age of Francis I and Henry IV in France, and the age of Henry VIII and Elizabeth in England; India in the track of the Portuguese, America in the track of Spain; trading companies in India, government colonies in North America: for, whilst French Canada and Louisiana were administered as detached *généralités* of France, the thirteen British and Dutch colonies on the east coast were allowed representative government under nominal control of the Crown.

In both countries a contest between the two immigrant nations was bound to come. It broke out at the same dates, and was carried on during the same years as the War of Austrian Succession and the Seven Years' War.

The Treaty of Paris in 1763 was one of the most disastrous

that France ever signed. Her continental gains under Louis XIV had not been diminished at the Treaties of Utrecht or of Aix; and they were not lessened now. But she lost at a blow most of her colonies in India and America, together with the only hope of regaining them—supremacy at sea. And whilst she wasted herself in a useless struggle on land, which only prepared the way for 1870 and 1914, British sea power and the British Empire came into being, as the deciding factor of nineteenth-century history. Such was the real significance of the Seven Years' War.

LECTURE XX

ENLIGHTENED DESPOTISM

I

The second half of the eighteenth century has been called the Age of the Enlightened Despots. Three rulers of the first rank and three of the second certainly deserve that name: Frederick the Great, Catherine the Great, Joseph II; Don Carlos (Charles IV of Naples, afterwards Charles III of Spain), Leopold of Tuscany (afterwards the Emperor Leopold II), and Gustavus III. All these rulers caught something from the ideas of the 'philosophers' which they tried to translate into political institutions. The ideas were enlightened: the government was despotic. The blending of these two ingredients was characteristic of the eighteenth century. It came too late to avert the French Revolution, but not too late to confine its full effects to France, and to postpone the fall of Monarchy in central and eastern Europe for a hundred and twenty-five years.

II

I suggested, when we were dealing with Louis XIV, that the most successful part of his government was his patronage of the Arts: that, whilst his generals impoverished France, and failed to win the Rhine frontier, his literary men were making French culture and the French language fashionable all over Europe. The easy-going government of Fleury, and the anarchy of Louis XV's later years, confirmed this influence, and gave it a fresh significance. French eighteenth century culture came to charm; it stayed to instruct. It began with *belles lettres*; it ended with political pamphlets. At a time when England was laughing over *Roderick Random*, *Tom Jones*, and *Tristram Shandy*, or sentimentalizing about *The Vicar of Wakefield*, the French public was wrinkling its brow over a work on political theory, a rationalist encyclopaedia, and a handbook for revolutionaries. Why was this? Because England, with its constitutional charters, its

Parliament, and its class-peace, could slowly adapt old institutions to new uses; whilst France, without a Constitution, without a Parliament, and without social unity, was intensely conscious of grievances which it could not remedy. Because Englishmen, living their political life with sub-conscious efficiency, became conscious students of human nature; whilst Frenchmen, consciously antagonistic to their political surroundings, had no taste for the criticism of life itself.

The Enlightenment (as it came to be called, from the German term *Aufklärung*) was the working out of ideas, mainly English in origin, by three schools of French writers—the Philosophers, the Economists, and the Encyclopaedists. All three groups had one characteristic in common. They had little political education, except what they got from their school histories of Greece and Rome; less political experience—they were mere spectators of the government of their country; and no political traditions outside the Monarchy—where tradition was the enemy. And so they had to fall back upon pure reasoning, and to reconstruct society and government according to the principles of Euclid.

Of the philosophers, three stand out, both by their own quality, and by the influence that they had on their times—Montesquieu, Voltaire, and Rousseau.

Montesquieu, born in 1689, made a name as a daring young man by his *Lettres Persanes* (1721), in which he set the fashion of satirizing French society under an Oriental disguise: so one might make the draught more palatable, and might save oneself from the Bastille. A few years later he visited England. He arrived a satirist: he returned a philosopher. His second book was an essay (anticipating Gibbon) on the causes of the decline and fall of the Roman Empire. His third, the result of twenty years' travel and investigation, came out in 1748, and was called *L'Esprit des Lois*. It gave a detailed analysis of the different forms of government, their causes, their principles, and their relative merits: it ended by condemning the French system of government, and by pointing to Limited Monarchy of the English type as the most likely to secure political liberty. The book had a huge sale, and was translated into every civilized tongue. Forty years later it became one of the text-books of the Revolution.

Voltaire was born in 1694, started life, like Montesquieu, as a satirist, and spent some part of his youth in the Bastille. Like Montesquieu he visited England, and came back with a changed mind. He announced his conversion to liberalism in his *Lettres Philosophiques* or 'English Letters' (1734), praising the Quakers, popularizing Locke, and upholding the ideas of Newton against Descartes. The Paris Parlement did its best to advertise the book by having it burnt by the common hangman. But it did not exercise much influence till its author became famous as a dramatist, a historian, and a writer of satirical romances. At sixty he was *le roi Voltaire,* a popular hero, the leader of every attack on tyranny and intolerance, the writer of innumerable letters and pamphlets, and unofficial adviser and publicity agent to half the Courts of Europe.

All his life (and he was eighty-four when he died) Voltaire was a hater of evil rather than a lover of good; a man who disbelieved in other men; who might shame them out of the wrong, but could not lead them into the right; whom you could honour for anything rather than himself. His influence on the eighteenth century was profound; but its effect was to strengthen the critical spirit which destroyed the old régime, rather than to provide the enthusiasm which constructed the new one.

If the part played by Voltaire in the political Reformation of the eighteenth century was like that played by Erasmus in the religious Reformation of the sixteenth, his Luther was Jean-Jacques Rousseau. Montesquieu and Voltaire were middle-class Hamlets, conscious that the times were out of joint, but uncertain how to put them right. Rousseau was a watchmaker's son of Geneva, a member of no class or nation, a moral and political tramp, who thought that he could take society to bits, as his father did an old watch, and put it together again in a new way.

Rousseau too came to England, but not till his best days were over, and his mind made up to the verge of insanity. He learnt nothing here. He imagined that his friends were plotting against him, and made enemies wherever he went. In return the average Englishman thought him a Bolshevist. Dr. Johnson once accused Boswell of keeping bad company, because he had been to stay with Jean-Jacques. 'My dear Sir,' protested *Boswell,* 'you don't call Rousseau bad company. Do you really think him a bad man?' 'Sir,' said Johnson, 'if you are talking jestingly of this, I don't talk with you. If you mean to be serious, I think him one of the worst of men; a rascal who ought to be hunted out of society, as he has been . . . Rousseau, Sir, is a very bad man. I would sooner sign a sentence for his transportation than that of any fellow who has gone from the Old Bailey these many years. Yes, I should like to have him work in the Plantations.' 'Sir,' asked Boswell, 'do you think him as bad a man as Voltaire?' 'Why, Sir,' replied the Doctor, 'it is difficult to settle the proportion of iniquity between them.'

Their 'iniquity' was, however, of different kinds. Montesquieu and Voltaire thought the People so bad that it must be kept in order by Kings, and Kings so bad that their power must be limited by the People—a rather cheerless basis for a political philosophy. The first article of Rousseau's creed was, 'I believe in Man.' He thought that all men were born free and equal and virtuous, and that it was the institutions of society which had made them wicked and enslaved. In politics, then—this is the doctrine of the *Contrat Social*—all that is needed is to recover the 'natural rights' of men and citizens by putting the 'general will' of the community on the throne. In education—this is the teaching of *Emile*—one has only to give free rein to the natural virtues and talents of the child: nowadays (I believe) they call it the 'Montessori System.' In morality, too, give full play to your natural instincts and emotions—see the *Nouvelle Héloïse,* the one novel whose sentimental fascinations upset the day's routine of that dry old German philosopher, Immanuel Kant. And in religion—that was the creed of the *Vicaire Sovayarde*—trust your heart against your reason: be a Theist with the Catholics rather than a Materialist with the authors of the Encyclopaedia. It is easy to see why Rousseau's view of life—so exciting, so romantic, so vague, so self-indulgent—went to people's heads, whilst Voltaire only went to their brains. A generation that had forgotten the New Testament discovered the Gospel according to St. Jean-Jacques: it was almost as unworldly, as inspiring, as revolutionary. Rousseau's Paris attic—'the abode of rats, but the sanctuary of virtue and genius'—became a place of pilgrimage. 'His talk,' says one worshipper, 'would have ennobled a bit of cheese'; and 'when he left me, I was conscious of the same void we feel after waking from a beautiful dream' [*Ligne*].

A dreamer—that is just what Rousseau was; and that was why his ideas captured a society of dreamers. But not those very wide-awake gentlemen, the Enlightened Despots, with their rival Gospel of St. Voltaire. They are for reason, he is for instinct. They are for reform, to prevent revolution: he is for revolution, without which there can be no reform. The two ideas overlap, with momentous results, in the French Revolution. But, at the moment we are speaking of, Voltairism holds the field.

As to the Economists of the Enlightenment, I need do no more than mention the Physiocrats. Rousseau preached the essential goodness of human nature: the Physiocrats expounded the essential goodness of the soil. Rousseau based politics on the natural rights of man: the Physiocrats based economics on the natural products of the earth—crops and minerals. Quesnay, born in the same year as Voltaire, originated this doctrine: it was formulated by Gournay as *Laissez faire et laissez passer*— 'free production and free distribution.' Their most distinguished disciples were Louis XVI's minister, Turgot, and (with a difference) our own Adam Smith.

The philosophers and economists of the Enlightenment spread their ideas in three ways—by their books, by their talk—especially in the 'salons' run by learned hostesses which were such a feature of eighteenth-century Paris—and by their articles in the Encyclopaedia. The Encyclopaedia was a universal dictionary—a 'general view (as the prospectus said) of the efforts of the human spirit in all spheres and in all ages'—with articles ranging from high questions of philosophy to the best way of making boots. It took twenty-one years to produce—the first instalment appeared in 1751, the last in 1772—and its editing was the patient and sometimes dangerous work of Diderot and d'Alembert. Unlike most modern encyclopaedias, it was a propagandist publication: it blessed what the philosophers loved, and cursed what the philosophers hated, especially the tyranny of the Church, economic Protection, and the arbitrary power of the Crown. Consequently it was twice suppressed on the ground that it encouraged rebellion against God and the King. But these views were made palatable by other articles on technical and scientific subjects. *Voltaire* describes (or invents) a pretty scene at the Trianon, when Louis XV, Mme de Pompadour, and their friends fall into dispute about the composition of gunpowder. They send for a copy of the confiscated encyclopaedia. It is brought in—twenty-one heavy folios—by three footmen. They all become absorbed in it, not only finding out how gunpowder is made, but also how the rouge that Mme de Pompadour uses differs from that patronized by the ancient Greek beauties, and the fair ladies of Spain. Something like that was happening all over France. Everywhere the trade in Enlightenment followed the flag of scientific knowledge, and influenced just those classes which were best able to profit by it. There were many subscribers to the Encyclopaedia among the professional classes, the educated tradesmen, and the more liberal clergy; and it was they who supplied the leaders of the Revolution.

III

But what we must particularly notice is the influence of the Enlightenment outside France, and in a different sphere of society. In Prussia, in Austria, and in Russia, the subscribers to the Encyclopaedia, the disciples of the French philosophers and economists, were not the clergy and the middle classes, but the crowned heads. The humblest lecturer hopes that he may have among his audience a future Prime Minister or two. The Encyclopaedists knew that they were lecturing to Frederick the Great, Joseph II, and Catherine of Russia—and moreover that these monarchs would forthwith put their ideas into practice.

IV

How did it all work out? Let us begin with Prussia. We left Frederick in 1763, victorious but exhausted, at the end of the Seven Years' War. He reigned another twenty-three years, and worked all that time, as only he could work, at the recuperation of his country. The main lines of his policy were already laid down by the genius of the Great Elector, and the unenlightened good sense of Frederick William I. But some new features were added by the philosophers, with whom Frederick was in constant communication. It was not enough to reorganize the army, to recolonize the country, to subsidize industry and agriculture, to impose new taxes, and to issue instructions as to the right way to do everything—if it were only how to light a kitchen fire. All that was according to the best traditions of the Hohenzollerns. Where Frederick showed his Enlightenment was rather in his scheme for compulsory education, in his extension of religious toleration to the Jesuits, in his judicial reforms—such as the abolition of torture—and in his codification of the law. Under such a system Prussia became one of the most efficient countries of Europe: but it remained one of the most corrupt. Berlin, says the British Ambassador in 1773, has no honest men in it, and no modest women. 'A total corruption of morals reigns throughout both sexes in every class of life' [*Harris*]; and a contemporary traveller observed that there were more prostitutes in Berlin, in proportion to the population, than in any other city in Europe [*Moore*]. That is an unpleasant footnote to the history of Enlightened Despotism.

V

In 1778 the same Ambassador moved from Berlin to St. Petersburg. There too he found the Enlightenment at work, and passed much the same verdict upon it. 'Great luxury and little morality,' he says, 'seem to run through every rank. Flattery and servility characterize the inferior class, presumption and pride the higher one. A slight though brilliant varnish covers in both the most illiterate and uninformed minds' [*Harris*].

The Empress who represented Enlightenment in Russia at this time was one of the most remarkable women of the eighteenth or any other century. Catherine II was the daughter of an undistinguished German princeling, an officer in the Prussian army, and had been brought up in the military-commercial atmosphere of Stettin. Her assets in life were a French governess, an ambitious mother, and a genius for making the best of things. When she was picked out by Frederick the Great and the Empress Elizabeth as a suitable bride for the Russian Grand Duke (rather as Marie Leczinski had been picked out for Louis XV, because she was a princess, and nothing more), she soon took her own future and the destiny of Russia in hand.

Her husband Peter turned out to be a drunken degenerate, with a weak man's passion for taking a strong line. Not only (as we have seen) did he reverse the Russo-Austrian alliance in 1762, and thereby save his hero the King of Prussia from defeat: he also tried to Prussianize the Russian army, and to Lutheranize the

Russian Church. The failure of these schemes gave Catherine her first clue to power. She could be popular in Russia if she became a Russian, and stood for the restoration of the national régime of Peter the Great. So she sent her German mother back to Stettin; she entered the Orthodox Church, and called herself Katherina Alexeievna; and she carried a snuff-box with a portrait of Peter on it, and was heard to ask herself, 'What would he say? What would he do?' [*Ligne*]. Catherine's second clue to power was the *coup d'état* which had put Elizabeth on the throne in 1741, and which, like every succession in Russia since Peter's time, had been the work of the army. She determined to use the same means. The officers of the Guard were won over. Peter was deposed, and subsequently put to death—not by Catherine's orders, but without her disapproval. His widow had no liking for the role of Regent for her son Paul: she made herself Empress, and remained so for thirty-four years (1762–1796).

Catherine had prepared herself for Empire by reading Voltaire, the Encyclopaedia, and the *Annals* of Tacitus. Montesquieu, she used to say, was her Breviary [*Guénin*]. As Empress she kept up a lively correspondence with Grimm and Diderot; wrote articles for a periodical edited by her friend Princess Dashkoff; and composed several volumes of plays and memoirs. She was a great collector of books, pictures, and objects of art; and was believed to patronize the literary men and painters of every country except her own. Sir Joshua Reynolds—in return for his *Discourses to the Royal Academy*—received a gold snuffbox, adorned with her profile in bas-relief set in diamonds, and containing a French inscription in her own handwriting. And Dr. Johnson was never so pleased as when he heard (though I believe it was a mistake) that she had ordered the *Rambler* to be translated into Russian, and imagined it being read 'on the banks of the Wolga' [*Boswell*].

But, though yielding nothing to her contemporaries in Enlightenment, Catherine realized better than they sometimes did the difference between political theories and the art of Government. 'In all your plans of reform,' she once said to Diderot, 'you forget the difference between our positions. All your work is done upon paper, which does not mind what you do to it: it is all of a piece, pliable, and presenting no obstacles either to your pen or to your imagination. But I, poor Empress, must work upon the human skin, which is terribly ticklish and irritable' [*Ségur*]. Catherine was, perhaps, too conscious of this difficulty, and too much discouraged by it: she started many reforms, but completed few. A Commission was appointed to codify the law, with Instructions drawn up by Catherine herself in such liberal terms that their circulation was forbidden in France. 'The nation,' she wrote, 'is not made for the sovereign, but the sovereign for the nation. Equality comes when the citizens obey the law, and only the law.' The deputies wept for joy to hear such sentiments: but they went home after 200 sittings without having decided anything. An attempt to reform the system of justice ended in the establishment of different courts to try different classes—one for the nobles, one for the bourgeoisie, one for the free peasantry—and none for the serfs. The abolition of serfdom was one of the first points in Catherine's enlightened programme: but under the pressure of the great landlords, without whose help it was impossible to govern the provinces, the lot of these 'dead souls' grew sensibly worse. Their right of appeal to the sovereign was taken away: their lords exacted more and more of their forced labour: and they could be bought and sold like cattle. In the St. Petersburg Gazette, during 1789, appeared this advertisement: 'For sale, a hairdresser, and a pedigree cow' [*Malet*].

Whatever her failures—and their seriousness was shown by Pugatcheff's rebellion in 1771-75—Catherine's reign influenced Russia only less widely than that of Peter the Great. In one of her letters to Grimm (dated 1781) she enclosed, half-humorously, statistics of what she had accomplished:

Governments set up under the New Scheme ..	29
Towns built	144
Conventions and treaties signed	30
Victories won	78
Noteworthy edicts ordering new laws or foundations	88
Edicts for the assistance of the people	123
Total ..	492

No one knew better than Catherine herself how little such figures meant, as against the huge apathy of Russia. And we cannot be surprised that in her later years she let herself live on her earlier reputation for energy and enlightenment, though she justified to the end the general belief that she was one of the most fascinating and intelligent women in Europe.

Catherine may be honoured, if in no other way, for one act of great courage. At a time when small-pox was as inevitable as influenza, and the newly-discovered safeguard of inoculation was thought to be flying in the face of Providence—it was actually prohibited in Oxford by the Vice-Chancellor and Mayor in 1774 —she invited an English surgeon to visit Russia, and insisted upon being inoculated, although the operation was still quite experimental, and everyone supposed that she would die of it. I think that was a finer stroke for Enlightenment than many that she learnt from the philosophers.

VI

Whatever Frederick's moral failings, whatever Catherine's wanderings from the straight path of enlightenment, it is Joseph II of Austria who affords the classic example of the difficulties of a philosopher on a throne.

For many years he was not his own master. From 1765, when he became 'Co-Regent,' to 1780, when his mother died, there were (it was said) three Kings of Austria—Maria Theresa, Joseph, and Kaunitz, the Chief Minister. The Empress-Queen was more than a popular and patriotic figure-head. She supervised the whole internal government of the country. And though (from Joseph's point of view) a dreadfully unenlightened person, she knew what Austria needed, and was able to secure her ends— the unification of its varied provincial interests, and the organization of imperial finance—without causing popular disaster. Kaunitz, the hero of the Franco-Austrian alliance, became a dry, able, eccentric old man, with a deep knowledge of international diplomacy. He was respectful to the old Queen, in his rude way; and indulgent to the young Emperor's new-fangled notions of government—but no more.

Joseph, then, had to play the part of philosopher-king without much support from the rest of the company. He was quite ready to do so. From an early age he had made Frederick the Great his model. He dressed like a soldier, 'in a plain uniform of white faced with red' [*Moore*], and lived in studied simplicity. He got up at five in the morning, and worked till twelve; and again from three to five in the afternoon. He drove in and out of Vienna in an open chaise; and travelled almost alone on horseback all over his domains, jumping off sometimes to show a peasant how to drive his plough, and putting up like any private traveller at the local inn. He was ready to lay down the law to anybody about anything—in these days he would have been a university lecturer. When his sister, Marie Antoinette, married Louis XVI he sent her a regular self-examination paper on her duties as wife and Queen; and when he visited her at Paris he found fault with almost everything he saw—'button-holing poor M. Campan, he spent more than an hour talking vehemently, and without the slightest reserve about the French Government' [*Campan*]. This weakness for setting other people right was turned by a rather too conscious 'love of his country, and of the well-being of the monarchy' (they are his own words) into an almost fatal passion. Although he refused to visit Voltaire, he was well up in the ideas of the philosophers, and had a cut-and-dried plan for reforming and reorganizing the whole state of Austria.

The Austrian peasants were serfs: they had to work three days a week without payment for their feudal lords: they had no justice but the feudal courts: they could not even marry without the lord's leave. Within six weeks of his accession Joseph did what Frederick and Catherine had not dared to do—abolished serfdom, and declared all his subjects to be free and equal before the judge and the tax-collector. He did it 'in the name of reason and humanity,' and because serfdom was 'contrary to human dignity and liberty.' He was right: it is. But the country was not ready for the change, and it was a complete failure.

Joseph's orderly mind was offended by the political divisions of his Empire. Reason demanded one capital—Vienna, and one Crown—that of Austria. So he abolished the separate coronation at Buda-Pesth, and placed the Hungarian crown among the royal jewels at Vienna. It was reasonable that a single state should have a single language. So he made German, the speech of the Austrian majority, the official language, and enforced it with disastrous results upon the minorities of Magyars, Italians, and Croats.

Reason prescribed religious toleration. Within a year of his accession Joseph issued an edict allowing liberty of worship to non-Catholics. There were two exceptions to this religious amnesty, which he also justified on philosophic grounds. The Contemplative Orders he suppressed: 'they could not be pleasing to God,' he said, 'because they were useless to their neighbours.' And if a Deist were found anywhere, he was to be given twenty-four strokes of the rod, 'not because he is a Deist, but because he professes a religion which he does not understand' [*Malet*]. This pontifical attitude gave Frederick an opportunity for jokes about 'my brother the sacristan,' and the Pope a reason for visiting Vienna, where he was shown round the imperial stables and dog-kennels, but made no impression upon the champion of Enlightenment.

It was not the Pope who wrecked 'Josephism,' but the people. The Hungarians objected to the loss of their crown, their language, and their liberties. They refused men or money for the Turkish war, till the Emperor was forced to give way, and allow them to remain unreformed. The Austrian Netherlands broke into open revolt against the attempt to reform their constitution, their finance, and their administration of justice. Joseph appealed to arms, and was beaten. Before he died, the rebels had formed themselves into the United States of Belgium. The revolt did not end until his successor gave them back their traditional liberties.

Joseph on his deathbed directed the procession of the Last Sacrament—methodical and autocratic to the end [*Ligne*]. But he died a disappointed man, and a subject for moralists. He proposed as his own epitaph, 'Here lies a prince whose intentions were pure, but who had the misfortune to see all his plans fail.' Why did they fail? Because he ruled, as philosophers reasoned, *a priori*; because he forgot the differences between Austrian, Hungarian, and Belgian character; because he mistook uniformity for unity, and tried to win people's minds without winning their hearts. His mother, Maria Theresa, used to blame him for his suspicious manner. 'Confidence is the great motive power,' she wrote to him (Sept. 1766); 'lack that, and you lack everything. Persuade people, as I do; don't try to force them.' And then, with a good deal of shrewdness;—'You are an intellectual flirt. You are always running after ideas, without any discrimination. A clever remark, a mere phrase, seizes your mind—in a book, or wherever you find it. You apply it on the first opportunity, without really considering whether it fits the case: rather like Elizabeth [her daughter] does with her good looks—she is quite content so long as *someone* is admiring her, and doesn't mind whether it's a prince or a footman' [*Arneth*].

It is easy to blame Joseph. But he did not altogether fail—notably in Austria itself, where he was, on the whole, content to carry on his mother's work. And it was in no small degree the Enlightenment that made possible until 1918 that strange medieval survival in the modern world—the Austro-Hungarian Empire.

VII

Most liberals are conservative in parts. The Enlightened Despots were as benighted as any of their predecessors in the matter of foreign policy. They inherited the idea of the Balance of Power, as formulated at Utrecht, and modified by the Diplomatic Revolution of 1756. They inherited *raison d'état* as the rule of statesmanship. They inherited the diplomatic methods of Louis XIV. If despotism placed them in the position of the wolf, enlightenment would not save the lamb.

In the eighteenth century Sweden, Poland, and Turkey formed a belt of weak states across Europe, separating the strong central powers (Prussia and Austria) from their increasingly powerful eastern rival, Russia. After the Treaties of Nystadt (1721), Vienna (1735), and Passarowitz (1718: though the Treaty of Belgrade in 1739 marked a temporary set-back for Austria), each of these states was marked out for attack and perhaps partition by its neighbours. Poland was the first and only complete victim. Sweden took warning from its example, and was saved by the energy of Gustavus III. The partition of Turkey was postponed, owing to the counter-attractions of Poland, and the confusion of the Napoleonic wars, until the nineteenth century; and even now it is incomplete.

The Partition of Poland is generally regarded as the classical crime of the eighteenth century. Before we judge it, we must see how it came about.

The opportunity came with the death of Augustus III in the same year as the Treaty of Hubertsburg (1763). Russia was already in virtual possession of Poland. Her political policy was to 'preserve its constitution,' i.e., the elective monarchy, 'liberum veto,' and right of 'confederation,' which kept it in a state of anarchy. Her religious policy was to support the 'Dissidents'— a minority of Greek Catholics—against the attempts of the Roman Catholic majority to deprive them of political rights and liberty of worship. At present (as her minister Panin frankly admitted in 1769) Catherine 'already possessed more territory than she was in a position to govern,' and the formal annexation of Poland was postponed. But she had no intention of sharing the spoil. Frederick, for his part, had long coveted that part of Poland—the valley of the lower Vistula—which cut off East Pomerania from East Prussia; all the more so, now that he had Silesia. He was already looking for some means of inducing Catherine to cede this territory. Meanwhile he, too, supported the anarchical 'constitution,' and championed another body of Dissidents—the Lutherans of West Prussia. Austria had no direct interest in Poland; but if there were a scheme of partition, she could hardly be left out of it: she would at any rate demand compensation' elsewhere. As to France: since about 1750 she had pursued two incompatible policies in Poland—that of the official Foreign Ministry, and that of Louis XV's 'Secret Diplomacy.' Shortly before the death of Augustus III, Choiseul, as Foreign Minister, drew up a memorandum on the Polish situation, and submitted it to de Broglie, the chief agent of the 'King's Secret.' The manuscript still exists, with *de Broglie's* comments upon it. Both statesmen admit that France has political and commercial interests in Poland—political, because Sweden, Poland, and Turkey are the traditional enemies of Austria; commercial, because Poland has great natural resources, which await development. Then they diverge. Can the Polish government be reformed? No, says Choiseul: Yes, says de Broglie. Choiseul was right. Will Poland be partitioned? No, says Choiseul, because the Powers are too jealous of one another: Yes, says de Broglie, because their greed will overcome their jealousy. De Broglie was right. Would partition be a danger to France? No, says Choiseul, because Russia and Prussia would

THE POLISH QUESTION

quarrel over the spoil, and (so far as the Balance of Power is concerned) cancel out: Yes, says de Broglie, because their common crime would unite them against the rest of Europe. Here neither was right. They did not foresee the complications caused by the Turkish question, or by the addition of Austria to the partitioning Powers.

On the death of Augustus III, Russia and Prussia gave his throne to Stanislas Poniatowski, a Polish noble with liberal tendencies, and 'enlightened' friends in Paris; a man conscious of the almost fatal weakness of his country, but not strong enough to save it. Besides, he had been a lover of Catherine, and could not be openly disloyal to her: and he had against him the so-called 'patriot' party, who played into the hands of the partitioning Powers by opposing any step of political or religious reform. In 1771 an attempt to enforce religious toleration led to the forming of the 'Confederation of Bar.' Russian troops were sent to suppress the Confederation. Choiseul, by way of forwarding (as he supposed) French interests, dispatched Dumouriez (twenty years later the victor of Valmy) on a mission of help to the rebels, and induced Turkey to declare war on Russia.

But the Poles would not be saved, and the Turks could not save them. *Dumouriez* found his allies—the confederate nobles —patriotic, but quite undisciplined. 'Their manners were Asiatic —astonishing luxury, mad extravagance, dinners of immense length, cards and dancing their only occupations. They expected the French envoy to provide them with funds, and were horrified when he declined to do so, and hurt at his blaming their luxury and frivolity at a time when their countrymen were in danger, and their relations languishing in Siberia.' Their military forces consisted of 16,000 or 17,000 cavalry, 'badly armed, badly mounted, without discipline or obedience,' under eight or ten independent leaders, who spent their time quarrelling with one another. There was no artillery, and for a long time no infantry, because the nobles refused to arm their serfs. Even against the 25,000 scattered troops which were all that the Russians had, to police a country larger than France, these irregulars could do nothing. Matters were not made easier for the French envoy by his having to carry on his negotiations in Latin.

As for the Turks, they had lost their old skill in fighting. Their army had no bayonets. Its Mohammedan gunners mutinied because they were given ramrods finished with pig's-skin; or refused to plant their batteries properly, because (they said), if it was the will of Allah that the cannon-balls should hit the enemy, they would do so as well from one position as from another. The Turkish fleet was quite unwieldy—it was said, because the crews wore such big turbans that the ships had to be built dangerously high between decks to accommodate them. The Turkish admiral was pictured in a sugar-loaf hat some two feet high— presumably he stayed on deck [*Malet*].

The consequent successes of Russia on two fronts alarmed both the rival Powers. Joseph had no wish to fight Catherine for the possession of the Lower Danube: Frederick could not allow a partition of Turkish territory without compensation for Prussia. In this emergency he proposed the partition of Poland, which might enable him to seize the coveted territory between East Pomerania and East Prussia. Catherine would have preferred to keep the whole of Poland, but was prepared to give up part of it to avoid Austrian opposition in Turkey. Joseph and Kaunitz would have preferred Turkish to Polish territory; but their proposals were vetoed by Russia. Maria Theresa protested that the Austrian gains were 'purchased at the price of honour, of the glory of the monarchy, of the good faith and religion which are our peculiar possession' [*Sorel*]. But she was in bad health, and worried by the growing estrangement between herself and her son [*Herzelle*]. In the end, as Frederick cynically remarked, 'she wept, but she took.'

And so the crime was carried through. In 1772 at St. Petersburg, 'in the name of the Most Holy Trinity,' and 'to secure Poland from total dissolution,' Austria annexed Galicia and Zips with 2½ million inhabitants: West Prussia (except Danzig and Thorn), with 700,000 people, went to Frederick; and Catherine occupied part of Lithuania, with a population of 1½ millions The partition was carried out in characteristic fashion. The Russians practised 'slaughter, pillage, burning, violation, and holding to ransom in the name of religion . . . Wily and fanatical, using guile and violence in turn, they behaved like the Tartar conquerors.' The Austrians 'marked out boundaries with gravity and minuteness; planted, took up, and replanted their eagles; rummaged archives, compiled and posted up methodical recitals of their titles and ancient rights.' Frederick treated his new territory 'as conquered country, taxable and corvéeable at will.' Even before the treaty of partition was signed, he practised deportations of the Polish population. 'The King of Prussia,' wrote a resident in the country in 1771, 'has caused to be taken from Poland nearly 7,000 girls of from sixteen to twenty years of age, and he demands that from every tract of so many acres there shall be delivered to him a maiden or girl, with a cow, a bed, and three ducats of money— the bed to be a feather bed with four pillows, and two pigs being added to complete the dowry': and these girls, dowry and all, were transported to Prussian Pomerania, where there was a deficiency of pigs and peasants [*Sorel*].

VIII

What were the results of the Partition of Poland? First, it cast discredit on the 'Enlightened Despots,' and on the 'Enlightenment' itself. They were proud of their work—'the first example which history furnishes (as Frederick complacently remarked) of a partition so regulated, and peaceably terminated, between three Sovereigns': and it was flattered by imitation— the attempt to partition Bavaria in 1779, the second and third partitions of Poland in 1793 and 1795, and (to go no further) the Gargantuan rearrangements of the Napoleonic wars. But Europe called it a crime, and has grown increasingly ashamed of it.

Secondly, the disappearance of Poland brought Prussia and Austria face to face with Russia. The 'Russian danger' became a permanent factor in central European politics. 'It will need the whole of Europe,' said Frederick to Joseph in 1769, 'to keep those gentry within bounds. I shall not be alive: but in twenty years' time it will be necessary for both of us to join in alliance against Russian despotism.' Thus was born a fear that led to 1914.

Meanwhile, though partition might be easy, assimilation was likely to be very difficult. Russia, indeed, in the first and second partitions, was absorbing districts that belonged to her by right of religion and nationality. The frontier between Russia and Poland in 1793 practically coincided with that set up by the Treaty of Versailles (1918). But Prussia by all three partitions, Austria by the first and third, and Russia by the third, found themselves in control of large populations which they have never been able to assimilate. Poland became a cradle of music and revolution.

IX

After the partition of Poland, that of Turkey was only a question of time and opportunity. The Turks had got a footing in south-eastern Europe through the dissensions of the Balkan peoples: they kept it through the quarrels of the Central Powers. They were nomad conquerors, not settlers or civilizers. Their rule was that of a military garrison, efficient only in time of war. Their faith and discipline, embodied for fighting purposes in the Janissaries ('regular' troops) and Timars (military fiefs), were of a simplicity that must either conquer or decay.

The Turkish tide had twice flowed and twice ebbed over the Hungarian plain during the fifteenth, sixteenth, and seventeenth centuries. Its low-water mark, since 1456, had been Belgrade: its high-water mark in 1529, and again in 1683, had been under the walls of Vienna. Since the last date it had ebbed rapidly. Only Austrian weakness and French intrigue, during the War of Polish Succession, had enabled the Turks to maintain their footing at Belgrade in 1739. It was France again that, carrying on a policy which was as old as Francis I, urged Turkey into war with Russia (as we have just seen) in 1770. The result upset all the French calculations. Within two years of the partition of Poland, Catherine dictated the Treaty of Kutchuk Kainardji (1774), the starting-point of the whole modern Russo-Turkish question. By this treaty Russia, the self-appointed heir of the Eastern Empire, whose Tsars aimed at continuing the Roman succession at Byzantium, whose religion was that of the Greek Christians in Turkey, and whose churches bore the emblem of the cross triumphant over the crescent—Russia not only gained Azof, the independence of the Crimea, and the freedom of navigation in the Black Sea, but also established a right of intervention on behalf of the Christian population of European Turkey.

Only one step remained—the actual partition of Turkish territory. Catherine and Joseph formed a partnership for this purpose, and drew up a plan (1781). Russia was to have the north shore of the Black Sea as far west as Odessa. Moldavia and Wallachia (representing the bulk of modern Rumania) were to form a free state under the protection of Austria, which would also annex northern Serbia and Bosnia, including Belgrade. The rest of the Balkan peninsula was to be a Greek Empire under the protection of Russia, and with its capital at Constantinople. In 1787 the two monarchs went on their 'Arabian Nights' tour through the Crimea, and entered Sebastopol under a triumphal arch bearing the inscription, 'To Byzantium.'

When our period ends, in 1789, Russia and Austria are both at war with Turkey, and the fear of their success is bringing England, France, and Prussia into alliance against them. Sweden under Gustavus III has barely avoided the fate of Poland, and is once more arming against Prussia. Poland is being encouraged to revolt. France is organizing Turkish resistance.

We are back at the old diplomatic game. Here is the board, with its rigid squares, its rules for every move, its exact balance of power. One of the usual openings has been made, and met with the orthodox answer. The pieces begin to move. Suddenly a new force puts its hand on the board, and sweeps them all away.

LECTURE XXI

LOUIS XVI

I

On May 10th, 1774, in his gilded bedroom at Versailles, Louis XV at last lay dying of small-pox. It was a virulent case; the whole palace seemed infected; hardly anyone but the King's old sister would go near him. It was already late in the evening, and it was known that he could not last long. The ante-chambers were full of courtiers, and the palace square full of horses and carriages. The watchers in the King's room had put a lighted candle in the window, which they were to blow out at the moment of his death, as a sign to the waiting crowd below. At last the light wavered, and went out. The Dauphin and his wife, who were waiting in an inner room, heard in the square outside the shouting of orders and the rattling of harness as the bodyguard and equerries mounted and got ready to depart; and in the Palace itself a noise like thunder, as the crowd of courtiers deserted the ante-chamber of the dead King to do their homage to Louis XVI. It is said that Louis and Marie Antoinette threw themselves on their knees in floods of tears, and exclaimed, 'O God! Guide us, protect us: we are too young to reign!' [*Campan*].

The new King was twenty years old, the new Queen nineteen. They had already been married four years; but Louis was still a dull, awkward, shy boy—his clothes often untidy, his hair in disorder, and his hands black from working at keys and locks. His voice was either gruff, or, if he were excited, broke into shrill sounds. He was a heavy eater, but in no other way a sensualist: a keen sportsman, who hated any other shedding of blood. His vices might have been virtues in a private man: his virtues were vices in a King. He could never play a dignified part at Court functions. An Englishman who was presented at Versailles in 1774 said, 'The King receives the presentations with less attention than one should naturally show to a cat or a dog, because he does not even seem to look at you' [*Keith*]. 'He was so short-sighted,' says another visitor in 1787, 'that he could not recognize anyone at three paces. He was a fat man of medium height, with high shoulders, and the worst form that you could imagine. He had the air of a peasant, and there was nothing lofty or royal in his mien. He was always embarrassed by his sword, and did not know what to do with his hat . . . He held himself badly, and waddled; his movements were brusque and ungraceful; and his shortsightedness caused him to squint.'

Louis' mind was only less awkward than his body. He was indeed fond of reading, especially English books and periodicals: he could translate Milton, and enjoy (with some qualms) the earlier volumes of Gibbon's *Decline and Fall*. He had a talent for geography, and was fond of drawing and colouring maps. He knew something of French history, and could criticize Molière. Nor was he without ability for business. Ministers who met him in Council remarked that he could read his correspondence and attend to the business of the meeting at the same time. His memory for a point of detail was often better than theirs.

Upon two subjects his usual silence and indecision would suddenly give way to definite opinion and clear speech. One was religion: the other was the happiness of the French people. One of his Ministers had inserted into a state document some phrase about the King's happiness being troubled by disorders in the provinces. 'You must change that phrase,' Louis suddenly remarked; 'you mustn't make me speak of my happiness: I can't allow such an untruth to pass. How do you suppose I can be happy, when nobody in France is? No, Sir, the French people are not happy—I see that only too well . . . They will be one day, I hope: that is my fervent desire. Then I shall be too. Then I can speak of my happiness—not before.' Louis' eyes, as he spoke, filled with tears, and his Ministers looked at one another in embarrassed surprise [*Moleville*]. But while Louis' instincts were mature, the reason that should have guided them was rudimentary. His intelligence (said his brother-in-law of Austria) was as chaotic as the universe before God said 'Let there be light.' His ideas (said his brother of Provence) were as elusive as a handful of oiled billiard-balls. He had no power of concentration, or of initiative. He shrank from any decision that would affect twenty-five million people. 'The King,' said his wife, 'is not a coward; he has plenty of passive courage; but he is overwhelmed by an awkward shyness, a distrust of himself, due as much to his education as to his disposition. He is afraid to command, and dreads most of all speaking to a crowd' [*Fersen*]. 'Nobody would have been happier as King of England, where he could have known for certain the voice of public opinion, and followed this infallible guide' [*de Staël*]. No one could have been less fitted, just at this moment, to be King of France.

Of the Queen, Marie Antoinette, it is difficult to speak dispassionately. Her tragedy was that she had to be a queen. Nature had made her a brave, charming, warm-hearted, and indiscreet girl, who only wanted to be happy, and to make others happy. From the first she became the victim of persons and policies that conspired to ruin her life. She was born on the day of the disastrous earthquake at Lisbon. She was married as a pledge of the unpopular alliance between France and Austria. She was thrown, at an age when she should have been at school, into the dullest and most dissolute Court in Europe. Her French tutor (de Vermond) was a fool, her Austrian ambassador (Mercy d'Argentau) a pompous old gossip, and her lady of honour a stiff and boring person who deserved her nickname of 'Madame l'Etiquette.' She had an unfortunate facility for making secondrate friends. Soon after her arrival in France, Choiseul, the Minister who had arranged her marriage, was dismissed; and she became the butt of all the gossip and intrigues of the anti-Austrian party. Everything she did must be wrong. Her slightest indiscretion was magnified into a scandal, her mildest witticism into an insult. An evening concert, a country ride, or a private play at the Trianon, was good enough material for writers of libellous and indecent verse. One thing might have atoned for all else; and the lack of it was not her fault: for eight years Louis failed to give her a child. When at last she appealed to French sentiment as a mother she had alienated it as a queen. She had set herself against the democratic feeling of the country by securing the dismissal of reforming Ministers: she was suspected of the unforgivable sin of preferring another country to her own, and of influencing French policy in the interests of Austria. And so Paris, which in a chivalrous mood might have been expected (as Burke said) to 'draw a hundred swords in her defence,' found her a traitor, and turned her life into a tragedy.

II

While Louis XV's body was hurried to its grave, crowds surrounded the residence of Louis XVI, from sunrise to sunset, shouting 'Vive le Roi!' A fashionable jeweller made a fortune by the sale of snuff-boxes on which appeared a portrait of the young Queen framed in black shagreen leather, with the inscription, 'Comfort in chagrin.' Poets wrote congratulatory odes. Ladies wore bunches of wheat, and other symbols of abundance, in their hair. Never was such enthusiasm [*Campan*]. It seemed the beginning of a golden age. 'A young, virtuous, and benevolent King, who had no other thought but that of the happiness of his subjects, and no idea of authority except that founded upon justice, gave by his own example a fresh stimulus to all these generous ideas' [*Ségur*]. 'I blush to think,' wrote Maria Theresa, 'that after thirty-three years of reigning I have not done as much as this dear prince has done in thirty-three days.' Someone chalked up 'Resurrexit' on the statue of Henry IV, the best of French Kings.

Louis had certainly begun well. He had chosen the best body of Ministers that France had seen for many years—not, indeed, Choiseul, who was identified with 'philosophy,' and the attack on the Church; nor Machault, the enemy of the Parlements; but Maurepas, who had been out of office for thirty disastrous years, and was to play the part of Lord Melbourne for the young sovereigns; Vergennes, Choiseul's lieutenant in Turkey and Sweden, and one of the ablest of foreign ministers: Malesherbes, an enlightened reformer, as Home Secretary; and the famous economist Turgot, the philosophers' nominee, as Controller-General of Finance. *Condorcet,* writing to Voltaire, welcomed this last appointment as 'the happiest possible event for France, and for human reason. There has never entered into any King's Council,' he went on, 'a man who combines to so high a degree virtue, courage, disinterestedness, the love of public good, enlightenment, and zeal. Since this event I have been sleeping and waking as peacefully as though I lived under the laws of England. I have almost ceased to take an interest in public affairs; I am so sure that they can't help going well.'

Turgot was likely to need all his talents, and all the loyalty of his friends. The country was terribly in debt. It was showing a deficit on every year's budget, and spending in advance a series of imaginary surpluses. Terray, Louis XV's last Finance Minister, had said that there was no remedy but to declare a national bankruptcy. In point of fact there was plenty of money in the country: it needed not so much wit to discover, as courage to extract it. Turgot believed that the situation could be saved partly by reducing expenditure, and partly by encouraging trade and agriculture: his programme was 'No bankruptcy, no new taxation, no loans.' He boldly attacked the expenses of Versailles. He abolished the regulations that restricted the trade in corn, and the 'corporations' that obstructed the flow of labour. He taxed the landlords, instead of commandeering the peasants' labour, for the upkeep of the roads. And he designed a system of representative local government, which, if it had been carried out, might have supplied some of that political responsibility and social solidarity for lack of which France was drifting into revolution. But Turgot moved too fast for prevailing opinion. His reforms destroyed too many vested interests. The Paris Parlement, which Louis, with more generosity than wisdom, had recalled, refused to register the new edicts, and did so in terms which showed how unfit it was to be the champion of the people. The clergy, it declared, did their duty to the State by charity, education, and public worship; the nobility, by advising the Crown, and fighting in the King's army; and 'the lowest class of the nation, which cannot render such distinguished service to the State, does its part by the payment of taxes, by industry, and by the work of its hands.' Louis XIV himself could not have put the case for privilege more benightedly. Turgot threw himself on public opinion, and forced his reforms through by a *lit de justice*. At the moment he seemed to have succeeded. 'Thanks to God and the King,' wrote Voltaire (April 3, 1776), 'here we are already in the Age of Gold—and up to the neck in it!' But he had underestimated the strength of privilege. The very next day the Swedish ambassador wrote home: 'M. Turgot is up against a most formidable league, composed of all the nobles, all the Parlements, all the financial interests, all the ladies at court, and all the faithful' [*Malet*]. His hope was in the King: but he made the mistake, in dealing with Louis, which Mr. Gladstone is said to have made in dealing with Queen

Victoria—he addressed him as though he were a public meeting: he lectured too much, persuaded too little. 'Never forget, Sire,' he said, 'that it was weakness which laid Charles I's head upon the block.' No one likes to be told that he is weak, especially when he is conscious of being so. Louis, urged by the Queen and the Court party, posed as a strong man, and gave Turgot his dismissal. With him went Malesherbes, despairing of the Government. 'Maurepas,' he said, 'laughs about everything; Turgot doubts about nothing; I doubt about everything and laugh about nothing—what a Ministry!' [*Guénin*].

III

This was in 1776. Philosophy having failed to save France, recourse was had to finance. Necker, who remained Louis' chief minister for the next five years, was a Swiss banker, whose credit stood high in the financial world, and whose wife was noted both for her social philanthropy and for her political 'salon.' The philosophers disliked him. Condorcet wrote to Voltaire, 'Necker succeeding Turgot is like Fénelon followed by the Abbé Dubois,' and resigned his appointment at the Mint. Necker's vanity alienated many who admired his honesty. As to his views—they were so often put in print by Necker himself, or by his daughter Madame de Staël, that they were known almost to weariness. A practical business man, rather disdainful of theories, he had visited England, and come back with an admiration for English institutions. What struck him most of all was 'the influence of publicity upon national credit, and the advantages offered by representative government for putting public finance on a sound footing.' From that time onwards 'he thought that economy, and the publicity which guarantees the keeping of promises, are the foundation of order and credit in a great empire; and just as, in his view, public morality ought not to differ from private, so he believed that public finance could be carried on, in many respects, by the same rules as that of the individual household. To equalize receipts with expenditure: to arrive at this balance by cutting down expenses rather than by increasing taxation: and, when war unhappily became inevitable, to pay for it by loans carrying guaranteed interest, or by fresh economies, or by a new form of taxation—those were M. Necker's first principles, and his last' [de Staël].

It was the War of American Independence, here referred to, which became the first cause of the failure of Necker's policy; for it dissipated at once the products of past and the prospects of future economies. A second cause was the publication of the *Compte Rendu au Roi*, a Budget Statement (1781). Necker's aim was to take the country into the confidence of the crown, and to strengthen its credit by proving the sound condition of the national finances. But most of the Statement consisted of criticisms directed against the Civil List, and the system of taxation, and of drastic suggestions for reform. What caused most offence was the exposure, in a work of which 100,000 copies sold in a few weeks, of the pensions and other payments made to members of the Court. The public had always suspected that large sums of money were wasted in this way: now they learnt that the pension list cost them as much as the fleet and the colonies put together [*Malet*]. For instance (these examples are quoted from the *Livre Rouge* published by the National Assembly a few years later) there was M. Blanchet, who received 4,727 livres 'in consideration of his past services,' and 4,727 livres 'in consideration of his future services'; or M. de Gallois de la Tour, who had 22,720 livres in three payments—the first 'as First President and Intendant of Provence,' the second 'as Intendant and First President,' and the third 'for the same considerations as those above mentioned.' An annuity of 6,000 louis was given to the hairdresser of Mlle d'Artois, though that princess had died at the age of three. Payments were even promised, if not made, to persons who did not and might never exist—such as 4,000 livres to 'the person who shall marry Mme de Baschi, the mistress of Monsieur the King's brother' [*Mercier*]. Necker's attack on the Civil List made him popular with the crowd; at Court it could only increase his unpopularity. A third cause of his failure was his revival of Turgot's scheme for local government. A beginning was made in Berry (1778) and Mantauban (1779). Provincial Assemblies were set up, consisting of members of the clergy, nobility, and commons nominated by the Crown. They had no power, except to talk, and to report. But among the resolutions sent up by the Assembly of Berry were two which savoured of revolution. One demanded 'a brotherly partition of taxes,' and the abolition of the *corvée*; the other claimed that the members of the provincial Assemblies should be elected 'by the mass of those whose interests were at stake' [*Malet*]. Maurepas, who disliked Necker, took the opportunity to work on Louis' fears, and the banker followed the philosopher into retirement.

After philosophy and finance came Calonne, the Court candidate. Because he was clever he was supposed to be profound—in England we more often argue the other way: he was at any rate perfect in the art of political window-dressing. His policy was to pacify privilege by increasing the Civil List, and to improve the credit of the country by encouraging expenditure. Luxury was a sign, if not a source, of prosperity. The more money the nation spent, the readier other nations would be to lend it fresh supplies. Acting on this comfortable doctrine, Calonne made Necker's war loans a permanent part of his budgets, and borrowed more money in three years of peace than his predecessor had borrowed in five years of war. Having thus restored the country to a state of bankruptcy, he turned round and said that the only remedy was to put in force at once the whole Turgot-Necker programme—a universal tax, abolition of the *corvée* and of internal Customs, free trade in corn, and a complete system of provincial Assemblies. When the Parlement objected, recourse was had to the Notables—an ancient body which represented the privileged classes, and which, it was hoped, might be more amenable. Paris was sceptical: someone put up a poster announcing a performance by M. de Calonne's company at Versailles of a Grand Drama entitled 'Confidence Misplaced,' with a curtain-raiser called 'Forced Consent'; the performance to end with 'The Purse with a hole in it,' an Allegorical Ballet composed by the Manager [*Malet*]. The event was as expected. The Notables did indeed approve of the provincial Assemblies, the abolition of the *corvée*, and free trade in corn: but they refused to accept the proposed taxation, so long as they were in ignorance as to the origin and amount of the public debt: and many of them demanded the summoning of the Estates General. The King, once more under Court pressure, dismissed Calonne.

The wits published the usual epigrams. One was headed, 'Today's Barometer,' and went on, 'The People—variable: the Parlement—rain: the Clergy—stormy.' The mountain of the Notables, said another, is in labour, and will bring forth a mouse —or else a new Controller-General [*Guénin*].

And so it did. De Brienne, Archbishop of Toulouse, was the Queen's nominee, and a leader of the opposition. But even he could suggest no alternative to the Turgot-Necker programme: and a last attempt was made to carry it through. The Notables resisted, and were dissolved. The Parlement refused to register, and was sent into exile. Mob-riots broke out, and the Queen was publicly abused as 'Madame Déficit.' Thousands of people were thrown into prison. At last, when money must be raised somehow, Brienne recalls the Parlement (1787), and promises, if they will register his new loan, to summon the Estates General in 1792. 'Summon it,' they cry, 'in '89.' The only reply is a command to register the loan. The King's own cousin, the Duke of Orleans, rises to protest (it is the one creditable act in his career): 'That's all wrong!' he cries. 'It's all right,' retorts the King: 'It's all right, because it is my will.' And with this last gesture of a dying absolutism Louis leaves the House. With Orleans exiled, and two of their members in prison, the Parlement made a last bid for the popular support which their opposition to the new taxes was rapidly alienating. 'France,' they declared, 'is a monarchy governed by the King in accordance with the laws'; and these laws guard two fundamental rights—the right of the nation to vote Supply freely by means of regular meetings of the Estates General; and the right of the individual not to be arrested without being at once brought before a properly constituted court. These English rather than French sentiments were met by fresh arrests, and the arrests by fiercer resistance. With only a few thousand pounds left in the Treasury, Brienne made a final appeal to the last hope of the monarchy—the Church Assembly. That too, like the Notables and the Parlement, demanded the immediate summoning of the Estates General. The King gave way, and agreed that they should meet in May, 1789. Brienne was dismissed, and Necker recalled.

During the seven years of his retirement, and the failure of all his schemes, Necker had bitterly regretted his resignation. 'Ah!'

he exclaimed, when they told him of his recall, 'if they had only given me these fifteen months that the Archbishop has had! Now it is too late' [*de Staël*]. In fact, it was too late by fifteen years—the fifteen years of Louis XVI's reign. Influences were at work all the time—the King's feebleness, the opposition of the Queen and Court, the demand for financial publicity, the cry for political representation, and the revolt of the people against the *ancien régime*—which neither philosophy nor finance, neither persuasion nor compulsion could control. Necker's recall, and the summoning of the Estates, meant not reform, but revolution.

IV

There was another side of Louis XVI's government that in happier times might have outbalanced the financial disasters to which (as things were) it only added fresh weight—I mean the foreign policy of Vergennes.

Vergennes inherited Choiseul's belief that England was the enemy, and that France had a future overseas. He kept up the Austrian alliance, but took care that it should not involve him in a continental war. He manœuvred France back into its old position as European referee. Meanwhile he got ready for the next round in the fight with England, an opportunity for which was already in sight.

Vergennes' continental policy is best illustrated by the Bavarian Succession question, and the affair of the Netherlands. The first is like one of those round convex mirrors which reflect a whole room: it sums up the eighteenth century. Bavaria, blocking the upper Danube valley, commanded the main routes from Austria to France, and from Austria to Italy. It had always been coveted by the Hapsburgs. To Joseph II, an eager imitator of Frederick the Great, it seemed another Silesia. In 1777, when Frederick had grown old, Catherine was involved with Turkey, and Louis was preoccupied with the American War, the perfect opportunity presented itself. Maximilian Joseph, the Elector of Bavaria, died childless, and the succession passed to Charles Theodore, the Elector Palatine, representing another branch of the family. Joseph at once put forward claims, based upon a fifteenth-century document of doubtful value, to the parts of Eastern Bavaria which he particularly needed; and persuaded Charles Theodore to acknowledge his rights, in return for the Order of the Golden Fleece, and a handsome allowance for his illegitimate children. So far so good. Unfortunately, in his zeal to imitate Frederick, Joseph forgot that Frederick might not be flattered by imitation. The conqueror of Silesia was now posing as a reformed character, and at once came forward as the champion of political freedom. A curious correspondence followed, in which Joseph defended his right to make any arrangement he pleased with Charles Theodore, and Frederick accused him of playing fast and loose with the Constitution of the Empire. In the summer of '79 words gave way to war, and both sides marched their armies into Bohemia. Soon a position of stalemate was reached, practically without fighting; and in the autumn the Prussian army went home again, after no greater exploits than plundering the fields and orchards of the invaded territory; so that it was called the 'plum and potato war.'

Meanwhile Maria Theresa, who disliked the whole business, suggested terms of peace behind Joseph's back. Frederick was agreeable, but insisted upon 'compensation' for the trouble he had been put to. In return for the succession to the duchies of Ansbach and Bayreuth, he allowed Joseph to keep a strip of Bavarian territory—the so-called 'Quarter of the Inn' (*Innviertel*) at the angle of the Inn and Danube. This was the Treaty of Teschen; it was negotiated through the good offices of France and Russia, both of whom had kept out of the war; and it did much to restore the prestige of France as an international referee.

Joseph was disappointed with the result of his schemes, and displeased at the failure of France to support him. A few years later he made a fresh attempt to secure Bavaria, by a plan to which he hoped Vergennes would not object. The Austrian Netherlands had always been more an embarrassment than an asset to the Emperor. They were a long way off. They resented being reformed. They could not be developed commercially without rousing the jealousy of England and Holland. By the Treaty of Fontainebleau (1785), Joseph had indeed forced the Dutch to give up the Barrier Forts which they had held since 1714; but his subsequent attempt to open the navigation of the

Scheldt, in spite of all that Marie Antoinette could do to influence Louis, had been defeated by the French Foreign Minister. Joseph turned once more to the compliant Charles Theodore, who agreed to exchange Bavaria for the Netherlands, which he was to rule under the title of King of Burgundy—a fantastic bit of antiquarianism, which would also have upset the Balance of Power in Germany. Vergennes would have none of it, and Frederick set himself to organize a Fürstenbund, or League of German Princes, the object of which was to maintain the settlement of Westphalia, and to protect its members against the unlawful aggression of Austria. In face of this attitude Joseph gave way. His second failure was a second victory for Vergennes.

V

It was also the last and most peaceful victory of Frederick, who died the next year. Many kings outlive their glory: he had outlived his shame. He had become a Protestant hero, and the champion of German liberty. It is said that the Bavarian peasants, after their delivery from Austria, set up a new image in their cottages, and said their prayers to 'Jesus, Maria, and Frederick.' In the next century Treitschke proclaimed Frederick to be the founder of Pan-Germanism, and Carlyle made him a model for English schoolboys. If we are to judge him as an epitome of later Prussianism, there is no more to be said. If he stands on his own claims, the efficiency of his government is balanced by the lowness of his view of life. Frederick the Great is also Frederick the Cad.

Maria Theresa, who in 1778 lamented that she had lived twelve years too long, died in 1780. Out of touch with the Enlightenment, which then seemed to be ruling the world, she outlived the Enlightened Despots in the affection of the common people, who disliked philosophers and reformers, and knew her to be a good woman and a great patriot.

Joseph died soon after Frederick, in 1790. Only Catherine, of the Big Four, lived through the French Revolution, to die in 1796—less hard-working, and more open to flattery, in her later years, but still a grand and fascinating figure in a world which was rapidly passing away.

VI

The third and most serious part of Vergennes' foreign policy was his participation in the War of American Independence. The causes of the war do not concern us here; but so far as the Colonies were fighting for democratic principles, and for the right to settle their own taxation, their cause appealed at once to the younger generation of France; whilst the Government saw little but an opportunity for helping in the humiliation of England. The Declaration of Independence roused fresh enthusiasm. Beaumarchais, the d'Annunzio of his times, organized a gun-running scheme, by which the Insurgents were supplied with war material from French arsenals. French officers, largely from the younger nobility—de Lauzun, de Noailles, de Ségur, de Lafayette—sailed to America, and served in Washington's army. Burgoyne's capitulation at Saratoga (1777) brought France officially into the war.

The treaty of alliance was negotiated at Paris by Benjamin Franklin of Boston—printer, journalist, postmaster, inventor, and statesman, whose straight unpowdered hair, round fur cap, large spectacles, and noble sentiments made a deep impression upon a society unaccustomed to self-made men. The Anglo-American war thus became Anglo-French; it was Vergennes' ambition to make it Anglo-European. He easily obtained the help of Spain. Then, by exploiting the discontent of the maritime powers with the English practice of searching neutral ships for contraband of war, he induced Catherine of Russia to head a League of Armed Neutrality, including also Denmark, Prussia, Sweden, Holland, Austria, and Portugal. England was completely isolated. The capitulation of Cornwallis (1781), the naval successes of Guichen and d'Orvilliers in the West Indies, and of Suffren off India, the loss of Port Mahon, and the siege of Gibraltar, brought us very near to disaster. But Rodney turned defeat into victory, Gibraltar was relieved, and Vergennes, being short of funds, and nervous about the Turkish situation, consented to proposals of peace. By the Treaty of Versailles (1783) the United States confirmed their independence, Spain recovered Florida and Minorca (but not Gibraltar), and France once more fortified Dunkirk. The Treaty of Paris was avenged. French prestige stood higher than it had done for forty years.

VII

At any other time a successful foreign policy would have saved the situation at home. But now the American victory turned to a disaster for France. The country was irretrievably bankrupt. English trade, helped by a commercial treaty drawn at the end of the war, quickly out-distanced French. Most significant of all, American republicanism came home with the French army. Against such influences there was no solidity in French society, or government, or throne, to offer any resistance.

When the crisis of the Revolution came, the kings' statues in Paris were pulled down and broken to bits: and it is said that the crowd, who expected to melt them down into an infinite supply of copper money, stood round angry and astonished; for they were all hollow inside, no thicker than a single coin [*Mercier*].

LECTURE XXII

CONCLUSION

I

With the meeting of the Estates General at Versailles in May, 1789, our period of history comes to an end, together with a good many institutions and ideas to which Europe had grown accustomed during the previous three hundred years. Two tasks remain. One is to estimate the causes of the French Revolution. The other is to summarize what we have learnt about the permanent character of the various States of Europe.

As to the first, many volumes have been written, and many views propounded. At the time, each class of society, as the fashion is, supposed its own grievances to be the most urgent, and had its own explanation of the catastrophe. The orthodox put it down to the Encyclopaedia; the Ministers, to the influence of Court intrigue; the Parlements, to their arbitrary treatment by the Crown; the philosophers thought it would not have happened if they had been in power; the commercial classes, if trade had not been so bad; the peasantry, if it had not been for feudalism and over-taxation [*de Ségur*]. Looking back at the situation, we can safely say that no one cause stood alone, no one class was entirely to blame. The whole country had been long drifting into Revolution.

II

The first class of causes may be called intellectual; and at the head of them comes 'the revolutionary spirit in France before the Revolution.' This spirit goes back at least as far as the Fronde: the demands made by the Paris Parlement in 1649 were singularly like those made by the Estates General 140 years later. It was the *frondeur* attitude towards the arbitrary regime of the Crown and of the privileged classes which developed, under the misfortunes of Louis XIV's later years, and under the misgovernment of Louis XV, into a definitely revolutionary movement. 'When Louis XV died, France was not merely revolutionary in its ideas, but also in its temperament' [*Rocquain,* cp. *Aubertin*]. Under Louis XVI an outbreak was inevitable.

To the natural growth of resentment against misgovernment was added the artificial stimulus of 'philosophy.' It is significant that the influence of Montesquieu, Voltaire, and the Encyclopaedists began to be felt at the very time, in the middle of the eighteenth century, when the *frondeur* spirit became revolutionary. And its effects were all the more disturbing because the French writers, unlike their English originals, had no practical experience of politics, and had never seen a revolution. They tested their political principles, not by the experiment of self-government, but by the uncertain analogies of Greek and Roman history. Instead of using principles to reform practice, instead of trying to make the actual order of society more ideal, they built up in their imagination a heavenly Paris—only that the jewelled gates and streets of gold were replaced by the will of the people and the natural rights of man—and proposed to substitute this glorious fabric, ready-made, for the France of Louis XV. Rousseau was the arch apocalyptist. Readers who, like Mme Roland, had been brought up on Plutarch, Holbach, Helvétius, Raynal, and d'Alembert, were transformed by the *Contrat Social* from reformers into revolutionaries.

For those who could not read philosophy there was always the stage. In 1784 appeared a play which Napoleon once described as 'the Revolution already at work'—Beaumarchais' *Mariage de Figaro*. The hero and heroine were a footman and parlourmaid, who criticized their masters with considerable freedom. 'They say it's a difficult job to be a courtier,' remarks Suzanne. 'Difficult?' replies Figaro: 'Why, I can tell you the secret of it in three words—receiving, taking, asking—that is all.' 'The magistrate on the bench,' says another character, 'forgets himself, and looks only to the Law.' 'Yes,' retorts Figaro, 'a law which is kind to the rich, and cruel to the poor.' And the play ends with a song of which one verse runs thus:

'It's merely a matter of how you are born,
If A is a shepherd, and B is a King:
Luck gives one man glory, another man scorn:
But capacity changes it all—that's the thing.
Here's a dozen odd Kings that we fawn on and flatter;

If one dies, we shan't miss him—it really won't matter.
But there *is just* one King for whose sake we'd deport all
The rest—that's King Voltaire—and he is immortal.'

The intellectuals could afford to flirt with such sentiments: among the mob they inflamed a fatal passion.

Another influence that has to be reckoned with is that of English ideas—not merely those mediated by the 'philosophers,' but those popularized by social intercourse between the two countries. Between 1763 (the end of the Seven Years' War) and 1789 (the outbreak of the Revolution) a great many people crossed the Channel in both directions. There was hardly a literary man in London who had not travelled in France, hardly a man of fashion at Paris who had not come into contact with English ideas in his own country, or in ours. There were said to be 40,000 English people living in France in 1788. Dr. Johnson, the most unimpressionable of travellers, visited Paris in 1775, and astonished the natives by going about in London dress—brown clothes, black stockings, and a plain shirt. He saw the King and Queen dine at Fontainebleau, and the animals in the menagerie at Versailles. He went over Santerre's brewery, one of the sights of Paris, little knowing how soon its proprietor would be a ringleader of the Revolution, and command the troops at the execution of Louis XVI. The Doctor refused to write a book on so hackneyed a subject as French travel; but recorded his opinions of French society. 'The great in France,' he observed, 'live very magnificently, but the rest very miserably. There is no happy middle state as in England. The shops in Paris are mean: the meat in the markets is such as would be sent to a gaol in England.' Hence good cooking is a necessity rather than a virtue. He is offended by the French habit of spitting, and by other nasty accompaniments of nice manners. At a party the footman puts the sugar into the coffee with his fingers, and, when the teapot won't pour properly, blows down the spout [*Boswell*].

At the beginning of the eighteenth century the French had regarded Englishmen as gloomy barbarians, who cut off their Kings' heads and their horses' tails; and our pamphleteers had declaimed against the importation of French lace and French dancing-masters. Now everything was changed. 'Since these people despoiled us in the Indies and in Africa,' says a French writer, 'we have taken from them many things—their gardens, their Vauxhall, their Ranelagh, their dark dramas and their terrible comedies, their whisk [whist], their punch, their horse-races, their jackets, and their wages.' English simplicity in dress had a levelling influence: the French nobleman now wore his own hair and a narrow-tailed coat, like any commoner, and drove about in a cab. More serious forms of imitation followed—heavier gambling, a rage for racing, English clubs, which largely displaced the 'salons,' and a taste for duelling and suicide. This last was regarded as a specially British habit: 'An Englishman who travels,' wrote Diderot, 'is often only a man who goes out of his country to kill himself elsewhere.' Rousseau's campaign for a return to Nature was backed by knowledge of English country houses, English gardens, English nature-poetry, English novels of human sentiment, English philanthropy. Gray's *Elegy*, Young's *Night Thoughts*, Sterne's *Tristram Shandy*, and Richardson's *Clarissa Harlowe* were eagerly translated and assimilated. And in eighteenth-century France to be natural was to be revolutionary [*Lockitt*].

Even more important was the influence of English political ideas. The partiality for the British Constitution shown by Montesquieu and Voltaire was now more widely spread, if less well informed. Mirabeau, the first statesman of the Revolution, was one of many who regarded England as the home of political liberty, and who were working for a constitutional monarchy of a broadly English type.

The only influence comparable to that of English ideas was that of the American revolution. The English influence was spread over a long period: it affected mainly the literary men and the nobility: it was mixed with a good deal of suspicion towards a traditionally hostile neighbour. The American influence came suddenly: it affected military men and adventurers, who did not commonly read Rousseau, or study the British Constitution; whilst to those who stayed at home distance lent enchantment to the view of liberty. 'Our youth,' says *Mme Campan*, 'flew to the wars waged in the New World for liberty, and against the rights of thrones. Liberty prevailed. They returned triumphant to France, and brought with them the seeds of independence.

Letters from military men were frequently received at the Palace of Versailles, and their seals bore the thirteen stars of the United States surrounding the cap of liberty; and the Chevalier de Passy, one of the most esteemed poets of the day . . . published an epistle to the citizens of Boston, in which were the following lines:

' "You, happy people, freed from Kings and Queens,
Dance to the rattling of the chains that bind
In servile shame the rest of human-kind." '

Anglomania gave way to Americomania. Whist went out of fashion, and Boston came in: a small affair, perhaps, 'but a noteworthy sign of the great convulsions into which the whole world was so soon to be thrown; and I (says *de Ségur*) was far from being the only one whose heart beat at the sound of the awakening of liberty, and the attempt to shake off the yoke of arbitrary power.'

When the Revolution came, its first practical reforms followed the English model; but its abstract Declaration of Rights was borrowed from America; there lay just the difference between the two influences.

III

Another class of causes of the Revolution may be called political, and may be summed up in the statement that before the Revolution France had, properly speaking, no Constitution, and that it was the primary object of the Revolution to provide one. The government of the old régime had been arbitrary, impotent, and anarchical: the government of the new régime was to be legal, efficient, and systematic.

It had been arbitrary in the sense that its limits were not fixed by law, but could be enlarged by caprice; and that its methods were subject to no appeal or redress. The commonest instance of this was the *lettre de cachet*—an order for your arrest and detention 'during the King's pleasure,' which might be signed by a Minister at the instance of a private enemy, and against the execution of which there was no remedy, unless a still higher authority interested himself on your behalf. Even under Louis XVI's mild rule, *lettres de cachet* were still issued at the rate of seventy or eighty a year. In such ways a government which was one of the most ineffective in the world was also one of the most despotic, and became a school in which the leaders of the Revolution learnt only too well the lesson of tyranny.

Arbitrary in intention, the government was in effect impotent. It is only a new monarchy which can do what it likes—a King of Prussia or a President of the United States. The old monarchies are slaves of tradition and routine. Louis XVI, with all his liberal intentions, was the Prisoner of Versailles. And if he had taken a strong line, or appealed to force, who would have supported him? Ultimately the army. But the army could not be trusted. Its character had been deteriorating since the middle of the century. The American War had infected it with democratic ideas. The spread of freemasonry was destroying discipline, and encouraging a revolutionary equality. And the unfortunate edict of 1781, which made it impossible for commoners to secure commissions, was a new and special cause of discontent.

This mixture of arbitrariness and impotence was the tragedy of Louis XVI's government. It might have mattered less if the administration of the country had been decentralized. But it was at once centralized and chaotic. For administrative purposes France was divided first into forty old *gouvernements* under noble Governors, and secondly, into thirty-six new *généralités*, under Intendants, cutting across the old division. For purposes of taxation there were two systems: all the central provinces (the *pays d'élection*) were assessed by officers of the Crown; the outlying provinces (*pays d'état*) were assessed by their own deputies. For the *gabelle*, or salt-tax, there were seven groups of provinces, and each had a different tariff. For judicial purposes the country was divided into two parts by a line running roughly from Geneva to the middle of the Bay of Biscay. South of this line justice was administered according to the *droit écrit*, based on the old Roman law: north of this line you came under the *droit coutumier*, which might be any one of 285 local codes—'you changed your laws, with your horses, at every stage on the road' [*Voltaire*]. Once more, the thirteen central provinces of the Seine and Loire valleys formed a Customs Union called the 'Five Great Farms,' within which goods could circulate duty free: but each of the other nineteen provinces had its own customs barrier, and its own tariff. Finally, to complete the confusion, there was no recognized system of weights and measures: each province, almost each parish, had its own.

Every old country, England not excepted, shows anomalies of this kind: they are not necessarily fatal to good government. But in France they became so, partly because there was no attempt to decentralize control, and partly because local enmities and independence grew like weeds in the garden of national unity. When the provincial deputies presented their *cahiers* at the Estates General of 1789, it was found that Alsace denied its incorporation in the French nation, that the people of Provence would not recognize the French King except under the title of 'Count of Provence,' and that Navarre expressed its readiness to unite itself with France so soon as that country had a government as good as its own [*Champion*]. This lack of real unity under a show of uniformity was one of the surest causes of the Revolution.

IV

It is no less certain that one of the immediate causes was Finance. National bankruptcy (as we have seen) decided the summoning of the Notables, and of the Estates General. National bankruptcy was the lever with which the Commons overturned the old régime. Over-taxation and unjust taxation were their special grievances. Unjust taxation, because the privileged classes were largely exempt, and the wealthy could afford to compound with the tax-collector, whilst the poor and unprivileged were fleeced in proportion to their apparent means—one must either be very rich, or pretend to be very poor. Over-taxation, because, what with the *taille*, the *capitation*, and the *vingtième*, over 50 per cent of the poor man's income went direct to the State; because, in addition, he had to pay an indirect tax on salt (the *gabelle*) and on wine (the *aides*), and could be punished either for drinking more than four bottles of wine a year, or for eating less than six pounds of salt. The *gabelle* was enforced by an army of 50,000 officials: every year 30,000 people were imprisoned for offences under the salt-tax laws, and more than 500 hanged, or sent to the galleys [*Malet*].

V

But society can put up with a good deal of misgovernment and over-taxation, so long as there exists a happy relationship between class and class. It was the lack of this which was the most serious fact in the situation. When the Revolution came, it was not content to limit the arbitrary power of the Crown, to decentralize provincial government, to secure popular control over taxation: but it set itself to destroy the relics of feudalism utterly; and feudalism had come to mean social inequality and social privilege, beginning in class feeling and ending in class war.

French society for 500 years past had been divided into three curiously stable classes—clergy, nobility, and commons. The first two, numbering about 600,000 of the population, were 'privileged': the third, numbering about twenty-four millions, was 'unprivileged.' Privilege meant partly such honorary distinctions as admission to Court; partly exactions, such as the levying of feudal dues; partly exemptions, as for instance from taxation.

Of the 70,000 clergy (not including 60,000 monks and nuns) 10,000 were bishops and other dignitaries, generally rich, and 60,000 *curés* and *vicaires,* generally poor. The church lands were reckoned at a fifth of the whole country, and the value of their rent, plus feudal dues and tithes, at 500–550 million francs per annum [*Malet*]. Not more than 6 per cent of this huge wealth went to the upkeep of churches, schools and hospitals, in charitable gifts, or in grants to the Treasury. There were bishops with incomes ten times as great as those of the present English sees; and country clergy who starved on incomes of £30 to £70 a year. Needless to say, there was no love lost between the two classes; whilst the rich and privileged ecclesiastics shared the special odium of the rich and privileged aristocracy.

The old nobility (*noblesse de l'épée*) also fell into two classes—the *grande noblesse* of 1,000 families, and the *petite noblesse* of 99,000 families. The former monopolized such honorary privileges as Court sinecures, high military commands, provincial governorships, and foreign embassies. They were also the absentee landlords of large estates, which they often left unvisited and uncultivated, whilst they exacted feudal dues from their tenants to meet the cost of their establishments at Paris or Versailles. The *petite noblesse* were as proud as they were poor, bringing up large families in their tumble-down country *châteaux,* and sending their superfluous sons into the army, their daughters into nunneries. Here again there was little love lost between the two classes. Challenging both, and popular with neither, was the new nobility (*noblesse de robe*), which had acquired its titles by purchase or by merit, and held them in virtue of work done for the Law or Government of the country. This class numbered some 40,000, was proud of having won its privileges, and represented the exclusiveness of the *noblesse d'épée*.

Below this distinct but disunited minority of the privileged classes stood the great majority of the population—the unprivileged Commons or *Tiers Etat*. The time of their disunity was to come. For the moment their three classes of Bourgeoisie, Artisans, and Country Labourers stood together on their lack of privilege and hatred of feudalism.

In spite of war and misgovernment the eighteenth century had not been an unfavourable time for the French middle class. Much of the intelligence of the country, and most of the ready money, was in the hands of the merchants, tradesmen, and financiers; with whom, for wits, if not for wealth, must be classed the teachers, doctors, lawyers, and other professional men, numbering altogether, I suppose, some 100,000. This class suffered more than any other from the financial insecurity of the country: it was more conscious than any other of its exclusion from society, and from political life. Its grievances and ideas were the mainspring of the Revolution.

The two-and-a-half-million artisans were no more than a tenth of the whole population, and could not play the part that they made their own in later Revolutions, except in Paris, and in the industrial cities of the Midi.

Elsewhere they were swamped by the peasantry, or Country Labourers, who numbered no less than twenty-one out of the twenty-five millions of the population. About a million of these, mostly in Brittany and the Franche Comté, were still serfs, bought and sold with the land: many were landless labourers earning from 10*d.* to 1*s.* 8*d.* a day: some were *métayers* who shared profits and losses with their landlord: most were tenants paying some kind of feudal rent for the use of the land: others, perhaps half a million in all, were 'peasant proprietors,' owning a few fields round their cottages. But whether tenant or proprietor, it was the peasant upon whom fell the heaviest burden in the country—taxation, feudal dues, conscription, *corvée*: he was the

'State mule,' said Richelieu a century and a half earlier: at last he was growing restive under his load.

Social disunity, then, and social unrest were the most fundamental causes of the Revolution. The order of social privilege should correspond to the order of social service: in eighteenth-century France the one exactly inverted the other. The classes were upside down. At the Paris Carnival in 1789 some young men got themselves up to represent the three Orders, and paraded the streets in a hired carriage—the coachman dressed as an abbé, the footman wearing the badge of nobility, and two common people riding inside, to represent the Third Estate [*Dorset*].

VI

Looking back at all these points—the growth of revolutionary ideas, weak but arbitrary government, over-taxation, bankruptcy, and social inequality—one cannot doubt that France was ready for revolution. Yet if one had been alive then, it might well have seemed improbable. Bad as things were, they were in many respects better than they had been for three-quarters of a century. The country was more prosperous at home. Its prestige stood higher abroad. The Conservatives grumbled, as they always do: but to the Liberals it seemed a time of progress, the beginning of a golden age. 'In truth,' writes *de Ségur,* 'when I recall that age of deceptive dreams and learned follies, I compare the state in which we were then to that of a man standing on the top of a tower, his head giddy with the sight of an immense horizon, the moment before a fearful fall ... We were proud to be Frenchmen, still more proud to be Frenchmen of the eighteenth century, which we looked upon as an age of gold which the new philosophy had brought back into the world.'

It was perhaps more than a coincidence that at this moment of inflated hopes an ingenious paper-maker hit on the idea of filling a paper bag with hot air, and sending it up into the sky. Soon Montgolfier had manufactured a gas balloon large enough to lift a man, and proposed to make his first ascent from the garden of the Tuileries. 'The good and kind heart of Louis XVI was terrified at this rash act, and at first tried to oppose it. At the moment when every eye was fixed on the two men who were so hardy as to brave, in their frail bark, the winds, and the immensity of space, and perils hitherto unknown, there came an order from the Minister, forbidding them to start. But the courage of the aeronauts, and the impatience of the crowd that had been summoned to enjoy this trial of genius, overcame every prohibition. The cord was cut, the balloon rose majestically, and we watched the aerial navigators set out upon their voyage through the sky' [*Ségur*]. Need I expound the parable? Within a few hours the gas gave out, and Montgolfier came to earth again. Within a few years the ideals of the enlightenment, inflated with philosophy, and floating in the air, ended in Revolution.

VII

The French Revolution was the deathbed of the eighteenth century; and here, if at all, I must attempt to write its obituary notice.

The Old Regime was dead. Its likeness might survive in the new generation, but not itself. Never again would Europe believe with the same naivety in the divine right of kings. Never again would statesmen so frankly recognize *raison d'état* as the rule of international policy. Never again would territories and populations be so freely annexed and exchanged, or thrones be placed so confidently at the disposal of carpet-bag kings. The Old Regime was dead. Why? Because its old governments (such as the Bourbons and Hapsburgs) were more interested in diplomacy than administration, and were out of touch with the mass of their people; whilst the new governments (the Enlightened Despots) adopted political and social reform in the spirit in which rich employers sometimes adopt profit-sharing schemes, or build model villages for their workmen—because it is 'good for business.' They believed in reforming people, but they did not believe in the people they reformed. They consulted foreign philosophers as to what ought to be done: they did not consult their own people as to what they wanted. In a word, the Old Regime disregarded and exploited the force which created it—I mean, nationality. Despotism, however enlightened, ruling for the people but not by the people; conscription, conquest, partition; disregard for national rights, disbelief in human nature—the whole system was growing out of touch with the people, and that just when they were being educated by commerce, philosophy, and political persecution to realize their power.

Why did the Revolution begin in France? Because, on the whole, the Old Regime was less of a burden there than elsewhere. Outside France government was more enlightened, but it was also more despotic. In France the old monarchy still rested, however precariously, upon its two supports—a feudal society and a Catholic Church; but during the long anarchy of Louis XV's reign it had ceased to be effective; and there was growing up in the minds of the educated classes, and even in the sentiments of the crowd, an alternative system, ready to take its place. The French people would put up with any crimes on the part of its rulers, provided that they really ruled. A lazy King, an unemployable upper class, absentee bishops and landlords, inefficient officers, ministers who did not administer—these they could not forgive. Governments die of weakness, as well as of wickedness. It was not any intolerable oppression that made France destroy the Old Regime, but the feeling that it was utterly out of date and unreal.

There was another reason. England in the eighteenth century was also suffering from absentee landlords, and from worldly bishops who seldom visited their dioceses. The English middle classes were prosperous, the lower classes terribly poor. The new city populations were unenfranchised, trade unions were illegal. The whole machinery of government was in the hands of employers and landowners; whilst the philosophers and economists explained that social inequality, and the exploitation of the poor by the rich, were a law of nature. Why was there a revolution in France, then, and not in England? Partly because we had carried through our political revolution a century before, in 1688; and a social revolution without a political one loses half its seriousness. Partly—and this is the essential point—because there was not in England that gulf between the upper and lower classes of society which in France exacerbated every other grievance. A recent historian speaks of the 'alliance between the spirit of aristocracy and the spirit of popular rights, each taking the other entirely for granted,' which existed in England before the Industrial and French Revolutions. This alliance, he says 'was native to the soil of England. It was sanctified by custom, sport, and hospitality, deeply pledged in the punch-bowl, renewed in the hunting-field and at the race meeting. It was the natural offspring of a healthy society based on widely diffused small properties, and on the absence of very obvious economic oppression of class by class. The political spirit of the eighteenth century was based not on the equality but on the harmony of classes. Poor and rich together took a patriotic pride in our "free constitution," which they continually contrasted with the slavery of continental countries' [*Trevelyan*]. There was much social inequality, then, and some economic oppression, in both countries. What prevented revolution in England was the recognition of the social duties of the rich and of the political rights of the poor: it was the absence of this recognition which made the French Revolution inevitable. Liberty does not depend upon the institutions of a country, but upon the spirit in which they are administered. Democracy is not a constitution, but a state of mind.

But why did the Revolution come when it did, and not before? The answer seems to be, owing to the prosperity of the second half of the eighteenth century. France had never again been in such a state of misery as it was during the last years of Louis XIV: but then there had been no class to propose a remedy, or to lead a revolt. During the first half of the eighteenth century Law's System and Fleury's laissez-faire Government did much to improve the position of the middle classes. During the second half of the century, in spite of misgovernment and defeat, the country as a whole recovered its vitality and prosperity. But why should this improvement make a revolution more, instead of less, likely? Because it is not misery and oppression as such that cause revolution, but the realization that you are miserable, and have power to resent it. It is not when things are at their worst, but when they have become a little better, that men see how bad they have been. In France 'the destruction of part of the medieval institutions of the country made what was left a hundred times more odious . . . Louis XVI's smallest act of arbitrary power became more unbearable than the whole tyranny of Louis XIV' [*Tocqueville*]. When the Revolution came, its heart was at Paris and in the central provinces, where reform had gone further than anywhere else; or in commercial cities like Marseilles, which had benefited most from improved conditions of trade. Nowhere was the old régime more oppressive than in Brittany and La Vendée; and it was just there that the people rebelled against the revolutionary Government.

How did Paris come to play so large a part in the Revolution? Because it was a capital without a King. Its geographical position, the size of its population, and (most of all) the centralized character of French society and the French Government, made it more of a capital than any of its rivals. 'At the time of the Fronde [when it had last led a revolt against the Government] Paris was still only the largest city in France: in 1789 it is already France itself' [*Tocqueville*]. 'The local people,' reports *Arthur Young* in July, 1789, 'daren't have any opinion of their own, until they know what Paris is thinking.' But the more Paris became the arbiter of fashion, and the maker of public opinion, the less it remained the home of the King, or the centre of the Government. Versailles had become, since Louis XIV's time, both Windsor and Whitehall. A seat of federal government, such as Washington or Canberra, may be built in a desert: its stands for the Balance of Power—a good eighteenth-century principle. But the seat of a centralized monarchy should be at the chief centre of population. What is lost in detachment is more than gained in knowledge of the people. It was a bad day for France when Louis XIV built Versailles. Under Louis XV it became 'a home of lost causes,' a symbol of every prejudice the philosophers attacked, and of every privilege the people hated. Meanwhile Paris, knowing nothing of Government, took the *Contrat Social* for a political manual; and knowing nothing of monarchy, made a king of Voltaire.

VIII

It has often been disputed, how far a historian may philosophize. If he confines himself to reporting events, he is no better than a super-journalist. If he derives, from the few events he has studied, principles that are to explain the whole range of history, he is likely to cut his facts to the pattern of his fancy. But at least he must always be ready to generalize, when the evidence seems to justify it; otherwise there can be no system of historical knowledge, no science of history.

CONCLUSION

We have perhaps studied three centuries of European history in sufficient detail to justify an attempt to generalize; but only to this extent, that we should ask what, if any, are the permanent characteristics of the national states whose history we have been investigating. And I believe that we can summarize what we have to say in this dogma: it is as difficult for a nation to change its character as it is for an individual.

What has been the essential issue of French history, from 1494 to 1789, from Charles VIII to Louis XVI? Always the question of Monarchy—of the relation between a King and his people, between a King and other Kings. Not constitutional monarchy, with powers defined by a charter, or limited by a Parliament: but mystical monarchy, accepted as a miracle, and accountable to God alone. '*Roi* is a word which conveys to the minds of Frenchmen the ideas of benevolence, gratitude, and love; as well as those of power, grandeur, and happiness... They consider him as their friend, though he does not know their persons; as their protector, though their greatest danger is from an Exempt or *Lettre de cachet*; and as their benefactor while they are oppressed with taxes. They magnify into importance his most indifferent actions; they palliate and excuse all his weaknesses; and they impute his errors or crimes to his ministers, or other evil counsellors, who (as they fondly assert) have for some base purpose imposed upon his judgment, and perverted the undeviating rectitude of his intentions. They repeat, with fond applause, every saying of his which seems to indicate the smallest approach to wit, or even bears the mark of ordinary sagacity. If he happens to be a little indisposed, all Paris, all France is alarmed, as if a real calamity was threatened. At a review the troops perform their manœuvres unheeded by such of the spectators as are within sight of the King—they are all engrossed in contemplation of their Prince... At Mass it is the King, not the priest, who is the object of attention. The Host is elevated; but the people's eyes remain fixed upon the face of their beloved Monarch.' So wrote an English traveller at the end of Louis XV's reign—one of the worst in French history [*Moore*]. And such was the spirit which made it possible for a power originally based on popular support against the tyranny of the nobles to side with the privileged classes against the people. Royal Absolutism easily suppressed provincial rights, and the Parliamentary veto. But 'though the nation abdicated its rights, it did not abdicate its opinions' [*Sorel*]; and much the same grievances were expressed from the fourteenth century to the eighteenth. The Huguenots found the Monarchy intolerant, the Frondeurs found it tyrannical, the Philosophers found it arbitrary and inefficient: but none of them doubted that France should have a King. This confidence in Kings, as often abused on the one side as it was renewed on the other, is the clue to French history. The French people were the King's family, the French territories were the King's estate. It was the King's business to rule the one and to defend the other. Perhaps also to extend it. Here the 'natural frontiers' policy might justify conquest (up to the Rhine) as a means of national defence; in much the same way as the Revocation of the Edict of Nantes might justify persecution as a means of national unity. Louis XIV did not misread his people's desire for orthodoxy and glory: but he miscalculated the loyalty of the upper classes, and the endurance of the lower. He revived against Catholic France the hatred which Englishmen had felt towards Catholic Spain. He involved his country in interminable wars on the Continent, and abdicated to England the throne of the sea. After his reign absolute Monarchy could go no further: it fell ill and died. But centralized tyranny reappeared in Robespierre's government; Danton was an exponent of the 'natural frontiers' policy; Napoleon satisfied the desire for glory to a degree undreamed of by Louis XIV; and there has been plenty of evidence in later events that the French character and policy have outlived, and are likely to outlive, every change in the government of the country.

IX

What permanent part did England play in the three hundred years between the Renaissance and the Revolution? To the average continental observer, I think, we seemed to be 'a nation of shopkeepers,' an insular Poland, and a home of liberty.

'England,' writes *Sorel,* 'is a commercial island,' and its whole policy hangs on this fact. Its *raison d'être* is political economy. War ruins trade; so England does not fight willingly: but, when it does so, it is with 'a grave and concentrated passion, and an animosity all the more stubborn as its motives are egoistical'; and when it makes peace, it is with an eye to finance rather than to glory. Where did French policy have to reckon with English hostility? Nowhere in central Europe, except when family interests gave James I a walking-on part in the Thirty Years' War, or the unpopular possession of Hanover involved us in the wars of Frederick the Great. Not there; but at Antwerp, Dunkirk, Gibraltar, Minorca; in India, in the North American Colonies, or on the trade routes of the Southern Atlantic. We fought for markets, we fought for the freedom of our trade at sea, we fought for the mastery of the English Channel. That was our 'natural frontiers' policy.

Again, when the 'close season' of the religious wars was over, when Britain's long feud with Louis XIV came to an end, and Voltaire informed the world that we were a civilized nation, English society seemed to Frenchmen as vicious as their own, but less refined; and English methods of government (though liberal) as unstable as those of Poland itself. It became a political maxim with Frederick the Great to have no dealings with a nation whose foreign policy might change after every general election. Joseph II took the American revolt for a sign of the break-up of the British Empire.

But it was the Enlightened Despots themselves who were on the edge of disaster. They argued in terms of the old Europe, whilst a new Europe was growing up round them, and a new political system was almost ready to take their place. The people, tired of being reformed, was about to take charge of its own destiny. France was to carry out the experiment: but the formula came from England—England, whose people, 'feeling themselves free, worried less about looking equal' [*Sorel*].

Our status in the family of nations was that of an eccentric and impolite elder brother, whose wealth makes him a good ally, and whose knowledge of the world enables him to give sound advice.

X

Perhaps, however, the best example of national character is Spain. In the course of three hundred years we have seen Spain under good Kings and under bad—certainly most of them were bad; and under reforming as well as unreforming ministers. It seems to have made no difference to the character of the country. Isolated from the rest of Europe, proud, ignorant, and fanatical, the Spanish people kept its mind as inviolate as its soil—and still, so far as humanly possible, keeps it so. You can read about the sixteenth or seventeenth century in a history book: you can experience them by travelling in Spain.

Italy, again, has the same character throughout our three centuries. In the eighteenth century as in the sixteenth, it has no national unity, and takes little interest in the nomad princes who occupy its thrones—though Turin, according to no less an authority than Lord Chesterfield, was one of the most elegant Courts, and Tuscany by general consent one of the best-governed states in Europe. The only hope of a united Italy lies in another French invasion, and in the ambitions of the Kings of Sardinia, whose consistent policy it has been to profit by the quarrels of their French and German neighbours.

Germany again, at any time from the sixteenth to the eighteenth century, shows how difficult it is to change national character. In the sixteenth century German feudalism does not burst inwards, like an electric lamp, but outwards, like a balloon. The formation of its new Society and Government is not centripetal, as in France, but centrifugal. 'Imperium in imperio,' the bugbear of French politics, is the maxim of German. The Holy Roman Empire is a mosaic of small states forming an intricate pattern round certain larger units. In the seventeenth century their separatism is sanctified by the Treaty of Westphalia. In the eighteenth it reappears in Frederick the Great's Fürstenbund. There is no German nation, no German patriotism. No movement, whether religious or political, can occupy Germany except by conquering its three or four hundred principalities in detail. Liberty in the eighteenth century, like Lutheranism in the sixteenth, is inconceivable apart from the Princes.

Hence the success of the two overgrown principalities, Austria and Prussia. Austria, with the same population as France, had none of its compactness or uniformity. It was a miniature edition of Europe, split by racial and religious differences, nervously maintaining its own balance of power, and dependent for survival less upon its army than upon its diplomatic service. 'It lived in Europe, by Europe, and for Europe. A blunder in foreign policy could destroy it; a clever stroke was enough to restore it . . . Its eclipses, its aberrations, its settings and risings again, all result from the same cause; so does its invariable power of recovery—the secret of its whole history' [Sorel].

Prussia is the antithesis of Austria. A new and self-made country, under new and self-made Kings, it knows what it wants, and pursues its policy with single-minded ruthlessness. It is no use to point out that its population is the mixed offspring of the inter-marriage of Slavs and Teutons, and of French and South German immigrations: there is no doubt about its permanent Prussianism. It is no good saying that the battle of Rosbach, the foundation-stone of Prussia's military success, was won by a Frenchified king and an army of foreign mercenaries against troops which were mainly German: there is no questioning the ingrained efficiency of Prussian militarism. The basis of Prussian power, throughout our period, is successful estate management: the national industry (as Mirabeau remarked) is war. The weakness of the system flows from the same source as its strength—centralization. Its vices are those of a vulgar man who by unscrupulous methods has made himself unhealthily rich. It has still (at the end of the eighteenth century) to become a nation, and to learn the meaning of patriotism. It will only learn by adversity.

Finally, at the far end of Europe, we have Turkey, Poland, and Sweden—the counter-weights of French diplomacy during the sixteenth and seventeenth centuries, in the eighteenth no longer moved by France, but by Russia. Russia rises as Turkey falls, and at first seems to be another inroad of barbarians. But there is this difference. The Turks are an army which falls to bits when it ceases to advance. The Russians are a state, with the germ of a national culture. The policy of the Tsars is simple enough—religious expansion southwards at the expense of Turkey, political expansion westwards at the expense of Poland, and commercial expansion north-westwards at the expense of Sweden. Its social indifference and incoherence made Russia as impervious to Enlightenment in the eighteenth century as in the twentieth, an early prey to Communism.

XI

When we look at Europe in this way, and notice how, in one country after another, national character and policy persist from the end of the fifteenth to the end of the eighteenth century, we cannot fail to be impressed by the strength of nationalism, and its claim to be the ruling principle of political science. This is the first lesson of modern European history: and none is more necessary nowadays; for it explains the disaster of 1914—the nemesis of nationalism; and it leaves no illusions as to the barrier of habit and tradition that must be broken down before any international system, such as a United Nations Organization, can take the place of the Balance of Power.

There is another lesson of history to balance this—ultimately, perhaps, to outbalance it. Literature is international, science is international, religion is international, the struggle for political freedom is international. There have been moments during our three hundred years—Luther's Reformation, the Revolt of the Netherlands, or the French Enlightenment—when international ideas seemed to break down national boundaries. There have been movements or institutions—the Catholic Church, Humanism, Commerce, or the American colonies—which have held the promise of a larger unity.

As long as men can remember, their rulers have been kings, their loyalty national, and their ultimate argument war. No sensible statesman makes light of such heredity. But he need not despair. The history of the Renaissance, of the Reformation, and of the French Revolution, shows that no political or ecclesiastical institutions, however venerable, can permanently defy a moral idea, once it has captured the conscience and imagination of the people. In man himself is the remedy for the evils of mankind.

LIST OF BOOKS

ACTON, Lectures on Modern History.
—— The History of Freedom, and other Essays.
ALLEN, The Age of Erasmus.
AMADIS OF GAUL (E.T. by Okes, 1619).
ANNUAL REGISTER.
ANSPACH (Margravine of) Memoirs (Paris, 1826).
ARMSTRONG, Charles V.
—— Elizabeth Farnese.
—— The French Wars of Religion.
ARNETH, Maria Theresa und Marie Antoinette. Ihr Briefwechsel, 1770-80.
—— Marie Antoinette, Joseph II und Leopold II. Ihr Briefwechsel, 1775-92.
—— and GEFFROY, Correspondance secrète entre Marie-Thérèse et le Comte de Mercy-Argenteau.
ATKINSON, Michel de l'Hôpital.
AUBERTIN, L'esprit public au XVIIIe siècle.
AULARD, Etudes et leçons sur la Révolution française.
AUTRICHE, Recueil des Instructions données aux Ambassadeurs, etc. (ed. Sorel).
AVENEL, Lettres, instructions diplomatiques, et papiers d'état du Cardinal Richelieu.

BADOARO (see GACHARD, Relations des Ambassadeurs Vénitiens).
BAIN, Slavonic Europe.
—— The Daughter of Peter the Great.
BAINVILLE, Histoire de France.
BASTIDE, The Anglo-French entente in the 17th century.
BATIFFOL, Le Siècle de la Renaissance.
—— Marie de Médicis.
BEARD, The Reformation of the 16th century (Hibbert Lectures, 1883).
BEAUMARCHAIS, Le Mariage de Figaro.
BEAZLEY, Russia from the Varangians to the Bolsheviks.
BERNIS (Cardinal de), Memoirs and Letters (E.T. by Wormeley).
BERTRAND, Louis XIV.
BESENVAL, Mémoires (ed. 1821).
BOSSUET, Oraisons funèbres (ed. Larousse).
BOSWELL, Life of Johnson (ed. Everyman).
BOURGEOIS, Manuel historique de politique étrangère.
BRADBY, The Great Days of Versailles.
BRANTOME, Livre des Dames (E.T. by Wormeley).
BRIDGES, France under Richelieu and Colbert.
BROGLIE (De), Frédéric II et Marie-Thérèse, 1740-42.
—— Le Secret du Roi (E.T. 1879).

336   LIST OF BOOKS

BRUNNER, Correspondances intimes de l'Empereur Joseph II avec Coblenz
    Kaunitz, 1767-90.
BURCHARD, (Joannes), Diarium, 1483-1506.
BURCKHARDT, The Renaissance in Italy.
BURKE, History of Spain.
BURNET, History of My Own Times (Oxford, 1823).
BUVAT, Journal de la Régence (ed. Campardon).

C.M.H. (Cambridge Modern History).
CAHEN, Les querelles réligieuses et parlementaires sous Louis XV.
CALVIN, Letters (ed. Bonnet, E.T. by Constable).
CAMPAN (Madame de), Mémoires (ed. Barrière).
CARLYLE, Frederick the Great.
——— The French Revolution.
CATHERINE II, Mémoires (ed. Herzen).
CATT (Henri de), Memoirs of Frederick the Great (E.T. by Flint).
CHAMPION, La France d'après les cahiers de 1789.
CHAMPOLLION-FIGEAC, La Captivité du Roi François Ier.
CHEVERNY (Comte de), Mémoires sur les règnes de Louis XV et Louis XVI.
CHRISTIE, Etienne Dolet.
CHESTERFIELD, Letters to His Son.
——— Letters to Lord Huntington.
CHOISEUL, Mémoires.
CLARK, The Dutch Alliance and the War against French Trade, 1688-97.
COLLINS, Voltaire, Montesquieu, and Rousseau in England.
COMMINES, Mémoire sur les règnes de Louis XI et Charles VIII (ed. Buchon).
CONDORCET, Correspondance (Paris, 1847).
CONSTITUTIONES Societatis Jesu (E.T. 1838).
CONTARINI, see GACHARD, Relations des Ambassadeurs Vénitiens.
COUPLAND, Wilberforce.
COURTIN, Nouveau traité de la civilité qui se pratique en France parmi les
    honnestes gens (1679).
COX, Memoirs of Horatio, Lord Walpole, 1678-1757.

DALLINGTON, A Method for Travell shewed by taking the view of France as it
    stood in the year of our Lord, 1598.
D'ARGENSON, Journal et Mémoires (ed. Rathery, E.T. by Wormeley).
DASHKOFF, Memoirs of the Princess Dashkaw (ed. Bradford).
DEFFAND (Madame du), Lettres à Voltaire (ed. Trabucco).
DE RETZ, Mémoires (ed. Renaissance du Livre).
DE STAËL (Madame), Oeuvres (Paris, 1820).
DOLLINGER, Studies in European History.
DORSET, Despatches from Paris, 1784-90 (ed. Camden Society).
DOUAIS, L'Inquisition.
DOUMIC, Saint-Simon.
DUBOIS, Mémoires (E.T. by Dowson).

Duclos, Secret Memoirs of the Regency (E.T. by Maers).
—— Mémoires secrets sur les règnes de Louis XIV et de Louis XV (Paris, 1791).
Dumouriez, Mémoires (ed. Barrière).
Dyer, John Calvin.

Edict of Nantes. Edict du roy sur la pacification des troubles de ce royaume, donné à Nantes au mois d'Avril 1598 (Paris, 1644).
Eliot, Turkey in Europe.
Epistolae Obscurorum Virorum (Francoforti ad Moenum, 1581).
Erasmus, Select Letters (ed. Allen).
—— Familiar Colloquies.
—— In Praise of Folly.
Evelyn, Dairy (ed. Everyman).

Fersen (Count Axel), Diary and Correspondence (E.T. by Wormeley).
Fisher, The Republican Tradition in Europe.
Fletcher, Gustavus Adolphus.
Frederick (the Great), Mémoires (ed. Boutaric et Campardon).
Franklin, Memoirs of the Life and Writings of Benjamin Franklin (ed. Everyman).
Froude, Life and Letters of Erasmus.
Fugger Newsletters, 1568-1606 (ed. Klarwill, E.T. 1924).

Gachard, Relations des Ambassadeurs Vénitiens, etc.
—— Correspondance de Charles Quint et d'Adrien VI.
Gardiner, The Thirty Years' War.
Gougeaud, La Marine de Guerre—Richelieu et Colbert.
Grant, A History of Europe.
Guenin et Nouaillac, L'Ancien Régime et la Révolution.
Guicciardini, Storia Fiorentina.

Hammond, The Village Labourer.
Hanotaux, Richelieu.
Harris (Sir James, Lord Malmesbury), Diaries and Correspondence.
Harrison, William the Silent.
Hassall, Louis XIV.
Hausset (Madame du), Private Memoirs of Louis XV (E.T. 1895).
Hemon, J. J. Rousseau.
Henault, Mémoires (1855).
Henri IV, Lettres d'Amour (ed. Lescure).
—— Recueil de Lettres missives (ed. Berger de Xivrey).
Herouard, Journal du Roy Louis XIII.
Hodges and Hughes, Select Naval Documents.
Hodgetts (Brayley), Catherine the Great.
Howard, English Travellers of the Renaissance.
Hume, Spain, 1479-1788.

INFORMATION for Pilgrims unto the Holy Land (1498, ed. Duff).

JACKSON, Zwingli.
JOURNAL D'UN BOURGEOIS de Paris, 1515-36 (ed. Lalanne).

KEITH, Memoirs (ed. Smyth).
KIDD, Documents of the Continental Reformation.

LANE-POOLE, History of Turkey in Europe.
LANZ, Actenstücke und Briefe zur Geschichte Kaiser Karl V.
LAVISSE, Histoire de France.
—— Vue générale de l'histoire politique de l'Europe.
—— The Youth of Frederick the Great (E.T. by Simeon).
—— et RAMBAUD, Histoire générale.
LEA, History of the Inquisition in Spain.
LESCURE, Correspondance secrète inédite sur Louis XVI, etc., 1777-92.
LETTENHOVE, Lettres inédites de Marie-Thérèse et de Joseph II, 1763-81.
LETTRES ROYAUX (ed. Cassati).
LIGNE (Prince de), Mémoires, etc. (E.T. by Wormeley).
LOCKITT, The relations of French and English Society, 1763-1793.
LODGE, Students' Modern Europe.
LORD, The Regency of Marie de Médicis.
LOUIS XIV, Mémoires (ed. Dreyss).
—— Oeuvres (Paris, 1806).
LOUIS XV, Correspondance secrète (ed. Boutaric).
LOYOLA, Letters and Instructions (E.T. by O'Leary).
LUPTON, Life of John Colet.
LUTHER, Three Primary Works (ed. Wace and Buchheim).
—— Table Talk (E.T. by Hazlitt).

MACAULAY, History of England.
—— Critical and Historical Essays.
MACHIAVELLI, The Prince (ed. Everyman).
—— History of Florence, etc. (ed. Bohn).
MAGNE, Scarron et son milieu.
MAHAN, The Influence of Sea-Power upon History.
MAINTENON (Madame de), Correspondance (E.T. by Wormeley).
—— Lettres à (ed. Mélange des Bibliophiles).
MALET, Cours complet d'Histoire.
MALLESON, Prince Eugene of Savoy.
—— Loudon.
MARGARET, Marguerite de Valois, Mémoires et Lettres (ed. Guenard).
MAZARIN, Lettres du Cardinal de Mazarin à la Reine, etc. (ed. Ravenel).
MEDAILLES sur les principaux événements du règne de Louis le Grand (Paris, 1702).
MERCIER, Tableau de Paris (Hambourg, 1781).

MOLEVILLE (Bertrand), Mémoires Particuliers (Paris, 1816).
MONRO, His Expedition with the worthy Scots Regiment (called Mac-Keyes Regiment) levied in August, 1626 . . . collected and gathered together at spare-houres, by Colonell Robert Monro, etc. (London, 1637).
MONTAGU (Lady Mary Wortley), Letters, 1709-60 (ed. Everyman).
MONTESQUIEU, Lettres Persanes (ed. Dent).
MOORE, A view of Society and Manners in France, Switzerland, and Germany (1779).
MORITZ, Travels through Several Parts of England, 1782.
MOTLEY, The Rise of the Dutch Republic (ed. Everyman).

NINON DE LENCLOS, Lettres (ed. Garnier).
NORMAND, La Bourgeoisie française au XVIIIe siècle.

OGLE, The Marquis d'Argenson.
OLDHAM, The Renaissance.
OXENSTIERN (Comte Jean), Lettres Intimes (ed. Wrangel).

PAGET (Stephen), Ambroise Paré.
PALATINE (Princess), Correspondance (E.T. by Wormeley).
PATTISON (Mark), Isaac Casaubon.
—— Essays.
PEARSALL SMITH, Life and Letters of Sir Henry Wotton.
PEPYS, Diary (ed. Everyman).
PERKINS, France under the Regency.
—— Louis XV.
PETER MARTYR, Opus Epistolarum (ed. Amstelodami, 1570).
PHILIPPSON, La Contre-Révolution religieuse au XVIe siècle.
PONIATOWSKI, Correspondance inédite de Stanislas-Auguste-Poniatowski et Madame Geoffrin.
POOLE, The Huguenots of the Dispersion.
PREVOST, Manon Lescaut.
PRIULI (?), see GACHARD, Relations des Ambassadeurs Vénitiens.
PUTNAM, William the Silent.

RAMBAUD, History of Russia.
RANKE, History of the Popes.
REDDAWAY, Frederick the Great.
RICHELIEU, Mémoires (ed. French Historical Society).
—— Maximes d'Etat, ou Testament Politique (Paris, 1764).
—— Maximes d'Etat et Fragments Politiques (ed. Documents Inédits . . . Mélanges III).
ROCA, Le règne de Richelieu.
ROCQUAIN, L'esprit révolutionnaire avant la révolution.
ROMIER, Les origines politiques des Guerres de Religion.
—— le Royaume de Catherine de Médicis.

Rousseau, Du Contrat Social.
Rulhiere, Histoire ou Anecdotes sur la Révolution de Russie (Paris, 1797).

Saint Simon, Mémoires (ed. Renaissance du Livre).
Saussure (de), A Foreign View of England, 1725 (E.T. by Van Muyden).
See, Les idées politiques en France au XVIIIe siècle.
Seebohm, The Era of the Protestant Revolution.
Sedgwick, Ignatius Loyola.
—— The Oxford Reformers.
Segur (Marquis de), Souvenirs et Anecdotes sur le règne de Louis XVI (ed. Funck-Brentano).
Servita, History of the Inquisition, a pious, learned, and curious worke, necessary for Counsellors, Casuists, and Politicians, translated out of the Italian copy by Robert Gentilis (London, 1639).
Sevigne (Madame de), Lettres Choisies (ed. Larousse).
Sichel, Catherine de Medici.
Sismondi, History of the Italian Republics (ed. Everyman).
Smith (Preserved), Martin Luther.
Smollett, Travels Through France and Italy, 1766 (ed. World's Classics).
Somervell, Studies in Statesmanship.
Sorel, The Eastern Question in the 18th Century (E.T. by Bramwell).
—— L'Europe et la Révolution Française.
Squire, William the Silent.
Stanhope, Spain under Charles II (ed. Mahon).
Stevens, Gustavus Adolphus.
Stirling (Maxwell), The Cloister Life of the Emperor Charles V.
Strachey, Queen Victoria.
Strickland, Life of Queen Elizabeth (ed. Everyman).
Stryienski, Le dix-huitième siècle.
Stubbs, Lectures on Mediaeval and Modern History.
Sully, Memoirs (E.T. 1819).
Symonds, The Renaissance in Italy.
Syveton, Ripperda.

Taine, L'Ancien Régime.
Temperley, Frederick the Great and Kaiser Joseph.
Thomas, Marlborough and the War of Spanish Succession.
Thompson (Francis), Ignatius Loyola.
Thompson (H. L.), History of Christ Church.
Tiepolo, see Gachard, Relations des Ambassadeurs Vénitiens.
Tilley, Studies in the French Renaissance.
Tocqueville (de), L'Ancien Régime (ed. Headlam).
Toland, An Account of the Courts of Prussia and Hanover (1702).
Topin, Louis XIII et Richelieu.
Torcy, Mémoires (E.T. 1757).
—— Journal Inédit (ed. Masson)

TOYNE, Albrecht von Wallenstein.
TREVELYAN, British History in the Nineteenth Century.

VAISSIERE, Gentilhommes Campagnards de l'ancienne France.
VAST, Les grands traités du règne de Louis XIV.
VAUBAN, Dîme royale (ed. Michel).
VILLARS, Mémoires de la Cour d'Espagne sous le règne de Charles II.
VOLTAIRE, Le siècle de Louis XIV.
—— Précis du siècle de Louis XV.
—— History of Charles XII (ed. Everyman).

WACE and BUCHHEIM, Three Primary Works of Luther.
WALISZEWSKI, La dernière des Romanov.
—— Autour d'un trône.
—— The Romance of an Empress.
WEISS, Papiers d'Etat du Cardinal de Granvelle.
WHITTALL, Frederick the Great on Kingcraft.
WILHELMINA, Mémoires de Frédérique Sophie Wilhelmine de Prusse (1812).
WILLERT, Henry of Navarre.
WILLIAM, Correspondance de Guillaume le Taciturne (ed. Gachard).
WILSON, History of Magdalen College.
WRAXALL, Memoirs of the Courts of Berlin, Dresden, Warsaw, and Vienna, 1777-79.

YOUNG (Arthur), Travels in France and Italy (ed. Everyman).
YOUNG (Norwood), Life of Frederick the Great.

INDEX

ADRIAN of Utrecht, and Luther, 57: as Pope, 60
AIX-LA-CHAPELLE, Treaty of (1668), 200: (1748), 265
ALBERONI, 220
ALPINE PASSES, 9, 27
ALVA, in the Netherlands, 86: recalled, 88
'AMADIS OF GAUL,' 67
AMERICA, discovered, 13: its gold, 14: War of Independence, 312: its influence on France, 317
ANNE, of Austria, 157
ANNE, of Russia, 247
ASCHAM, Roger, describes Charles V, 40
AUGSBURG, Peace of, 126: League and War of, 201
AUGUSTUS II and III, of Saxony, 258
AUSTRIA, ambitious, 10: in 1618, 128: at Peace of Westphalia, 165: in 1715, 208: in 1740, 259: in 18th cent., 331

BACON, Roger, 16
BALANCE OF POWER, in 16th cent., 41
BALTIC trade question, in Thirty Years' War, 133
BAVARIAN Succession, War of, 309
BEAUMARCHAIS, 'Mariage de Figaro,' 315
BELLEISLE, 260
BESTUJEF, 248
BOHEMIA, begins Thirty Years' War, 131
BOURGEOISIE, their rise, 11: French, in 17th cent., 160: in 18th cent., 322
BRANDENBURG, its geography, 249: in Thirty Years' War, 250: for later history, see PRUSSIA
BRANTÔME on Catherine de Medici, 102
BRESLAU, Treaty of, 263

BRIENNE, 308
BROGLIE, and the 'King's Secret,' 294
BURGOYNE, General, on the Prussian Army, 273
BURGUNDY, divided, 5: disputed between Francis I and Charles V, 41; for later history, see FRANCHE COMTÉ
BURNET, Bishop, on Louis XIV, 193
BUVAT'S 'Journal,' 213

CALAS case, 231
CALONNE, 307
CALVIN, his fears for Protestantism, 46: his 'Institutio,' 97: at Geneva, 98: his letters, 100
CALVINISM, and Lutheranism, 98: in Germany, 128: in France, see HUGUENOTS
CANADA, Cartier's Colony, 47: Champlain, 122
CARLOS, Don, 221-2
CARLYLE, on 18th cent., 210
CATEAU CAMBRÉSIS, Treaty of, 42
CATHERINE I, of Russia, 247
CATHERINE II, the Great, 287: educates herself, 288: an 'enlightened' reformer, 289: is inoculated, 290: her death 311
CHAMBERS OF REUNION, 200
CHARLES II of SPAIN, 168
CHARLES V, EMPEROR, his character and looks, 39: his rivalry with Francis I, 36–47: his empire, 39, 44: ambitions, 41: wars, 41: dealings with Luther, 57: piety, 58: difficulties, 58: the causes of his failure, 43: his retirement and death, 45
CHARLES VI, Emperor, and Elizabeth Farnese, 221: his Pragmatic Sanction, 259
CHARLES VIII, of France, his marriage, 5: Italian ambitions, 27: he invades Italy, 29

344 INDEX

CHARLES X, of Sweden, 239
CHARLES XI, 240
CHARLES XII, and the Regent, 218: and Peter the Great, 240
CHOISEUL, on Louis XV, 224: his Polish policy, 294
CHRISTIAN IV, of Denmark, 132
CHRISTINA, of Sweden, 238
CONCILIAR MOVEMENT, 21
COLBERT, 179: 'Colbertism,' 180, 183: and the navy, 182: other activities, 183
COLET, 3
COLIGNY, 106
COLUMBUS, 14
COPERNICUS, 15
CORCOVA, and its mosque, 6
COUNTER-REFORMATION, 63–77: Wars of, 78
COURTIN, on good manners, 177
CROCODILE, preserved, 34

D'ALBRET family, 113
D'EON DE BEAUMONT, 235
DE L'HÔPITAL, and his policy, 104
DE RETZ, on the Fronde, 158, 161: his 'Memoirs,' 163
DEVOLUTION, War of, 199
DIPLOMATIC REVOLUTION (1756), 270
DRAGONNADES, 192
DU BARRY, Madame, 229
DUBOIS, 213
DUMOURIEZ, on Poland, 295
DUTCH WAR (1672), 200

ECCLESIASTICAL RESERVATION, 127
EDICT OF RESTITUTION, 135
EIGHTEENTH CENTURY, its character, 209
ELIZABETH, of Russia, 248
EMPIRE, The, in 1494, 9: for later history, see AUSTRIA
ENCYCLOPAEDIA, 285
ENGLAND, in 1494, 4: at Treaty of Utrecht, 203: English influences in France, 18th cent., 236, 316: why no revolution in 18th cent., 325: national reputation, 329
'ENLIGHTENED DESPOTISM,' 281–299: Why it failed, 324
'EPISTOLAE OBSCURORUM VIRORUM,' 51

ERASMUS, on reading, 2: his Greek Testament, 52
ESCURIAL, 79
EVELYN, on Louis XIV, 169
EUROPE, in 1494, 1–12: in 1715, 205–9

FARNESE, Elizabeth, Queen of Spain, 219: her policy, 220: her old age, 222
FERDINAND II, Emperor, 129: his policy, 135
FEUDALISM in 16th cent., 121
FLEURY, 226: his government, 227: his Polish policy, 258: in 1740, 260
FONTENOY, Battle of, 264
FOUR ARTICLES of Bossuet, 188
FRANCE, in 1494, 4: national character, 5: constitution, 37: under Francis I, 38: 'encircled' by the Hapsburgs, 40: entente with Turkey, 45: Wars of Religion, 95: in 1715, 205: under Louis XV, 235: in 1748, 265: ally of Austria, 272: in 1757, 279: under Louis XVI, 318: taxation system, 320: class war, 321: monarchism and national policy, 324
FRANCHE COMTÉ, seized by Louis XIV, 200
FRANCIS I, of France, his character and kingdom, 36, wars, 41: Italian wars: 29: rivalry with Charles V, 36–47: Turkish alliance, 45: treatment of Protestants, 95
FRANCO-AUSTRIAN enmity in 16th cent., 36, 45: in 17th cent., 142: it disappears, 208: alliance, see DIPLOMATIC REVOLUTION
FRANKLIN, Benjamin, 312
FREDERICK WILLIAM, the Great Elector, 250
FREDERICK I, of Prussia, 251
FREDERICK WILLIAM I, of Prussia, his character and home life, 251: government and army, 252: his death-bed, 253
FREDERICK II, the Great, his character, 266: education, 266: accomplishments, 267: idea of kingship, 268: way of life, 268: philosophy, 269: accession and aims, 259: invades Silesia, 260: betrays France, 263: ally of England, 271: invades Saxony,

INDEX 345

275: talks of suicide, 276: a 'Protestant hero,' 278: an 'enlightened despot,' 286: and the Bavarian Succession, 309: on Elizabeth Farnese, 221: the Great Elector, 250: Poland, 256: Seven Years' War, 277: his death, 311

FRENCH REVOLUTION, Causes of the, 314–323

FRIDESWIDE, Saint, buried with Mrs. Martyr, 64

FRONDE, The, described by de Retz, 158: by Louis XIV, 170: and English Civil War, 160: its results, 162

FÜRSTENBUND, 311

GALILEO, nearly burnt, 15: his discoveries, 15

GALLICANISM, 187

GERMANY, in 1494, 8: national character, 23: divisions, 58: in 1618, 126: in 1648, 147: in 18th cent., 331

GRANVELLA, recalled from Netherlands, 84: accuses William the Silent, 85

GREEK culture rediscovered, 21

GUISE family, its reputation, 101

GUNPOWDER introduced, and its effects, 16

GUSTAVUS ADOLPHUS, his education and ambitions, 136: intervention in Thirty Years' War, 137: dealings with Richelieu, 143: last campaign and death, 146

HANOVER, Question of, 271

HENRY II, of France, and Charles V, 42: his foreign policy, 43

HENRY III, of France, described by Sully, 110

HENRY IV, of Navarre, 113–125: his youth, 113: letters, 114: speeches, 115, 118: reading, 121: becomes heir to French throne, 110: King, 111: a Catholic, 111: his religious policy, 115: government, 118: industrial views, 121: 'ten wishes,' 122: 'Great Scheme,' 123: opinion of Catherine de Medici, 102: assassination, 125

HOHENZOLLERN character and policy, 248

HUGUENOTS at Geneva, 99: in France, 99: at Court, 103: granted the Edict of Nantes, 116: how treated by Richelieu, 151: by Louis XIV, 191

HUMANISM, 20

'INDEX LIBRORUM PROHIBITORUM,' 76

INDULGENCES, 49: traffic in, 56

INQUISITION in Spain and Italy, 71: fails north of the Alps, 72: to be judged fairly, 72

INTOLERANCE, 62

ITALY imports foreigners, 7: in 1494, 8: national character, 23: wars of 16th cent., 25–35: in 1715, 207: in 18th cent., 331

JANSEN and JANSENISM, 189: under Regency and Louis XV, 229

JESUITS, 65–71: their discipline, 68: their expulsion, 231

JOHN, Don, in the Netherlands, 89

JOHNSON, Doctor, on Rousseau, 283: on French manners, 316

JOSEPH II, Emperor, 290: his reforms, 291: 'Josephism,' 292: Bavarian Succession question, 309: and the Netherlands, 310: his death-bed, 292

JULIUS II, Pope, his Leagues, 29: militant, 33

KAUNITZ and the Diplomatic Revolution, 271: in later life, 290

KUTCHUK KAINARDJI, Treaty of, 298

LAW, John, his System, 214: its results, 216

LECZKINSKI, Stanislas, in Poland, 258: in Lorraine, 258

LEFÈVRE, 95

'LETTRES DE CACHET,' 318

LISBON earthquake, 275

LORRAINE question in 1733, 261

LOUIS XII of France, and his Italian claims, 27: invades Italy, 29

LOUIS XIII, his youth, 140: his relations with Richelieu, 155

LOUIS XIV, his Minority, 157–168: Home affairs, 169–186: Church policy, 187–196: Foreign policy, 196–204: education, 169: influenced by the Fronde, 171: character and ideas, 171: 'Memoirs,' 170: hard work, 174: Court, 175: supports Colbert, 181: patronizes literature 183: treatment of Jansenists, 190: and Huguenots, 191: influenced by Madame de Maintenon, 196: Spanish obsession, 198: Imperial ambitions, 198: his wars, 199: dynastic disasters and death, 204: Lord Acton on, 184: estimate of his reign, 205

LOUIS XV, 223–237: his character, 224: marriage, 226: mistresses, 228: extravagance, 232: eggs and dogs, 234: reading, 234: and the Jansenists, 231: and the Parlement, 233: the 'King's Secret,' 234: foresees 'the deluge,' 237: in 1740, 260: his death, 300: and burial, 229

LOUIS XVI, his looks and character, 300: accession, 303

LOYOLA, Ignatius, reads romances, 66: is converted, 67: founds the Jesuit Order, 83

LUTHER, his character, 53: books, 53: views, 54: popularity, 59

LUTHERANISM persecuted by Francis I, 95: its political separatism, 128

MACHIAVELLI, 28
MADRID, Treaty of, 42
MAGDALEN COLLEGE in 1494, 3
MAINTENON, Madame de, 196
MARGARET, daughter of Catherine de Medici, 103: marries Henry of Navarre, 114: describes Huguenotism at Court, 103: the Massacre of St. Bartholomew, 107: her end, 114

MARIA THERESA of Austria, her character, 261: situation in 1740, 262: appeal to the Hungarians, 262: and Silesia, 273: and the French Alliance, 272: her old age, 290: and death, 311

MARIE ANTOINETTE, 302
MARTYR, Peter, and his wife at Christ Church, 64
MATHIAS, Emperor, 129

MAUPEOU, 233
MAXIMILIAN I, Emperor, married, 5: ruler of Austria, 10
MAZARIN, his character and tastes, 157: succeeds Richelieu, 157: on the 'Frondeurs,' 161: his wealth, 163
MAZEPPA, 241
MEDICI, Catherine de, 101: and the Massacre of St Bartholomew, 106
MEDICI, Mary de, 125
MILITARY Art in Italian Wars, 30: in Thirty Years' War, 133, 137
MONARCHY in 16th cent., 11: in France, 328
MONRO, Colonel, describes Breitenfeld, 139: Gustavus Adolphus's answer to Richelieu, 145: and his death, 146
MONTAGU, Lady Mary Wortley, travels in France, 227
MONTESQUIEU, 282
MONTGOLFIER, and his balloon, 323

NANTES, Edict of, 116: revoked, 194: results, 194
NAPOLEON, and Charles V, 59
NATIONALISM in 1494, 11: and Internationalism, 333
'NATURAL FRONTIERS' of France, 32: under Richelieu, 142: under Louis XIV, 197
NAVARRE, 113
NECKER, 105: his 'Comte Rendu,' 306: recalled too late, 309
NETHERLANDS, under Charles V, 81: under Margaret of Parma, 82: revolt of 78–94 results, 92
NIMUEGEN, Treaty of, 200
NOBLESSE, French, in 16th cent., 121: under Richelieu, 152: in 18th cent., 321
NOTABLES, in 1560, 103: in 1787, 307
NYSTADT, Treaty of, 241

OLIVA, Treaty of, 239
OLIVARES, 167
ORLEANS (the Regent), 211 (the Revolutionary, 308
OXFORD in 1494, 2: education then, 3: Renaissance, Reformation, and Counter-Reformation at, 63

INDEX 347

PALATINE, Princess, and her letters, 212
PAPACY, and the Reformation, 22: and the Italian wars, 33: and finance, 48: and Protestantism, 60: and the Council of Trent, 73
PARACELSUS, 1
PARÉ, Ambroise, 31
PARIS, its part in French history, 327 Treaty of (1763), 279
PARIS, Brothers, 265
PARLEMENT de Paris, its pretentions, 159: part in the Fronde, 160: controversy with Louis XV, 233
PARMA, Margaret of, 82: Alexander of, 89
PARTITION TREATIES of Louis XIV, 202
PASCAL, his 'Lettres Provinciales,' 190
PAUL III, Pope, patronizes the Jesuits and Inquisition, 71: writes to Francis I, 96
PAULETTE, 120
PETER the Great, his childhood, 243: character and looks, 244: policy and reforms, 245: result of his reign, 246
PETER III, of Russia, 277, 287
PHILIP II, of Spain, his character and looks, 79: policy, 80: fanaticism, 80: and the Flemings, 82: enforces the Inquisition in the Netherlands, 84: outlaws William the Silent, 90: ruins Spain for religion, 91
PHILIP III, 167
PHILIP IV, 167
PHILIP V, and the French succession, 219: uxorious and melancholy, 220
PHILIP, Don, 221
PHILOSOPHERS, French, 282
PHYSIOCRATS, 235, 285
POISSY, Synod of, 104
POLAND, in 17th cent., 254: causes of its weakness, 254: coveted by its neighbours, 257: succession war, 258: First Partition, 293: results, 297
POLTAWA, Battle of, 241
POMPADOUR, Madame de, 228: her rouge, 286
PONIATOWSKI, Stanislas, King of Poland, 295
PORT ROYAL, 189
PRAGMATIC SANCTION of Charles VI, 259
PRESS, French in 18th cent., 236

PRINTING, discovered, 18: results, 18
PROTESTANTISM, its characteristics, 61
PRUSSIA in 17th-18th cent., 248-253: national policy, 332: for early history, see BRANDENBURG
PYRENEES, PEACE of, 168

REFORMATION, 48-62: helped by wars of 16th cent., 46: its causes, 48: and results, 61
REGENCY, French, 205-222: its government, 213: finance, 214: foreign policy, 217
RELIGIOUS ORDERS decadent, 50
RENAISSANCE, 13-24: summarized, 20: and the Italian wars, 34
RICHELIEU, 140-156: his 'Memoirs,' 141: foreign policy, 142-4: Thirty Years' War, 146: Valtelline policy, 148: home policy, 151: deals with Huguenots and nobles, 152: navy, army, finance, 154-5: relations with Louis XIII, 155: death-bed, 156
RIPPERDA, 221
ROLAND, Madame, 315
ROME rediscovered, 20
ROUSSEAU, 283: and his ideas, 284
ROUVIGNY, 'Old,' interviews Louis XIV, 193
RUDOLPH II, Emperor, 129
RUSSIA, in 17th cent., 241: geography and character, 242: national policy, 332

ST. BARTHOLOMEW, Massacre of, 106: described by Margaret of Valois, 107
SAINT-SIMON, on Peter the Great, 244
SAVONAROLA, 33
SEA-POWER, in 16th cent., 47: Richelieu on, 143, 154: in 1715, 208: in Seven Years' War, 279
SEVEN YEARS' WAR, Armies in, 273: strategy of, 275: fighting in, 276: causes of Prussian success, 277: results, 278: colonial war, 279
SILESIA, question of, 260: First Silesian War, 260: Second, 264
SOLYMAN the Magnificent, 44

INDEX

Spain, under the Moors, 6: in 1494, 7: national character, 7: and American gold, 14: under Philip II, 79: at Peace of Pyrenees, 168: causes of decline, 166: Succession question, 201: War of Succession, 203: in 1715, 207
Stage, French, in 18th cent., 236
Stanhope on Charles II, 168
States General of 1560, their demands, 104
Sully describes himself, 119: his Ministry, 120
Sweden in 17th-18th cent., 238–241: weakness of its Empire, 239

Telescope invented, 16
Teschen, Treaty of, 310
Testament, Greek, printed, 19: influence on Reformation, 52
Tetzel, 56
Thackeray, 'Barry Lyndon,' 274, 278
Thirty Years' War, 126–139, 146–148: its four periods, 131
Travel in 15th cent., 2, 4
Treasury of Conversion, 192
Trent, Council of, 73
Triple Alliance (1717), 219
Turgot, 303
Turkey, its advance in 16th cent., 44: rise and fall of power, 298: in 18th cent., 332: army and fleet, 295: its Partition planned, 298

'Unigenitus,' Papal bull, 191: 'Billets de Confession,' 230
United Provinces in 17th cent., 92
Utrecht, Treaty of, 203: its main results, 205: Union of, 90

Valdes on Luther, 57
Valtelline, 148
Vauban and Louis XIV, 174: his 'Dîme Royale,' 184
Vergennes, 309
Versailles under Louis XIV, 175: Treaty of (1783), 312
Voltaire, on the Age of Louis XIV, 282: Maria Theresa, 262: Battle of Fontenoy, 264: the Prussian army, 273: the Encyclopaedia, 285

Wallenstein, 133
War in modern history, 25
Westphalia, Peace of, 163
William the Silent, his character and looks, 83: declares against Alva, 86: and Spain, 88: dealings with Don John, 89: under a ban, 89: assassinated, 90: estimated, 91
Wotton, Sir Henry, on Galileo, 16
Worms, Diet of, 57